*f*P

AMERICAN
SPARTANS

*The U.S. Marines: A Combat History
from Iwo Jima to Iraq*

JAMES A.
WARREN

FREE PRESS

New York   London   Toronto   Sydney

FREE PRESS
A Division of Simon & Schuster, Inc.
1230 Avenue of the Americas
New York, NY 10020

For information regarding special discounts for bulk purchases,
please contact Simon & Schuster Special Sales: 1-800-456-6798
or business@simonandschuster.com.

Designed by Elliott Beard

The flag-raising silhouette used throughout the book is adapted from the
U.S. Marine Memorial, Arlington National Cemetery.

Manufactured in the United States of America

10   9   8   7   6   5   4   3   2   1

Library of Congress Cataloging-in-Publication Data

Warren, James A.
    American Spartans : the U.S. Marines: a combat history from Iwo
Jima to Iraq / James A. Warren.
        p. cm.
    Includes bibliographical references and index.
    1. United States. 2. Marine Corps—History—20th century. I. Title.

VE23.W38 2005
359.9'6097309045—dc22   2005054292

ISBN-13: 978-0-684-87284-1
ISBN-10:   0-684-87284-6

IN MEMORY OF MY BROTHER,
PAUL DANIEL WARREN,
1959–1999

Contents

Contents

Introduction

Go tell the Spartans, thou that passest by,
That here, obedient to their laws, we lie.

*Translation from the Greek of a tablet marking the grave
of Spartan warriors in fifth-century BCE Greece*

0640, February 19, 1945
The Bonin Islands, 660 miles south of Japan

The tranquil silence of a Pacific Ocean dawn is shattered by the percussion of the big guns of a huge American naval armada—battleships, cruisers, destroyers—joined by a host of landing craft that have been converted to rocket- and mortar-firing gunboats. Not long after the first shells punish the barren landscape of Iwo Jima, a Japanese island fortress of a mere eight square miles in the middle of the western Pacific Ocean, several squadrons of Marine and navy fighter-bombers join in the fray, dropping their high-explosive payloads on preidentified Japanese strongpoints.

At 0905, the first troop-bearing amphibious tractors—called amtracs by the U.S. Marines—make the pivotal transition from sea to shore

1

along a three-hundred-yard front to the northeast of the island's most ominous terrain feature, 556-foot Mount Suribachi. The sun is bright, the sky an all but cloudless azure blue. The sea is calm.

The first waves of seventy thousand American assault troops debouch from the amtracs and secure a tenuous foothold along the shore. Lieutenant General Tadamichi Kuribayashi's well-disciplined Japanese garrison, a mixture of army and navy units, hold their fire according to plan, waiting patiently until the first waves of Marines are closely packed together on the shoreline—as many as two men per yard of beach, most lying prostrate in the fine, black volcanic sand.

Kuribayashi later remarked to Imperial General Headquarters that "the violence of the enemy's bombardments is far beyond description."[1] Initial Japanese resistance was very light. Only desultory fire greeted the invaders. The terrain gave the Americans more problems than the enemy that first hour, as men and tracked vehicles struggled to mount the three terraces above the beach. Feet sank in the soft volcanic ash up to calf level, but at least the infantry could move up and off the beach. Tracked vehicles of all sorts had grave difficulties moving at all in the soft ashen sand.

By 0930 hours six thousand troops were ashore. A brilliantly executed rolling barrage from naval guns hit Japanese positions about four hundred yards to the front of the rushing assault troops. Colonel Harry Liversedge's 28th Regiment landed at the southern end of the line on Green Beach, and pushed inland across the neck of the island with a view to severing its head, Mount Suribachi, from its body. The 27th Marines, under Colonel Thomas A. Wornham, were sorting themselves out on the beach, preparing to jump off for the south end of the airstrip. American senior officers were particularly nervous about the fate of the 25th Regiment, which faced the cliffs of the rock quarry: any number of Japanese weapons were housed there and could fire into the Marines from their right flank.

Just before 1000, as one American infantryman would later put it, came "curtain time in hell."[2] The vast array of Japanese guns, placed on

Suribachi and across the broken terrain of ridges, plateaus, and ravines to the front and north of the invasion beaches, opened fire: coastal guns, field artillery, mortars, machine guns, the odd sniper and rifleman. A wall of deadly steel fell upon the exposed American troops. Scores of American infantrymen died in the first minutes. As sergeants and officers urged their men forward off the beach toward the steep terraces ahead, the fury of the Japanese fire intensified, targeting both the men and their transports and supply ships.

Soon the shoreline was awash in wrecked and twisted steel, severed limbs, and shredded bodies. The surf was red with blood of the wounded and the dead.

The next hour was one of the most harrowing of the Pacific war—a conflict with a great many harrowing hours. Incoming fire was escalating fast. Reports from the regimental commanders ashore to Generals Holland M. Smith and Harry Schmidt aboard the flagship USS *Eldorado* were terse: "Catching all hell from the quarry. Heavy mortar and machine-gun fire. Troops inland two hundred yards but pinned down." From the center of the landing beaches came another: "Taking heavy casualties and can't move. . . . Mortars killing us."[3]

The thirty thousand Americans who stormed from the sea onto the volcanic ash of Iwo Jima's beaches that sunny morning of February 19, 1945, to do battle against twenty-one thousand highly trained, resolute Japanese soldiers were members of an extraordinary military fraternity of amphibious soldiers. These Marines, most of them not yet twenty-one years of age, were enduring the first hours of a struggle that would conclude, for the lucky ones—you had to be lucky to survive Iwo—thirty-six days later. Each hour would seem to last a day; each day, a week. For each of the men who survived, the battle would prove to be a searing, life-defining experience.

Memories of combat would remain with them until death: the perpetual crack of small arms, the whine of Japanese rifle rounds zipping to their right, their left, and overhead. The thump of the mortars, the spray of ash and debris when a satchel charge was tossed into a pillbox, and the thunderous, percussive blasts of artillery and naval gunfire. The tedium and drudgery, punctuated by moments of sheer terror, that attended the routine of taking out one enemy bunker, one tunnel, one enemy platoon after another. The lack of sleep. The emotional and physical burden of simply getting through another day amid the ever-increasing numbers of eviscerated, stinking corpses, both American and Japanese.

There were moments of horror and moments of inspiration—inexplicable acts of suffering, selflessness, stupidity, waste, and courage. And those who survived the horrors of Iwo would remember and mourn the men they had known as friends and brother Marines. A total of 6,318 Marines and sailors died to wrest the island, and the three airfields that were its only military asset, from the Japanese.

To have fought at Iwo Jima is to have taken part in the battle that cost more Marine lives than any other. Iwo figures in the American popular imagination as the defining battle of the Marine Corps, for it showcased in dramatic fashion all the qualities we think of when we utter the words "United States Marine." More than any of the Corps' many bloody engagements over two centuries of combat, it is Iwo that has cemented the bonds of affection and respect that Americans feel for the Marine Corps. The photo of five Marines and one navy corpsman raising the flag on Mount Suribachi—an image we have all seen hundreds of times—still moves us. It symbolizes not only the Marine Corps' values and resolve, but also Americans' collective strength, both moral and physical, and our willingness to sacrifice for noble causes.

Legend has it that America's Marines, modeled on a unit of British soldiers who kept order aboard ships of the Royal Navy, were first recruited at Tun Tavern in Philadelphia, on November 10, 1775, and fought in the Revolution. Officially, the organization did not come into continuous operation until July 11, 1798, when the U.S. Congress established a Corps of Marines, to be manned by some 350 officers and men, headed by a commandant, and meant to serve aboard the vessels of the newly formed U.S. Navy. Nonetheless, November 10 remains the birthday of the culture of the Corps.

The Marine Corps is a unique military organization. It has the distinction of being the only military service in the world designed to operate across the entire spectrum of military activity—from conventional, set-piece battles to guerrilla war to humanitarian relief missions to evacuation of civilians from war-torn foreign shores to peacekeeping. It undertakes these missions with tightly knit teams of varied strength and size on land, on sea, and in the air.

Since 1952, the Marine Corps has been charged by the U.S. Congress with the solemn responsibility of maintaining this country's "force in readiness," meaning, as Marines themselves often say, that the Corps is America's crisis response, our "911" military force. The deployed, operational forces of the Marines all over the world, known collectively as the Fleet Marine Force (FMF), must be ready to plan and execute its missions within as few as six hours. The scope of the Corps' operations is daunting: doctrine has it that the Marines must be prepared to deploy up to two hundred miles inland from the coast. Yet in Iraq and Afghanistan, they have successfully operated well over four hundred miles from the sea.

Most of the Corps' "first strike" missions are carried out by one of seven Marine expeditionary units (MEUs). With about twenty-two hundred Marines, it's the smallest of the Corps' independent air-ground task forces. At any given moment there are a minimum of two of these units afloat and on call, sailing aboard groups of ships (from three to seven vessels) especially designed and equipped to bring combat power to bear from sea to shore.

Because of their renowned performance in storming beaches during World War II on islands such as Guadalcanal, Tarawa, Okinawa, and, above all, Iwo Jima, the Marines are known as shock troops—meaning they are highly spirited and aggressive soldiers trained to storm enemy defenses along a stretch of shoreline, secure a beachhead, and clear the way for heavier, conventional forces to follow. Yet they are a great deal more than that, too. The Marines are highly flexible and adaptable soldiers—among the world's most versatile and spirited.

Not even the Corps critics, and there have been more than a few, quarrel with the notion that Marines tend to attract men (and increasingly, today, women) with a penchant for adventure and adversity, for testing their physical and moral courage. Marines pride themselves on adhering to a traditional code of values centered around duty, honor, and commitment to their fellow Marines.

Young Americans today join the Marine Corps for much the same reason they did sixty years ago. "If you want to fight," a classic Marine Corps recruiting poster has it, "join the Marines." Another poster of 1950s vintage describes with terse precision what the Corps offers that so many young American males find alluring. A painting of a stern Leatherneck sergeant in dress blues stares out at the viewer with martial bearing and abundant self-confidence. The tagline above his head: THE UNITED STATES MARINES. The tagline below: WE BUILD MEN. The Marines offer people a chance to test their mettle and become part of something larger than themselves, about which they can be proud.

In the course of researching this book, I spent a number of weeks in the field and in the classroom with Marines of all ranks, and interviewed more than 150 active-duty and former Leathernecks, both professional officers and those men, officer and enlisted alike, who served one or two hitches and then went back to civilian life. The Marines fit no stereotype. They are a varied lot. Yet Marine history and culture bind them together like a close family. And the history of the Corps from World War II to the present is inextricably bound up with the story of the U.S. exercise of power to shape world politics and events.

American Spartans is an interpretive history of the Marine Corps from the Corps' bloodiest battle, Iwo Jima, up through the fall of Baghdad in April 2003. The narrative begins with Iwo Jima for a number of reasons. Iwo was the supreme test of the mission that created the Marine Corps we know today—a force of 175,000 men and women who serve as America's crisis response team. The amphibious assault mission had its origins in the Spanish-American War at the turn of the twentieth century. With scant resources and no doctrine to speak of, a handful of Marines set out to master a kind of fighting most military strategists had consigned to the scrap pile. Fortune, in this case, favored the Marines, for it was the amphibious assault techniques and tactics they developed and taught that won World War II in Europe in the West, and in the Pacific war as a whole, in 1945. The Marines were the masters of amphibious conflict. They began work in earnest on amphibious warfare in classes at the Naval War College in Newport in 1901, and continued to perfect doctrine, tactics, and equipment through the battles of World War II, in Quantico, Virginia, and at other installations on the East Coast.

Leaving aside the battle as an event in military history, Iwo looms large in America's understanding of the identity of the Marine and his Corps. Indeed, Iwo lies at the center of how Marines define themselves. Attacking from the sea is what Marines do. And they do it to win. Marines never quit. Iwo Jima proved that. Individual units remained effective combat organizations despite taking more than 50 percent casualties in the field.

The rigorous demands on body and soul required by the amphibious assault in the age of the airplane and the machine gun were perhaps *the* driving force in creating the highly spirited, adaptable soldier required by a military organization whose main mission from 1945 until today has been that of armed intervention on foreign shores. Building on its experiences in World War II and its deployments as colonial infantry in the so-called banana wars, the Marines transformed themselves from an obscure navy police unit of fewer than 10,000 men into an independent military service of more than 170,000 people with its own air force.

Thus reinvented, the Marine Corps played an extraordinarily active role in American foreign policy, particularly in those places where anarchy, violence, and a great many guns were involved. By the close of the twentieth century, the Marine Corps had established itself as the most formidable and experienced expeditionary force in modern history.

The Marine Corps prides itself quite correctly on its worldliness and its adaptability. It has earned the right to be proud on both counts. An admiring public understands as a matter of course that Marines are tough fighters with a superb track record in battle. Less well appreciated is the Corps' capacity to anticipate changes in warfare and to innovate. The Marine Corps is an exceptionally imaginative institution. Its list of major military innovations includes close air support of infantry, the amphibious assault, and, of course, the helicopter assault, which debuted in the Korean War in the fall of 1951.

In addition to describing major Marine operations, changes in doctrine, and missions, this book will assess the Corps' contributions to the wars it has been called on to fight, the myriad operations—peacekeeping, humanitarian relief, evacuation of Americans and foreign nationals from a host of imploding nation-states—in which it has been involved, and its contributions to military art and science.

The narrative focuses on ground combat, and I've tried to give the reader a sense of what the ordinary infantry Marine endured in the field in each of the five wars discussed in the book.

American Spartans begins with an exploration of what makes the Corps tick—its unique and fascinating culture. The remainder of the chapters cover Marine participation either in individual wars or over discrete periods of history.

It should be said at the outset that I see the Marines' experience of the last sixty years largely as a success story, but a stormy and at times controversial one. This success rests on a number of pillars, including the Corps' remarkable facility to transmit its values and habits of mind effectively to more than thirty thousand new recruits a year. On the individual level, the transformation that recruits undergo at the recruit depots in Parris Island, South Carolina, and San Diego, and in the officer candidate schools in Quantico, Virginia, is both profound and, in the vast majority of cases, permanent. Few indeed are the former Marines who do not retain a strong emotional connection to the institution. Fewer still are those former Marines who do not value what they learned at the hands of their drill instructors and fellow Marines.

Marine culture is paradoxically deeply committed to *both* tradition and change. It demands adherence to a code, to a way of comporting oneself, and it places immense value, or so it seems to me, on the power of belief to effect results in the real world. Commitment to. a force or entity larger than themselves—for example, discipline, sacrifice, and individual courage, or the Marine Corps itself—is absolutely essential to the Marine way. The Corps teaches that focus on one's selfish needs and wants at the expense of those of the unit, or the Corps as a whole, will lead only to woe.

Marines also believe ardently in the power of history—that one's present must be guided by the past, and, indeed, that Marines must learn and revere the history of the Corps if the organization is to remain strong and vital. Remembering, commemorating, are highly developed arts in the Marine world.

Both of these notions—believing in something transcendent and believing in the value of history—are deeply imbedded in that mystical quality that Marines think of as what sets them apart: Marine esprit de corps. Just what is esprit? Few veteran Marines would quarrel with the definition put forward by Major General Fred Haynes, a veteran of Iwo Jima, where he helped plan the assault on Mount Suribachi, who went on to fight in the Korean and Vietnam wars. Haynes is a lanky eighty-four-year-old who grew up in Plano, Texas, and joined the Marines in 1941 after reading a classic book about World War I Marines in combat called *Fix Bayonets!* by John Thomason. He retired from the Marines in 1977, having the unusual distinction of commanding two divisions—the 2nd at Camp Lejeune, North Carolina, and the 3rd on Okinawa. "Esprit," Haynes said,

> it's a lot like love. It's impalpable. You cannot touch it. You cannot exactly get your mind around it, but you certainly know it when it's there. Marines trust one another. You have this animating spirit, this belief in the guy on your right and the guy on your left. They've all been through a similar kind of training, and it's tough training done by people who have been in some pretty tight spots. You understand that these guys

[Marines in general] know their job, and they will cover you and you them. It's a belief, too, that you can't beat us because we're in it until the end, and we're in it together as Marines. You may knock a few of us off, but, if you do, watch out. If you kill Marines, one thing is for sure, there will be other Marines coming along soon, and they will keep coming until they find you.[4]

Almost sixty years after Fred Haynes fought on Iwo Jima, another Marine major general named James Mattis sent a message to the entire 1st Division, a unit he commanded on the eve of its attack on Saddam Hussein's Iraq in March 2003. It expressed the same essential ideas. As it happens, General Haynes is a close friend of General Mattis. They are part of the same family—the Marine Corps family:

You are part of the world's most feared and trusted force. Engage your brain before you engage your weapon. Share your courage with each other as we enter the uncertain terrain north of the Line of Departure. Keep faith in your comrades on your left and right and Marine Air overhead. Fight with a happy heart and a strong spirit.

For the mission's sake, our country's sake, and the sake of the men who carried the Division's colors in past battles—who fought for life and never lost their nerve—carry out your mission and keep your honor clear. Demonstrate to the world there is "No Better Friend, No Worse Enemy" than a U.S. Marine.

This book, in the end, tells the story of a small group of men and women who have maintained this spirit from the time of Fred Haynes to that of James Mattis: the U.S. Marines.

ONE

"THE INDEFINABLE INNER STRENGTH"

Elements of Marine Corps Culture

June 2000, Stone Bay, near Jacksonville, North Carolina

A forty-something military historian from New York City drives along a coastal road accompanied by a burly public affairs staff sergeant of the United States Marine Corps. Their destination: Scout Sniper school, USMC, Fleet Marine Force, Atlantic. All Marines, the historian knows, are riflemen. The rifle is at the core of the Marine Corps' tumultuous history, its organizational mind-set, and its ethos.

Here at Stone Bay, adjacent to Camp Lejeune, the main base of the 2nd Marine Division, rifle marksmanship becomes high art. It is a brilliant, humid North Carolina summer afternoon. The landscape of bright-green piney woods running along the shoreline of the Atlantic Ocean seems too pretty and serene a place to learn how to kill a human being at a thousand yards with a single shot. The goal of the Scout

Sniper course is to find out which highly trained marksmen "pack the gear" to earn the right to call themselves snipers.

On the winding road that leads into the firing ranges, there are large signs at intervals in brilliant scarlet and gold, the official colors of the Corps, bearing terse inspirational quotes. One sign jumps out: "You can't hurt them if you don't hit them."

Its author is the Marine's Marine, the indomitable Lewis B. "Chesty" Puller. Puller won five Navy Crosses, the highest award for valor awarded by the Department of the Navy, in campaigns from the banana wars in the Caribbean of the 1930s, through the Pacific theater in World War II, and on to the Chosin Reservoir in Korea. Puller is the only Marine in history to have won five Crosses. His aggressive style of leading from the front, his gruff refusal to entertain defeat even in the most dire circumstances, and insistence that "if you're a Marine, you are *all* Marine" have combined to make him both legend and symbol of America's Corps of Marines. Every year on the anniversary of his death, a contingent of Leathernecks travels to Saluda, Virginia, and places a fresh wreath on his grave.

As the sniper class is about to begin, a young corporal, one of eight Marines in the class, comes running across the field adjacent to the rifle range. He is late. Class begins at 1400 and it is 1405. The instructor, Gunnery Sergeant K. S. Stewart, is a cordial and enthusiastic veteran of fifteen years in the Marines. He has a passionate interest in rifles, cartridges, windage, and muzzle velocity. He shouts out in playful reproach to his errant student, whose cheeks are bright red and awash in sweat,

"Corporal, you look real tired!"

The corporal responds with pluck, in Pulleresque fashion: "Oh, hell, Gunny, I'm not tired. I just felt like getting me a little extra PT [i.e., physical training]!"

Gunny Stewart chuckles and replies, "Ah-huh . . . Well, there's nothing wrong with getting stronger!" The tardy corporal is promptly ordered to take up his M-16, assume the prone position, and get to work.

"Getting stronger" is something of a Marine Corps mantra. The most obvious form of strength one notices among Marines is physical. Marines are, by and large, younger, fitter, and more intimidating than typical army soldiers. The strength you cannot see, though, is more important. It lies in the spirit of comradeship and brotherhood that bonds these Americans from widely diverse backgrounds into something bigger than themselves, something that commands respect. They are part of a world-renowned tribe of warriors.

Marines see themselves as members of the finest fighting force on earth, and they will be happy to tell you so. If you spend time among them, you may very well find it hard not to believe they are right.

The Marine Corps is committed to a demanding and explicit warrior code. The code brings a set of values—loyalty, discipline, boldness, frugality, persistence, courage—both physical and moral—and, of course, pride. Pride in one's country, in the Corps, in one's unit. It also demands that you put aside your personal objectives for those of the mission and the institution. Candor, directness, and self-criticism are highly encouraged and much in evidence in the Marine Corps world. Respect for others and personal discipline are seen as essential, and violators are punished.

History plays a far more important role in the lives of Marines than it does in their army and navy counterparts. Marines feel a deep obligation to live up to the high standards set by their forebears at Belleau Wood, Tarawa, Iwo Jima, the Chosin Reservoir, and, more recently, in the superb performance of the 1st Marine Expeditionary Force in the second Gulf War.

The Corps' code, deeply anchored in history, gives Marines an abiding self-confidence and sure-handedness in their operations that other military professionals find impressive, even unique. The obstacles to accomplishing the mission always seem small next to the Marines' "can do" approach to their martial trade.

Marines have exhibited this jaunty "can do" attitude as long ago as the first decades of the twentieth century, when they performed so effectively in the Philippine Insurrection of 1899 to 1903; or in the

Caribbean counterinsurgencies of the 1920s and 1930s, during which Marines ran the governments of Haiti and Nicaragua; or, most famously, in several horrendous battles on the Western Front in World War I, where German troops admiringly called them "Devil Dogs." General Smedley Butler, one of two Marines to win the Medal of Honor twice, captured this confidence in a letter to General John A. Lejeune, then the commandant of the Marine Corps:

> We have a class of men in our ranks far superior to those in any other service in the world and they are high-spirited and splendid in every way. They joined because of our reputation for giving them excitement, and excitement from a marine's standpoint, can only be gained by the use of bullets and the proximity to danger.[1]

Even today, it is the rifleman who preoccupies the thinkers and innovators at Quantico's Warfighting Laboratory, where those who are charged with making the Corps a more effective force today than it was yesterday reside. As the key yearly HQMC publication *Concepts and Issues* (2003) puts it:

> Throughout our history, the Marine Corps has always known that people, not weapons, technologies or systems, ultimately determine operational success during wartime and other contingencies. Our core values of honor, courage and commitment are powerful ideals deeply held by all Marines. They are the foundation of our ability to fight and win—today and in the years to come—just as they have been for more than 200 years.[2]

The Marine Corps has remained committed to a traditional, human-centered, and moral—as opposed to technological—view of war, and its training regimen and institutional ethos reflect this outlook on the Corps' main activity, which is to fight and win battles.

Since the late 1980s, the Marines' basic doctrine has been spelled out in a manual of just over one hundred pages entitled *Warfighting*, but the ideas expressed in that small volume draw very much on the concepts that have been passed down in writing and by word of mouth from generation to generation of Marines. *Warfighting*, a sort of bible of Marine thinking and culture, holds that that modern war is especially chaotic, violent, and fast moving. It therefore requires quick, intuitive decisions, and great strength of will, character, and endurance. War at its fundamental level is

> a clash of opposing human wills. . . . War is an extreme trial of moral and physical strength and stamina. . . . No degree of technological development or scientific calculation will diminish the human dimension in war. Any doctrine which attempts to reduce warfare to ratios of forces, weapons and equipment neglects the impact of the human will on the conduct of war and is therefore inherently flawed.[3]

Because war is a struggle between opposing wills, it is shaped by the inconsistencies and oddities that characterize human behavior. And because war invariably involves bloodshed and all manner of suffering and stress, it is inherently unpredictable and uncertain.

The Marine Corps doesn't attempt to mitigate uncertainty with complex systems and specialized tactics, custom-made for each of the more than twenty missions it might be required to undertake. Instead, it accepts that chaos, fear, danger, and uncertainty are permanent features of combat. "Because we can never eliminate uncertainty," says *Warfighting*, "we must learn to fight effectively despite it. We can do this by developing simple, flexible plans, planning for likely contingencies, developing standard operating procedures, and fostering initiative among subordinates."

Since modern war especially is "not the monolithic execution of a single decision by a single entity but necessarily involves near-countless independent but interrelated decisions," the Marine Corps categorically rejects the principle of centralization of control and decision making in combat.[4] A Marine captain will tell his platoon leader to reduce a position, but he will leave the decisions concerning how to complete the mission to the leader himself. A very great deal depends on the individual Marine confronted with life-and-death decisions.

The Corps has always favored speed, audacity, and initiative in its fighters, and never more so than today, when success and failure in war, writes the former commandant, General Charles Krulak,

> will rest, increasingly, with the individual Marine on the ground—and with his ability to make rapid, well-reasoned, independent decisions while facing a bewildering array of challenges and threats. These decisions will be subject to the harsh scrutiny of both the media and the court of American public opinion. In many cases, the individual Marine will be the most conspicuous symbol of American foreign policy. His or her actions may not only influence the immediate tactical situation, but have operational and strategic implications as well.[5]

Surprisingly, despite the Marines' emphasis on men, not technology, and their somewhat traditional and conservative views of history, they have an admirable record of anticipating changes in modern warfare and staying ahead of the curve. The Corps' leadership since the turn of the nineteenth century has worked tirelessly to adapt their training, equipment, and doctrine to new potential threats on the horizon.

There was nothing inevitable about this trajectory of events. The modern Marine Corps has its origins in the emergence of the United States as a Pacific power in the wake of the Spanish-American War. In the decades between 1900 and 1930, a few visionaries among the Marine officer corps foresaw the need for advance naval bases in the Pacific in a war against Japan, and they set about the painstaking business of developing the amphibious assault against a hostile force dug in ashore. Before the Marines began developing doctrine and equipment for such assaults, they had been conducted more or less on the fly, with whatever boats and equipment a navy had at its disposal.

The U.S. Army might very well have taken up the amphibious war business. It was by no means obvious that the Marines would take up the challenge. But the army lacked the inclination, while the Marines—or, more accurately, a few very smart Marines—saw that amphibious specialization could provide the service with a means to grow and a raison d'être to ensure its survival.

While fighting guerrillas in Nicaragua in the 1920s and 1930s, the Marines laid the crucial groundwork for the close air support doctrine of World War II. Building on decades of experience in the conflicts they came to call derisively the "banana wars" on behalf of American diplomacy from 1900 through the early 1930s in the Caribbean, the Corps in 1940 published the classic manual for American forces on coping with the peculiar political and military ambiguities of guerrilla conflicts. The *Small Wars Manual* is still widely read by militaries around the world today.

When the atomic bomb made the World War II–style amphibious assault obsolete, the Marines responded with an entirely new kind of approach: "vertical envelopment." The new doctrine called for the first wave in any assault to land behind the enemy in helicopters dispatched from widely dispersed ships beyond the horizon—too far from land to be vulnerable to attack by land-based artillery. At the time the faculty at Marine schools in Quantico began to devote serious consideration to vertical envelopment, the Corps had not a single helicopter in its inventory.

Today, the Marines are innovating yet again, this time taking a leading role in developing effective doctrine and training for the "Three-Block War." The idea is this: soldiers in a given operation today will on one block perform humanitarian relief; other soldiers will keep hostile groups apart in peacekeeping operations on the next block; and on the third block of the same conflict, soldiers—or Marines—will engage in mid-intensity combat.

"Two critical elements in the Marines' culture, our way of doing things," said Major General Haynes, "are adaptability and imagination. As I look back on what we've done, and the way we did it, I'd have to say imagination played a very big role indeed."[6]

To understand Marine culture, one has to look at the boot camp experience, for it is at boot camp, as a contemporary slogan one hears around Marines today has it, "where the difference begins."

"A lot of people think the physical part of boot camp is tough, really brutal," said Seth Haines, a thirty-one-year-old former reconnaissance sergeant who served five years in the Corps before leaving to earn a degree in history from Columbia University. "But for me, and most Marines I know, it was the emotional harassment and stress that was the toughest part. It's that key boot camp experience that sets the Marines apart from the army, and it's an experience all Marines share."[7]

Boot camp today consists of thirteen weeks of sixteen-hour, highly stressful days at one of two recruit depots, Parris Island, South Carolina, or San Diego, California. The harassment and intense instruction of boot camp have two objectives: to break down the self-centeredness and selfishness of the recruit (the "egoectomy," in Corps parlance), and to build all recruits into disciplined, physically fit, and "squared away" Marines who believe wholeheartedly in their country, their Corps, and their unit.

Marines do not leave boot camp ready to join the operating forces and fight. Rather, they depart as Believers—young Americans who have absorbed the basic spirit, tenets, and mind-set of the Marines, living and dead, who have come before them. No one has written more perceptively about recruit training than Lieutenant General Victor H. Krulak, whose book, *First to Fight*, is a classic exposition of what makes the Corps tick. I have never met a Marine officer who hadn't read it. Krulak writes:

> In the Marines, recruit training is the genesis of the enduring sense of brotherhood that characterizes the Corps. In that twelve-week period [the book was written when recruit training was one week shorter than it is today], an almost mystical alchemy occurs. Young adults from diverse areas of the country and backgrounds are immersed in an environment wherein they are able to perceive, understand and finally accept as dogma the essential Marine Corps virtues.[8]

In the trials of boot camp, the marches, the endless hours of close order drill, the continual harassment, and the weeks of rifle range work, recruits begin to develop the self-confidence and resilience essential for success in combat. The Corps demands that its recruits accept a set of basic tenets. Prominent among them is the notion that the Marine Corps is the greatest fighting force in the world; that the reason the Corps performs so well on the battlefield is that Marines hold fast to the old verities of duty, honor, and loyalty to country and Corps; that Marines will never leave a fellow Marine wounded or dead on the battlefield; that fortune favors the bold of heart; that ordinary young men and women can enter the brotherhood if they give themselves over to the teachings of the Corps; that the deadliest weapon in the world is a Marine with his rifle.

The training at the Parris Island and San Diego recruit depots, for the vast majority of Marines, has a positive effect that lasts a lifetime. Scores of former Marines who have written of their experiences in boot camp or talked in interviews for this book spoke of boot camp as a transformative experience. Not a few said it was the most important period of their lives, the watershed event. The former governor and U.S. senator from Georgia, Zell Miller, reflected on his experience at Parris Island as

> the turning point in my life. Everything that has happened to me since has been at least an indirect product of that decision [to join the Marines], and in the twelve weeks of hell and transformation that were Marine Corps boot camp, I learned the values of achieving a successful life that have guided and sustained me. . . . The best analogy I have heard describing what it is like to go through Marine Corps boot camp is that it is the closest thing to a birth experience grown men will ever go through. The main difference is the gestation period is compressed into three instead of nine months.[9]

Running the show are the most motivated among the highly motivated: the drill instructors (DIs). The DI is a teacher, a counselor, a strict disciplinarian, and a role model who functions in loco parentis for his platoon of recruits. At his best, he is a model of the small-unit leader the Corps holds up as the ideal Marine: tough, fair, smart, compassionate, and a passionate believer in the Corps. He would never ask a recruit to do something he would not do himself.

This brotherhood continues to develop throughout the Marine's tenure in the Corps as his knowledge and experience of the traditions and customs of the Corps expands. Officers all receive their initial education and training at the Marine Corps base at Quantico, Virginia. First there is the officer's version of boot camp, either at a ninety-day Officer Candidate Class or in the Platoon Leader's Course taken in the summers by college students who have opted to become Marines upon graduation. Then, all officers attend a six-month intensive course of study called the Basic School. At TBS, as Basic School is known throughout the Corps, even Marines who will become pilots and intelligence specialists must learn how to run a platoon on the ground and master all the basic skills of the infantryman: land navigation, terrain appreciation, the platoon in the defense, and small-unit tactics, among others.

One needs to spend only a few days among units in training exercises to see that Marine culture prizes adaptability, boldness, and self-criticism. Sergeants and officers invariably gather their men together immediately after the conclusion of a training exercise and talk about what went right and what did not. On many occasions I heard Marine officers and noncoms criticizing their own performance as well as that of the men in their charge. "The Corps is famous for its self-confidence and bravado, but in fact it is a very self-critical organization," said First Lieutenant Chad Gill, a Naval Academy graduate and intelligence officer attached to the 13th MEU during a night-raid training operation in the Mojave Desert in 2003.[10]

The Marine Corps in the field in training exercises is one big encouragement machine. Everyone is there to do his or her part, and to help you do yours if you need help. Marines are ceaselessly encouraging one another to "go for it," constantly confirming that "you're trackin'." They often express approval and support not with words, but with a kind of infectious growl, either an "Urrrrghhh!" or "Hurrrrah!"

"Not only must we not stifle boldness or initiative," *Warfighting* asserts, "but we must continue to encourage both traits in spite of mistakes. On the other hand, we should deal severely with errors or inaction or timidity. . . . We must not tolerate the avoidance of responsibility or necessary risk."[11]

Wherever Marines are being trained, at whatever level, talk of character building and values is never far behind. Words like *pride, discipline*, and *persistence* permeate Marine discourse. Marines have their own language, with scores of sayings and slang words. The Corps has been referred to derisively as a kind of military cult, and more dispassionately as a kind of military "denomination." Indeed, there are some striking similarities between the Marines and a religious order. Both require a transformation for full membership, a kind of rebirth. Both require the willing acceptance of a core set of beliefs. Both require an enduring commitment to a cause greater than oneself. For the Marines, stories of Iwo Jima, the Chosin Reservoir, Hue, and Chesty Puller are sacred. They serve as scriptures do for religious groups.

"Ah, yes, the Marines. They are a remarkable group of people," said Dean Alberto Coll, a former Defense Department undersecretary who has taught many of the outstanding majors and lieutenant colonels in the Marines for more than a decade at the Naval War College in Newport, Rhode Island. "They remind me of the Jesuits."[12] Dean Coll is not the only person to make this connection. Marine general Anthony Zinni, who rose to perhaps the most prestigious theater command in the American military—Central Command, covering nineteen countries in the Middle East and Asia—once remarked, "What we were doing was not a job, not even a profession, but a calling. For me, joining the Marines was the closest thing to becoming a priest."[13]

The Jesuits and the Marines share the qualities of steadfastness and an unwavering commitment to their creeds and their mission in the world. Both groups are dedicated apostles of their own institutions, their own "way."

It is this religious dedication to their Corps and its work that has prompted critics to label the Marines as fanatics and extremists, as war lovers. The Corps demands a very high level of commitment from its people, in part because it has always felt besieged by critics and the bureaucratic forces of the Department of Defense that have so often threatened to eviscerate their service, and in part because their experience tells them that this deep commitment gets the job done on the battlefield. "To the Marine," writes one Corps veteran of World War II:

> The Corps is his religion, his reason for being. He cannot be committed up to a point. For him, involvement is total. He savors the traditions of his Corps and doubts not the veracity of them. He believes implicitly that he must live up to those epics of physical and moral courage established by those who preceded him. He believes that his Corps is truly unique—that it is the most elite military organization ever devised, and that he, as an integral part of that organization, must never bring disgrace or dishonor upon it.[14]

"When I meet a man who is a former Marine," said James Webb, among the most highly decorated Marines of the Vietnam War and now a best-selling novelist, "I automatically trust him. And that trust has never failed me."[15]

The Marine Corps has been taken to task by journalist Thomas Ricks in his fascinating book *Making the Corps*, published in 1997, for its increasingly outspoken disdain for the consumerist values and "me first" ethos that prevail in American society. Ricks sees a yawning gap developing between an increasingly isolated Marine Corps and the postmodern America it serves. He is certainly correct about the gap in value systems, but to this observer, the Marines are a long way from giving up on the nation they serve. They see themselves as exemplars of a different and better way. They see the Corps and its values as a beacon of hope for the country, particularly for its young people.

Consider some of the differences between the culture of the Marines and the army, navy, and air force. The Marines are held together by their common identity as Marine riflemen. People in the other services tend to identify much more closely with those who do a similar type of work rather than with their service brothers and sisters as a whole; for example, the tank troops identify with other tankers, and helicopter pilots with other aviation people. But the Marines' first loyalty is to the Corps as a whole. "In the Marines, there is a saying," quipped Captain Justin Wilson, a mild-mannered and intelligent operations officer at the Basic School in Quantico. "You are either in the infantry or a jock strap—you're in support of the infantry."[16]

Another distinguishing feature of the Marines, and one that helps explain "the Marine mystique," is the tight bond between officers and enlisted men. James Webb grew up as an air force brat and, after service in Vietnam, went on to serve briefly as secretary of the navy. He believes, as do many close observers, that there is a real difference between the way officers and enlisted people relate to one another in the Marines and how they do so in the other three services. The Marine Corps may have three full divisions and three air wings, but its sensibility is shaped and governed by thinking about small-unit fighting—about closing with the enemy with small arms. Far more so than their counterparts in the larger services, Marine officers are judged and rewarded by their performance as leaders of men in the field, in combat, as opposed to staff work or advanced-education performance. To have it said that an officer "takes good care of his Marines" or that he "is coolheaded under fire" is tantamount to saying that he is an exemplary U.S. Marine. In the other services, with the exception of elite units such as the army's Airborne units and the Rangers and the navy's SEALs, this sort of outlook is far less in evidence.

In the *Marine Corps Manual* of 1921, General John Lejeune wrote a set of guidelines on relations between officers and enlisted Marines. All Marine officers today know the passage and take its essence to heart:

A spirit of comradeship and brotherhood in arms came into being in the training camps and battlefields [of World War I]. This spirit is too fine a thing to be allowed to die. It must be fostered and kept alive and made the moving force in all Marine Corps organizations. . . . The relation between officer and enlisted men should in no sense be that of superior and inferior nor that of master and servant, but rather . . . should partake of the relationship between father and son, to the extent that officers, especially commanding officers, are responsible for the physical, mental and moral welfare, as well as the discipline and military training of the young men under their command who are serving the nation in the Corps.[17]

Warfighting echoes Lejeune's writing in stating: "Relations among all leaders—from corporal to general—should be based on honesty and frankness regardless of disparity between grades. . . . Seniors must encourage candor among subordinates and must not hide behind their grade insignia. Ready compliance for the purpose of personal advancement—the behavior of 'yes-men'—will not be tolerated."[18]

Yet another key pillar of Marine culture is the pervasiveness of the institution's colorful history in its daily functioning and mind-set. The Marines use their history as a lure to bring new people into the fold, to reinforce basic lessons taught at all levels of training, to establish continuity, and to dramatize the effectiveness of its time-tested methods of "making Marines." Classes at the Basic School begin with a reading of a Medal of Honor citation and a brief commentary by the instructor about the relevance of the heroic actions described in the citation.

In a week of classes at the Basic School, this observer was struck by the enduring presence of the past in the lectures on "The Platoon in the Offense," "Land Navigation," and "Terrain Features." James Webb remarked, "People say you fight for your buddies. That's true, but that's a floor, not a ceiling. People say you fight because you're well trained and well led. That is also true. But the truly great military organizations have fought well because they hold themselves accountable to their own history and traditions."[19] So it is in the U.S. Marine Corps.

Another former Marine officer, Robert A. Wehrle, who served in the infantry between 1972 and 1982, offered an anecdote that says much about the use of history in the Marines. Years after leaving the Marines,

Wehrle was running in a charity benefit race at the Marine base in Quantico, Virginia, on the same course he had run during his days at the Basic School. As he made his way forward on the course, he noted a Marine gunnery sergeant running near him, calling out the names of Medal of Honor winners, which were printed on signs at intervals along the trail. The sergeant's son, a boy of twelve or so, was running, too, and he asked his father why he called out the names. The gunny's answer was "all Marine": "Because we want these men to know that we will never forget them, or what they did." [20]

The Marines enjoy an unusually close relationship with the American public. Both the Marine Corps in general and the individual Marine occupy a unique place in the American imagination. Marines have long understood that their existence is contingent on preserving their high name and public reputation. It is essential that the Marines of today hold to the high standards of performance of the past; if they do not, if the American people's reverence and respect evaporate, the brotherhood believes, the Corps will falter, and its missions will be handed over to its sister services.

The affection and respect that Americans have long felt for their Leathernecks rest in large measure on the Marines' steadfastness, their reliability, their record of sacrifice, and their bravery in combat. Yet this doesn't fully explain the feelings we have for the "Devil Dogs."

We see Marines as a breed apart, even among the millions of people in the other arms of the military who serve with heroism and distinction. Among all our people in uniform, argues one scholar, the Marines have become the American samurai, a warrior class whose existence and character have long been governed by fidelity to a demanding martial code and tradition. Americans are proud of the Corps, because for all its emphasis on discipline, struggle, and sacrifice, our Marines (unlike the Japanese samurai class) are not drawn for the most part from the elite, but from Everywhere, U.S.A.—from small country towns in West Virginia, from Iowa farms, from New York City's rougher neighborhoods, and in very large numbers from Texas and California.

Each year more than thirty thousand young Americans enter the Corps. More than 50 percent of them are younger than twenty-one. The vast majority, more than 90 percent, are males. One of the truly outstanding Marine officers of the postwar era, General Robert Barrow, has written perceptively on the relation between the Corps and the American people, as in his description of why young men are drawn to the Marine Corps:

> First, many, if not most want desperately to believe in something. Most of us want one or more strong personal commitments—religion, home, community, or some other institution which would extract from us involvement and strong beliefs. In today's world, the opportunity for such positive commitment has waned significantly and many young people look around them in vain for such opportunities. For many, the search ends with the Marine Corps.
>
> Second, there is an inherent need in all males of the animal world to prove their masculinity or manliness. . . .
>
> In the past [this need was fulfilled] by . . . opening the new frontier, "going to sea," or other forms of adventure. . . . The opportunity for legitimate proving of one's manliness [today] is shrinking. A notable exception is the Marine Corps. The Marine Corps' reputation, richly deserved, for physical toughness, courage and demands on mind and body, attracts those who want to prove their manliness. Here too their search ends.[21]

The values and characteristics that comprise Marine Corps culture, and the organization of the contemporary Corps, are in large measure a product of the Marines' most distinctive military mission: amphibious warfare and, more specifically, the most harrowing, complex aspect of that type of military operation: assault from the sea against a heavily defended beach. This was not a mission that especially concerned the Marines for the first 125 years of their existence. Even when it first emerged as a strategically vital capability, a great many senior officers in the service took little or no interest in involving the Corps. Yet its impact on the future history of the Corps has been staggering. Amphibious warfare provided the Corps with an institutional raison d'être. The rigors and formidable challenges such operations posed demanded a spirited force of infantrymen who prized courage, physical stamina, and aggressiveness—traits the Marines already thought of as at the core of their identity, and traits that, in the wake of the brutal island assaults conducted by the Corps in World War II, became synonymous with the Marines in the public imagination. What's more, the organization and training necessary to conduct successful amphibious operations produced general-purpose infantrymen with the right mix of mobility, combat power, and logistical support to conduct independent, limited operations on foreign shores without leaving a large political "footprint." For a country with enormous diplomatic and geopolitical interests, such a force was to prove indispensable, as we shall see. In exhibiting an early interest in fighting effectively on beaches when most military organizations and authorities dismissed such operations as impossible in the age of the machine gun and military air power, the Marines became the spearhead of American diplomacy.

The most knowledgeable historians of Marine amphibious operations in World War II argue that 1933 was the most crucial turning point in the Marine Corps history. It was in September of that year that the chief of naval operations and the commandant of the Marines, Major General John H. Russell, agreed to reorganize the Marine Corps around the Fleet Marine Force. The FMF contains the three divisions and three air wings that together today form the Marines' deployable combat forces. Its presence and organization assure the supremacy of amphibious operations in Marine Corps thinking, planning, and operational mind-set. Until that time, no small percentage of senior Marines had resisted the emphasis on amphibious training in favor of either the light infantry role the Corps had performed in the Caribbean or regular land operations. The creation of the FMF meant that more than half of the Marines in uniform would be either attached to the fleet while it was out to sea, ready to conduct amphibious operations on short notice, or back at home training for such sea duty. It meant, in short, that amphibious training would no longer be conducted at irregular intervals. The best minds in the Corps at the Marine Corps base in Quantico, Virginia, focused on producing the first written, systematic treatise for amphibious operations in military history.

The Tentative Manual for Landing Operations (1937) laid out both the theory and practice of such operations. It broke down the subject into six discrete parts: command relationships; naval gunfire support; aerial support; ship-to-shore movement; securing the beach; and logistics, especially the unique problems associated with loading and distributing ammunition, food, heavy weapons, and vehicles.

In the years between the manual's first publication and the amphibious campaign against the Japanese in the Solomon Islands, the officers at Quantico painstakingly refined the details, procedures, tables of organization, and equipment necessary for bringing forces ashore. Much of the work was carried out on sand tables containing miniature shorelines, and in the field with "notional" equipment, which injected an unfortunate element of artificiality in the training. There was no choice: the navy of the 1930s lacked adequate transport, tank lighters, and the amphibious tractors that were essential to ensure success. Nonetheless, by the outbreak of the Pacific war, the Marines had worked closely with New Orleans boatbuilder Andrew Higgins to produce the workhorse Landing Craft, Vehicle and Personnel (LCVP), with its ramp at the bow, a vessel that General Holland M. Smith (who led the Marines in their drive across the Pacific through Iwo Jima) would claim "contributed more to our common victory than any other single piece of equipment during the war."[22] The Marines attributed the failure of the British at Gallipoli in 1915 largely to the lack of an amphibious vehicle that could cross from sea to shore and keep moving inland, thereby reducing congestion on the beach and keeping a steady flow of supplies to the front lines. Here, too, they found a solution by adapting Donald Roebling's amphibious "alligator" (designed initially for travel in the Florida Everglades and in hurricane rescue work) to military purposes. The amphibious tractor, or "amtrac," could negotiate coral reefs, carry infantry, machine guns, or even a 75mm howitzer that could fire on enemy positions as it made its way shoreward.

The work of these officers laid a foundation for the successes not only of the Marine Corps' campaign across the Pacific, but of the Allies' amphibious landings in North Africa, Italy, and France, including the largest amphibian invasion of history, D-Day, June 6, 1944. Marine training teams were attached to a number of the army's divisions slated for amphibious operations, and the doctrine used by the army at Normandy and elsewhere had been developed and refined by the Marine Corps.

With each assault conducted against the Japanese, the Marines refined the core amphibious doctrine as laid out in *The Tentative Manual*. At bloody Tarawa, they learned of the necessity of having sufficient amtracs to bring all waves of infantry ashore, as hundreds of Marines had to wade into the beach from chest-deep water under scathing machine-gun fire. At Peleliu, they learned that the most effective way to reduce strongly fortified Japanese positions was with tank-infantry-demolition teams. And that waterproof radios for every unit were essential to prevent chaos on the beach. Large-caliber, heavily fortified enemy gun emplacements could not be knocked out with long-range naval bombardment. Pinpoint, close-in fire from destroyers, cruisers, and battleships, directed by a spotter on the ground, was required.

The early amphibious operations of the war in the Solomons were of course puny compared with those of Iwo Jima and Okinawa, but the underlying doctrine for all the operations—the basic principles and prerequisites for success—had all been worked out before the war commenced. The differences between the early campaigns and the assault on Iwo Jima, the "supreme test" of amphibious operations, were not in the doctrine employed

but rather in the means to put existing doctrine into effect. . . . The modifications wrought between 1942 and 1945 in the art of amphibious warfare did not seriously affect underlying principles. Those modifications, the production of materiel, particularly landing craft and weapons, and secondly in the refinement of certain techniques which had clearly been conceived before the war but which needed the experience of combat itself to achieve any degree of perfection.[23]

The amphibious assault is similar in objective and follows the same principles of fire and maneuver as a basic ground assault. But at command level, amphibious operations require mastery of a highly specialized set of procedures and coordination of landing craft and fleet protection both from sea and air. Ground troops must disembark in landing craft at regular intervals, widely dispersed, and their movement ashore must be very closely coordinated with naval gunnery fire and air attack. Special ammunition for these naval guns had to be developed, and the absence of artillery meant that enemy positions up high on cliffs sometimes had to be reduced by air power alone, the trajectory of most naval guns being too flat to aim high. Specialized beach parties, composed of both sailors and Marines, had to be able to communicate with the fleet to manage both the type and flow of supplies and equipment as required by rapidly changing circumstances on the shoreline and the urgent needs of the infantry assault commanders.

Ironically, the Marine Corps has not conducted a major assault against a hostile shore since the Inchon landing in September 1950, when the 1st Marine Division spearheaded General Douglas Mac-Arthur's attack on the west coast of Korea. Yet the Corps has been continually training its operational forces to bring combat power from sea to shore, continually working on the capacity to conduct "forced entry" against a hostile enemy. As we shall see in the coming pages, the amphibious assault of today has been vastly transformed by changing technologies. General Chuck Krulak put it this way in an address he gave shortly before his retirement:

Ultimately a global superpower must possess the ability for unilateral action. A key requirement in this capability is to project power ashore in the face of armed opposition. In the past, forcible entry from the sea was defined by amphibious assaults that focused on establishing a lodgment on the beach and then building up combat power for subsequent operations. Forcible entry is now defined as the uninterrupted flow of forces located far over the horizon directly to decisive objectives, wherever and whenever we desire.[24]

The amphibious assault, World War II–style, belongs to the past, but forcible entry from the sea is an indispensable—even vital—capability for the United States. Effective implementation of foreign policy rests squarely on our ability to quickly project military forces with real power anywhere. Marines are the masters of such amphibious operations.

The other mission to emerge out of the Spanish-American War—that of expeditionary service—also proved critically important in the construction of Marine culture and the growing importance of the Corps as the spearhead of American foreign policy. A colorful but little remembered history (except by Marines and former Marines) reveals the Corps as a colonial infantry force, working at the behest of the Department of State in the Caribbean, Central America, and China between 1900 and 1939. Marine forces undertook a great many operations of varied duration and complexity in these areas, ranging from rescue missions of American citizens in danger, to constabulary duties to ensure elections and stanch civil strife, to more ambitious missions, such as running governments in both Haiti and Nicaragua. American motives for these frequent interventions were by turns cynical and idealistic, and quite often a mix of the two. Here Marines landed on foreign shores to save lives, but also to guarantee the existence of repressive regimes friendly to U.S. policies and business interests. In both Haiti and the Dominican Republic, small units of Marines, companies and platoons, chased well-organized guerrillas and roving gangs of bandits out for plunder. The Marines Corps was the primary governing institution in the Dominican Republic from 1916 to 1926, and in Nicaragua between 1926 and 1933. In the latter nation, the Marines fought alongside local constabulary forces they had trained in a protracted guerrilla war against Augusto Sandino. Between 1907 and 1912, Cuba enjoyed no less than eight interventions. The customs house of Veracruz, Mexico, was seized against stiff resistance in house-to-house fighting in the wake of a hostile Mexican government's jailing of a boat party from a U.S. Navy ship in Mexico.

The jungles, villages, and towns of these countries proved an excellent training ground for hundreds of regular officers and enlisted men who went on to serve with distinction in World War II, then transmitted the lessons of their experiences to a new generation of younger Marines who would lead the Corps in both Vietnam and Korea.

By 1940, the Marine Corps had accumulated a vast reservoir of knowledge about politico-military operations short of full-scale war. Most of the fighting in the "banana wars" was carried out by companies, platoons, even squads serving with local forces. Scarcity of men, matériel, and transport fostered improvisation and initiative at low levels, as did the neglect by the diplomats who had called for Marines in the first place to resolve politico-military disputes. It was in the jungles and countryside of the Caribbean and Central America that the Marine Corps came to accept the principle that quick, intuitive decisions on the ground by corporals and sergeants were far preferable to sitting on one's hands until orders came down from the colonel ten miles away at the command post. Here it was that Marines began to develop a well-earned reputation for being a spartan, small-unit, infantry-centered military institution that does more with less.

The lessons of the Marines' colonial infantry service were distilled in a manual in 1940 that every serious student and practitioner of brushfire conflicts, peacekeeping, peacemaking, and occupation duty recognizes as a minor classic: the *Small Wars Manual*. Few are the Marines and infantry-minded American soldiers today who do not own a copy of this book.

Both a reference handbook on tactics, organization, and equipment and a repository of down-to-earth wisdom gained the hard way on how to think about such conflicts, its authors begin by pointing out that small wars "represent the normal and frequent operations of the Marine Corps." The line between military and political responsibilities in their execution is always blurred. Hence: "There is mutual dependence and responsibility which calls for the highest qualities of statesmanship and military leadership."[25]

Drawing on this vast reservoir of experience, the Marines transformed themselves from a small, fringe segment of the navy into the most worldly military service in history. The scores of interventions among the peoples of the world in times of crisis that compose so much of the Marines' operational history have given the Corps an admirable institutional self-confidence and flexibility that few, if any, other military organizations can match. In this sense they very much resemble a unit the Marines have trained with, and fought beside, in the Middle East on a few occasions: the French Foreign Legion. Like the men of the Legion, the Marines are an elite force maintained in a high degree of readiness. The Marine Corps and the Legion both have a long and close relationship with the people who pay their bills and depend on their capabilities. The critical difference, of course, is that the Marines are indigenous to the country they serve, which makes their relationship to the public deeper, more complex.

Because the Corps has been involved so intimately in America's relations with other peoples and nations in times of crisis, the Marine story is a vital part of the twentieth-century American experience. The Marines are America's "Strong Men Armed."[26] Men armed with weapons, and with the "indefinable inner strength"—a term coined by *New York Times* journalist Drew Middleton—that comes from holding fast to a set of time-tested beliefs, a brotherhood, and a history. In the end, the awesome power of the U.S. Marines comes not from their rifles, their hovercraft, their F-18s, or their nine regiments of infantry, but from the proud and resilient hearts of all Marines, past and present, warriors united in their commitment to the five-syllable Latin expression seen in the banner above the eagle on their emblem: *Semper Fidelis*. Its English translation: Always Faithful.

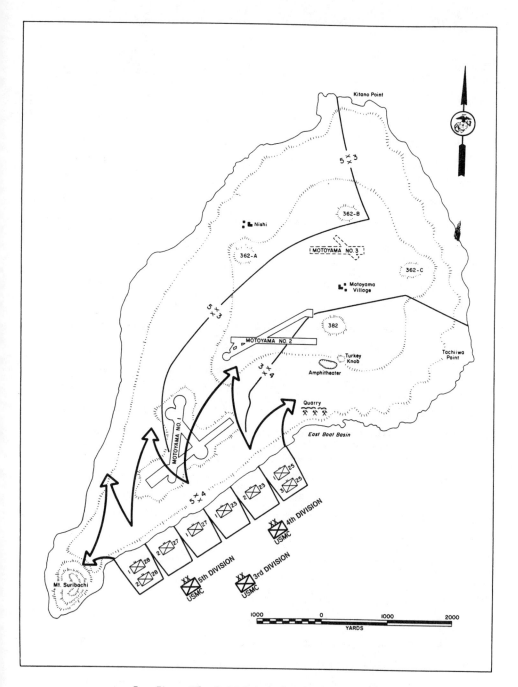

Iwo Jima: The Initial Assault of February 19th

Adapted from Joseph Alexander, *Closing In: Marines in the Seizure of Iwo Jima.*
Washington, D.C.: USMC, 1994.

TWO

THE SUPREME TEST

The Battle of Iwo Jima

When it was all over, more than twenty-five thousand young American men were wounded or dead. Casualty rates in the infantry regiments reached an astonishing 75 percent. Fewer than 250 Japanese soldiers out of a force of more than twenty-one thousand survived the fighting. Admiral Chester Nimitz, commander of the central Pacific theater, would remark even before the end of the fighting: "Among the Americans who served on Iwo Jima, uncommon valor was a common virtue." Many U.S. Marines who survived the battle would have said much the same about the Japanese. They, too, fought with tremendous tenacity.

The Joe Rosenthal photo of the flag-raising on Mount Suribachi, the most famous American photograph of World War II, is inspiring and moving. But the image takes on its full power only when one grasps the appalling horrors and savagery of the fighting that both preceded and followed the planting of that flag on Suribachi's peak.

It was a tiny, stinking island. Bereft of clean water and all but the hardiest vegetation, Iwo Jima was perpetually windswept and chock-full of sulfur, lending the air there a smell of rotten eggs. It "wasn't worth fifty cents at a sheriff's fire sale," one veteran of the campaign remarked.[1]

Before the war, intelligence reports indicated that a few hundred industrious Japanese settlers had tried to grow pineapples and other crops in Iwo's arid, volcanic soil, but their efforts had come to nothing, and most returned to Japan. Isolated 660 miles from Tokyo, Iwo Jima looked much like a pork chop when viewed from the air.

The optimists on the American planning staff had predicted the impending battle might take as little as four days. Marine lieutenant general Holland "Howlin' Mad" Smith, the man who had commanded the Leathernecks in their great amphibious sweep westward from the Solomons all the way up to the Marianas Islands in the central Pacific, was less sanguine: "The eve of D-Day at Iwo Jima found me unable to suppress a deep emotional surge. The imminence of action and responsibility for the most appalling operation we had yet undertaken weighed heavily."[2]

Smith had good reason to worry. Iwo would prove to be the bloodiest operation of the Pacific war for the Marines, and the only engagement in that conflict in which more Americans would fall than Japanese. Fred Haynes, the retired Marine Corps major general who was the operations officer of the 28th Marine Regiment, and thus one of a handful of officers who planned the assault on Mount Suribachi, reflected on the battle fifty-five years after the island had been wrested from the Japanese: "I'm a veteran of three wars. None of the other battles I've seen or even heard of compare to Iwo Jima. There's never been anything like it since. . . . It was the definitive event of my life."[3] Historians Jeter Isley and Philip Crowl suggest that the attack on this barren island fortress was nothing less than "the classic amphibious assault in recorded history."[4]

The Marines had engaged in some extremely tough combat in their naval march across the Pacific. At Tarawa, Bougainville, Tinian, Guam, and Saipan, they smashed through increasingly sophisticated island defense systems manned by Japanese troops imbued with the samurai's code of Bushido. The Japanese warrior saw surrender as bringing dishonor on himself, his family, and the emperor. In two and a half years of savage combat, each side had toughened, and there was no love lost between the combatants. Atrocities were committed on both sides. The defensive system built by the Japanese engineers and soldiers on Iwo outclassed those encountered in early campaigns. The American planning staffs at the corps and division levels knew that General Tadamichi Kuribayashi, a sixth-generation samurai and one of Tokyo's most gifted generals, a master of defensive strategy, commanded the garrison on Iwo. For more than six months his men had burrowed into Iwo's rocky crust, preparing hundreds of interconnected blockhouses, pillboxes, covered artillery emplacements, and ingeniously camouflaged machine-gun nests. Most of these were built almost flush to the ground. Aerial reconnaissance identified well over seven hundred emplacements, but those figures turned out to be about 30 percent too low. And then there were the caves and hundreds of machine-gun positions and mortars.

Imposing Mount Suribachi, the extinct volcano that dominated the southern end of the island and the beaches where the assault force would come ashore, bristled with coastal artillery and other fortifications. Across the island, Kuribayashi had developed three main defensive belts, each with interlocking fields of fire focused on the approaches to the main fortifications. There were about thirteen thousand yards of tunnels, ensuring fast and unimpeded movement belowground between various fighting positions. Some major installations had walls of concrete five feet thick.

The Marines asked the navy for nine days of prelanding bombardment. For a variety of reasons—among them limited ammunition and the navy's desire to prepare its ships for an even larger amphibious operation in early April against Okinawa, a much larger island in the Ryukyus, to the north—they got only three days. There is still a residue of bitterness between the Marines and the navy over the decision. Hundreds of fortified positions survived the shelling. Other misfortunes preceded the beginning of the battle. Twice, the landing was postponed due to unexpected delays in General MacArthur's campaign to regain the Philippines and the consequent shortfall of amphibious shipping.

Nonetheless, Iwo had to be taken. In the last several years, a heated and very interesting debate has arisen over whether or not Iwo was, in effect, worth its cost in Marine blood, and whether or not interservice rivalries may have significantly shaped the Joint Chiefs of Staff (JCS) decision to invade Iwo rather than a less well defended target that would offer similar strategic benefits.

Thus far the controversy has had the salubrious effect of bringing up a fresh set of questions about the efficacy of the unorthodox manner in which U.S. strategy was formed during the Pacific war. The ongoing debate among Iwo scholars shows that of the myriad reasons given for attacking Iwo by various military commands, some proved far more compelling than others, given the benefits of hindsight. But the new scholarship thus far has utterly failed to demonstrate that the decision to seize Iwo was essentially wrongheaded or grounded largely on false assumptions or cynical interservice rivalries. It certainly does prove the key planners worked with incomplete information and were capable of miscalculation.

Ironically, however, the recent scholarship makes it clear that one of the key benefits the Joint Chiefs of Staff envisaged from seizing the island—namely, that American fighters on Iwo would be able to escort B-29s on the way to bomb Japan, thereby saving countless lives and planes—never truly panned out in the end. Iwo proved too far from Japan for the escorts to be effective. But there was a compensating, and largely unforeseen, benefit of seizing tiny Iwo: it made an immense contribution to air-sea rescue of B-29 crews because it cut in half the fourteen-hundred-mile distance between the Marinas Islands B-29 bases and Japan. Therefore, it aided morale of the B-29 crews considerably. As General George Marshall's report to the secretary of war put it, "Iwo fields saved hundreds of battle-damaged B-29s, unable to make the full return flight to their bases. . . ."[5]

Another bulletproof rationale for taking the island was that American fighters on Iwo could intercept Japanese planes attempting to attack the B-29 bases in the Marianas. Between November 1944 and early January 1945, seven Japanese raids had destroyed eleven B-29s and severely damaged another eight. Other compelling reasons for undertaking the invasion were outlined by the Joint War Plans committee in a document dated October 18, 1944: "In effect, this operation would contribute toward lowering Japanese ability and will to resist by: (1) establishing sea and air blockades; (2) conducting intensive air bombardment; and (3) destroying enemy air and naval strength. The capture of this island would help make feasible [the] ultimate invasion of the industrial centers of Japan." [6]

Thus there would be no surprise attack on Iwo Jima. Kuribayashi had been expecting the Americans to land since late 1944. No one, certainly not the leaders of V Amphibious Corps (VAC), had doubts that the Japanese were well dug in and ready. John Lardner, veteran correspondent for *The New Yorker* who was with the task force as it headed north, commented: "The Marines headed for Iwo spoke more flatly . . . of the expectation of death than any assault troops I had been with before." [7]

Preparations for the attack on Iwo Jima were the most elaborate of the Pacific campaign to date, and part of a step-by-step strategy. Work began in earnest in the early fall of 1944, after the American Joint Chiefs of Staff and President Franklin D. Roosevelt vetoed General Douglas MacArthur's plan to invade Formosa in preparation for the attack on Japan proper. It was agreed that MacArthur's rival in the Pacific theater, Admiral Chester Nimitz, commander in chief, Pacific Ocean Areas, would prepare a multidivision navy-Marine task force and drive into the Bonin Islands to secure an air base before taking Iwo. With that task accomplished, the fleet would press closer to Japan, by invading an island that dwarfed any of the tiny Bonins: Okinawa. The Marine air squadrons emplaced on conquered Iwo would protect the right flank of the Okinawa invasion force and attack enemy ships attempting to reinforce and resupply the large Japanese army garrison on that island.

The commanders of Operation Detachment—the official designation for the assault on Iwo—were a seasoned group. They had fought together as a team on many earlier island campaigns. Admiral Raymond A. Spruance, the strategist who had commanded the carrier force during the watershed naval battle near Midway Island in June 1942, was in overall command of the operation. His Fifth Fleet's 497 ships assigned to support the Marines formed an impressive armada, on a scale that would have been unthinkable even a year earlier: in addition to a wealth of specialized support and supply vessels of one sort or another, there were four command ships, eight battleships, twelve aircraft carriers, forty-three amphibious transports, sixty-three LSTs (Landing Ship, Tank) and thirty-one LSMs (Landing Ship, Medium).

Vice Admiral Richmond Kelley Turner was the most experienced tactical commander of amphibious forces in the world. Irascible, never a favorite with the press, Turner was designated by Spruance to command the Joint Expeditionary Force, Task Force 51. Turner would give the order to "land the landing force" on D-Day morning. He would be in tactical command of the operation until the Marines had firmly established a beachhead.

Lieutenant General Holland Smith, age sixty-three, knew Operation Detachment would be his last campaign as a U.S. Marine. Designated as commanding general of the grand forces, Smith was the first to admit that Major General Harry Schmidt was the officer who would run the battle once the Marines were ashore. Schmidt had been appointed commander of V Amphibious Corps by Smith himself. And Schmidt and his operations staff did all the corps-level planning. "I think they asked me along only in case something happened to Schmidt," said Smith.[8]

Schmidt's landing force consisted of three of a greatly expanded Marine Corps' six divisions—the 3rd, 4th, and 5th. Schmidt had commanded the 4th Division in the attack on Kwajalein atoll, in the Marshall Islands, and at Saipan, in the Marianas. On little Tinian, his daring landing on a "back door" beach had succeeded brilliantly: the Marines took the island with minimal casualties.

The division commanders, too, were combat veterans of the Pacific war and World War I. Graves Erskine was forty-seven and the youngest major general in the Corps. He assumed command of the 3rd Marine Division in October 1944 after it had captured Guam. He had fought in

France in World War I and seen action in Haiti, the Dominican Republic, and Nicaragua.

At Iwo the 4th Marine Division would be making its fourth landing in less than thirteen months. They were commanded by Major General Clifton B. Cates. Twice wounded in action in World War I, he had been awarded the Navy Cross for bravery. At Guadalcanal, he commanded the 1st Marine Regiment, a particularly tough unit. That regiment had repulsed a ferocious attack on Henderson Field and paid a heavy price for it.

Major General Keller E. Rockey commanded the 5th Marine Division. He had distinguished himself in combat at Château Thierry in the last year of World War I and had earned a Navy Cross in combat. His division was the only one of the divisions slated to attack Iwo that had never fought as a unit before. About 40 percent of its officers and men were combat veterans, though, many from the disbanded paratroop and raider battalions of the Corps.

Task Force 58, under Vice Admiral Marc A. Mitscher, with its fast carriers and battleships, would strike the Japanese home islands in a diversionary attack soon after the landing commenced. Admiral Spruance felt it a necessary precaution to draw Japanese airpower away from the Fifth Fleet sailing off the island. The Marines objected to Mitscher's commandeering of all of their own fighter squadrons and two of the battleships originally slated to bombard the island for his raid. The complexity and scale of the logistical effort required to bring the combat power of three divisions to the shores of Iwo Jima was in at least one sense even greater than that required for the invasion of France the year before. This time there was no England, no fully industrialized supply base even remotely near Iwo Jima to support the invasion. Men and material had to be brought to bear at the right time and place from all over the Pacific Ocean.

In the course of their drive across the Pacific, the Marines had learned many lessons about the use of amphibious vessels of all shapes and sizes; about the coordination and placement of supporting arms; about the proper mix and placement of infantry, engineers, and artillery in the complicated orchestration of the assault from the sea; and about the storage and disbursement of fuel, food, and ammunition. More than twenty thousand troops from the navy, army, and Marines supported the eight infantry regiments involved in the actual fighting. These included Seabee battalions, which for the first time would come ashore with the early waves of assault troops to remove obstacles and cut roads into the terraces just beyond the landing beaches. Army DUKW (referred to as "Duck," this military acronym stands for: D—the model year 1942; U—amphibious; K—front-wheel drive; W—rear-wheel drive) drivers, mostly black soldiers, would haul in all manner of war-fighting material, including the critical 155mm howitzers that were too big and heavy to come ashore in Marine amphibious tractors. And then there were the vital Naval Shore Parties tasked with creating order out of chaos under heavy fire on the beach amid the steady two-way traffic of LSTs, Marine-laden amtracs, and LCMs carrying the vital Sherman medium tanks. Most of those steel-plated behemoths had 75mm guns, but others were equipped with the relatively new flamethrowers capable of shooting jellied gasoline into pillboxes.

No assault in Marine history was so well rehearsed. On Hawaii, where the 4th and 5th Divisions were encamped, models of Suribachi and other critical terrain features were constructed by Seabees and Marine engineers. Infantry fire teams, platoons, and companies conducted fire-and-maneuver attacks ceaselessly for weeks. The 3rd Division, on Guam, conducted similar drills. On that island, Marines sharpened their combat skills in mopping-up operations, flushing out scores of Japanese stragglers who fought on long after organized resistance had come to an end.

Advancements in aerial intelligence gathering and communications systems used by the Marines to control the vast array of armor, infantry, air, and naval weapons would prove indispensable in overcoming the island fortress. Each Marine division had a group of enlisted communications specialists of Navajo Indian descent who could be counted on to relay messages in their native language between different echelons without their being understood by the Japanese. Aerial reconnaissance allowed the navy-Marine planners to construct a detailed map of the island's major fortifications and gun emplacements—or at least of the 70 percent of them that had been spotted. A precise grid system was applied to the entire island, and each ship was assigned its own area and targets to shell.

In the end, however, Iwo would prove to be a test not so much of new systems and organizational adaptation as of the individual fire teams, squads, and platoons. The fire team was (and is) the smallest individual unit in the Marine Corps table of organization. At Iwo, the fire team consisted of four Marines. Three fire teams plus a squad leader formed a squad of thirteen.

The fire team consisted of a leader, typically armed with an M-1 Garand .30-caliber semiautomatic rifle or a carbine; a Browning Automatic Rifle (BAR) bearer; the BAR man's assistant, who carried ammo for that weapon; and a private with an M-1. In a demolition squad, one of the fire teams was composed of a bazooka man, two BAR men, and an M-1 rifleman. Its job was to neutralize enemy fire while the other two squads of its platoon tried to destroy the enemy position with either satchel charges or flamethrowers. Three squads and one leader—typically a first or second lieutenant—formed a platoon. Each platoon consisted of two rifle and one demolition squads.

If there was a weaknesses in preparation for the operation, it was with the replacement system, for each division contained more than twenty-five hundred replacements, the vast majority of whom had been insufficiently trained in infantry assault techniques. The reason for the failure was simple: the Marine Corps had expanded far too rapidly to maintain its prewar standards of small-unit training. The result, according to Major General Fred Haynes, was that "the replacements hadn't trained with our units. They were put in where and when needed. We put a white stripe on the back of their helmets to signal to the regular guys to look out for them. But a great many of those young Marines died very soon after going into the line."[9] Nor were the support Marines fully competent in infantry tactics, though many of them turned in credible combat performances.

The forbidding terrain of Iwo favored the defenders. Vice Admiral Turner, not a man given to hyperbole, said it was "as well defended a fixed position as exists in the world today."[10] The Japanese displayed great resourcefulness and skill in exploiting the natural topography of the island. Yet General Kuribayashi had no illusions that he would reign victorious against the Americans. He approached the battle with a distinct sense of fatalism. He knew that talk of reinforcements was empty. The Americans had control of the sea lanes and air above the island, and the Japanese navy didn't have enough planes, pilots, or aircraft carriers to both seriously challenge the gigantic American armada and protect the shoreline of the home islands. While serving in the Japanese embassy in Washington in the 1920s, he had written to his family: "The United States is the last country in the world Japan should fight. Its industrial potential is huge and fabulous, and the people are energetic and versatile. One must never underestimate the Americans' fighting ability."[11] He told his wife before departing for the island that he expected to die there, along with most of his twenty-one thousand defenders. His objective was to turn Spruance into Pyrrhus, by killing so many Marines that Washington would lose heart and reverse its plans to invade the homeland. When it was all over, Holland Smith would remark that "of all our adversaries in the Pacific, Kuribayashi was the most redoubtable."[12]

During the vast majority of the earlier encounters between the Marines and the Imperial Army, the Japanese had attempted to crush the Americans before the Corps established a beachhead. This time, despite the resistance of his senior staff, Kuribayashi ordered his units to hold their fire until the Americans were tightly packed along the landing beaches. Harry Schmidt's scheme of maneuver for conquering the island fortress was not subtle. The 4th and 5th Divisions would each assault with two regiments abreast under a rolling barrage of naval guns and rocket-firing gunships. The 5th's 28th Regiment would be on the far left (southernmost) part of the beach, tasked to break through the defenses on the neck of the island, sealing off the defenders of Suribachi from the main force of Japanese to the north. The 2nd Battalion, 28th Marines (2/28, in

44

standard military nomenclature) would then pivot left and square off to attack the many enemy defensive positions around the base of Suribachi. Meanwhile, the 27th Regiment would join the 4th Division in an attempt to punch their way up the terraces to take Airfield No. 1 by end of day one. The 25th Marines, on the far right, had as their initial objective the unenviable task of securing the high ground surrounding a rock quarry on the coast. Until they had done so, it would be impossible for the rest of the assault force to pivot to the north. The 3rd Division would remain in its transports as a reserve until those objectives were secured, at which point it would land between its sister divisions to spearhead the drive to break the first and what was thought to be the strongest defensive belt on the island, just north of the main airfield on the large piece of level terrain in the center of the island known as the Motoyama Plateau. Then it would be a matter of each regiment slugging it out against a series of entrenched strongpoints within its zone. Commencing on February 16, the three-day bombardment, planned and commanded by Vice Admiral William H. P. Blandy, who also supervised minesweeping, air bombardment, and the efforts of the Underwater Demolition Teams (UDTs) to clear the shoreline of obstacles, took out scores of heavy weapons threatening the landing force. Not enough, it would turn out. On day two, the UDTs, precursors of the navy's SEALs (Sea, Air, Land teams), swam toward the landing beaches under cover of twelve LCI (Landing Craft, Infantry) gunboats. The UDT men, thought by the Marines to be "half fish and half nuts," made a heartening discovery: there were no mines. Nor were there any other obstacles to prevent boats from reaching the beach.

The LCIs paid dearly for the effort to cover the swimmers. Apparently mistaking the gunboats for the invasion itself, the big Japanese coastal guns opened up on them. All twelve boats were hit, and there were heavy American casualties. On one vessel alone, seventeen men were killed. The commander, Lieutenant Junior Grade Rufus H. Henry, was wounded three times, but he managed to steer out of harm's way and get his wounded aboard a destroyer. Henry won the first of twenty-seven Medals of Honor awarded during the campaign. A number of the coastal guns that opened fire were pinpointed by sharp-eyed spotters, and were knocked out before the landing commenced.

On day three of the bombardment, Blandy went along with the Marines' request and focused all his weapons on defenses that threatened the immediate landing area. It was perhaps fortunate that the Marines didn't know the results of Blandy's work. Of 915 primary and secondary targets identified by intelligence, only 194 had been damaged or destroyed.

Well before first light on February 19, the assault Marines were out of their beds and preparing themselves for the most harrowing event in their lives. More than five hundred would be dead by the end of the day, and another two thousand wounded. After a steak-and-eggs break-fast—for those who could eat at all—it was onto the decks of the transports to await orders to man the landing craft. It was good weather for a landing, with moderate seas, a seven-knot breeze, and excellent visibility. As the business of orchestrating the waves of 830 amtracs and scores of LCMs and LSTs got under way, the sun was shining brightly on the vast armada, and the outline of the island loomed. To correspondent John P. Marquand, Iwo "never looked more aesthetically ugly than on D-Day morning, or more completely Japanese. Its silhouette was like a sea monster with the little dead volcano for the head, and the beach area for the neck and all the rest of it, with its scrubby, brown cliffs, for the body."[13] The unloading of the landing craft came off without a hitch. The initial assault wave was assembled at the line of departure offshore by 0830, and they went in in good order.

The first wave of Marines reached the shore under the cover of an enormous pounding of naval guns. Initial Japanese resistance was very light: only desultory fire greeted the invaders. The terrain gave the Marines more problems than the enemy that first hour, as men and tracked vehicles struggled to mount the fifteen-foot-high terrace above the beach. Feet sank in the soft volcanic ash up to the knee, but at least the infantry could move up and off the beach. Tracked vehicles had grave difficulties moving at all.

As described earlier, six thousand Marines had made shore within twenty minutes at most. Raking fire from naval guns, regulated by aerial spotters, kept the beach clear ahead of the advancing soldiers. The 28th Marines under Colonel Liversedge came ashore at Green Beach and proceeded to move inland toward Mount Suribachi at a fair pace. The 27th, led by Colonel Wornham, massed on the beach and solidified their plan to move to the south end of the airstrip. There was discussion among the officers concerning the dangers facing the 25th Marines from the cliffs opposite them, in which it was presumed a large number of Japanese were concealed, fully armed and waiting to attack.

Then the full fury of battle broke loose. Kuribayashi unleashed his heavy weapons on the tightly concentrated assault troops, with devastating effect. Preregistered fires pummeled everything that moved. It seemed like every shell killed or wounded at least one Marine, or disabled a combat vehicle. Within minutes hundreds of Marines were killed. Major Frederick S. Karch, who twenty years later would command the first Marine battalions to land in Vietnam, wondered how anyone could live through such an intense pasting.

The challenges of the hour that followed were among the most severe in the Pacific war. The Japanese counterattack intensified quickly. Generals Smith and Schmidt, who watched from the USS Eldorado, heard reports from the commanding officers that the situation was dubious. An hour and a half into the invasion, the 25th, on the right flank, had advanced only two hundred yards. It took the 3rd Battalion the entire day to staunch the fire from the quarry. Twenty-two officers and five hundred enlisted men were killed or wounded.

There was at least some good news amid mounting casualties from the opposite side of the beachhead: the 28th's 1st Battalion had crossed the neck and set about trying with some success to dig in. Both division commanders called in their reserve infantry units that first day. The 5th Division's 26th Marines got the call around noon, and Cates's 24th Marines were ashore by late afternoon. Both regiments had a tougher time getting ashore than did the first waves to hit the beach in the morning.

On the increasingly congested shoreline, beach parties struggled desperately under mortar and machine-gun fire to preserve some semblance of order. Rising tides caused a number of landing craft to breach; others foundered in the surf, having been damaged by Japanese coastal guns. A number of tanks got ashore that morning, but without Marsden Matting (a mesh that allowed vehicles to cross over soft or muddy terrain) they could not negotiate the black sand and climb the terraces in search of some sort of defilade until proper assaults could be organized with supporting infantry. The tanks had to be pulled by bulldozers up the terrace. Four of the 5th Division's tanks took direct hits within minutes of their first advance toward the front line. Sergeant Thomas Gallant described what happened when one of the behemoths was hit by an armor-piercing tank round: "It punched through the cold armor plate as a finger is punched through putty, making a hole all the way through the thickest part." The entire crew was killed instantly, transformed into "a jellied, liquified mass blended into a viscoidal sticky fluid."[14]

By 1100 the beach was strewn with so much detritus that Admiral Turner was forced to close it off until a modicum of order was reestablished. One Marine correspondent later described the scene: "It was as though the owner of a toy factory had gone berserk and strewn handfuls of heads and limbs over a miniature island. Except for the puttee-tapes of the Japanese or the yellowish leggings of the Americans, it was hard to identify the fallen of either side. From it all rose the intensifying reek of death."[15]

Amid the mayhem, however, there was no widespread panic. Platoons and companies struggled to organize themselves and press the attack forward. Americans and Japanese blasted away at targets seen and unseen amid the plaintive cries of wounded Marines, and shouts by men for ammo, water, and machine-gun support. Along the beach Seabees and Marine pioneer units attached explosive charges to landing craft, stalled and damaged trucks, Jeeps, and half-destroyed amtracs to clear them from the beach. It was imperative to land some of the artillery to repulse the expected night attack. A number of 105mm howitzers fell into the sea, as the DUKWs transporting them swamped in the afternoon's heavy surf.

Among the hundreds of Marine dead that first day was the Marine Corps' first Medal of Honor winner in World War II. Gunnery Sergeant "Manila John" Basilone, a brawny machine gunner who had served with distinction on Guadalcanal and had refused to stay home for a publicity tour as the Marine Corps had wanted, was killed instantly along with four members of his squad by an artillery shell just as he was pushing his men forward in attack.

On the island's neck, just north of Suribachi, it seemed that everyone had a brush with death before nightfall. One B Company Marine reached the western coast of the island and paused to inspect himself. The Japanese had shot the heel off one of his boondockers. He had bullet holes in his pack and through his dungarees. His skin hadn't even been nicked. The 1st Battalion had gotten across the neck so fast that a U.S. destroyer off the western beaches mistook some Marines for Japanese and fired several five-inch shells, striking the cliff just below where three Marines were trying to dig in.

Fire on the beach remained extremely heavy; with the exception of the 28th Marines, progress toward the first major objectives was discouragingly slow. Marines tried desperately to dig in to the black sand to shield themselves, but to no avail. It was like trying to dig into a barrel of wheat. From Suribachi, on the left flank, from the Motoyama Plateau to their front, and from the cliffs above the rock quarry on their right came direct fire of all varieties, and from deep in the island's center a steady flow of accurate artillery rained down. In the afternoon, *Time* correspondent Robert Sherrod was aboard a landing craft when he met an exhausted Marine returning from a morning's fighting. The Marine said, "I wouldn't go in there if I were you. There's more hell in there than I've seen in the rest of this war put together."[16]

One thousand casualties were evacuated to navy ships before nightfall. Japanese artillery continued to blast away through that first harrowing, chilly night, resulting in a steady flow of Marine casualties. Yet much to the surprise of the thirty thousand Americans, the Japanese did not launch a counterattack. In the morning, as Sherrod described the scene, the Marines faced "a nightmare in hell. About the beach . . . lay the dead. They had died with the greatest possible violence. Nowhere in the Pacific had I seen such badly mangled bodies. Many were cut squarely in half. Legs and arms lay fifty feet from any body."[17] All hopes for a quick campaign faded out that first night.

D plus 1—February 20—was, by and large, a discouraging day of little gain and continued heavy casualties. The consolidation of forces was frustratingly slow due to continued congestion and chaos on the beach. One battery of 155mm howitzers, the heaviest in the Marine arsenal, made it ashore and commenced firing by late afternoon. The 4th Battalion of the 12th Marines, an artillery unit with twelve 105mm howitzers, lost ten of its guns in heavy surf. Near the rock quarry the 24th and 25th Marines continued to slug it out with Japanese infantry firmly ensconced in the crevices and caves in the cliffs. As dusk settled they broke through most of the strongpoints, only to be hit by friendly fire in the form of both an air strike and naval fire. About one hundred casualties resulted.

There was one major accomplishment that day. The 21st Marines of the 3rd Division entered the battle and pushed across the western end of Airfield No. 1, while the 4th Division conquered the eastern end of the main runway, taking heavy casualties from the welter of camouflaged antitank guns protecting the field.

The critical objective of the next three days of the battle was Suribachi. The Americans couldn't push through the main line of resistance in the north until the "hot rocks," as the Marines called the volcano, were fully subdued. The tactics used in its capture were essentially those used throughout the campaign to reduce hundreds of strongpoints all over the island. The sheer number of well-protected caves, blockhouses, and antitank weapons severely restricted the use and effectiveness of supporting fires, as the Marines were invariably so close to the enemy that long-range guns were as likely to inflict friendly casualties as enemy ones. Where supporting arms could be used, it was largely to temporarily neutralize enemy fire rather than to destroy enemy positions outright. Once the fire from the Japanese position was cut off by tanks, artillery, or close air, the assault teams went into action, maneuvering so the men could get close enough to burn out the defenders or blow them up with satchel charges.

To reach the base of the mountain, wherein the defenders manned a network of strongpoints connected by tunnels, required the reduction of more than sixty blockhouses on the approaches alone. Perhaps fifty more were emplaced within the mountain, facing the attackers, in the first hundred feet of Suribachi's elevation. Higher up was a series of caves impervious to American artillery. The 28th gained but two hundred yards that day, overrunning about forty strongpoints en route. A cold rain added to the misery, and tanks were not able to join the infantry until very late in the day. Because they could not find protected positions to rearm and refuel. Indeed, there was precious little shelter anywhere on the island . . . except for the Japanese.

On D plus 2, the 1st Battalion, 28th Regiment—each Marine regiment had three infantry battalions—made good progress as it sought to maneuver around the western perimeter of the base. In the center, the 3rd Battalion cracked Japanese defenses, but the 2nd Battalion, whose mission was to reach around the base on the eastern side—with the landing beaches directly behind them—ran into devastating fire, first rifles and machine guns, then mortars. As the official history of the operation puts it: "The noise and fury increased until the hearing of the attacking Marines was numbed and their thinking impaired. It seemed as if the volcano's ancient bowels had suddenly come to life and the men were advancing into a full-scale eruption."[18] The shells fell and fell, in greater numbers. One Marine who made the assault that day would later write:

> We were now part of a real hell-bent-for-leather attack, the kind the Marines are famous for. . . . There seemed nothing ahead but death. . . . It is in a situation like this that Marine Corps training proves its value. There probably wasn't a man among us who didn't wish to [God] he was moving in the opposite direction. But we had been ordered to attack, so we would attack. Our training [had] imbued us with a fierce pride in our outfit, and this pride helped now to keep us from faltering.[19]

Earlier that day, the Third Platoon of Company E, 2/28, supported by three tanks, distinguished itself with a furious rush to within yards of the base of the volcano. A tough young Marine private from Montana cattle country, Donald Ruhl, who the day before had charged a block-house and captured it single-handedly, killing nine enemy soldiers in the process, threw himself on a hand grenade, absorbing its full impact and saving the life of his sergeant in the process. He received the Medal of Honor posthumously.

Next day, the 28th Marines, having painstakingly sealed off many fortified positions, continued to hammer away with the help of artillery and tanks. By late afternoon, the regiment's 1st and 2nd Battalions' patrols linked up at the southern tip of the island, and Japanese resistance from the mountain's slopes had all but evaporated.

A less-happy development came in the form of an order from Admiral Turner to Marc Mitscher, directing Task Force 58 to depart from the area. They were off to attack Honshu and Okinawa. Mitscher, much to the chagrin of the V Amphibious Corps command staff, took all eight Marine fighter squadrons from the scene. From here on in, all close air support for the Marines was flown by navy pilots, who, for all their courage and dedication, lacked the Marine airmen's extensive training in close-air-support techniques. Many Marines claimed that the quality of the air support in the battle suffered as a result.

D plus 4—February 23—was cold, the island again windswept and rain-drenched. In the 28th's zone, it fell to the 3rd Platoon, E Company, 2nd Battalion to scale the ugly volcano and secure the summit. There were no signs of resistance as the forty Marines cautiously made their way up a winding, steep trail, struggling on hands and knees to retain their balance, with flankers on both sides warily on the lookout for hidden enemy gun emplacements. The platoon's irrepressible, beloved leader, Lieutenant Keith Wells, had been badly shot up earlier in the fight. As his men struggled forward in full view of thousands of Marines to the north and sailors aboard the ships of the fleet, Wells was recuperating in a hospital ship. The Texas native had often opined that given fifty men who weren't afraid to die, he could take any position. Now his platoon was about to take a very prominent piece of real estate, making history in the process. They were minutes away from raising the American flag on the summit of Mount Suribachi. It would be the first flag-raising on Japanese soil in World War II, for Iwo was technically a part of the prefecture of Tokyo.

The 28th's Regimental Journal reports that the 3rd Platoon reached the summit at 1018. First Lieutenant Harold Schrier, a tall twenty-four-year-old former Marine Raider, was the first over the lip of the summit. Not a shot had been fired on the ascent. Destroyed rocket launchers, artillery pieces, and several unmanned machine guns lay about the summit.

Schrier ordered the men to find something in the debris to use for a flagpole. His battalion commander, Lieutenant Colonel Chandler Johnson, had given him a flag and told him to plant it on the volcano's crest. A piece of drainage pipe was located, and at 1031 Johnson's flag appeared above the crest. As soon as it was visible, shouts and cheers from tired Marines went up the length and breadth of Iwo Jima; ships blew whistles and horns. For every American on Iwo, it was a moment they would remember until the day they died. Now the Marines had the advantage of the high ground, and they could move on to the next phase of the operation—the drive to the north—without the awful burden of being chewed up by fires from both their rear and front. Aboard the *Eldorado*, James Forrestal, secretary of the navy, turned to General Holland Smith. Deeply moved, he said, "Holland, the raising of that flag on Suribachi means a Marine Corps for the next five hundred years."[20]

The flag also caught the attention of the Japanese, who quickly opened up on the crest with pretty much every weapon that had the range. Suddenly, several enraged Japanese emerged from their camouflaged fighting holes near the crest. They were dispatched by Marines of Schrier's platoon. A few minutes later the 3rd Platoon made a grisly discovery: 150 Japanese soldiers, realizing that the American conquest of Suribachi was imminent, had killed themselves inside a bunker about one hundred feet below the summit.

Early that afternoon, Chandler Johnson, fearing that "some son of a bitch is going to want that flag," sent a runner to obtain a larger replacement and secure the first flag for his battalion.[21] That larger flag, obtained from *LST 779*, went up in a short ceremony at 1430 as Joe Rosenthal, an AP photographer, snapped off a series of pictures. One of them caught five Marines and a navy corpsman just as they struggled to raise the larger banner. The image, an instant icon, remains a defining symbol of the U.S. Marines. The official history of Iwo Jima summarizes the event succinctly in a Churchillian phrase: "For the Marines on Iwo, the capture of Suribachi marked the end of a beginning; for General Kuribayashi's well-entrenched main force, it was the beginning of the end."[22]

The tactical key to defeating the Japanese in the north lay in breaking through the defensive belt in the relatively flat tableland that lay behind (to the north of) Airfield No. 2. Here, on the Motoyama Plateau, Kuribayashi emplaced many of his larger-caliber weapons—dual-purpose antiaircraft guns, the feared 47mm antitank guns, a large percentage of his two artillery and three heavy mortar battalions, which included weapons capable of hurling 700-pound barrel-shaped projectiles into the Marines' lines. They were inaccurate, but accuracy mattered little on Iwo at this point, for American fighting men were everywhere in the small amount of terrain they had captured.

The landscape of the plateau "comprised a weird-looking array of cliffs, ravines, gorges, crevices and ledges. Jumbled rock, torn stubble, small trees, jagged ridges and chasms sprawled about in a crazy pattern."[23] The Japanese had constructed tunnels for a thousand yards with more than a dozen entrances, and there were also many natural caves. As usual, the Japanese had taken great care to ensure that mutually supporting machine-gun and antitank blockhouses and pillboxes lined the natural avenues of approach to the plateau.

It was essential to crack the defensive line and reduce the positions on the plateau because many of the guns were sited onto the ravines, ridges, and cliffs along both coasts of the island. The 4th and 5th Divisions were assigned to drive up the east and west coasts respectively. By February 24, two of the 3rd Division's regiments were placed in the center of the Marine line. Unless the 3rd Division's Leathernecks broke into the plateau and reduced those positions, the regiments moving along the coast were sure to be decimated on the flanks. As V Amphibious Corps operations officer Edward A. Craig explained, if the Marines broke through the enemy's defensive belt behind the airfield, it would enable "our forces to envelop enemy troops on the right and left flank and to continue the attack down the rocky corridors and ridgelines on our flanks instead of assaulting frontally these ridges and cross compartments." [24]

By the time the 28th had secured Suribachi, the other Marine regiments had fully secured Airfield No. 1. However, progress in the effort to crack into the heart of the first defensive belt system behind it was discouragingly slow. Gains on February 21 through 23 had averaged only one hundred to two hundred yards per day, and casualties were heavy, particularly among the 4th Division's units, where the terrain precluded any armor support to speak of.

The camouflaging of Japanese heavy guns had prevented Marine and navy counterbattery fire from taking out as many heavy-weapon positions as Schmidt and his Marines would have liked. And the Japanese had fine visibility of Marine units as they assaulted, as well as excellent command and control.

The next day, February 24, General Schmidt ordered a three-regiment attack against what turned out to be the main defensive line to the north of Airfield No. 2. The 26th, 21st, and 24th Marines attacked (left to right) in the direction of the plateau after a full hour of artillery and air preparatory fires, with every tank that could be mustered from all three divisions in support. The bombardment hardly made a dent in the Japanese resistance. For two days small groups of Marines raced across the runway of Airfield No. 2 supported by tanks, but invariably they were driven back, and many Shermans were knocked out by highly skilled Japanese antitank crews in the rising ground to the north. Meanwhile, General Erskine's 12th Regiment, his artillery, continued to make its way ashore piecemeal.

It fell largely to the 21st Marines under Colonel Hartnoll J. Withers on D plus 5—and to the tanks of all the divisions that supported their attack—to finally break the Japanese defenses around Airfield No. 2. It was defended by the crack 145th Infantry Regiment under Colonel Masuo Ikeda. Ikeda had ringed the airfield with scores of pillboxes and reinforced concrete bunkers with walls as thick as five feet. Without question, the 145th was among the very best enemy units on the island. It was here that the 21st had to break through the main line of resistance.

The pillboxes and bunkers that dotted the rising piece of land between Airfields No. 2 and 3 were well covered on the flanks by machine guns and infantry, and the approaches were mined. Here as elsewhere frontal assault was the only option. Like every infantry regiment on the front lines, the 21st had been battling against a seemingly endless series of enemy positions since it had come ashore on February 21. Often the pressure to reduce large emplacements required that spider holes and snipers be bypassed, and the Marines thus took fire from the front, the flanks, and often from the rear. The steady thump of antitank fire made crossing the runway next to impossible.

Japanese artillery from the north pounded the attackers as they moved up the airfield. The defensive positions had to be taken in detail. And they had to be taken by tired Marines who had slept at best fitfully for a few hours over the course of three days. Indeed, few Marines anywhere on the island could sleep, because there was still no area of any size out of the range of Japanese mortars and artillery.

On February 23, a twenty-one-year-old corporal from 1/21 named Herschel W. Williams destroyed six pillboxes with his flamethrower, single-handedly, covered by four riflemen. It was the kind of initiative that gave heart to even the most tired and battle-weary of his brothers. His Medal of Honor citation stated that the corporal "daringly went forward alone to attempt the reduction of devastating machine-gun fire from the unyielding positions. . . . He fought desperately for four hours under terrific enemy small-arms fire and repeatedly returned to his own lines to prepare demolition charges and obtain . . . flamethrowers, struggling back, frequently to the rear of hostile emplacements, to wipe out one position after another."

The 21st Marines' attack on the morning of February 25 was supported by eight tanks. It ground to a halt rapidly, though, as five of the armored vehicles ran over mines or were struck with antitank fire within the first five minutes. Fifteen crewmen were killed or wounded. Only a screen of smoke enabled the three remaining tanks to retreat to the line of departure on the west side of the runway. Now two companies of 3/21 had to advance, somehow, across eight hundred yards, without armor, under heavy mortar fire, and attempt to knock out a series of enemy pillboxes and other emplacements en route. Their objective: one of the more formidable of the enemy's strongpoints on elevated land just north of the junction of Airfield No. 2's two runways. From there the Japanese commanded the entire airfield. Shortly after reaching the perimeter of the intersection both company commanders were dead—one the victim of a grenade, the other of a sniper.

The Marine Corps prides itself on accomplishing its missions, no matter the obstacles, and what happened next was a demonstration of Marines upholding that tradition. A first lieutenant named Raoul Archambault took command, gathered the platoon leaders together, and organized both companies for an assault—uphill against a well-defended belt of antitank positions, pillboxes, and trenches. The Marines broke across the runway under cover of a mortar barrage and naval gunfire, heading for where they thought the emplacements might be. The apertures in the pillboxes were difficult to detect. On the first try, a platoon or so scrambled to the top, only to encounter a wall of fire from two pillboxes on the flanks and a trench full of enemy riflemen. They were driven back to the base of the hill. The Americans regrouped, brought the wounded to the rear, and tried again, this time under artillery fire. They pushed forward only twenty-five or thirty feet when the Japanese unleashed a furious counterattack. The exhausted and outnumbered Marines withdrew to the other side of the runway.

Again the men of 3/21 regrouped. Naval gunfire was called in on the ridge. Then off again they went, reaching the crest against light opposition. But before they could dig in, the Japanese unleashed another counterattack. Savage, no-holds-barred fighting erupted on the crest. Men were bayoneted, strangled, clubbed with entrenching tools. Wild screams, Marine and Japanese war cries, and rebel yells meshed with the groans of the dying and wounded. In ten minutes, it was all over, and the U.S. Marines held the ridge, this time for good. Lieutenant Colonel Wendall Duplantis, Archambault's battalion commander, had observed the action from nearby. It was, said the colonel, "the most aggressive and inspiring spectacle I ever witnessed." [25]

Casualties were very heavy; they continued to be in the 21st for the next week, as one grim assault followed another. On March 2, when the commander of 2/21 took a bullet in the knee, his unit was taken off the front. It had three hundred effective men remaining out of the twelve hundred who had first crossed from ship to shore.

On the same day that the 21st Marines conquered the ridge at the intersection of the airfield, General Schmidt's remaining battalion of 155mm howitzers came across the beach. It was welcome news among the division commanders, for the Marines were woefully short of fire support as a result of the density and strength of the fortifications they had encountered. Schmidt's scheme of maneuver called for a steady advance across a front of about four thousand yards in the middle of the island. Fearing the destructive power of Japanese flanking fire, the Marine commander decided against fully concentrating his combat power in the center for a dramatic breakthrough. Instead, he placed half the organic artillery of the 4th and 5th Divisions at the disposal of the 3rd Division in the center, which also got a higher percentage of the V Amphibious Corps' 155mm howitzer fire for most of the brutal days of killing and destruction that lay ahead. Erskine's division would make the main effort in the center, but the entire line was meant to move forward more or less at the same pace.

Rockey's 5th Division now girded itself to push forward against the elevated strongpoints known as Nishi Ridge and Hills 362A and 362B, and then the Gorge. Each was a hornet's nest manned by Japanese soldiers whose water supply was growing short but who otherwise were of good morale, ready and willing to die for their emperor.

Cates's 4th Division would spend the next three weeks in a series of driving, bloody assaults against a devilish set of man-made and natural interlocking strongpoints dubbed the Meatgrinder. Its components: Hill 382; an escarpment shaped like a lopsided football known as the Turkey Knob; a rockstrewn natural depression called the Amphitheater; and the remains of Minami village, the blasted dwellings of which offered excellent cover to its defenders. Here the Japanese guns placed in defilade were virtually impossible to detect—even after Airfield No. 1 had been repaired by the Seabees, allowing for the fragile but reliable light observation planes of VMO-4, a Marine observation squadron, to fly over Japanese positions.

On D plus 6 it was the typical assault routine: artillery air and naval prep fire, followed by an early-morning jump-off for the infantry regiments on the line. As usual, the intensive preattack shelling inflicted marginal damage. In the 4th Division's zone, the 23rd Marines took heavy fire immediately after leaving the line of departure. Four of the six Shermans supporting the drive were knocked out early in the day; the remaining two were rendered immobile by the soft sand in front of Hill 382. One platoon clawed its way to the top of the hill, but enemy fire was so heavy that no other elements of the lead platoon's company could exploit this early advance. After several hours of hand-to-hand combat, the platoon had to withdraw. February 25 was a harbinger of ominous things to come for the 23rd Marines and the entire 4th Division. Five hundred Marines fell that day in and around the Meatgrinder. The next day, 1/23 got to the base of Hill 382. Again casualties were alarmingly high.

For the 5th Division to make serious progress in its drive up the western edge of the island, the 3rd Division had to steadily reduce the heavy weapons—and machine gun–bearing pillboxes—firing down on them from the plateau. This they began to do in earnest, albeit slowly, on February 25. The next day, the 5th Division's regiments pushed into broken terrain, a series of ridges and ravines, and made three hundred yards, taking over two wells the enemy desperately needed. A Japanese counterattack was broken by naval gunfire and Marine artillery. Then the main effort in the 5th Division's sector fell to the 27th Marines, who struggled hard and long to gain another two hundred yards.

The last day of the month found two of the 27th Regiment's three rifle battalions at the foot of heavily fortified Hill 362A. There the fire was so intense that no further movement could be made. The capture of the hill itself took two agonizing days of brutal fighting, much of it by the 28th Marines. Here, on March 2, the proud battalion that had raised the flag on Suribachi lost its commander, Lieutenant Colonel Chandler Johnson. He was killed by an artillery shell that "cut the top of his head off right above the eyes, all the way to the back of the neck, and the piece was hanging from [his] collar like a bucket lid," recalled Marine Private Art Stanton.[26] Hill 362A also took the lives of three of the Suribachi flag raisers. Marine engineers played a vital role in this operation, as the avenue of approach to 362A was strewn with mines and anti-tank ditches and treacherous cave outposts that had to be attacked with satchel charges and flamethrowers. The Third Battalion, 29th Marines destroyed sixty-eight such positions on March 1 alone.

The reward for such impressive progress was more combat and plenty of it, for the even more formidable obstacles of Nishi Ridge and 362B lay ahead. Colonel Thomas A. Wornham, commander of the 27th Regiment, remarked that these strongpoints had interlocking fields of fire the likes of which he'd never seen. Still, by March 10 — D plus 19 — the 5th Division had seized Hill 362B and occupied all but a small piece of land in their zone of operation in the northwest sector of the island. Along the way Marines of 3/26 had secured a small hill north of Nishi Ridge when the entire escarpment exploded in a deafening roar, killing or maiming some forty Marines in an instant. The Japanese had blown up one of their own major underground command posts.

The 3rd Division faced less broken terrain in late February and early March but no less ferocious resistance. The terrain was more amenable to tanks than was the area of operations of the 5th Division. Trouble was, the Japanese were extraordinarily good marksmen with antitank guns. Erskine's 3rd Division began to make significant progress on February 27, thanks in large measure to its having assembled an array of supporting fires to suppress Japanese return fire during Marine advances. Before the infantry broke into the assault, no fewer than eight battalions of artillery, supplemented by air strikes, saturated the Japanese strongpoints with ordnance. The 9th Marines lost eleven tanks on February 27 while clawing their way to the base of Hill Oboe and the summit of Hill Peter. The next day elements of the division broke through the main defensive belt about 200 yards north and 750 yards due west of the northern end of Airfield No. 2 and pushed past the ruins of Motoyama village, occupying what was left of it by late afternoon. With the fall of the village and the area immediately surrounding it, no longer could the enemy sit atop the central ridge and place observed fire on every inch of lower Iwo—and the thousands of U.S. Marines who were busy supporting the fighting at the front, and building a formidable military city on the conquered southern end of the island.

Now General Erskine faced the difficult task of seizing Airfield No. 3 and pushing his advance toward the northern coast of Iwo Jima. North of that airfield the ground rose into a saddle flanked by two hills. The hills formed the northwest and southeast corners of the Motoyama Plateau. Since caves there commanded the terrain to the south, naturally Kuribayashi had fortified them to the maximum possible extent. The unenviable task of crossing this killing ground fell to the men and officers of the 9th and 21st Marines, and they would pay for every yard gained. The first two days of the assault came to no good end. The 9th Marines fared a bit better, as they battered their way slowly and deliberately to the base of Hill 362B. Dead and wounded Marines were strewn all about the battlefield. The next day, March 5, was declared a day of rest by General Schmidt. It couldn't have come soon enough for the exhausted men on the line.

By now there was no question the Marines would prevail on Iwo Jima. It was only a question of how long it would take, and how many Marines would die, before the island was secured. The attack pressed forward. On March 6, the 3rd Division front was taking flanking fire from the 5th Division's zone—northwest of Airfield No. 3. It was time for something a bit different. Erskine's operations officer worked out a daring plan with Lieutenant Colonel Harold C. Boehm, the commander of 3/9 to conduct a surprise night attack with no artillery cover. At 0500 hours the men of 3/9 gathered themselves together and moved out in silence toward the sleeping Japanese and Hill 362C. It seemed to work. The initiative earned the 3rd Battalion four hundred precious yards of terrain. A great many very startled Japanese were shot or burned to death by Marine flamethrowers en route.

Yet in the morning, it was clear that the 3rd Battalion had not reached its planned objective, but rather Hill 331 instead. The jump-off point for the battalion had been farther to the rear than anyone had realized. Thus, the battalion found itself in the awkward position of being smack in the middle of some very angry Japanese soldiers. Boehm decided to press forward in any event, and at 0715, 3/9 saddled up and moved out in assault. Four hours later, the battalion, having encountered savage resistance from all sides, reported back to the regiment's command post: Hill 362C was owned and occupied by the U.S. Marines. Boehm's Marines had bypassed many of the strongest positions during its surprise night attack.

For the next several days the 9th and 21st Regiments pressed forward indefatigably. The twisted draws and ravines severely limited the use of armor, and casualties continued to be heavy. This greatly concerned General Erskine, who later remarked that

> the infantry battalions were now beginning to feel the presence of the large number of replacements, manifested by a sharp drop in combat efficiency. These men were found to be willing but very poorly trained. . . . The faulty teamwork, resulting from lack of small-unit training, was also a definite hindrance to the operation of the . . . battalions. Many

needless casualties occurred in these replacements because of a lack of knowledge of the proper use of cover and concealment.[27]

On March 8, 3/9 attacked toward the east from Hill 362C and managed a four-hundred-yard advance. Now the 3rd Division was beginning to approach the northeast shoreline, and the remaining Japanese were feeling the weight of heavy and continuous combat. By the afternoon of March 9, both 3/9 and 1/21 had run patrols all the way down to the beach, and by nightfall the 3rd Division held eight hundred yards of the northeastern shoreline. The tired, sleep-starved Marines of Erskine's division sent a canteen of seawater to General Schmidt for "inspection." Enemy territory had been decisively split in two by the 3rd Division's advance. Kuribayashi's tough soldiers and sailors now held only about one square mile, no more.

While this action was taking place, the weary 4th Division, on the right, had captured a key strongpoint in their area of operations: Hill 382. In the fight for "the Hill," as it was thereafter known among the survivors, one young Marine from New York State put on an extraordinary display of fighting prowess. Private First Class Douglas Thomas Jacobson used a bazooka and everything the Marine Corps had taught him about infantry fighting to reduce sixteen discrete enemy positions and one of the few light tanks the enemy had on the island. The statisticians credited Jacobson with killing seventy-five Japanese in one day. He won the Medal of Honor for his dangerous work, and lived to tell the tale as well.

Hill 382 finally fell on March 2—at which point the combat effectiveness of the 4th Division's assault companies stood at a very weak 50 percent. This was very serious, for the nature of the Meatgrinder was such that all its strongpoints needed to be assaulted simultaneously for any one of the battalions to make real headway.

The Amphitheater and Turkey Knob remained in Japanese hands. The next day, the 23rd Marines attacked positions north of the Amphitheater, hoping to link up with 2/25 in an encirclement of the enemy stronghold before mounting a frontal assault on the blockhouse atop the Knob. The approach to the Knob had been mined, but an engineer platoon finally managed to clear one avenue, and the Marines inflicted enough damage on the position to reduce the fury of its fire. It took Cates's men another six days of methodical attacks, one position at a time, to reduce this devil's den of Japanese resistance.

The last week of fighting around the Meatgrinder was punctuated by several night infiltrations into Marine lines by the enemy. The second of these turned out to be the most formidable counterattack of the entire campaign. The 25th Marines, on the right of the division's line, with the 23rd and 24th on their left, bore the brunt of this attack. The latter two regiments, as they pushed forward slowly in an east-southeast advance, threatened "to envelop [enemy] forces, which would be compressed in an area bounded by the sea in the east and the 25th Marines in the south. For all practical purposes, the northern wing of the 4th Division formed a hammer while the . . . 25th Marines would serve as the anvil." [28]

The commander of Japanese forces in this area was a proud samurai and champion swordsman, Captain Samaji Inouye. Late in the evening of March 8, he gathered his troops together, most of whom were members of naval units, and ordered them to break through the enemy's lines, head toward Suribachi, and destroy as many American Marines and aircraft as possible.

At 2300, the attack commenced in silence, with the main effort directed toward the boundary between the 23rd and 24th Regiments. Suddenly the Marines were greeted with the haunting cries of "Banzai!" as Japanese sailors tossed grenades and flung themselves forward into the American lines. Some had mines attached to their bodies and blew themselves up when they were close upon the Americans. A vicious, hand-to-hand melee followed for several hours. One of 2/23's rifle companies ran out of ammunition at about 0100. A Jeep with a trailer full of ammo managed somehow to move through enemy-infested roads and deliver its cargo. Sporadic fighting, coupled with the cries of the wounded, continued until dawn. Some 700 Japanese dead lay about the lines in the morning. The 4th Division had suffered 90 Marines killed and 250 wounded.

By March 10, all three Marine divisions had secured their core objectives: the 3rd had broken through to the sea; the 4th had effectively reduced the series of Meatgrinder strongpoints, though small pockets of resistance had been bypassed here and elsewhere on the island; and the 5th had backed Kuribayashi and virtually all of his remaining organized units into the area around Kitano Point.

The previous night, more than six hundred miles from the battle raging on Iwo, a horrific milestone in world military history was unfolding. Three hundred B-29 bombers unleashed firebombs on Tokyo. Seventy-two thousand Japanese citizens perished in one night, as sixteen square miles of the capital city—twice the real estate that comprised Iwo—went up in a hellish blaze. The next target of Admiral Nimitz's drive toward the home islands of Imperial Japan, Okinawa, had already been effectively isolated from resupply from either Kyoto or Formosa. On that island in the Ryukyus, Japan's 32nd Army and its legions of Okinawan laborers were preparing thousands of pillboxes, concrete gun emplacements, and defensive belts all around the large number of east-west ridges in the southern half of the island. They were under constant attack by U.S. Navy, Army, and Marine aircraft as they toiled.

All that remained on Iwo, now that the Japanese defensive belts had been cracked, was to reduce the isolated pockets of resistance. Perhaps three thousand of the original twenty-one thousand enemy soldiers remained alive. Short of water, isolated from one another with little command and control, these brave men, practitioners of Bushido to the end, held on and fought with a grim determination that earned the admiration of many a Marine.

A flag-raising ceremony on March 16 marked the declaration that organized resistance was at an end. Unfortunately, it was not—far from it. Ten more days of heavy, steady combat followed in the northern end of the island.

By this point in the battle, the Seabees and engineers had transformed the southern two-thirds of the island into a combination military airport and city. Asphalt plants, desalination stations, more than ten miles of roads, tank farms, barracks, and, less happily, morgues and three cemeteries sprang up.

Cushman's Pocket, a hornet's nest east of Airfield No. 3, was at last reduced by the 9th Marines on March 16. The Pocket, named after the commander of the 2nd Battalion, 9th Marines, Lieutenant Colonel Robert Cushman, a future commandant of the Corps, was a concentrated maze of pillboxes, concrete bunkers, and machine-gun pits. Holland Smith departed the island that day. His long and distinguished combat career in the Marines was over. It was surely a day of high emotion for Smith, one of the greatest amphibious soldiers of the twentieth century.

The last week of organized resistance found the much depleted 21st Marines, under Colonel Hartnoll Withers, executing the final assault on the extreme northern tip of the island. General Erskine was just behind the front, keeping an eye on progress despite his having contracted pneumonia. Erskine gave two captured Japanese a message for Colonel Masuo Ikeda, who commanded the defense in this sector of the island, explaining that U.S. forces had control of all but a small area near Kitano Point and calling on the colonel to surrender. His message contained no hyperbole: "The fearlessness and indomitable fighting spirit which has been displayed by the Japanese troops on Iwo Jima warrants the admiration of all fighting men. You have handled your troops in a superb manner but we have no desire to completely annihilate brave troops who have been forced into a hopeless position. Accordingly, I suggest you cease resistance at once. . . ."[29]

It was another offer the Japanese preferred to turn down. Fighting dragged on in the 5th Division's zone, centering on the Gorge, south of Kitano Point, an eight-hundred-by-three-hundred-yard pocket known as Death Valley. Here tank-bulldozers cut paths for Shermans, which in turn were followed by infantry rifle and demolition squads. Toward the end of fighting in the Gorge, a Marine tank-bulldozer driver was suddenly assaulted by a single furious Japanese soldier carrying a satchel charge. The dozer driver raised his plow just as the enraged Japanese closed in on the earthmoving behemoth, then slammed it down, cutting the enemy soldier in two before the charge went off. "Did you see what that Nip bastard tried to do to me!" the American exclaimed before deserting his dozer and walking out of the Gorge; the Sherman tankers looked on incredulously.[30] The next day, he was back on the job, clearing debris and dirt so the tanks could do their job.

The final enemy cave in Death Valley was demolished on D plus 34—March 25. The evidence suggests that on this day, or perhaps the day following, General Kuribayashi took his own life. His final campaign was a bravura performance. His defense was remarkably astute and disciplined throughout the thirty-six-day struggle. The general's only significant tactical error had been committed what seemed a lifetime ago to the combatants: the day before the invasion he had ordered Suribachi's big guns to fire on the preinvasion gunboats covering the preinvasion insertion of navy UDT swimmers, mistaking them for the first wave of the assault.

While organized resistance may have been on its last legs on March 25, it was not dead. That night three hundred well-coordinated enemy soldiers and sailors managed to infiltrate American lines. They reached all the way to the tents of the VII Fighter Command, a newly arrived army unit adjacent to Airfield No. 1, and took a terrible toll on the sleeping pilots. Some surprised Seabees and members of a Marine pioneer outfit sorted themselves out rapidly, formed a skirmish line, and attacked the raiders. It was a distressing and confused nightlong melee. By morning, all three hundred Japanese lay dead. One hundred American lives were lost, and two hundred more Marines, army pilots, and sailors were wounded.

Endurance—astonishing endurance, in terrible circumstances—was everywhere in evidence among the American and Japanese forces. Men somehow managed to carry on long after they might have been expected to fold. The navy corpsmen attached to the Marines are held in universally high esteem by the Marine veterans of Iwo. Chuck Tatum, a machine gunner in the 5th Division, reflected on a particular incident in a documentary film made about the battle, *Iwo Jima: Red Blood, Black Sand*:

> The bravest men I ever saw were U.S. Navy corpsmen . . . even though they were Navy we considered them Marines. Almost every one was decorated, and probably over 50 percent lost their lives. They were angels of mercy. [A fellow Marine got shot in the head] and I called the corpsman to come over. He says, "He's gone." And then the corpsman kinda sat down with his head against a rock, and he was crying, but there were no tears in his eyes, and he said, "I can't go on. I can't see any more wounded. I can't see anybody else killed." I tried to put my [arm around his shoulder] and comfort him . . . then somebody hollered, "Corpsman! Corpsman!" and he got up and grabbed his medical pouch and worked on another guy.[31]

On March 26, organized resistance was again declared at an end, this time by General Schmidt. Still, an army garrison that came ashore as the Marines departed in the last few days of March would continue for the next two months to find and kill hardcore Japanese who refused to quit. "In view of the character of the defense and the stubborn resistance encountered, it is fortunate that less seasoned or less resolute troops were not committed," said Admiral Spruance.[32]

The cost in blood had been shockingly high: 6,318 Marines and sailors were killed or died of wounds as a result of the battle. Well over nineteen thousand others were wounded. About twenty-one thousand Japanese died at the hands of the Marines and their supporting arms. Twenty-seven Medals of Honor were awarded. As an episode in military history, Holland Smith said after it was all over, Iwo Jima "proved the falsity of the theory that regiments or battalions that were decimated can never win battles."

Iwo Jima is the most famous battle in the storied history of the Marines. It was proof of the Corps' unique, highly aggressive style. It has also become a landmark in the American people's conception of the Corps as a martial institution second to none. Some people were horrified at the casualties, and along with heaps of praise from a grateful nation there emerged some strident voices castigating the senior leadership of the Corps for its willingness to assault concrete bunkers with human flesh day after miserable day.

But soon after the guns fell silent, the critics' voices subsided, and the vast majority of Americans were left with an enduring affection and respect, even reverence, for the courage and fortitude of their Marines.

The Seventh Bond Drive, for which President Franklin D. Roosevelt selected the Suribachi flag image as a symbol, raised more funds than any previous drive. And the flag-raising image was soon on postage stamps, paperweights, posters, and billboards in theaters. It was visible in more than one million retail-store windows, sixteen thousand movies theaters, fifteen thousand banks, thirty thousand railroad stations, and on five thousand billboards along highways.

As the Pacific war approached its conclusion, Americans knew that the Marine Corps was a very special organization, peopled by ordinary young Americans who had become fierce warriors, men who lived to fight: America's Spartans. General Lewis Walt, who won a Navy Cross in the Pacific and commanded all the Marines in Vietnam in the early years of the ground war there, believed that the amphibious nature of the Marine Corps accounted for a number of the characteristics that separated the Corps from other elite fighting organizations. Those qualities, he wrote, were "the aggressiveness inherent in an elite assault force; the versatility acquired by officers and men who must stand ready to land anywhere at any time, on short notice; and the high professional quality of a force that must understand ground, naval and air operations equally in order to fulfill its obligations."[33] When Americans look at the iconic Rosenthal photograph of those six men raising the Stars and Stripes, they are seeing all these characteristics. Little wonder that the photo and the moment it captures are among the most inspiring in our history.

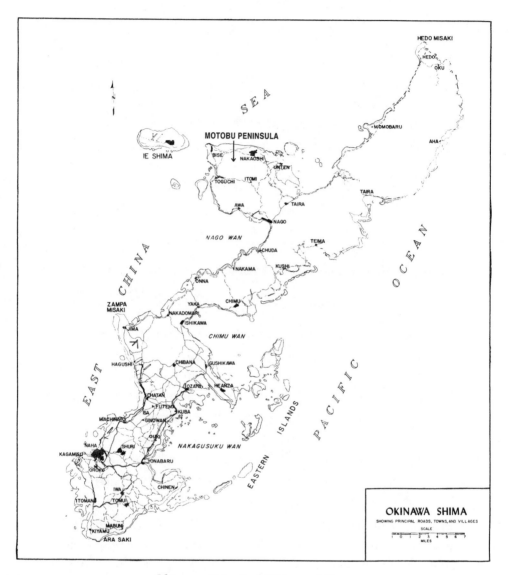

Okinawa: Principal Cities and Towns

Adapted from Benis M. Frank and Henry I. Shaw Jr., *Victory and Occupation: History of U.S. Marine Operations in World War II*, vol. 5. Washington, D.C.: Government Printing Office, 1968.

THREE

THE FINAL STRUGGLE

Okinawa and the Legacies of the Pacific War

Even before the last Japanese had been ousted from his tunnel on Iwo, the last and longest American campaign of the Pacific war was well under way. The battle for Okinawa began two years and seven months after the United States' first offensive in the Solomon Islands. Where the first steps had been tentative and small scale, the final campaign was enormous. In the spring of 1945, a naval task force assembled to invade Okinawa, just 350 miles from Japan's home islands. An astonishing 1,213 ships were deployed in Operation Iceberg to bring troops, trucks, tanks, and material ashore and protect the fleet in support of the land campaign. There was even a British fleet covering the western flank of the operation. The U.S. Army Air Forces pasted the island for weeks to prepare it for the arrival of the Tenth Army, which had a landing force of six infantry divisions, including the 1st Marine Division under Major General Pedro Del Valle. On top of all this amphibious power, the navy's submarines were active in intelligence gathering throughout the area of operations, and in sinking enemy supply ships making their way toward the Ryukyus.

In the battle for Okinawa, the U.S. Marines would play a critical but not leading role. Marine Corps land and air forces were important partners of the U.S. Army and Navy in the enterprise; Okinawa was a model of interservice cooperation. It was also the costliest single battle in the Pacific in terms of lives lost. The U.S. Tenth Army, including the 1st and 6th Marine Divisions, sustained more than seventy-six hundred deaths. The U.S. Navy lost almost five thousand sailors in horrific battles against kamikazes, subs, and bombers. These numbers paled in comparison to the Japanese, who lost as many as a hundred thousand soldiers and perhaps forty thousand civilians. Okinawa had a profound effect on the way ordinary soldiers and policy makers thought about what sort of fighting was likely to follow in the expected assault on Japan itself.

Planning for Operation Iceberg had begun in earnest with Admiral Nimitz's warning order of October 9, 1944, designating Admiral Raymond Spruance as overall commander of the Okinawa campaign, and Vice Admiral Richmond Kelley Turner, the navy's supreme wizard of amphibious warfare, as commander of the Joint Expeditionary Force. U.S. Army general Simon Bolivar Buckner, son of a distinguished Confederate general of the same name who had fought Ulysses S. Grant at Fort Donelson, was commander of the Tenth Army—the combat force designated to engage the Japanese 32nd Army under Lieutenant General Mitsuru Ushijima.

About two months later came the operation plan from Nimitz's staff, ordering Spruance to capture Okinawa's airfields and naval bases, defend those bases from air and ground counterattack, and ultimately gain control over the entire Ryukyu Islands area. That chain of islands stretches for about eight hundred miles between Kyushu, one of Japan's home islands, and Formosa. Okinawa is the largest of the Ryukyus, and a joint force in control of that island was enviably placed not only to invade Japan, but also to control important sea-lanes.

The original plan developed in the fall of 1944 called for a three-phase operation in which the small islands fifteen miles west of Okinawa were to be seized for artillery bases and fleet anchorages about a week prior to the main landings (Phase One). Then, the southern half of sixty-mile-long Okinawa would be taken (Phase Two). Finally, Phase Three called for occupying the less-populous northern half of the island along with Miyako Island, halfway between Okinawa and Formosa, and another tiny island about two hundred miles southeast of Okinawa called Okino-shima.

This plan did not survive for long once the action began to unfold in April. Japanese resistance in southern Okinawa was so resolute that the northern half was captured first, and a variety of considerations led Spruance to bypass the two islands slated for capture in Phase Three.

The story of Okinawa is one of coordination of massive numbers of troops, with Marines coordinating with army units in a manner quite unlike the Corps' go-it-alone mystique. One of the units to participate in the ground operation was the oldest and most storied Marine division, the highly regarded 1st Division, whose regiments had performed so well in France in World War I, and at Guadalcanal, Bougainville, and terrible Peleliu in the Pacific war. The 6th Marine Division was also involved, and was the newest in the Corps and the only division to be formed outside the continental United States in Marine history. General Lemuel Shepherd had activated the unit in September 1944 at Guadalcanal. It was hardly a greenhorn combat organization, though. It contained the reconstituted 4th Regiment, with many of its officers veterans of the Solomons fighting and the Guam campaign. The 22nd Regiment had fought at Eniwetok and Guam, and the 1st Battalion of the 29th Marines had been in heavy fighting on Saipan.

The Marine divisions were part of III Amphibious Corps, commanded by Major General Roy S. Geiger, a pioneer Marine aviator. Geiger was a combat veteran of World War I and the commander of the 1st Marine Air Wing during Guadalcanal. Another Marine, Francis P. Mulcahy, was to head another of the three main elements of Buckner's Tenth Army: the tactical air force, which included U.S. Army Air Force's squadrons as well as the 2nd Marine Air Wing. The third major component of the Tenth Army was XXIV Corps, under Major General John R. Hodge, U.S. Army, which consisted of three army infantry divisions and supporting units. The total number of Americans participating in Operation Iceberg numbered an astonishing 541,000 men.

Before the main event, the Kerama Islands, to the southwest of Okinawa, were seized. This preliminary attack was the brainchild of Admiral Turner, who saw the value of having a protected anchorage for repair and resupply facilities before undertaking an ambitious amphibious operation. Much of the terrain on these islands was mountainous or trackless brush. About a thousand Japanese soldiers and Korean laborers defended four of the eight main islands. It took the army's 77th Infantry Division five days to secure the islands. Resistance was generally light, and the Marine Corps' role was limited to a series of night reconnaissance landings by Major James L. Jones's Fleet Marine Force Reconnaissance Battalion. An unexpected bonus of this operation was the discovery and destruction of more than three hundred suicide boats the Japanese had planned to drive into the American ships.

Dawn of April 1 found more than 430 transports off the Hagushi landing beaches on the west coast of Okinawa. Their cargo comprised 180,000 Marine and Army assault troops and their combat gear. They were joined by nine hundred other vessels of all sizes, from minesweepers to gunboats, cruisers to tankers.

American intelligence had predicted strong resistance once the LVTs (Landing Vehicle, Tracked) in the armada hit the shoreline laden with infantry. The beaches were just west of two important airfields, Yontan and Katena. No one on Nimitz's staff expected Ushijima to surrender them without putting up a fight, yet that is what he did. His plan was to let the Americans land, and then hit the fleet from sea and air. Much to the amazement and relief of the landing force, only sporadic mortar, artillery, and rifle fire greeted their arrival on the shoreline. By evening, the Tenth Army had landed no less than eight regimental combat teams abreast along the landing beaches. Support troops and artillery were also ashore in significant numbers. The beachhead was three thousand to five thousand yards deep and covered with more than fifty thousand American troops by day's end.

It was an auspicious beginning for everyone, except the men of the diversionary force off the east coast. They executed their feint, but kamikazes scored direct hits on an LST and a troopship. A 2nd Division operations officer, Lieutenant Colonel Samuel G. Taxis, lamented, "We had asked for air cover . . . but were told the threat would be incidental."[1]

Ushijima recognized the futility of attempting to defeat outright so powerful a landing force at the shoreline. Iwo Jima had demonstrated beyond a doubt that the Americans could execute the amphibious assault in all its complexity with both greater efficiency and power than any other force in history. The huge armada that lay off the coast could not be prevented from orchestrating its planned operation of bringing more than a hundred thousand men from ship to shoreline. "A decisive land battle was to be avoided at all costs," wrote historians Jeter Isley and Philip Crowl, "until kamikaze planes, aided by the now battered surface fleet, could destroy or rout the American naval forces. Then once deprived of naval gunfire and logistical support, the enemy could be lured into the mountainous country south of Machinato and bled to death in futile attack."[2]

The Tenth Army's scheme of maneuver called for III Amphibious Corps to fight their way across the island to the east coast along with elements of XXIV Corps. The 1st Marine Division, which landed just south of the 6th Marine Division, would secure the waist of the island and prepare defensive positions in the neck of the southern zone, while the 6th pivoted to the north and moved by motor and foot up the Ishikawa Peninsula and then into the thinly populated and mountainous country in the north. Meanwhile, XXIV Corps was to pivot south and break through the series of three defensive belts ably prepared by the enemy.

By the end of April 3, the 1st Marine Division had crossed the neck of the southern half of the island and seized the Katin Peninsula, severing the island in two. The planners had slated this objective for the eleventh day of the campaign. Buckner and Geiger wondered, with some apprehension, where the enemy was waiting. The mood among the troops, on the other hand, was upbeat as they traversed clay roads, craggy mountain passes, and rice paddies, singing such verses as "Don't you worry, Mother, your son is safe out here, no Japs on Okinawa, no sake, wine, or beer."[3]

The major Marine actions in the first month of the campaign involved the 6th Division. Its assault regiments pushed to the north at a very rapid pace, preceded by a mechanized reconnaissance force of tanks and infantry. Behind the reconnaissance units engineers easily dispatched the mines and obstacles meant to slow down the drive. By April 7, the 29th Marines had taken control of Naha, the island's capital city, against token resistance. On that same day the first aircraft arrived ashore in the form of Marine Air Groups 31 and 33. They were used sparingly at first, largely due to a paucity of suitable targets. At Naha, engineers and Seabee units worked to open up the port to supply ships.

One day before the Marines took Naha, however, came two ominous developments: the Japanese unleashed the first of ten major kamikaze attacks against the fleet, and the army units pushing south ran into the first serious resistance on the ground.

It was at around this time as well that 6th Marine Division reconnaissance units detected the location of the main Japanese garrison in the north. The enemy had gathered in strength in the center of the Motobu Peninsula, in the craggy hills and ravines dominated by a twelve-hundred-foot mountain called Yaetake. There, Colonel Takeseko Udo's fifteen-hundred-man force was waiting in caves and fortified pillboxes, protected by a welter of machine-gun nests lining the avenues of approach. The enemy had an ample supply of 20mm cannon and naval guns on the mountain. Six-inch guns threatened any traffic that sought to move up road on the west coast of the peninsula. These same guns were also capable of hitting Ie Shima, a small island off the coast of the peninsula meant to be taken by the 77th Infantry Division later in the campaign.

76

The 29th Marines formed into three lines—one battalion each—and marched northwest toward Yaetake. Almost immediately they ran into heavy resistance. Their supporting tanks were of little use on the broken and twisted terrain. After several days of difficult, confusing fighting by the 29th, General Shepherd realized that one regiment was insufficient to reduce the stronghold. He called in the 4th Marines and ordered them to push the attack forward from positions on the eastern edge of the peninsula.

On April 13, 1/29 took very heavy casualties as it moved into the northern sector of enemy-held territory. The first concerted attack against the main position on Yaetake commenced on April 14. Shepherd used an unorthodox tactic: the 4th Marines, with 3/29 attached, attacked in an easterly direction from their line of departure on the west coast, while the 29th Regiment pushed westward from the east side of the mountain. Such a maneuver meant that the supporting artillery units had to be very careful not to drop rounds into attacking Marines.

By noon of April 14, the 4th Marines had taken a key ridge thirteen hundred yards to the west of Yaetake. As the Marines pushed farther west in an attempt to reach the next ridge, enemy resistance stiffened noticeably, despite plentiful naval gunfire, artillery, and close air support. A major problem in the dense, hilly underbrush was identifying the enemy's main firing positions. "It was like fighting a phantom enemy," wrote one Marine officer in the 4th Regiment. It was a precursor of Vietnam: Japanese soldiers would hold off firing until the headquarters element of a platoon or company crossed their front. Such was the experience of Company G, 4th Marines as it pushed into the broken ground near a terrain feature called Big Nose: "They had us right where they wanted us for a long time. We were fighting like blind men."[4] In the first ambush that day the company commander, the executive officer, and three other Marines were felled by fire, and, after that, "it was just one damned ambush after another."[5]

Still, the ridge was taken that same afternoon by Company G. A frontal assault combined with envelopment from the right flank did the trick. The 29th Marines met with less dramatic success that day as they attacked a series of positions along the Itomi-Taguchi Road. Initially the attack to the west bogged down, so 1/29 reoriented the axis of the advance to the southwest, where they could make good use of the high ground. They made eight hundred yards before halting for the night's bivouac. On April 15, the enemy got a good bead on the American positions and poured 20mm cannon fire into the 29th Marines. A Japanese infiltration inflicted thirty-five casualties on 2/29 before the attack was halted at around 1700.

And so it went: American advances, Japanese ambushes; Americans pinned down under heavy fire; Japanese retreats—all essentially a stalling tactic to allow Japanese air and sea forces to attack the U.S. fleet. On April 20, General Shepherd finally declared the peninsula secured.

One key to beating the Japanese was to secure their airstrips in order to open up the skies to friendly planes. The army units spent April conquering the group of small islands off the east coast beaches so as to clear access to Nakagusuku Bay. Then the veteran amphibians of the 77th Division began their attack on Ie Shima, off the west coasts, in mid-April. The importance of this island lay in its three airfields, which General Mulcahy very much wanted for his long-range fighters. Aircraft flying from those fields would be of immense help in protecting the fleet from the "divine wind" of the kamikazes. The fighting on Ie Shima proved unexpectedly rough. It took the 77th Division's soldiers five days to clear out the enemy from their entrenched positions there, at a cost of 239 men killed and 879 wounded. The Marine Corps provided scouts to reconnoiter an islet six hundred yards southeast of Ie Shima in preparation for the landing of army artillery batteries to support the main landing, which was a full-scale amphibious assault with naval gunfire and close air support.

For most of April, Marine aircraft squadrons were very active in fleet protection operations. Even before other tactical aircraft made their way ashore, four Marine fighter squadrons flew from the carriers *Bennington* and *Bunker Hill* to challenge the kamikaze attacks. In the second large kamikaze attack, Marine pilots from *Bunker Hill* shot down twenty-five planes, and *Bennington*'s Marines accounted for twenty-six shootdowns. In the fourth major kamikaze attack, on April 22, Marine pilots destroyed thirty-five enemy fighters and bombers.

Two days before the 77th Division achieved its objective on Ie Shima on April 13, General Hodge's XXIV Corps began a three-division, island-wide coordinated assault against the outer ring of the Naha-Shuri-Yonabaru line in southern Okinawa—the most formidable defensive line encountered by Americans in the Pacific war. From east coast to west, the Japanese had made great use of the terrain. Ridges, draws, and ravines were studded with heavy weapons, and the main fortified emplacements and caves were covered by mutually reinforcing machine-gun nests, mortars, and very often the 47mm antitank gun, which was highly effective against Sherman tanks. Most of the ridges ran in an east-west direction. The road network was poor, and what there was of it was heavily mined. The Americans attacking these positions, writes one historian of the campaign, found themselves entering killing zones "of savage lethality. . . . In typical fighting along this front the Japanese would contain and isolate any American penetration by grazing fire from supporting positions, then smother the exposed troops on top of the initial objective with . . . preregistered heavy mortar shells until fresh Japanese troops could swarm out . . . in a counterattack."[6]

The main strongpoint faced by XXIV Corps' 27th, 96th, and 7th Divisions was the Kakazu Ridge complex. The cost in casualties resulting from just a three-division offensive front was too great. The attacks bled the American infantry dry. April 19, 1945, is not a day remembered with fondness by army veterans of Okinawa. Japanese mortar and artillery fire was extremely heavy and accurate. Once the assault began, Japanese weapons ripped into U.S. companies as they crossed the high ground while mortars and artillery hit them in the defiles and the avenues of approach. In the 27th Division's zone, an attempt was made to bypass the strongpoint on Kakazu Ridge: thirty tanks pushed around the ridge and drove into Kakazu village. But the armor was unsupported by infantry, and the Japanese dispensed with the Shermans easily. Only eight tanks returned. It took five days of continuous artillery, armor, and infantry pressure to crack the core positions of the outer ring. Not until April 27 was the zone clear on the western end of the line.

General Buckner soon realized he lacked sufficient combat power to crack the line. He requested help from the Marines' 1st Tank Battalion, but General Del Valle demurred. His tanks and infantry had trained too exhaustively to be pulled apart and placed piecemeal into the cauldron of a full-scale land campaign. Ultimately, Buckner agreed not to split up Del Valle's division, much to the relief of senior Marine leadership on the island and in Washington as well, for the Corps was itching for a battle in which all its air and ground assets could work together as a team; very little of the close air support in previous Marine battles had been supplied by the Marine air wings. But Del Valle and Geiger knew that their rapid success in the north would be rewarded with a call to the front, and soon. And so the call came: on April 24, General Geiger was given the order to release a Marine division from III Amphibious Corps and put it in reserve for the Tenth Army. The 1st Marine Division would join in the effort to break the back of the defensive belts on the western end of the front, relieving the much-depleted 27th Division. A few days later, the 6th Marine Division would enter the fray, at which point the Tenth Army offensive would become a full two-corps drive with XXIV Corps on the east (left) and III Amphibious Corps on the west (or right).

Even before the 1st Marine Division saddled up for the march south, Admiral Turner pressured Buckner to reassess his "straight down the middle" strategy of coordinated frontal assaults across the entire island. The Fifth Fleet off the coast was hit hard. He wanted Buckner to speed up the ground campaign. General Geiger and Marine Commandant Alexander Vandegrift joined Turner in urging the army commander to order the Marines to undertake an amphibious assault on the enemy's rear. General Buckner was a competent and respected leader, but he was cautious by nature, and he had no experience with amphibious warfare. Buckner feared that the logistical train of the Tenth Army could not properly sustain a two-front battle and vetoed the amphibious assault. Marines ever since have argued that the ground casualties in the campaign ultimately were far higher than they would have been had Buckner agreed to a second amphibious assault. Ironically, just a couple of days after Buckner's late April decision, General Ushijima ordered a very large portion of his force facing the beaches the Marines would have attacked in a second landing along the eastern coast, the entire 24th Division and the 44th Mixed Independent Brigade, to displace to the Shuri Line. Therefore, it seems likely that a second major amphibious assault behind the Shuri Line would have brought the killing to an end much faster.

In the Japanese 32nd Army's command post in Shuri Castle, the question of whether to mount a counterattack had been debated for several days. The chief of staff, Lieutenant General Isamu Cho, a man with a strong inclination for the offense, argued for a massive counteroffensive by the newly arrived 24th Division, coupled with enveloping attacks from the sea on both coasts. He believed Japanese forces could isolate the 1st Marine Division in the west and break the momentum of the American onslaught against the line.

The Japanese opted for the counterattack, which commenced at 0500 on May 4 with a series of ambitious kamikaze attacks. It met with almost immediate disaster. Many lead assaulting elements were hurt by their own supporting fires, but American artillery inflicted the lion's share of the damage on the attackers. Twenty-eight battalions of U.S. artillery smothered the approaches to the American lines with devastating effect. On the west coast, in the 1st Marine Division's zone, about seven hundred Japanese raiders in small boats attempted to land right in front of Company B, 1st Battalion, 1st Marines. They approached the shore undetected—until they were within shouting distance of the beach, at which point the intruders let loose with screeching battle cries. Historians Charles Nichols and Henry Shaw described what followed: "Mortars and heavy machine guns sited to cover the reef began firing at the crowded barges, some of which carried as many as a hundred men. Rifle grenadiers . . . found targets in the open boats. Soon a weird half-light from flares, tracers, and burning barges suffused the area. Riflemen and machine gunners fired at bobbing heads in the water and raked the reef to stop the . . . attackers."[7]

A few Japanese infantrymen managed to get ashore, where they were rapidly killed. More than four hundred were destroyed before they could reach shore by Marine rifle and machine-gun fire. The raiders on the east coast met a similar fate at the hands of army units.

The failure of the counteroffensive, according to Colonel Hiromichi Yahara, convinced General Ushijima of the futility of additional offensive operations on the ground. More than six thousand Japanese perished on May 4. The loss of precious artillery pieces compounded the disaster.

During the first several days of the enemy counteroffensive, the 1st Marine Regiment had pressed forward with their own attack, reaching the north bank of the Asa River at a cost of 649 casualties. The entire 1st Marine Division made slow but steady progress as it knocked off enemy strongpoints in detail, that is, one at a time.

Buckner wanted yet more combat power to breach the Japanese defensive belt. The morning of May 11 found the 6th Marine Division on the line on the far right, or western, flank of what was now a very well-supported two-corps force stretched across the entire island. General Roy Geiger had command of III Amphibious Corps, deployed along the western half of the main line of resistance, or MLR. General Hodge's XXIV Corps was positioned along the eastern half. General Buckner called for a four-division assault across the entire front.

To the 1st Marine Division fell the unenviable task of breaching a series of ridges, hills, and draws in front and just to the west of the city of Shuri. The most significant of these, running north to south, were Dakeshi Ridge, Wana Ridge, and steep, narrow Wana Draw. Numerous cliffs and caves dotted the ground, and the approaches were well covered by machine guns, mortars, and mines.

In two weeks of furious combat along a nine-thousand-yard front,

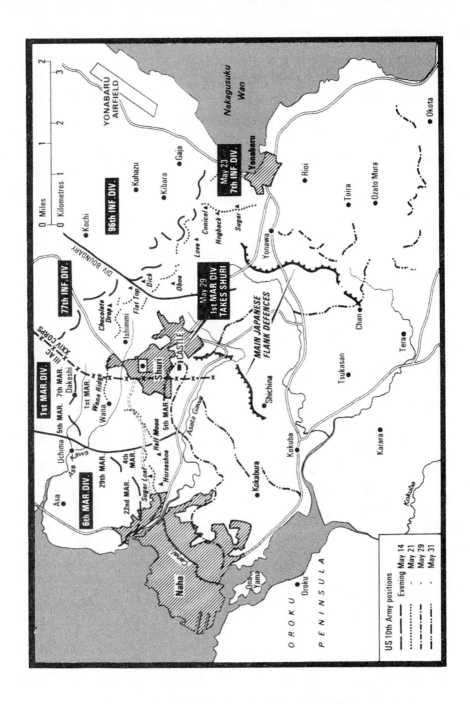

The Assault on the Shuri Line, May 1945, Okinawa

Source: Joseph H. Alexander, *The Final Campaign: Marines in the Victory on Okinawa*.
Washington, D.C. USMC, 1996.

the two armies tore into each other with enormous supporting artillery fire, and in the case of the Americans, considerable air support, not to mention fourteen- and sixteen-inch shells from battleships offshore. Much of the fighting was conducted in driving, cold rain and knee-deep mud. Trench foot, pneumonia, and dysentery were as common as artillery barrages.

The 6th Marine Division's regiments lost entire companies in attacking the Sugar Loaf Hill complex, which included Horseshoe Hill, to the south, and Half Moon Hill, to the southeast. The division's after-action report paints a grim picture of the scene:

> The sharp depression included within the Horseshoe afforded mortar positions that were almost inaccessible to any arm short of direct, aimed rifle fire and hand grenades. . . . Likewise, an attempt to reduce either the Horseshoe or the Half Moon would be exposed to destructive, well-aimed fire from Sugar Loaf itself. In addition, the three localities are connected by a network of tunnels and galleries, facilitating the covered movement of reserves. As a final factor in the strength of the position it will be seen that all sides of Sugar Loaf are precipitous and there are no evident avenues of approach into the hill mass. For strategic location and tactical strength it is hard to conceive of a more powerful position than the Sugar Loaf terrain afforded. . . . Troops assaulting this position presented a clear target to enemy machine guns, mortars and artillery emplaced on the Shuri heights to their left and left rear.[8]

Despite the fact that the 22nd Marines were at only about 60 percent combat efficiency, they were ordered to take the hill at any cost on May 14. With Company K of 3/22 attached, 2/22 assaulted behind a line of tanks and an artillery smoke screen. Two hours after jump-off, just before 1730, some forty men of Companies F and G found themselves at the base of the hill under the command of Major Henry A. Courtney Jr. It was progress of a sort, but they were too few to take the hill. Grenades, snipers, and mortar fire were coming at them. At 2300, Courtney's Marines took the crest, hurling grenades all the way up at the Japanese defenders on the reverse slope. Just before midnight, Courtney was killed. Two hours later, when reinforcements from Company K arrived, there were only seven of the original forty Marines still alive. The Japanese counterattacked that morning with fresh troops, and the Marines were forced to withdraw shortly after 1100 on May 15.

That same morning the 29th Marines joined the badly depleted 22nd Marines in the fight. All attempts to retake the crest were beaten back handily that day. May 16's plan of attack hinged on the ability of the 29th Marines to seize Half Moon Hill, east of Sugar Loaf—at least temporarily—so as to relieve pressure on 3/22, which was to make the main attack on Sugar Loaf. With tanks providing direct-fire support, two companies of the 29th Marines raced forward to the northern slope of Half Moon and began to dig in. In midafternoon, the Japanese mounted a furious counterattack against those companies, hitting the Leatherneck positions from multiple flanks. Again, withdrawal was the only option. The division report describes the fighting of May 16 as the bitterest of the Okinawa campaign. It left the 22nd Marines in such bad shape that they had to be taken off the line; combat efficiency was down to 40 percent.

The day after the battered 22nd Marines left the scene of battle, the Japanese defenders showed no signs of diminished resolve. Company E, 2/29 assaulted twice and was twice turned back. The Marines attempted to sweep around the hill and attack from the southeast, but that slope proved too steep to climb. The axis of advance shifted to the northeast slope. Three times the leading elements of the assault reached the crest by that route, but the Marines never reached the top of Sugar Loaf in sufficient numbers to resist the enemy counterattacks. A fourth attempt succeeded in gaining a foothold, but withering fire from the adjacent hills drove the Marines back. The fury of the combat around Sugar Loaf was described by historian William Manchester, himself a member of the 29th Marines, in his moving memoir of the Pacific war, *Goodbye, Darkness*:

Infantry couldn't advance. Every weapon was tried: tanks, Long Toms [eight-inch howitzers], rockets, napalm, smoke, naval gunfire, aircraft. None of them worked. . . . The Japanese artillery never seemed to let up, and every night Ushijima sent fresh troops up his side of the hill. We kept rushing them, moving like somnambulists, the weight of Sugar Loaf pressing down on us, harder and harder. . . . In that smog, grappling with whatever came to hand, we were like blind men trying to identify an elephant by feeling his legs. . . . The fighting was sometimes hand-to-hand . . . the [knife] being a more practical implement for ripping out a man's guts than a rifle. . . . At close range the mustard-colored Japs looked like badly wrapped brown-paper parcels. Jumping around on their bandy legs, they jabbered or grunted; their eyes were glazed over and fixed, as though they were in a trance. . . . Had I not been fasting I'm sure I would have shit my pants. Many did. . . . We were animals, really, torn between fear—I was mostly frightened—and a murderous rage at events.[9]

It fell to Company D, 2/29 to take and hold Sugar Loaf, finally, on May 18. All about the battlefield was the stench of death and cordite. A company of Sherman tanks split into two groups and snaked around the hill from both sides. Their steady fire on the reverse slopes, coupled with the strong resolve of the Company D infantry, ultimately broke the back of the Japanese defenders. One hundred fifty Japanese imbedded in Sugar Loaf's caves and fighting holes broke out of their positions and began to flee down the reverse slope, right into the Shermans' field of fire. Lieutenant Donald R. Pinnow, manning one of the tanks, recalled, "We pumped a few more shells into the caves when suddenly the Japs began running from the crest. . . . We fired . . . and blew them all over the landscape."[10] Fortunately, the fight for Half Moon Hill and Horseshoe Hill was easier; they were taken in three days by a fresh regiment, the 4th Marines. Shepherd's men were finally able to cross the Asato River and head into the town of Naha. By May 24, the division was on the outskirts of the town and it was soon taken.

While the 6th Marine Division was fighting its way past the western anchor of Ushijima's main defensive belt, the Marines of the 1st Division just to the east found themselves enmeshed in a meatgrinder campaign against the enemy on Dakeshi Ridge, Wana Ridge, and Wana Draw.

The 7th Marines were up against the outpost positions in front of Dakeshi. On May 11, Colonel Edward W. Snedecker's three battalions found themselves blasting away with the "corkscrew and blowtorch" method — explosive charges and flamethrower demolition teams — against the clever defensive system of Dakeshi Ridge complex. The scheme of maneuver that day called for a double envelopment of the ridge: 1/7 swung around one side; 2/7 approached the other; and 3/7 poured in fire from the front. Pushing through heavy mortar and machine-gun fire, 2/7 managed to gain the crest of the ridge that day. What's more, they held it against a furious counterattack. From the crest of Dakeshi, the Marines had a fine view of all the Japanese positions that blocked their path from Shuri to Naha — the heart of the Shuri Line.

Unfortunately, Dakeshi was just the opening act for a brutal eighteen-day effort to crack through the main line of defense. In those eighteen days, the 1st Marine Division's front would move a grand total of twelve hundred yards. Torrential rains severely limited the deployment of tanks in support, and the infantry paid dearly for their absence. Mud was everywhere. So, too, were suffering and death, and in the days that followed Marines developed a kind of stoic fatalism — a sense that it was only a matter of time before it was their turn to be on the wrong end of the bayonet fastened to the end of a Japanese Arisaka bolt-action rifle or of some lethal piece of shrapnel from the omnipresent artillery.

Here and throughout the remainder of the drive through the Shuri defensive belt, the movement of both III Amphibious Corps and XXIV Corps ultimately depended on the infantrymen with flamethrowers and satchel charges. The infantry's success, though, was contingent on the accurate application of armor, artillery, air cover, and powerful naval gunfire; the ships in particular had been called in to knock out 47mm antitank positions hindering the attack.

On May 17, 2/5 pressed its attack against the mouth of the Wana Draw, while 3/7 attacked Wana Ridge with two companies to the north of the draw. Company I was successful in seizing a piece of flat land leading directly to the western nose of the ridge itself. Its sister unit, Company K, attacking to the east of Company I with the support of no fewer than fourteen tanks, including two "Zippo" flamethrowing vehicles, reached the ridge just northeast of Wana village. But the Japanese used smoke grenades to hinder the tanks. Withering fire from both flanks and the front ultimately forced Company K to withdraw to the safety of Dakeshi Ridge, where American armor and artillery could protect them.

On May 20, Marines from 3/1, under Lieutenant Colonel Stephen V. Sabol, experimented with an innovative tactic. They struggled to pull large drums of napalm up the north side of the ridge; once they were on the crest, they split the drums open and rolled them down into the draw right on top of enemy positions. Then the Leathernecks dropped white phosphorous grenades into the napalm. It worked well. Unfortunately, the Marines could be sure that the following morning there would be more Japanese in the same positions. The Japanese were masters of night infiltration and movement, often covering their reinforcements with small-unit attacks to divert the Americans' attention.

The Wana complex proved to be a major drain on the manpower of the infantry regiments. The 7th Marines alone lost five hundred men in the first five days of fighting around Wana. According to historian Joseph H. Alexander, during the fighting between May 11, the date of the first attack on Wana, and May 30, the 1st Marine Division lost two hundred Marines for every one hundred yards of terrain it gained.

A particularly hairy part of the fighting for the infantry in the draw involved the crossing of the open floor in their attacks on the walls. It was a terrifying experience. Eugene Sledge recalled his own initiation into the killing ground:

> Our massive artillery, mortar, naval gunfire and aerial bombardment continued against Wana Draw on our front and Wana Ridge on our left. The Japanese continued to shell . . . everybody in the area, meeting each tank-infantry attack with a storm of fire. . . . We had been under and around plenty of "heavy stuff" at Peleliu, but not on nearly so mas-

sive a scale or for such unending periods of time as at Wana. . . . We left the field and slid down a ten-foot embankment to the sloping floor of the draw. My feet hit the deck running . . . the Japanese machine guns rattled away. Bullets zipped and snapped around my head, the tracers looking like long white streaks. I looked neither left nor right but with my heart in my throat raced out, splashed across a little stream, and dashed up the slope to the shelter of a spur. . . . Once behind the spur . . . I slowed to a trot. The veteran ahead of me and a little to my right slowed up, too. We glanced back to see where the two new men were. Neither one of them had made more than a few strides out in the draw from the other side. One was sprawled in a heap, obviously killed instantly. The other was wounded and crawling back.[11]

The torrential rains began to fall on May 21, and seldom let up for the next few days. The Shuri Line, already a godforsaken landscape of destruction, stench, and death, was inundated in mud. Tanks and amtracs were rendered useless. Streams and rivers overran their banks, and Marine boondockers and dungarees were immersed in ooze.

Then came some very welcome news. Aerial observation in the zones of the 1st and 5th Marines spotted a vast enemy retreat from the Shuri Line on May 26. General Ushijima had given the order to evacuate the Shuri defenses and retreat to his final defensive ring on the Kiyamu Peninsula. A rear guard would remain to slow the pace of the inevitable American breakout to the south. A few units among the retreating Japanese took a pounding at the hands of American aircraft and artillery, and hundreds died on the roads and in the fields to the south of the defensive line. Perhaps five hundred trucks and artillery pieces were destroyed as well. But the vast majority retreated in good order and with fine discipline. Under pressure from the navy to bring an end to the ground campaign, General Buckner urged his two corps commanders to aggressive action on May 27:

Indications point to possible enemy retirement to new defensive position with possible counteroffensive against our forces threatening his flank. Initiate without delay strong and unrelenting pressure to ascertain probable intentions and keep him off balance. Enemy must not repeat not be permitted to establish himself securely on new position with only nominal interference.[12]

When the directive was issued, the 6th Marine Division was attacking successfully into Naha, the 1st Marine Division had just conquered Hill 110 overlooking Wana Draw, and the Third Battalion, 1st Marines had reached Wana Ridge's crest twice, only to be driven off by ferocious enemy fire.

From then on, progress was steady. The army seized Yonabaru, at the eastern end of the main defensive line. The 96th Division took Conical Hill, the anchor of the defense in the east. The 6th Marine Division in the west made great progress in its effort to invest Shuri town. Meanwhile, the 1st Marine Division's 5th Marines captured the village of Asato. One day later, that regiment drove forward against comparatively light resistance toward the ridge just above what had been the command post of the 32nd Army—Shuri Castle. At 0930 on May 29, Lieutenant Colonel Charles W. Shellburne requested permission to send a company of Marines into the castle grounds, despite its being officially in the zone of the 77th Infantry Division's attack. General Del Valle knew he would receive flak from the army for granting the colonel that permission, but he was willing to take it. He justified his decision by arguing that the army division might very well have taken considerable casualties if it invested the castle from the eastern flank—far more than his Marines did in approaching from the west. Soon after receiving the order, a company from 1/5, commanded by a Marine officer from South Carolina, entered the castle grounds and raised the Confederate Stars and Bars above the heights. It took several days to get the Stars and Stripes up to the castle to replace the Confederate banner.

The Shuri Line had at last been fully breached. As it collapsed, General Shepherd succeeded in convincing Buckner to permit him to launch a surprise amphibious assault against some five thousand Japanese army and navy troops on the Oroku Peninsula. These men were ably commanded by one of the last of the Rikusentai—the Special

Naval Landing Force—Rear Admiral Minoru Ota. Shepherd's battle-weary 6th Marine Division had to defeat this enemy force to reach the Naha airfield.

Shepherd reckoned that the Marines would bring the fight to a quick end if he avoided the expected axis of attack, moving down toward Kokuba and then pivoting northwest into the heart of the penin-sula by ground movement. Instead, he would cross the estuary separat-ing Naha from Oroku by landing craft supported by artillery, come ashore north of the town of Oroku, and from there drive west toward the Naha airfield.

The 4th Marines, under Colonel Alan Shapely, were chosen as the main assault unit. Despite having less than two days to plan this compli-cated operation, the landing—the very last amphibious landing con-ducted against a hostile shore in World War II—went off very well. Complete surprise was achieved as the Marines hit the enemy on the flank. It took the 4th and the 29th Marines two days to seize the airfield, but eight more days of combat followed, some of which was at close quarters and savage.

Many Marines came to view death as inevitable after seeing so many of their comrades taken during a long and brutal campaign. Charles Owens of the 1st Battalion, 7th Marines had been in the thick of the fighting at Dakeshi Ridge, where more than a hundred men in his bat-talion had died. He commented, "The battle for Kunishi Ridge was the hardest fighting I ever saw. . . . The only way off was to be killed or wounded. . . . We just knew we were going to die on this ridge. There was no sleep. The replacements who reached us were either very old or very young and not well trained. Before you got to know them, they were dead."[13]

Just as the last battle of the Pacific war was coming to an end, Gen-eral Buckner fell victim to an enemy artillery shell while he was observ-ing the advance of the 8th Marines. General Geiger assumed command of the Tenth Army, becoming the only U.S. Marine ever to hold com-mand of a field army. On June 21, General Ushijima followed the dictates of Bushido and committed suicide. American troops of the 7th and 96th Divisions were just a few hundred yards from his last command post in a cave near the sea at Mabuni. That same day, General Geiger announced the end of organized resistance on the island. It was all over save the mopping-up operations and the burying of the dead.

The battle for Okinawa was the largest and most destructive engagement of the war in the Pacific. Casualty figures vary. Approximately 142,000 Japanese lost their lives—about 40,000 of those dead were civilians. The Tenth Army reported 7,374 killed or died of wounds, and 31,807 were wounded in action. There were some 26,000 non-battle casualties as well. During eighty-two days of ground operations the U.S. Pacific fleets and attached British carrier forces sustained unprecedented losses of men and ships. Four thousand nine hundred seven seamen lost their lives, while 4,824 were wounded in action. Thirty-six ships were sunk; 763 Allied aircraft were lost to enemy fire, most of it to kamikaze attacks. The 1st Marine Division reported 1,115 men killed in action and 6,745 wounded, while the 6th Division reported 1,622 killed in action and 6,689 wounded.

When Japan surrendered in the wake of atomic bombs in August 1945 on Hiroshima and Nagasaki, all six USMC divisions were deep into the planning stages for the invasion of the Japanese home islands. No Marine who had fought in Okinawa was saddened by President Truman's decision to use these weapons of mass destruction. There would be no more invasions. Much to their happy surprise, Okinawa's war was over.

During World War II, the Marine Corps expanded to twenty-five times its prewar size. At war's end, the Corps counted 485,000 officers and men in its ranks. A total of 669,000 people served in the Marines during the conflict. The Corps still accounted for only about 5 percent of the U.S. armed forces during the war years. The Marine Corps fought some of the toughest battles in the Pacific. After the loss of Wake Island in the first weeks of the conflict, it was never again defeated on the battlefield.

Yet it could be argued that the Marine Corps' greater contribution to World War II was in the realm of doctrine as opposed to combat. Long before the Pearl Harbor attack, a coterie of Marine officers had refused to accept the conventional military wisdom of the 1920s and 1930s— that the amphibious assault against a hostile enemy was doomed to fail in the modern age of the machine gun and the fighter-bomber. The disastrous British campaign at Gallipoli in 1915 confirmed this view in the eyes of the U.S. Army. The senior leadership of the Marines after World War I, led by Commandant John A. Lejeune and Major General and Assistant Commandant John H. Russell, by contrast, saw Gallipoli as a case study that could be improved.

The work of Russell and Lejeune was taken up by other Marines at Quantico, resulting in the groundbreaking 1934 publication of *Tentative Manual for Landing Operations*. Here for the first time the complex process was broken down into its essential parts, and key problems were isolated for study. The *Tentative Manual* was far from the last word in amphibious operations, but it put forward a new vocabulary and helped to structure new ways of thinking. It stirred the navy into participating in the ongoing discussions: When should command be turned over to the ground commander? Could preparatory naval gunfire and air bombardment be simultaneous? What was the optimum size of the amphibious boats or tractors required to bring the landing force ashore with its heavy weapons and supplies?

The *Tentative Manual* was refined in light of field experimentation and published by the navy as *Landing Operations Doctrine, United States Navy* (1937). Between May 1941 and August 1943 it was further revised three times, and the U.S. Marines used it to train most of the army commanders who led amphibious operations in both the European and Pacific theaters of war. The Marine Corps spearheaded the development of American amphibious operations before and during World War II. Had they not done so, many of the great battles of that conflict might have ended in disaster.

Marines were an expeditionary outfit, and they lived up to that name: 89 percent of the enlisted men and a remarkable 98 percent of the officers who served in the Corps during World War II were posted overseas. No other service could boast figures even remotely that high.

The rapid expansion of the Marine Corps had, of course, created problems. The newly minted Marines thrown into Iwo and Okinawa had not been as well trained as had the select few who were accepted into the fold in the years before Pearl Harbor. And the war exposed some of the inefficiencies in the Corps' logistical and training apparatus as well as its equipment-procurement procedures. But, on balance, the expansion was managed by the senior officer corps with alacrity and sure-handedness.

From an institutional point of view, perhaps the most significant result of the explosive growth of the institution between 1942 and 1945 was the creation of a large population of reserve and former Marines who could spread the Marine Corps gospel to the American people in the postwar era. Commandant Alexander Vandegrift got to the heart of the matter when he said, "It is a notable fact that few men have ever left the Marine Corps without a feeling of undying loyalty toward it."[14] The veterans were not hesitant about displaying that pride in the years after the war. In the immediate postwar period, when many high-ranking officers and officials associated with the U.S. Army and the fledgling U.S. Air Force attempted to limit the size and capabilities of the Marines on the grounds of "efficiency," the men who had served in World War II consistently frustrated such efforts. No individual was more important in keeping public image and public relations front and center than John A. Lejeune, commandant from 1920 to 1929. "The future success of the Marine Corps," Lejeune wrote, "depends on two factors: First, an efficient performance of all the duties to which [the Marine Corps is] assigned; second, promptly bringing this efficiency to the attention of the proper officials of the government and the American people."[15]

Robert Denig and his band of public relations Marines took General Lejeune's statement very much to heart. So did the World War II Corps as a whole. At the height of the Pacific war, the Public Relations Division pumped out an astonishing three thousand stories a month for public consumption. Many of these were about individual Marines, designed for the local papers. The strategy worked: after the war, the public displayed a deep and enduring affection for the Corps that members of other services sometimes found puzzling and frustrating.

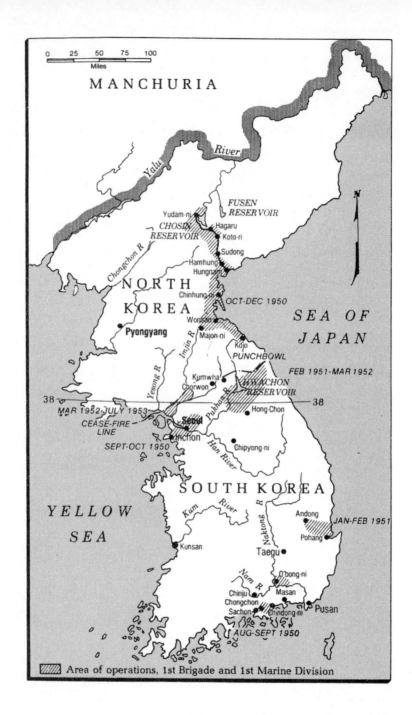

USMC Areas of Operations in the Korean War

Source: Allan R. Millett, *Semper Fidelis: The History of the United States Marine Corps*, revised and expanded edition. New York: The Free Press, 1991.

FOUR

TRANSITION AND CHALLENGE, 1945 TO 1950

Fourteen months after the secretary of the navy had told "Howlin' Mad" Smith that the raising of the flag over Mount Suribachi would ensure the Corps' survival for the next five hundred years, the commandant of the Marine Corps, Alexander Vandegrift, worried if it was true. Head-quarters Marine Corps (HQMC) in Washington was scrambling to maintain order and discipline amid a rapid and precipitous demobilization. Tough decisions were being made every day about the shape, structure, and personnel of a drastically reduced Corps. From a high of 485,000 men during the war, the active-duty Marine Corps was winnowed down to 155,000 by August 1946.

The Marines knew what they wanted to be in the postwar era: the nation's peacetime minutemen, a "force in readiness" with at least two battalions perpetually deployed at sea. One reinforced battalion with an aircraft squadron would sail the Pacific, and a similar ground-air unit would cruise in the Mediterranean or Caribbean. These forces would form the sharp edge of a Corps with at least three full divisions and three air wings. The Corps defined itself as a combined arms, ground-air force, capable of deployment on almost any coastline. Although World War II had not afforded the Corps the opportunity to prove the effectiveness of an all-Marine ground-air campaign, its leaders believed the drive across the Pacific had shown the Marines to be the best general-purpose military organization in the world. The skeptics—and there were many in the army and in Washington—rolled their eyes and said it was just so much Marine propaganda.

The pressures inherent in demobilization were not Vandegrift's only worry in May 1946, as the soft-spoken Virginian, hero of the first offensive at Guadalcanal in the summer of 1942, testified before the Naval Affairs Committee of the U.S. Senate. The subject at hand was Bill S.2044—one of the pieces of legislation put forward between 1946 and 1947 in the effort to streamline the functions of the U.S. armed services. Bill S.2044 caused considerable alarm at HQMC, for it appeared to threaten the Marine Corps with extinction, or a severe diminution in combat power and prestige at best. As Vandegrift put it:

> Marines have played a significant and useful part in the military structure of the nation since its birth. But despite that fact passage of the unification legislation as now framed will in all probability spell extinction for the Marine Corps. I express this apprehension because of a series of facts which I feel must now be placed in your hands as an important element in your deliberations. They may be summarized in one simple statement—that the War Department is determined to reduce the Marine Corps to a position of studied military ineffectiveness. . . . I know the War Department's intentions with respect to the Marine Corps are well advanced and carefully integrated. . . . And I also know that the structure of the unification bill as it now stands will provide perfect implementation of those designs. . . . In its capacity as a balance wheel Congress has on five occasions since 1829 reflected the voice of the people in examining and casting aside a motion which would damage or destroy the United States Marine Corps. . . . Now I believe that the cycle has repeated itself again, and that the fate of the Marine Corps lies solely and entirely with the Congress. . . . The Marine Corps,

then, believes it has earned the right to have its future decided by the legislative body which created it—nothing more. We have pride in ourselves and in our past, but we do not rest our case on any presumed ground of gratitude owing us from the nation. The bended knee is not a tradition of our Corps. If the Marine as a fighting man has not made a case for himself after 170 years of service, than he must go. But I think you will agree with me he has earned the right to depart with dignity and honor, not by subjugation to the status of uselessness and servility planned for him by the War Department.[1]

Vandegrift's statement drew much public sympathy and forced a delay in the efforts of the War Department, led by prominent senior army officers, to reorganize the armed services into a single department consisting of the navy, the army, and a new, independent air force. There had been several versions of this scheme advanced between 1944 and 1947, but the basic intention of the various plans put forward by executive committees and in proposed legislation were quite similar. On grounds of efficiency and streamlining, they sought to reduce duplication of functions and missions among the services, and to discard the Joint Chiefs of Staff (JCS) organizational structure that had orchestrated the victories over Japan and Germany.

That structure had required all members of the JCS to agree on major strategic and budget issues before making recommendations to the president. It had placed a premium on compromise among the services and ensured that the interests and views of each service got a fair hearing. Yet no Marine had served on the JCS during the war. The Corps' interests were supposed to be represented by the navy JCS representatives, Admirals Ernest King and William D. Leahy. When the JCS during World War II could not agree on how to attack a specific problem or a basic campaign plan, the president heard both sides of the issue, and then made a final decision. According to Admiral King, the number of times that happened could be counted on a single hand. The system, in other words, had worked.

The army, however, wanted to change things. Its reasons were rooted in a combination of organizational theory and substantial, long-standing resentment over the Marine Corps' siphoning off of missions, resources, and men for "land warfare" campaigns it saw as its own. The Senate bill that Vandegrift spoke out against was a variation of the McNarney Plan, named for Lieutenant General Joseph T. McNarney of the army, which had been discussed in Congress in May 1944 at the urging of the War Department. A red flag went up in Headquarters Marine Corps when McNarney requested that Congress grant the executive branch of government "broad authority to make change in an evolutionary manner . . . and that unnecessary involvement in unimportant details be avoided so that they will not confuse or delay a settlement of the overriding issue" of a streamlined single Department of Defense.[2]

Among the "details" that worried the Marines (and the navy) was a call for the overall military services chief to have direct access to the president on budgetary and strategic matters, bypassing a civilian secretary of defense and Congress. Under the current system, Congress had placed the budgetary power in the hands of two civilians—the secretary of war for the army and the secretary of the navy for the Marine Corps and navy. The Marines placed great faith in civilian control of the defense establishment for a good reason: Congress loved the Marines. Both the navy and Marines Corps were anxious that the concentration of budgetary and strategic power in the hands of one military officer, who would most often be either an army or air force general rather than an admiral, could lead to substantial reduction in the roles, missions, and budgets for the naval services. Another worry was the constant flow of evidence that the new air force advocates wanted to take over all military aviation assets, even those aircraft aboard the navy's aircraft carriers. There were middle positions in this dispute, too. Many reformers could see an argument for letting the navy keep its air arm, but were deeply skeptical of a discrete Marine air force. Even before the end of the war, the Marines learned that President Truman was in favor of a plan along War Department lines. Truman, an army artillery captain in World War I, had already earned a reputation for thinking the Marines were competing with the army, and that their rapid expansion to nearly half a million men during the war in effect meant they had transformed themselves into a second American army.

Just as 1945 came to a close, General Mike Edson, USMC, a hero of Guadalcanal and the liaison officer with the chief of naval operations, received copies of top-secret JCS documents concerning postwar reform. They contained shocking information about the army's view of the Marines' role in the new Department of Defense. They also harbored subtle hints that senior navy officers involved in the negotiations over the shape of the new department—officers who were meant to represent the interests of the Marine Corps—might be willing to compromise on protecting the combat power and missions of the Marines in exchange for guarantees that the navy could keep its planes. In documents JCS 1478/10 and 11, army general Carl Spaatz described the Marines' World War II operations as "patently an incursion" into the missions of the army and the Army Air Forces, and proposed that in the future "the size of the Marine Corps be limited to small, readily available and lightly armed units no larger than a regiment." Army chief of staff Dwight D. Eisenhower wrote in these same papers that the Marines in the recently completed world war had clearly duplicated the role of the army in fighting as regular ground-force units. He wrote, too, that, alone among the services, the Marines should not be "appreciably expanded" to meet the needs of the country in times of war.[3] As for Marine aviation, if it were essentially the same as naval aviation, meaning that all planes should be ship-based, he had no problem with its being retained. But he could not see a role for the sort of all-purpose aviation wing that the Marines envisioned as essential to fulfilling their mission as the nation's force in readiness. The loss of an independent air arm was widely interpreted as meaning death to the Corps' postwar self-image.

As the army's intentions concerning the Corps came more fully into view, the Marines put a loosely organized team of officers to work drafting papers and lobbying key political figures in Congress and in the national press. Edson was prominent among them. So was Lieutenant Colonel Victor H. Krulak, a highly energetic and brilliant Naval Academy graduate who had an uncanny knack for finding himself in the right spot at the right time. Indeed, wherever the critical debates and campaigns unfolded for the next twenty years, there was Victor "Brute" Krulak. He would play a vital role in the development of helicopter doctrine in the late 1940s and early 1950s. Before the war, Krulak had done important work on the amphibious tractor and landing-boat programs that were critical to the Marines' successes in the island assaults. Another member of what was soon dubbed the "Chowder Society" was Brigadier General Gerald C. Thomas, who had served as General Vandegrift's operations officer during the Guadalcanal campaign in 1942. Thomas taught history at Quantico and was known for his intellect and persuasive powers. Thomas brought on board Merrill B. Twining, another Naval Academy graduate, who had trained as a lawyer. And then there was Colonel Robert Hogaboom, who would in the late 1950s lead the board that revamped the FMF, and Yale-trained historian, Robert B. Heinl, who would go on to write a number of works of Marine history that were admired by Marines of many generations but criticized by some professional historians for lack of objectivity.

The Chowder Society soon came to see that unification under one department was inevitable. Thus they focused intense effort on preserving Navy Department autonomy within a unified Department of Defense, and most critically in securing specific legislative protection for the Marine Corps. With legislation on the books defining the Corps' roles, missions, and approximate size, no matter what the powers of the new defense secretary or the chief military officer of the United States, the Marines would be protected against General Eisenhower and those who shared his views, and against a future executive order of the president. In 1946, Congress merged the Senate and House committees dealing with the army and navy, respectively, into Armed Services Committees. While the new House committee was likely to be friendly to the Marines, the Senate committee looked decidedly pro-army. Members of the Chowder Society were also troubled by the appointment of Admiral Forrest P. Sherman as the department's chief negotiator in the legislative process, for he was himself a naval aviator more interested in saving the navy's planes than the Marines. Passionate testimony supporting the inclusion of language to protect the Marines in the next Senate unification bill, S.758, failed to change the bill. The bill did, however, preserve the extant Joint Chiefs of Staff planning system and a high degree of autonomy for the military departments—signal victories for the Navy Department as a whole, but cold comfort to the Marines, who continued to envision presidential directives and budgetary constraints leading to severe cutbacks of Corps combat effectiveness in the coming years.

Then came a stroke of good fortune. Rather than putting the House version of the bill before the House Armed Services Committee, the administration's House leaders put it before Congressman Clare E. Hoffman's Committee on Expenditures in the Executive Department. The administration fully expected that Hoffman, supposedly lacking interest or experience in military legislation, would turn the bill over to a subcommittee headed by James Wadsworth, a pro-army congressional expert on defense. But Hoffman was a good friend of the father of a member of the Chowder Society, Lieutenant Colonel James B. Hittle. Hittle persuaded the congressman to keep the hearings within the confines of his own committee. Hoffman, now tipped off about the army's true intentions, informed his colleagues that he could not report out the bill until he had seen the JCS 1478 studies. The army at first demurred, but congressional pressure ultimately led to their release. Once those papers were made public, Eisenhower's claim that neither he nor the army bore malice toward the Corps was shown to be something less than the truth. Americans have long favored the underdog, and when summary accounts of the JCS 1478 studies made their way into newspapers around the country, public support for the Marines' cause mushroomed. And the Marines were fortunate in having an unusual number of nationally prominent members of the press in their corner.

Pro-Marine newspapermen wrote stories containing convincing evidence that the Corps was under serious threat not only by those who argued for organizational efficiency, but also by certain people within the Truman administration with old grievances about Marine Corps arrogance and its drain of too many of the nation's most promising young fighting men from the army, which was supposed to do the nation's land fighting.

The Marine spokesmen in both congressional testimony and public statements argued that the restructuring would stifle healthy competition in the development of doctrine and equipment that would suit as many missions as possible. They pointed to victory in World War II to show that a decentralized system that afforded each service considerable latitude over how to construct its forces and execute a campaign had worked, and that despite the advent of the atomic bomb, and the inevitable changes in warfare that loomed ahead, there was no reason to dismiss the idea of decentralization. As for General Spaatz's claim about the Marine "incursion" into army missions, if the army was not prepared to execute the functions carried out by the Marine Corps, said one memorandum, "then clearly no incursion existed. . . . When the urgency arose for an amphibious expedition to seize Guadalcanal, although there were four Army divisions in the vicinity, it was the Marines who were assigned the task. . . . The Army was unprepared to conduct close air support . . . either before the war, during the war or at the end of the war."[4]

General Vandegrift went on to say that the thrust of the army plan was defective because it threatened Congress's own prerogatives concerning the conduct of war. The plan was based on the faulty assumption that the complexities of modern warfare justify an "extension of political-military control into fields of government which are essentially civilian in character." Wearying of the struggle and impatient for results, the president's special counsel, Clark Clifford, is said to have confided that "the issue of the Marine Corps has become the focal point of all opposition to the bill and unless some concession was given to the Marine Corps, the whole thing was liable to blow up. . . ."[5]

After months of drafting and redrafting and lobbying, the president signed the National Security Act of 1947. The idea of a single, all-powerful military chief of staff was gone. The act stated that the Marine Corps had primary responsibility for developing amphibious warfare doctrine and equipment; that it was a separate service within the Department of the Navy; and that it should include land combat, service, and aviation units. It went on: "The primary mission of the Marine Corps shall be to provide fleet marine forces of combined arms, together with supporting air components, for service with the fleet in the seizure or defense of advanced naval bases and for the conduct of such land operations as may be essential to the prosecution of a naval campaign."[6]

The act's becoming law was a cause for celebration among the Chowder Society—and indeed, for all Marines on active duty and in the reserves. Remarked General Vandegrift, "It is the first time in the history of the Marine Corps that the roles and missions have been spelled out in language that an eighteen-year-old could understand."[7]

General Vandegrift retired as 1947 came to a close. His successor, a tall Virginia Military Institute graduate named Clifton B. Cates, had fought with distinction at Belleau Wood as a young officer with the 4th Marine Brigade. Wounded three times during World War I, he had won the Navy Cross, the nation's second-highest medal for bravery under fire. By the time he assumed the commandancy, Cates had the unusual distinction of having commanded every level of infantry unit in combat from platoon all the way up to division. His tenure (1948 to 1951) was mostly a time when the nation was at peace, yet there were battles of a different sort fought in the vicinity of the Potomac River—the battles of the budget.

Marines have earned a reputation for being zealous to the point of paranoia in the defense of their service's missions and budget. In reviewing the first three years of Cates's tenure, it is easy to understand why. As Cates told correspondent Richard Tregaskis in 1948, his "biggest worry is to keep the Marine Corps alive, to keep it the potent element of national security it has been in the past, to develop its unique capabilities.

There are lots of people here in Washington who want to prevent that, who want to reduce us to the status of Navy policemen or get rid of us entirely."[8]

In Key West, a JCS conference to refine the principles of the National Security Act led to a March 1948 agreement to limit the size of the Corps to four divisions in wartime. The Corps had had six divisions in World War II. The Marines were even prohibited from forming a "second land army" in wartime. The commandant had not been allowed to attend the conference. In response, two prominent retired Marine generals, Holland Smith and Mike Edson, went on the warpath. Smith published *Coral and Brass*, a provocative autobiography, and Edson led a hard-charging campaign of correspondents and congressional supporters in public attacks against the Corps' detractors, with the air force a prominent target. Neither Edson nor Smith could bear to see President Truman succeed in his effort to strengthen the powers of the new office of secretary of defense and the JCS at the expense of the Navy Department as a whole.

Meanwhile, two new appointees, Secretary of Defense Louis Johnson and Chairman of the Joint Chiefs of Staff Omar Bradley, proved at best indifferent and often hostile to HQMC's modernization programs and general efforts to ensure that the Corps got its share of training resources.

The secretary of the army, Kenneth C. Royall, blithely suggested in public testimony in 1949 that President Truman should either make the army part of the Marines or the Marines part of the army. When Massachusetts senator Leverett Saltonstall asked Royall if he was advocating that the DOD abolish the Marine Corps and integrate its combat forces into those of the army, Royall responded without hesitation: that was exactly what he was proposing.

President Truman was determined to undertake cuts in the defense budget, and Bradley and Johnson, both of whom thought the amphibious assault to be an anachronism in the nuclear age, supported draconian cuts in the Marine Corps' personnel level and budget. Again, both the public and a host of pro-Marine organizations, such as the National Rifle Association (NRA) and the American Legion, protested strongly. With personnel already deployed in the cities and along the rail lines of northern China to keep peace between the sparring Nationalists and Communists, the Fleet Marine Force in mid-1948 could field only eleven battalion landing teams (BLTs)—a paltry number for the FMF, obligated by law to respond with a forcible entry capability in addition to evacuation and humanitarian missions in every corner of the globe. (A typical Marine division of the postwar era consisted of three regiments and nine infantry battalions, each of which could be detached and serve as a battalion landing team at sea, and supporting units of many types.)

In fiscal year 1949, Johnson cut a dangerously lean FMF even further —from thirty-five thousand Marines to about thirty-one thousand. The following year brought a further cut of 5 percent. He reduced the number of BLTs to a postwar low of eight. The number of air squadrons in the FMF dropped from twenty-three in 1948 to twelve in 1950.

The size of the Marine Corps as a whole—meaning the FMF, plus the supporting establishment for training and base maintenance—shriveled from ninety-two thousand in 1947, to eighty-three thousand in 1948, and then to just over seventy-four thousand in 1950. When Johnson threatened to cut the number of BLTs down to six in 1951, a deeply frustrated General Cates responded:

> It is not merely to be a question of cuts in men and money—although they are serious enough. We are being told in detail—and told by the Department of Defense—where and how these cuts are to be made— by striking into the heart of our combat forces. . . . I cannot agree that a cut so pointedly directed at reducing the combat strength of this highly effective organization is an economy.[9]

Cates and the senior officer corps were understandably apprehensive about the Corps' ability to meet its commitments and maintain a high standard of readiness with so few men and dollars. With the lion's share of the FMF concentrated at Camp Lejeune and with continuous deployments of BLTs with the Sixth Fleet in the Mediterranean, the Marines' capacity to respond to a crisis in the western Pacific was limited. Headquarters had no choice but to increasingly rely on the 4th Marine Division—the Marine Corps Reserves. The implications of that were clear: the Corps would not reach a fight in very much of a hurry. The planning problems were more acute when the JCS assigned the Corps two critical missions in the event of war against the Soviet Union. Should such a conflict erupt, the Marines were to seize naval and air bases in Iceland and the Persian Gulf, paving the way for air force bombers to attack Soviet cities and military targets from those bases. Next, two Marine divisions were to join the army in a ground war to capture the oil fields of the Middle East.

The Potomac battles in the postwar era pitted the Marine Corps against the fashionable ideas of the day. One of the most fashionable was that a military organization of combined arms, with a tradition of focusing on the foot soldier with his rifle, was an inappropriate luxury in a nuclear age where airpower would reign. Another much publicized notion that relied on sophisticated theoretical social-science scholarship was the notion that ordinary bureaucratic and business-management concepts of efficiency and organization could be applied with great effect to the "business" of war, and to the formation of military institutions. Time and again, the Corps found stiff resistance or skeptical indifference among those in the civilian defense bureaucracy. The Corps wanted to be robust and well funded enough to be an independent combined-arms service. In a defense establishment obsessed with nuclear-conflict scenarios and strategic bombing, this boutique operation seemed quaint and wasteful. As the Korean War would soon show, the Marine Corps was neither.

If the years after the Pacific war brought serious challenges to the institution's health, they failed to stifle the forward-looking, imaginative outlook that had characterized the best of the officer corps for most of the twentieth century. General Roy Geiger, who had commanded III Amphibious Corps on Peleliu and Okinawa and been a witness to the atomic tests at Bikini Island in 1946, had come to a sobering conclusion about what the bomb meant for the amphibious assault: a small number of atomic weapons could destroy an expeditionary Marine force as currently organized. He urged headquarters to use its most competent officers to develop a technique of conducting amphibious operations in the atomic age.

Vandegrift assented to Geiger's plea, forming a special board at Quantico under three generals to ponder how the Marines should redefine their amphibious landings.

The board formed its own secretariat under the direction of Colonel Merrill B. Twining. After about a year, the board put forth a sobering report: radical changes in doctrine and equipment would be required for future amphibious operations. The existence of atomic weapons made wide dispersion of forces essential. A number of options were considered, including the use of fixed-wing transports, gliders, or paratroop operations to transport ground forces to shore. Submarines were even considered. What most captured the board's attention and imagination, however, was the helicopter. Desultory experiments had been carried out with autogyros in Nicaragua in the 1930s. They were not very maneuverable, though, and the results were less than promising. When the board first seriously considered the helo as the indispensable new aircraft, the Marine Corps had not a single one in its inventory. The board was starting from scratch in creating a new doctrine, soon known throughout the Defense Department as "vertical envelopment."

Colonel E. Colston Dyer, a pilot with good connections to navy aviators who were experimenting with primitive helicopters, assumed a prominent place in the research process. He, along with Krulak, Hogaboom, and others, submitted a report in March 1947 that established the basic requirements for a helicopter program. Two types of craft would be required in the amphibious assaults of the future: an assault helo to deliver infantry, and a larger transport machine to provide those troops with beans, bullets, and heavy weapons. The latter type was at the time beyond the technological capability of either of the two most important helicopter companies of the time—Sikorsky and Piasecki—but the Marines were willing to bide their time. The Marine schools at Quantico began work in earnest on their doctrine even before they had the machines to test their theories. The goal was to take vertical envelopment from the drawing board to the littoral areas of the earth and to acquire and deploy helicopters that could carry serious payloads from the deck of an aircraft carrier to a point behind enemy forces along a hostile shore. Ideally, the assault craft would have a payload of about five thousand pounds and be able to fly at about one hundred knots at five thousand feet for two to three hundred miles.

In January 1948, Vandegrift activated Experimental Helicopter Squadron HMX-1 at Quantico. There it could draw on instructors and students from the Marine Corps schools, and be accessible to members of Congress and the DOD—the people who would be called upon to provide resources and approval for the fledgling program. The squadron and the special board worked for months on logistics, organization, and equipment, creating charts and tactics for an assault force of divisional size, integrating fixed-wing planes, traditional landing craft, and helicopter landings.

In May the test pilots of HMX-1 and a regimental combat team staff group gingerly lifted five HO3S-1 Sikorsky choppers off the deck of the escort carrier USS *Palau* sailing off the North Carolina coast, and flew a group of U.S. Marines into the pine forest training grounds at Camp Lejeune. Operation Packard I, the first field test of vertical envelopment, was under way. Each helo in the operation carried only three Marines. In Packard II, a grand total of sixty-six Marines were ferried ashore, where they established a command post with all supplies and equipment being delivered by fixed-wing craft. Packard II was hardly a spectacular or large-scale exercise, but it was a start. Victor Krulak was to write many years after the event that the most important objective of Packard II was "to create a state of mind among the students, instructors, the Navy and the observers, as to the dramatic tactical horizons of the helicopter." [10]

By year's end, Twining, Dyer, Krulak, and Hogaboom had written a manual of operations, *Amphibious Operations: Employment of the Helicopter (Tentative)*. Soon known throughout the armed services as PHIB 1, an abbreviation of "amphibious," this publication reflected the same "can do" spirit and confidence that undergirded the tentative manual of 1934 that had laid out the principles of the ship-to-shore amphibious assault that had conquered the Japanese.

The board was undeterred by naysayers both within and outside the Corps who pointed out that the machine the Marines wanted for its projected squadrons—to be operational in 1953—the Piasecki HRP, would cost close to $1 million each. They also faced a fixed-wing establishment that saw the helicopter program as a serious threat. Eventually, by the early 1960s, the army would surpass the Marines in helicopter doctrines and deployment and doctrinal development, but it was the Marines who pioneered it.

While desk-bound Marines worked political and PR battles, and toyed with helicopters, a different PR operation went into effect on the other side of the planet. After Hiroshima and Nagasaki, the Japanese surrender put General MacArthur in charge of a new, temporary empire in occupied Japan. Elements of both the 2nd and 5th Marine Divisions joined the 6th Marine Division in occupation duty. Their area of operations was the island of Kyushu, the southernmost of the two islands. There they repatriated Korean and Chinese laborers and joined the Japanese in helping to clear away vast amounts of rubble from the American bombing campaign. At Sasebo, a city of three hundred thousand that had been savaged by B-29s, Marines found the business section of the city leveled flat, and there were sixty thousand homeless. Refuse and rubble was general, as was the stench of untreated sewage. When the 2nd and 6th Marines came ashore at Nagasaki, the conditions were much worse. One grunt said with typical Marine candor, "It was a filthy, stinking, wretched hole, and the sooner we get out, the better we will all like it."[11]

Once fully established in the predictable rhythms of occupation duty, which included a great deal of guarding of installations, endless patrolling to ensure order, and performing small-scale cleanup projects, the Marines joined one of the most remarkable sea changes in attitudes between two peoples in world history. Soon the "duplicitous" and "savage" Japs appeared docile, and even childlike—in need of support, advice, and direction from their big Western brothers, the Americans. As the historian John Dower has pointed out, the cover of *Leatherneck* magazine's September 1945 issue "introduced a subtle and significant metamorphosis: it depicted a smiling Marine with an appealing but clearly vexed monkey on his shoulder dressed in the oversize uniform of the Imperial Army. Heretofore the Japanese had been depicted as apes and gorillas; immediately after the war they became transformed into clever, imitative, domestic pets."[12]

As legions of Marines and other service people who served in Japan have testified, the Japanese were good losers. Indeed, most ordinary Japanese welcomed the conquerors. For the Marines, occupation duty was relatively short. All but a few 2nd Marine Division units departed by February 1946, replaced by army units. There was, of course, the usual carousing that attends the occupation of a defeated enemy's home cities, but for the most part the Marines in Japan acquitted themselves with discipline and professionalism. General MacArthur, who ran the country for six years after World War II not unlike a regent and who was no great friend of the Marine Corps, remarked, "Their general conduct was beyond criticism. . . . They were truly ambassadors of goodwill."[13]

There did remain some hostile fire for the Marines in Asia—but not in Japan. The Marines soon had to go back to China, where they had been intermittently active for decades. Whether they arrived in ships at the mouth of the Hai River or in the railway station, throngs of boisterous Chinese greeted the 3rd Battalion, 7th Marines with cheers and wide grins. Children waved, laughed, and scurried about amid the novelty of seeing such large, tough-looking American troops. The 3/7 was in the vanguard of General Keller Rockey's III Amphibious Corps force of fifty thousand Marines en route to duty in war-wracked northern China.

The first landing of Marines in China had taken place in Canton in 1844 to protect an American trading post. In 1856, Marines had led a combined navy-Marine assault on several barrier forts manned by Chinese who sought to prevent the U.S. Navy from resupplying the U.S. legation in Canton. More famously, the Marines engaged in heavy combat in Peking and Tientsin in defense of American and other foreign nationals during the Boxer Rebellion in 1900. They stayed from 1900 to 1941, giving rise to the term *China Marines.*

The new deployment marked a departure, for postwar north China duty was the first of many inspired by the cold war. For the next four years ever-smaller numbers of Marines found themselves embroiled in the bizarre, highly unpredictable, and often violent landscape of China's civil strife. Sino-American diplomacy of this era was attended by more than a little naïveté on the part of American policy makers, and the costs of America's well-intentioned but wrongheaded policies were paid in large measure by Rockey's force of Marines. The China deployment would come to an abrupt conclusion in May 1949 with the Marines' evacuation of American dependents in Tsingtao, just as Mao Tse-tung's troops were about to crush the remnants of Nationalist resistance and give birth to the People's Republic of China.

The Marines had been sent to Hopeh Province and the Shantung Peninsula at the behest of the State Department, for it was a major objective of postwar U.S. foreign policy to ensure a strong, unified, and democratic China as a bulwark against the Soviet Union. According to U.S. intelligence, the Soviets had designs on mineral-rich Manchuria.

The publicly stated mission of the Marines put forward by Truman administration spokesmen was to orchestrate the surrender of several hundred thousand widely dispersed Japanese troops in the strategically essential northern industrial region of the country and to ensure the order and economic stability of the country as a whole. The diplomats instructed the Marines to assist the Nationalist Chinese government under Chiang Kai-shek in repatriating both the Japanese soldiers and more than 250,000 Japanese and German civilians who had joined Japanese forces in their invasion of the country in the early days of World War II.

The Nationalists, however, were only marginally cooperative. They had different priorities than the United States. They routinely ignored American military and political guidance, seeking to maximize their position vis-à-vis Mao's Communist guerrilla army by moving many divisions of troops into mineral-rich Manchuria and leaving only poorly trained militia forces to help the Marines dealing with Communist provocations and Japanese repatriation.

It was clear to Chiang Kai-shek and Mao Tse-tung—but to neither Truman nor his long-suffering diplomatic emissary to China, General George C. Marshall—that full-scale civil war for control of the entire country was inevitable. As events would soon prove, Chiang was as inept an army commander as he was a statesman. The Communists brilliantly exploited his weakness. Mao's People's Liberation Army (PLA) was highly disciplined and well led. As the months went by, they steadily gained the support of the peasantry, tossing away Marxist doctrine where practical to do so, and staying clear of engagements against the Nationalists in and around the cities where the Nationalist army enjoyed advantages against the lightly armed PLA.

Once the 6th Marine Division had set up headquarters in Tsingtao and the 1st Marine Division at Tientsin, General Rockey deployed his Marines along the railway lines between Tientsin and Tsingtao, and between Peking and Tientsin, to protect trains from sabotage and to ensure the delivery of coal to China's major cities. Without coal deliveries, Peking and Shanghai were in danger of economic collapse and wide-scale famine.

Even before Rockey's entire force had deployed, Mao had formed the correct impression that U.S. forces ostensibly in the region to keep peace and order in effect freed up Nationalist soldiers to challenge his growing strength and prestige. And so Mao ordered his commanders to conduct a low-intensity harassment campaign against the Marines' train patrols.

The days of relative peace for the China Marines were short. On October 6, while General Rockey presided over the surrender of fifty thousand Japanese on behalf of the Nationalist government, a detail of Marine engineers protected by a single rifle platoon came under heavy fire from about fifty Communist infantrymen while trying to clear the road between Tientsin and Peking. The Americans were forced to withdraw. Two days later, the engineers returned, this time with an entire rifle company—and air cover—and completed their mission without incident. Similar harassment occurred whenever the Marines traveled in vulnerable numbers throughout Hopeh and the Shantung Peninsula.

When Communist forces in the fall of 1945 attempted to block a Marine landing in the port of Cheefo on the Shantung Peninsula, Rockey wrote to Vandegrift that he "felt that any landing there would be an interference in the international affairs of China; that it would be bitterly resented by the Communists, and that there would be serious repercussions. Although the opposition would not have been very serious, there was apt to be some fighting, sabotage and guerrilla warfare thereafter."[14] Rockey promptly diverted the landing from Cheefo to Tsingtao to avoid trouble, but evidently the very presence of Americans was a thorn in the side of the Communists, for ambushes and harassment along the roads and rails continued. One Marine died and ten were wounded between October 1945 and January 1946.

Meanwhile, the 1st Marine Air Wing under Major General Claude E. Larkin was soon transporting the Nationalist 92nd and 94th Armies to Peking for billeting. Chiang's forces showed no inclination, however, to relieve the Marines strung out along the railways. To fill the gaps, the Marines rearmed a number of Japanese units and deployed them throughout the railway net. Regular air patrols were essential in support of III Amphibious Corps ground troops, and Marine fighter pilots were always at the ready when American infantry was patrolling outside the city boundaries or running security operations on trains.

The Marines administered the repatriation of some 630,000 Japanese soldiers and civilians during its deployment. This duty tested the diplomatic skills of III Amphibious Corps' officers, for both the Communists and the Nationalists were often reluctant to turn over Japanese with technical and military expertise, because they could be put to good use in the civil war. On November 14, Communist infantry stopped a train along the Peking-Mudkin line carrying Major General DeWitt Peck, commander of the 1st Marine Division. He was conducting an inspection of Marine outposts along the railway when the train was halted six miles north of Kuyeh by rifle fire. Peck ordered his escort platoon to return fire and called in reinforcements. The Communists continued sporadic fire until Company L, 7th Marines arrived on the scene and began to mortar the Chinese positions.

The reason for Communist hostility was not obscure. Chiang was using the Marines in Chinwangtao to protect his base of operations for attacks into Manchuria. In the wake of the incident, General Rockey contacted his superior, army general Albert C. Wedemeyer, in the hopes of securing permission to conduct air strikes. Wedemeyer's response conveys some notion of the complexity and awkwardness of the rules of engagement the Marines had to work under:

> If American lives are endangered by small-arms fire . . . it is desired that you inform the [Nationalist Chinese] leader or responsible authority in that village in writing that fire from that particular village is endangering American lives and that such firing must be stopped. After insuring that your warning . . . has been received and understood, should firing that jeopardizes American lives continue, you are authorized to take appropriate action for their protection. Your warning and action should include necessary measures to insure safety of innocent persons.[15]

Operating under such rules of engagement placed great pressures on Marine commanders to ensure discretion and fire discipline on the part of their men. It was a tough and thankless job, rewarded not by praise but by silence. With each incident, tensions and negative feelings toward the Communists increased. Matters were made more difficult by the departure of hardened combat veterans, who were replaced by inexperienced Marines fresh from training in the United States.

The months of frustrating duty rolled forward. In addition to their various security patrols, Marines were closely involved in support of General Marshall's continued efforts to broker peace between two armies increasingly bent on outright war. The Corps supplied six teams of truce negotiators to work with the Nationalists and Communist forces beginning in March 1946. The Marine teams quickly gleaned that the Nationalist troops were poorly led and lacking in motivation. The reverse was true of the Communists, whose land-distribution policies won them many friends among the peasantry.

General Marshall's efforts and the efforts of the Marines were confounded by a basic contradiction in American policy: the United States was officially neutral in the conflict between Mao and Chiang Kai-shek, but, in practice, Chiang was an ally, and Mao was not. The Nationalists won several victories in Manchuria in the spring of 1946, but they failed to accomplish the essential task: the destruction of the lion's share of Mao's forces. The fighting went on, punctuated by a series of fragile truces.

On July 26, 1946, came a major ambush of a Marine convoy near Anping, forty-four miles from Tientsin: nine supply trucks escorted by about forty men from the 11th Marines were attacked—just as they approached a roadblock of oxcarts—with small-arms fire and hand grenades by a force of three hundred Communists. A grenade killed the escort commander, Sergeant Douglas A. Corwin, among others. The Marines stood and fought a desperate battle for three and a half hours, while one Jeep in the rear guard managed to turn around and head back to Tientsin. Colonel Wilburt S. Brown's 11th Marine Regiment rushed a heavily armed four-hundred-man rescue patrol to the scene. By the time reinforcements arrived, four Marines were dead and ten wounded. Communist casualties were estimated at fifteen dead. The

Communists claimed that the Marines had opened fire on them, and refused to produce the officer who had led the attack. Thereafter, Marines patrolled only in considerable strength.

Thankfully, Anping was the last major engagement the Marines would endure in China, though harassment continued.

On April 5, 1947, a considerably emboldened PLA unit attacked a large Marine Corps ammo dump at Hsinho, killing three Marines and wounding eight in a fierce firefight. Eight more Marines were injured in another firefight while coming to their comrades' aid. The remaining Marine force in China, three battalions based at Tsingtao, was assigned to guard the U.S. naval base there. They were the force that evacuated the last American nationals from Tsingtao when Mao's Communists won a tremendous battle at Huai-Hai and conquered both Peking and Tientsin. By the end of May 1949, the last Marines had left China for good. But the Marines were destined to confront the PLA—and other Asian communists—in two major conflicts that would follow World War II: the Korean and Vietnam wars.

FIVE

THE KOREAN WAR

From Pusan Through the Capture of Seoul

August 2, 1950, Pusan, South Korea

Amid the anxious bustle in this grimy port city on South Korea's east coast, a tall U.S. Marine officer with close-cropped white hair stood on one of the docks looking seaward. He scanned the horizon for the first sign of U.S. Navy transports bearing the 1st Marine Provisional Brigade, which he was to command. Their mission was atypical for Leather-necks: they were sent to Pusan as reinforcements to help U.N. forces hold on to a small semicircle of real estate surrounding the port called the Pusan perimeter. The Communist forces of North Korea were on the verge of driving the U.N. troops off the Korean peninsula.

Brigadier General Edward Craig was one of the most highly re-garded officers in the Corps. A New Englander by birth, Craig pos-sessed an iron will, even temperament, and an excellent record of leadership in both combat and staff positions. Five years earlier he had served as operations officer for Harry Schmidt's V Amphibious Corps at Iwo Jima. Edward Craig was one of several senior officers who would take an undermanned and poorly funded Marine Corps into the Korean War.

A long chain of sobering events had brought General Craig to the seashore at Pusan. At the end of World War II, the Allies had divided the ancient nation of Korea at the 38th parallel. American army units took the surrender of Japanese occupiers and assumed control over the southern half of the 575-mile peninsula. The Soviet Union occupied the northern half in what was supposed to be a temporary arrangement. Once the Koreans could get back on their feet, they were expected to establish their own government through elections supervised by the United Nations. Yet by the late 1940s, Korea had became an object of intense focus as the cold war developed. The "temporary" arrangement of two Koreas had calcified into a permanent one. An authoritarian regime under Syngman Rhee, a Korean-born resident of the United States who had long been active in the campaign for an independent Korea, was soon installed in power in Seoul with American backing. The Soviets installed a totalitarian Communist regime under Kim Il Sung in Pyongyang.

In August 1948, the United States recognized Rhee's government as the sole legitimate authority in Korea after the Soviets refused to allow a U.N. legation into North Korea. Red Army forces pulled out of North Korea in 1948, but they left behind the nucleus of a strong force of Korean and Chinese veterans of Mao's People's Liberation Army, well armed with Soviet artillery and at least one hundred fine Soviet T-34 tanks. North Korea thus possessed far more formidable forces than the shaky, lightly armed constabulary force South Korea fielded. The Truman administration had been reluctant to provide the fledgling Rhee regime with tanks and artillery for fear it would mount an invasion of North Korea.

Throughout 1949, the North Korean People's Army (NKPA) conducted a number of raids into South Korea—officially known as the Republic of Korea (ROK)—including a surprise thrust into the strategic Ongjin Peninsula. By spring 1950, Kim Il Sung had gained both Mao's and Stalin's blessing to invade South Korea. His intention was plain enough: he sought to crush the Rhee regime and gain dominion over the entire peninsula. By the time of the invasion, he had 120,000 troops, including two highly trained PLA divisions, courtesy of Mao— the vaunted Korean Volunteer Corps. Soviet contributions included 122mm howitzers, one hundred aircraft, 76mm self-propelled guns, and eight Soviet advisers per division.

At 0400 hours on June 25 seven infantry divisions spearheaded by one armored division barreled across the 38th parallel dividing the two countries, blasting their way through the ROK army units dispersed along the Demilitarized Zone with alarming speed. ROK internal security units farther south were also cut to ribbons by well-coordinated attacks. The North Korean blitzkrieg gathered momentum rapidly. Seoul fell in less than four days. It was clear to U.S. military intelligence and to General Douglas MacArthur, commander of all U.S. forces in the Far East, in Tokyo, that without immediate U.S. military assistance, the North Korean People's Army would conquer the entire peninsula, and soon.

The Truman administration, caught off guard, reacted with alacrity. On the afternoon of June 25, a U.S.-sponsored resolution came up before the U.N. Security Council labeling Kim Il Sung's government as the aggressor in the conflict, and demanding the withdrawal of his forces. Since the Soviets were boycotting the Security Council at the time (for the United Nations' failure to seat Communist China), the resolution passed. On June 26 Truman extended the Truman doctrine, which pledged U.S. aid to "help free peoples to maintain . . . their national integrity against aggressive movements that seek to impose upon them totalitarian regimes," to the countries of Asia.

Truman ordered the Seventh Fleet to protect Formosa and called upon U.S. naval and air forces under MacArthur's command to come to the rescue of besieged forces of the Republic of Korea. Some fifty-two nations pledged support for a U.N.-led (but U.S.-dominated) effort to roll back the invasion. General MacArthur assumed command of all

U.N. forces in the region, and on June 29, Truman ordered American ground forces to deploy to South Korea.

The initial month of the war was a disaster. Elements of the U.S. Eighth Army in Japan were hurriedly deployed beginning on July 2; these units were at 70 percent of wartime strength. They were also an occupation army, with lax standards of discipline and little interest in training. In short, the American army in Japan had grown physically soft.

The American soldiers' World War II–era bazookas and 75mm recoilless rifles were completely ineffective against NKPA T-34 tanks. After several desperate hours, the initial engagements turned into a rout. First Lieutenant Philip Day Jr. remembered what happened when his platoon was ordered to withdraw under fire:

> When we moved out we began taking more and more casualties. . . . Guys fell around me. Mortar rounds fell around here and there. . . . Although we were young, we became exhausted just trying to run. This was a terrible time. . . . All around I saw enemy fire kicking up spurts of water. Guys stopped and removed their boots, threw their helmets away, stripped themselves of everything that slowed them down. . . . Everything had broken down and it was every man for himself.[1]

This task force of the 24th Infantry Division lost 185 men, killed, wounded, or captured. The rout had a devastating effect on the entire division psychologically. As word spread throughout the Eighth Army, a sense of impending disaster and panic sank in. By mid-July the Eighth Army, under Lieutenant General Walton H. Walker, had no other option but to trade South Korean real estate for time. Many army units broke and ran soon after making contact with advancing North Koreans, leading more than one reputable historian to call the early days in Korea among the darkest hours in the history of the U.S. Army.

By the end of July, the combined U.S.-ROK forces found themselves backed up into the southeast corner of the peninsula, hanging on tenuously to the port of Pusan. ROK army units set up a defensive line in the north, while the bewildered American divisions manned the fifty-mile western side of the perimeter. Counterattacks were not a viable option; U.N. forces were barely strong enough to hold on.

MacArthur's forces needed serious help, and fast. Ever since General Clifton Cates, commandant, USMC, and Lieutenant General Lemuel Shepherd, commander, FMF Pacific, had learned of the crisis, they had acted with the focus and speed of men possessed. They were determined to get the Marines into combat—and into the breach. It wouldn't be easy. They faced enormous logistical and personnel problems, for the Truman administration's budget cuts had left the Marines with a regular force that lacked the men, the equipment, and the amphibious shipping to respond rapidly to such an emergency with more than a single regimental combat team. Even deploying a unit of that size—about sixty-five hundred men and their equipment—all the way to Korea posed grave difficulties. The strength of the entire Corps stood at just seventy-four thousand. If the Marines were to play a major combat role in the Korean crisis, the reserves would have to be called up.

Luck and good military common sense combined to ensure that the Corps would indeed perform not only a prominent combat role in the critical year, but a gut-wrenchingly dramatic one that enhanced the institution's prestige and paved the way for the powerful, three-division, three-air-wing force that has played such a critical role in America's foreign-policy interventions ever since.

The critical decisions and frenetic activities the crisis engendered at FMF Pacific, Camp Pendleton, and the Pentagon all took place in July, and neither Cates nor Shepherd waited for orders from the JCS before they instructed their staffs to initiate planning, including the notification of reserve units that the call to active duty was imminent. Immediately they concentrated dispersed units of the FMF at Camp Pendleton and San Diego to form the nucleus of a powerful regimental combat team. Thousands of man-hours were expended at all echelons, from HQMC down to company level, in sorting out the myriad administrative and logistical details involved in sailing from San Diego before the

Pentagon had even ordered the call-up of the Marine Reserves and authorized the 1st Marine Division to go to war strength on July 25.

General Douglas MacArthur was instrumental in the decision to send the Marines from California before any army units left the American mainland. On July 10, as U.N. forces were engaged in the nasty business of trading real estate for time to build up combat power and get it to South Korea, MacArthur met with Lemuel Shepherd. The commander of all U.N. forces had a week earlier urgently requested the immediate deployment of a Marine regimental combat team. Recalling the fine performance of the 1st Marine Division in the New Britain operations of 1943 to 1944—when Shepherd had been assistant division commander—he said that he wanted that division once again. The only hope of a quick resolution of the conflict lay in undertaking a daring amphibious assault behind the enemy's front lines to cut off his supply line. Pointing with his pipe to the port of Inchon, west of Seoul, Shepherd, in a letter to historian Robert Heinl, recalled MacArthur's words: "If I only had the 1st Marine Division under my command again, I would land them here and cut the North Korean armies attacking the Pusan perimeter from their logistical support and cause their withdrawal and annihilation."[2] Could Shepherd pull together the entire division in time for a September 15 landing? He could. MacArthur need only ask the JCS for approval and Shepherd would start the ball rolling.

When MacArthur formally requested the Marine division for early September, the Pentagon demurred. It was too soon—such a rapid mobilization would result in an unacceptable weakening of the Fleet Marine Force Atlantic. MacArthur, who had told Craig that he himself had the utmost admiration for the Corps and would welcome its units to his command, was none too pleased. His response conveys how important he felt it was that the division participate in the operation:

Most urgently request reconsideration of decision with reference to the First Marine Division. It is an absolutely vital development to accomplish a decisive stroke and if not made available will necessitate a much more costly and longer operations effort both in blood and expense. . . . It is essential the Marine Division arrive by 10 September 1950 as requested. . . . I cannot emphasize too strongly my belief of the complete urgency of my request. There can be no demand for its potential use elsewhere that can equal the urgency of the immediate battle mission contemplated for it.[3]

Craig, as he gazed out to sea, knew his Marines would acquit themselves well once in a fight. What he did not know was where that fight might be. The commander of the U.S. Eighth Army had only informed the Marine general to be ready to deploy to the front by 0600 hours on August 30. The situation was too fluid, too chaotic, to know where the Marines might be brought into the fight, though the army general reckoned it would probably be somewhere in the southwest of the defensive line.

Craig's brigade had originally sailed from San Diego for Japan as the vanguard for the 1st Marine Division's amphibious assault on Inchon, which was somewhat reluctantly approved by the JCS soon after MacArthur's formal request. But the NKPA's successful end run around the left flank of the Eighth Army made its deployment directly to the fighting in southeast Korea essential.

Only one night after the brigade debarked from its ships at Pusan, Craig's Marines were ordered to the southwest corner of the perimeter. They would go into combat near Mansan, and along with attached army units, engage in the first sustained counterattack against the North Koreans. From August 7 through August 13, in torrid heat, the Marines fought a series of hard-won small-unit actions while driving west toward the towns of Sachon and Chinju. For the first three days, the brigade and attached elements of the 5th and 27th Infantry Divisions fought as part of Task Force Kean. The task force drove back the North Koreans, clearing an important road junction at Tosan.

On August 9, the North Koreans were retreating from Chinju, having taken heavy losses at the hands of both Marine ground forces and Marine air, in the form of Corsair fighter-bombers firing rockets and 20mm cannons. For the first time in the conflict, an enemy unit found itself up against American soldiers who refused to give ground and who possessed the confidence to win. Just outside of Chindong-ni on Hill 342, which rose above the road that constituted the Americans' main supply route, a platoon of G Company, 3rd Battalion, 5th Regiment Marines engaged in the first Marine combat of the Korean War. Their objective was the relief of an army company under heavy attack. By noon, an intense firefight was in full swing, but the Marines took the hill and beat off an NKPA counterattack at the cost of six dead and twelve wounded. Other hill fights followed as the North Koreans attempted to outflank the attacking task force and cut it off from its supply lines as it drove west. These attacks were pushed back, and the Marines were able to secure the road junction at Tosan.

As they pushed farther to the west, a reconnaissance unit from D Company, 2nd Battalion was ambushed in a defile called Taedabok Pass, but the Marines held on until tanks and mortar fire could provide supporting cover fire for an infantry assault that drove the enemy from his well-concealed position. Almost all of the fighting in the first week was on or near the hills that lined critical roads connecting the main towns to the west of the Pusan perimeter.

While the 1st Battalion, 5th Marines was busy trying to knock out a series of well-entrenched NKPA positions on Hill 250 east of Sachon on August 10, a reinforced North Korean platoon was spotted making its way toward a nearby hill to support their comrades on Hill 250. A single squad of Marines waited patiently for the enemy to advance to within seventy-five feet, and this promptly opened up with every weapon at their disposal, killing more than thirty enemy troops.

On August 11, Marine artillery began to shell Kosong, forcing an NKPA regiment to flee by truck. The convoy was caught in the open by Marine aircraft, and more than 140 trucks were blown up or deserted in what became known as the "Kosong Turkey Shoot." That morning, elements of 1/5 engaged in hand-to-hand fighting following a reckless

NKPA attack; the assault was ultimately turned back. The tide was turning in the Pusan perimeter, and in dramatic fashion.

Still, the Marines would face many successful night infiltrations carried out by units of the NKPA, many of which had fought alongside the PLA in their civil war. The Chinese, the U.N. forces soon learned, were masters of moving in close to enemy forces at night without detection. One such attack occurred on August 12, and cost many lives.

Meanwhile, in one of many firsts in Marine history to unfold in the Korean War, 1/5's sister battalion 3/5 attacked enemy forces in the opposite direction twenty-five miles to the rear, near Chindong-ni, the very place where the brigade had begun their impressive advance. The only way General Craig could direct both fights was by shuttling the twenty-five miles between units by helicopter. At Chindong-ni and to the east of Sachon, the fighting progressed well, and Craig felt confident of his unit's ability to push the enemy back to the west of Sachon and Chinju.

But the Marine "fire brigade," as it was now being called, was needed elsewhere, and Craig was ordered to turn over his positions to an army unit. The fighting would only get harder. Elements of at least one North Korean regiment crossed the Naktong River near where it converged with the Nam, putting them in position to cut off the main supply route of the U.N. forces. The resulting battle of the Naktong Bulge marked a step up in intensity and scale from the Sachon offensive. About seventy-five miles from Chindong-ni and to the west of Yongson, the bulge resembled the tip of a thumb jutting westward. It was surrounded on three sides by water and on the east by a valley. The eastern approaches to the enemy bridgehead were guarded by several long, twisting ridges, each with a series of crests and saddles. The Eighth Army's 24th Infantry Division wasn't prepared to take on this challenge alone.

Brigadier General John H. Hill worked out a complex plan to take the two critical ridges, Obong-ni and Cloverleaf, with General Craig and the U.S. Army regimental commanders. The Marines would jump off first, on the morning of August 17. Their objectives were Obong-ni Ridge, Hill 207, and Hill 311, all in the very heart of the bulge.

Obong-ni's six peaks bristled with North Koreans. By the end of the day, the 5th Marines stood triumphant on its spine, but not before four frontal assaults had badly mauled several companies of Marines, decimating a couple of platoons. The North Koreans also mounted a night counterattack that almost wrested the ridge back. On one of the frontal assaults, Captain John L. Tobin was hit by small-arms fire and severely wounded just as he was about to climb the fire-strewn slopes. His executive officer, Ike Fenton, recalled the scene:

> We hugged the right side of the road. John Tobin was on my left, the radio operator on my right. An enemy machine gun opened up and stitched John six or seven times. It also hit the radio operator. I wasn't scratched. . . . John did what any actor in a Western does when he gets shot in a barroom fight—staggers across the room, hits a wall and slowly collapses. John was knocked backward, hit the side of a cliff and slowly slid down to the ground. . . . All of a sudden it dawned on me that he had the only map in the Company that showed our objective. Immediately I knew I had to get the map before poor John bled all over it. . . . It shows you how you think in combat: here was a good friend of mine badly wounded and I thought about a map.[4]

One day later, the Marines and army infantry took the two hills, and controlled the ridge. The brigade had played a vital part in averting disaster within the Pusan perimeter. It retired to a bean field outside of Mansan, with the intention of taking on replacements, getting some well-earned rest, and preparing to join the rest of the 1st Marine Division for its key role in MacArthur's amphibious attack behind the enemy's lines at Inchon. But it was not to be, for the North Koreans, realizing that their defeat in the bulge had been due in large measure to committing their units piecemeal in attack, launched a massive assault, with the focal point being the 4th Infantry Division, deployed about four miles east of where the Marines had defeated the enemy at Obong-ni. For three days the Marines methodically attacked and bested the inexperienced NKPA 9th Division, pushing that unit back some eight thousand yards. Never again would the North Koreans mount a serious assault on the Pusan perimeter.

The 1st Marine Provisional Brigade had fought in three discrete engagements in two months against an enemy that had enjoyed nothing but success until its arrival. With the help of some U.S. Army units, the Marines had secured victory in all three battles. It was a huge boost in morale, both within the tattered ranks of the Eighth Army and on the home front. Now the North Koreans understood that not all U.S. units were manned with poorly conditioned and trained troops. As First Lieutenant Robert Bohn of G Company, 3/5, put it, "As we waited to board ship [to join the rest of the 1st Marine Division for the Inchon operation] the Company felt good about itself. We were veterans now and very confident. We'd kicked the shit out of the North Koreans."[5]

The very same day the brigade finished its second Naktong bulge engagement, September 5, the remainder of a now wartime-strength 1st Marine Division of twenty-four thousand Marines had at last formed up at Camp Pendleton. Its units had been gathered from far-flung bases and garrisons. The 7th Regiment was formed by redesignating the entire 6th Regiment from Camp Lejeune. One hundred thirty-eight reserve units, mostly infantry outfits, were called to active duty. One of the battalions of the 7th Marines was pulled in from its operations with the Sixth Fleet in the Mediterranean.

That day, too, a major story broke in the news, based on two letters that stirred a great outpouring of support for the Marine Corps. The first was by a congressman, urging President Truman to permit the commandant of the Marines a voice on the JCS. The second was Truman's reply. He dismissed the request, arguing, in effect, that the Marines were not a discrete service within the Department of the Navy and that the chief of naval operations could speak on the Corps' behalf on the JCS. He went on: "For your information, the Marine Corps is the Navy's police force and as long as I am President that is what it will remain. They have a propaganda machine that is almost the equal of Stalin's. . . . When the

Marine Corps goes into the Army it works with and for the Army and that is how it should be."[6]

The very next day Truman offered General Cates a public apology, yet Cates should have thanked him. By confirming his prejudice, he strengthened the resolve of the Marines and swung many people over to their side. Coming on the heels of the brigade's fine performance, Truman's ill-advised comment aroused new-found sympathy for the bravery and resourcefulness of the Corps.

There would be more bravery and a good deal of good luck attending the Marines' next fight, which was without question one of the riskiest operations in U.S. military history: Operation Chromite, the amphibious attack on Inchon, followed by the drive to recapture Seoul.

Vice Admiral James A. Doyle, protégé of the U.S. Navy's foremost amphibious specialist of World War II, Admiral Richmond Kelley Turner, was serving as commander of Amphibious Group 1, a Marine-dominated amphibious training team in the Far East, when North Korea invaded its neighbor. Now, in July, Doyle found himself in the unenviable position of having to prepare an operational plan for the invasion of Inchon, a grimy port about the size of Omaha on the west coast of Korea, just south of the 38th parallel. He had a mere eighteen days to work out the details. Typically, an invasion plan involving two divisions in assault took more than fifty days to complete. MacArthur had originally envisaged the 1st Cavalry Division hitting the beach on July 27, but the North Korean advances had put an end to that plan. So much pressure was placed on Walker's Eighth Army that the entire 1st Cavalry had to be ferried over to join the Eighth Army's defensive line. MacArthur nonetheless remained convinced that a great turning movement against the enemy's flank was the key to the conflict. From the port, an advance of only twenty miles would put U.N. forces on top of Seoul, not only a key psychological objective, but an important rail and road nexus.

MacArthur was confident about Chromite's chances of success. Neithcr Doyle nor the JCS shared his confidence, even if the weather held and the ship's captains could negotiate the tricky channel leading to the landing beaches. Archie G. Capps, one of Doyle's amphibious staff, nicely summed up the situation when he remarked, "We drew up a list of every natural and geographical handicap. Inchon had 'em all."[7]

MacArthur's first critical task was thus one of persuasion. Although his Joint Strategic Plans and Operations Group had worked out preliminary plans for three different landing sites, MacArthur himself never wavered from his preference: Inchon. Not even the Marines, with their well-established penchant for taking on the most difficult assignments with a "can do" attitude, were sanguine about the operation's prospects.

The reasons for the skepticism were many: Inchon had one of the highest tidal ranges among the world's ports—about thirty-two feet. Low tide revealed a harbor all but bereft of seawater, with soft, oozing mud-flats. A landing force of the size MacArthur needed could maneuver properly for only a few short hours at high tide, on only two particular days in September. Furthermore, the currents were very fast. The channel leading up to the landing zone was narrow. If one ship was immobilized or went aground, it could stop the whole operation. Not all the obstacles were hydrographic, though. The channel leading to the port was encumbered by tiny islands. The port was dominated by a fortified, cave-infested island called Wolmi-Do that had to be taken by a single battalion of Marines before the main force could proceed. And the beaches themselves were protected by high granite walls.

The invasion force was to include seventy thousand Marines and soldiers of X Corps. The navy wasn't at all confident that it could muster the shipping to bring off the operation and protect the fleet at the same time. What if the Russian fleet at nearby Port Arthur went into action? In July and August, many in Washington still thought the invasion of South Korea was merely a diversion for a full-scale Communist invasion of Western Europe. The Soviets might very well take aim at such a rich naval target if they were joining the war.

The JCS sent Army Chief of Staff J. Lawton Collins and Chief of

Naval Operations Forrest P. Sherman to Tokyo for a conference in late August to get the details of the operation from MacArthur and his staff. After listening for eighty minutes to unrelentingly negative briefings MacArthur rose up calmly and deliberately, and stated that the arguments just raised as to the problems posed by Inchon only confirmed his faith in the plan: the enemy would dismiss the probability of such an attack because of its very brashness. By analogy, he brought up General James Wolfe's dramatic assault on Quebec against the French forces there in the French and Indian War, when Wolfe and his soldiers scaled the heights of the walled city rather than attacking the more approachable riverbank north of the city where the French had committed their defenses. Discussing alternative sites on the west and east coasts of Korea, he argued that they offered insufficiently deep envelopment opportunities. Inchon was the right place to attack. He would seal off the southern half of the peninsula and disrupt the enemy's supply lines, paralyzing the North Korean forces facing Walker's Eighth Army. There are different accounts of the specific language MacArthur used in his comments that day, but the participants agree on its effect. The great general himself recalled in his memoirs that while the navy's reservations were "substantial and pertinent," they were not insuperable:

> My confidence in the Navy is complete, and in fact I seem to have more confidence in the Navy than the Navy has in itself. . . . As to the proposal for a landing at Kunsan, it would indeed eliminate many of the hazards of Inchon, but it would be largely ineffective and indecisive. It would be an attempted envelopment which would not envelop. It would not sever or destroy the enemy's supply lines or distribution center, and would therefore serve little purpose. . . . But the seizure of Inchon and Seoul will cut the enemy's supply line and seal off the entire southern peninsula. . . . This in turn will paralyze the fighting power of the troops that now face Walker. . . . Inchon will not fail. Inchon will succeed. And it will save 100,000 lives.[8]

One day before the big brass met, MacArthur met with the new commander of the 1st Marine Division, Major General Oliver P. Smith, who had just flown in from Camp Pendleton and was in the dark as to the objective his division would be charged with seizing. Here, too, the army general put on a masterful performance. Smith went into the meeting with the opinion that X Corps staff, heavily dominated by MacArthur's protégés, were cavalier in thinking that such a large amphibious operation could be sorted out in less than a month. MacArthur, puffing serenely on his pipe, told the Marine that he knew the operation would be somewhat helter-skelter. But, he said, the Marines would be up to the task. Besides, such an operation successfully carried out with the Marines in the vanguard would surely put an end to the Corps' recent struggles in carving out a respectable place for itself within the new Department of Defense.

Before his audience with MacArthur, General Smith sat down with General Edward Almond, MacArthur's chief of staff, and the commander of X Corps, and thus Smith's commanding officer. In World War II, Marine general "Howlin' Mad" Smith (no relation) had fired an army general under his command for lack of aggressiveness in reaching his objectives in combat, and the furor that followed the decision poisoned Marine-army relations for years. Almond and Oliver Smith's relationship during the next nine months only exacerbated the bitterness. Things got off to a bad start when Almond, fifty-eight, and a major general, referred to Smith, fifty-seven, and also a major general, as "son." Smith lacked the brilliant record in combat shared by so many high-ranking Marine officers who would lead the 1st Marine Division's regiments and battalions in Korea, and his habits—he seldom swore, never drank, and was a deeply religious Protestant from Texas—were certainly not typical of the average Marine. But he had a deep knowledge of military history, and would prove to be a leader with exceptional loyalty to his men and a deep commitment to achieving the objective. Other Marine officers sometimes referred to him as "the professor," but he was decidedly not Edward Almond's "son."

Smith was astonished when Almond brushed aside his concerns and reservations about the lack of planning time and the lengthy laundry list of obstacles confronting a force attacking a port such as Inchon as being essentially mechanical problems that would find easy solutions. Almond, after all, had never been involved in either leading or planning an amphibious operation of any scale. During the campaigns that followed, Almond's and Smith's personal dislike of each other would slide into a feud, in which the army officer would chide the Marine for being overly slow and cautious in combat, while the Marine general was equally outspoken about Almond's deficiencies: he was arrogant, ignorant of amphibious subtleties, erratic in his judgment, and overly emotional in front of the troops. Smith, along with most senior Marine officers, also resented the imposition of Almond's command on what was from both an operational and planning point of view essentially a Marine Corps–navy show. All the hard planning—and most of the risk—fell on the 1st Division.

Smith left the meeting, anxious to brief his staff and commence planning work for a major campaign. When Sherman and Collins returned to Washington, they recommended approval of the Inchon operation despite lingering skepticism and acute awareness of the insufficient time allotted to plan it. On August 28, the JCS gave MacArthur provisional approval for a campaign consisting of four broad phases, in the first three of which the Marines played the critical role: the invasion of Inchon and the establishment of a secure beachhead; the drive to Seoul and its capture; the severing of the enemy's lines of supply and communication; and, finally, the deployment of much of the combat strength of the division as an anvil against which the reinforced Eighth Army would hammer the trapped divisions of the retreating North Korean People's Army.

Even with the most intense and efficient planning schedule imaginable, the fact that only three weeks remained before the September 15 D-Day guaranteed that much would have to be left up to chance. One Marine veteran of the Pacific war would say about Chromite, "The whole thing was a rusty travesty of a World War II operation."[9] He was entirely correct. Among the 260 ships assembled in the armada were thirty LSTs of World War II vintage, which the Japanese had been using for commercial fishing. They still stunk of dead fish even when the Marines boarded them for the landing. A number of the more than twenty-nine thousand troops in the landing force, including the army's 7th Division Infantry, which was to follow behind the 1st Marine Division, came from sea to shore with their supplies not combat-loaded, meaning that if they ran into heavy opposition, they would not be able to obtain either ammo replenishment or heavy weapons very quickly. Procedure was thrown out the window: Smith's planners at division level prescribed a rigid scheme of maneuver for the attacking regiments because there was no time for the regimental staffs to work out the details themselves. Minesweepers were attached to the amphibious force, but there were too few of them to handle the heavy concentration of mines the intelligence people feared the force might very well encounter. Intelligence on enemy strength and disposition was negligible.

Chromite was derisively labeled "Operation Common Knowledge" because the press had caught wind that an invasion on the west coast of Korea was in the offing. The operation began inauspiciously as the ships of the amphibious task force departed Kobe, Yokohama, and Pusan early to avoid the worst of the roiling seas caused by Typhoon Kezia. Seasickness nonetheless gripped thousands of Marines and sailors. On September 13, a naval bombardment group cautiously sailed up Flying Fish Channel and spotted a minefield, sending tremors into the hearts of Admiral Doyle and his staff. Fortunately, the field was small, consisting of obsolete mines that could easily be detonated by small-arms fire. It was an early example of the good fortune that characterized the entire operation.

More good luck followed when the bombardment force of destroyers punished Wolmi-Do with more than a thousand rounds of five-inch gunfire. The main North Korean gun emplacements on the island opened up, exposing their positions. They inflicted damage on three destroyers and killed a lone naval officer, but by the next day virtually all the heavy defensive positions on Wolmi-Do had been knocked out. The

North Koreans apparently realized at about this time that the invasion was aimed at Inchon, and they rushed in two thousand reinforcements. Still, the port remained lightly defended with a grand total of about four thousand mediocre troops. The NKPA had gambled by deploying most of its forces farther south.

The nine ships assigned to Phase I of the operation, the seizure of Wolmi-Do, rendezvoused just after midnight on September 14. At 0520, after a breakfast of powdered eggs and canned apricots, the assault force, Companies G, H, and I of the 3rd Battalion, 5th Marines went over the side and climbed into their LCVPs. Twenty minutes later the guns of the support force, including two British light cruisers, shattered the tranquil silence. At 0615, a barrage of rockets hit Wolmi-Do, and then came the gull-winged Corsairs fighter bombers for the final softening up. At 0633 the first Marines scrambled onto the beach. It would take four waves to bring the entire force ashore.

First to hit land were elements of G and H Companies. The third wave ferried in ten tanks, including six Pershings. Resistance was light as the Marines made their way onto the landing beach on the northwest side of the islet. Company G quickly fanned out and headed for the high ground on Radio Hill. The fourth wave, consisting of Company I, stumbled into a bypassed platoon of NKPA troops, but they lacked weapons to challenge the American tanks and were buried alive by a Sherman with a bulldozer blade attached. Another group of North Koreans hid in a cave at the end of the six-hundred-yard causeway connecting Wolmi-Do to Inchon proper. One 90mm shell from a Pershing was all it took to get more than forty dazed enemy soldiers to give up. The last combat took place after 1000 on another islet south of Wolmi-Do, also connected to the main island by a short causeway. Here a well-coordinated assault by G Company with a little help from the Corsairs on station won the day. All told, seventeen NKPA soldiers were killed; seventeen of 3/5's Marines were wounded. Here again, as historian Clay Blair has pointed out, good fortune was very much with the U.N. attack force and particularly with the Marines, for the island had plenty of interconnected trenches, tunnels, and well-constructed gun emplacements. Had the North Koreans seen fit to man these emplacements with battle-tested troops, the outcome would have been very different.

Now Lieutenant Colonel Robert Taplett, commander of 3/5, ordered his men to dig in for the long day to follow and prepare themselves to support the main assault force. Taplett, having checked his defensive positions and sensing that the enemy was not going to mount a counterattack against Wolmi-Do, asked 5th Marines commander Colonel Ray Murray for permission to conduct a reconnaissance in force, or even an assault on Red Beach—where the remainder of the 5th Marines were slated to land when the tide came in once again at around 1700. His request was denied.

The plan for the main assault called for the 5th Marines to land on Red Beach, just north of Wolmi-Do, at 1730 and seize a three-thousand-foot arc, stretching from the northwest of the peninsula to the southeast, anchored by the inner harbor basin, to the southeast. Three miles south of Red Beach, Colonel Chesty Puller's 1st Marines would land at Blue Beach facing a suburban-industrial area. Puller's unit would push inland and cover the only road leading into the seaport, thus preventing reinforcements from entering the port or the defenders from extricating themselves. Without this leverage on Inchon's flank and rear, the Marines could easily be swallowed up by two square miles of dense urban area. With only about an hour and a half of daylight left following the initial landing, there was little room for error.

The initial waves of the main attack at Red Beach hit the seawalls of Inchon at 1731, just a few minutes after navy Skyraiders strafed the beaches that lay ahead of the assaulting Marines. It was raining and windy, and the sky had a foreboding cast. Up went the wooden scaling ladders, and after tossing a few grenades over the wall, the first Marines dashed for the hills that dominated the landing area, which needed to be secured fast to ensure a successful beachhead.

The 5th Marines had been chosen to hit Red Beach because, unlike the 1st Marines, they had ample combat experience as a unit. Theirs was the critical objective, because the port facilities had to be seized in good working order to ensure the buildup of enough combat power to conduct the drive toward Inchon along the Inchon-Seoul highway. Company E rapidly secured the right flank by taking the British consulate and the lower reaches of Observatory Hill.

Enemy fire was sporadic and light at first, except on the left flank, where stubborn NKPA soldiers in a bunker opened up with small-arms and machine-gun fire, felling several Marines immediately. First Lieutenant Baldomero Lopez, platoon leader, attempted to silence their fire with a grenade; he was shot before he could hurl the projectile. He smothered the grenade with his body to protect his men, and was awarded a Medal of Honor posthumously.

After the first three waves came ashore, the landing craft of additional waves began to get mixed together, causing confusion and turning the sequence of events in the attack plan on its head. It was one of a number of indications of haste in preparation, but a combination of drive and a willingness to improvise turned potential disaster into success.

Poor visibility and a temporary breakdown in communications led to a costly mistake that might have easily turned to tragedy. Because Companies C and D were delayed in attacking Observatory Hill, a handful of North Koreans were able to set up machine guns on the crest after the last of the suppressive fire had lifted. Their fire was joined by that of a few NKPA mortar crews. After an LST took a few NKPA rounds, its crew then opened up with 20mm and 40mm cannon fire, killing one 2/5 Marine and wounding twenty-three before the mistake was noted and fire lifted. As night fell, the 5th had achieved control over all its objectives with only very light casualties to show for its efforts.

Off Blue Beach, the LSTs carrying more than 170 Marine-laden amtracs came under enemy artillery fire, which obscured visibility. American and British naval gunfire also produced smoke and flames. Neither the guide boats nor the company commanders could see their objective amid the haze, smoke, and drizzle. Fast tides pulled LSTs and amtracs to and fro; many of the waves in the invasion force landed in no particular order, often far from their planned objective. The entire reserve battalion, Colonel Jack Hawkins's 1/1, mistook the tidal basin for the seawall of Blue Beach. His men took to the sea again and found the beach at last, save one platoon that marched overland and took a few NKPA prisoners along the way.

By day's end, thirteen thousand Marines were ashore. The casualties totaled 21 killed, 1 missing, and 174 wounded. Whatever opposition was left in Inchon proper opted to run rather than fight. After building up supplies and landing enough motor transport and tanks, the drive to Seoul commenced in earnest. Reinforcements flowed into the zone of action, as ROK Marines arrived to support the 1st Marine Division and the U.S. Army's 7th Division garrisoned the turf the Marines had secured in and around Inchon.

It would take the Marines five days to push into the outskirts of Seoul. Along the way they encountered a series of ambushes, tank attacks supported by infantry, and dug-in NKPA positions within towns and on hills that abutted the Inchon-Seoul highway. As the two regiments pressed toward the Han River, the last natural obstacle before Seoul, the resistance grew considerably more intense. Colonel Murray's 5th Marines, on the left (north) flank, opted to advance in a column of battalions, while Puller's regiment moved forward on a broad front south of the main highway.

Murray again had the critical first objective: the taking of Kimpo Airfield. Along the way his men destroyed six unsuspecting NKPA tanks. Once at the airfield, Murray's Marines went up against a hodge-podge unit of defenders consisting perhaps of three hundred troops from various North Korean regiments. On the night of September 17–18, the North Koreans attacked a single Marine outpost near the airfield four times in the space of two hours, supported by one tank. Then the NKPA force tried to envelop Company E with simultaneous attacks from the east and west. Nonetheless, in the morning, Lieutenant Colonel Harold Roise's battalion invested the entire airfield, including the high ground to the east.

Meanwhile, Colonel Puller's men encountered stiff resistance as they pushed through the town of Sosa, where the highway cuts through rugged, dusty red hills and ridges. Northeast of the town Lieutenant Colonel Thomas Ridge's 3/1 drove a force of North Koreans off Hill 123, although once the Marines had secured its crest, they were treated to a thunderous artillery barrage that wounded forty-four Marines. The next day, Puller's 1st Battalion motored north to relieve 5th Marine units on a series of hills that had to be taken in preparation for taking Yongdungpo, the industrial suburb of Seoul, just east of the Han. The 2nd and 3rd Battalions, 1st Marines pressed onward, assaulting North Korean positions on Hill 146 just south of the main highway, and running into mortar and artillery fire for their trouble.

Early on the morning of September 20, Lieutenant Colonel Allan Sutter's 2/1 encountered a battalion-sized enemy force supported by five T-34s rumbling westward out of Yongdungpo, about three miles from the suburb. With Company D on one side of the highway and E on the other, the enemy didn't have a prayer. Howitzers, infantry-manned weapons, and Pershing tank fire made short work of them. Two enemy tanks were victims of a single nineteen-year-old bazooka-bearing private named Walter C. Monegan Jr. He was also credited with breaking up a concerted enemy effort to overrun the 2/1 command post during the melee. More than three hundred enemy troops were killed in the engagement.

Before a three-battalion assault from the northwest, northeast, and center by Puller's regiment, Yongdungpo was shelled all night, and much of it was set afire. The next morning, Lieutenant Colonel Hawkins's 1/1 struggled against enemy forces on two hills that blocked the 1st Regiment's approach from the northwest. With covering fire from Company A on his left, Captain Robert Wray's Company C captured both hills with double envelopments.

On Hill 85, resistance was fierce, and several fire teams were completely pinned down as the enemy commander bent his flanks in a horseshoe shape to counter the double envelopment. A gallant charge by Lieutenant Henry A. Comminskey broke the resolve of the North

Koreans, though. The twenty-four-year-old from Hattiesburg, Mississippi, single-handedly attacked an enemy machine-gun position, killing four North Koreans with his .45 pistol, then ran down two more enemy soldiers, killing them, too.

Later that day—while the 2nd and 3rd Battalions attacked Yongdungpo from the southeast and made slow and costly gains against the NKPA's 87th Regiment—Company A, 1/1, under Captain Robert Barrow, a future commandant, was about to begin one of those small-unit actions that helps explain why the Marines have earned a reputation for steadfastness and boldness in small-unit infantry combat. Barrow decided to march his unit across a rice field east of the Kalchon River, a tributary of the Han, which ran along the western border of the Seoul suburb. In good order, with two platoons forward and one back, and Barrow's command group in the center, they made their way through the waist-high rice stalks—a scene that reminded more than one participant, of the famous Marine assault through the wheat fields of Belleau Wood.

After crossing the river on foot, the Marines were astonished that no enemy fire had scythed through their ranks. Barrow's men proceeded up a main thoroughfare right into the heart of Yongdungpo, effectively splitting it in two. Barrow set up defensive positions on a sausage-shaped dike, 30 feet high and 150 feet long, close to both the town hall and the main road junction where the highways from Kimpo and Inchon met.

Then, as darkness settled in, the Marines of Company A heard the sound of T-34s along a road paralleling the dike. "The squeaking and engine humming was drawing much closer, and as I crouched in my hole, I felt the ice-like shiver of pure fear," recalled Private First Class Morgan Brainard. "In the moonlight I could see its turret with the long gun on it slowly circling back and forth, like some prehistoric monster sniffing for prey." [10]

Five tanks attacked the company's position, the deep, concussive bark of the 85mm gun, of the T-34, sending shell after shell into the dike from only twenty-five yards away. Yet, not a single Marine was killed. The packed earth of the dike absorbed the shock of the shells, which were meant to pierce armor, not dirt. The T-34 crews were not so lucky. Once the Marines recovered, their bazookas blew the turret off one tank, destroyed another, and inflicted serious damage on two more. After five passes, the surviving NKPA tanks limped off.

All was quiet until 0100 on September 22, when a battalion of enemy troops commenced no less than five infantry assaults on Barrow's Marines. Displaying admirable fire discipline, these were each repulsed in turn. In the morning, Captain Barrow counted 210 enemy corpses. "Yongdungpo did for A Company what no other thing could have done in terms of unifying it and giving it its own spirit, a spirit that said, 'We can do anything,'" Barrow said later.[11]

When other 1st Regiment units joined in the assault, a great deal of relief and joy flooded through the ranks of tired Marines: the NKPA's 87th Regiment had vacated Yongdungpo.

The 1st Marines' attack into Seoul proper commenced at 0700 on September 25. The capital of South Korea was among the largest cities in Asia, with more than a million inhabitants in 1950. Many had fled in the wake of the North Korean invasion the previous June, but hundreds of thousands remained during the horrific street fighting following the investment of the city. There was nothing pretty or artful about the tactical solutions the Marines employed in their effort to oust the NKPA from hundreds of well-defended strongpoints. The Seoul operation was an unremitting series of rapid, short assaults by one or two fire teams at a time, supported by antitank weapons, tanks, and, often, strafing runs by aircraft. The planes doing the strafing belonged to the Tigers of Marine Night Fighter Squadron VMF(N)-542 and the Black Sheep squadron, which Major Gregory "Poppy" Boyington had made famous in World War II. On the very first day of the Seoul fighting, Black Sheep commander Lieutenant Colonel Walter Lischeid was killed in action.

As Marine planes cut through deadly North Korean flak, Puller's men grimly pressed on, knocking out one point of resistance—a fortified house with a squad of NKPA infantry, a barricaded street, a rooftop sniper's nest—at a time. At critical intersections along the Marines' line of advance, the NKPA had constructed barricades eight feet high and five feet thick, typically made of bags filled with rice. These strongpoints were reduced as they had been on Iwo Jima—by well-timed collaboration among tanks, infantry, and engineers, who cleared the streets of mines under infantry cover so that the armor could break through the barricades. Then, the fire teams and squads of tired, grim-faced Marines regrouped, checked their weapons, and did it all over again.

By the end of the day, the whole city stunk of cordite, napalm, sewerage, and burning flesh. Terrified cries of women and children mixed in with the moans of the wounded and dying.

At 2009 that night, a message was received at the 1st Marine Division CP from the operations officer of X Corps. The enemy was withdrawing to the north under heavy attack by U.N. airpower. "You will push attack now to the limit of your objective in order to insure maximum destruction of enemy forces. Signed Almond."[12]

The impetuous Almond was at it again. He was determined to take Seoul no more than three months to the day after the invasion, fulfilling his boss's promise. In his ambition to please he foolishly interpreted an intelligence report claiming a "massive evacuation" to mean the withdrawal of NKPA troops. General Smith was incredulous at the mistake. The overflight that produced the intelligence had occurred at night. It would have been impossible with the technology of 1950 to determine if a mass movement of human beings at night consisted of troops or terrified refugees.

Puller and Murray were given orders to execute night assaults against the better judgment of their Marine commander. The jump-off was set for 0115 the morning of September 26. Lieutenant Colonel Ridge's 3/1 had been in steady combat all day along Ma-Po Boulevard. He was so wary of the enemy that he took extra precautions to reinforce his front as night fell. He ordered his weapons company commander, Major Ed Simmons, to set up a formidable roadblock to cover every inch of his front with fire. Simmons was nothing if not thorough: he mined the road in front of the roadblock, and assigned a rifleman, a 75mm recoilless rifle team, a heavy machine-gun section, and a rocket squad to man the barricade. Ridge then protested so hard against the order to attack that he thought he might very well be relieved. He further delayed the attack by claiming insufficient support fire. Suddenly, as Ridge remembered it, "Ed Simmons was on the tactical radio with a voice at nearly high C and said, 'Enemy tanks are coming down the boulevard—they're about to hit us!' My response was 'Thank God!' whereupon Ed's voice dropped back to normal and he asked, 'What did you say?' Almost immediately thereafter, the battle was joined."[13]

A reinforced battalion of the NKPA's 25th Brigade had launched a counterattack along the main thoroughfare. Their target was the 3rd Battalion of the 1st Marine Regiment. Within seconds the entire boulevard erupted. No less than ten T-34s spearheaded the North Korean assault. The Marines countered with every weapon at their disposal. An attack on the division CP by a self-propelled gun was taken out by a 75mm recoilless rifle, but North Korean infantry surged forward en masse, undaunted. Marine artillery landed perilously close to friendly lines, but by 0315 or so, the artillery support slackened considerably because the tubes were too hot to fire effectively. At 0400, Colonel Puller, whose regiment had been engaged in steady and unrelenting combat for two hours, received the same unwelcome news: the 11th Marines' howitzers covering his unit from across the river in Yongdungpo had to call it quits temporarily for the same reason. Fortunately, an army artillery battalion was able to come to the Marines' aid, and an enemy assault on elements of the 1st Regiment was thwarted. When Chesty Puller showed up at Ridge's CP, he greeted his battalion commander in his typically gruff style, telling Ridge, "You'd better show me some results of the alleged battle you had last night."[14] Tom Ridge showed him seven tanks, two self-propelled guns, and eight antitank guns destroyed, and about four hundred enemy dead. Major Simmons's Browning heavy machine guns alone had fired thirty thousand rounds.

In the morning, the 5th Marines, to the northwest of Puller and

Ridge finally cleared the last of the enemy from the Hill 296 complex. Company I, under Captain Bob McMullen, swept downhill in a skirmish line at a good clip, while North Korean fire ripped across their front, felling two platoon commanders and several other Marines. The Third Platoon had to be committed early, and the whole company quickly fell upon two hundred well-entrenched enemy infantry, driving them farther down the slopes of the hill. After a welcome respite and a savage counterattack, the 5th Marines finally broke through the hills and onto the streets. Puller's 1st Marines were only too glad to have the additional muscle pressing on the enemy from the northeast. Staff Sergeant Lee Bergee of Company E, 1st Marines recalled the action on September 27:

> As we fought yard by yard up Ma-Po Boulevard, tanks led the way. I saw a North Korean soldier lying in the street. He'd been hit by a burst of white phosphorous. His body was still burning. I watched one of the tanks roll over him, crushing and grinding his body into the pavement. . . . At each barricade we had to annihilate the enemy, then reorganize, evacuate casualties, and wearily go on to the next. At the railroad station we found the still-warm bodies of women and children massacred by the North Korean secret police.[15]

The end of the battle was in view by midday on September 27. The 32nd Infantry Regiment of the U.S. Army had been committed by Almond. Its troops pressed in on the defenders from the southeast. The previous day, advance units of the Eighth Army linked up with the 7th Infantry Division of X Corps. The NKPA was in deep trouble—many units in the south had been decimated, and command and control had badly deteriorated. The Eighth Army had regained its confidence and strength, broken out of the Pusan perimeter, and pushed the bulk of the NKPA invasion force back toward the 38th parallel. Morale at MacArthur's headquarters in Japan was soaring, and for good reason. The Marines fighting in the streets could sense that the enemy's organized resistance was giving way. A vicious street fight broke out at the city's main intersection at around 1100 on September 27 where the major streetcar lines crossed to form an X near a large school. By that point, Lieutenant Colonel Taplett's 3/5 was attacking toward two NKPA flags flying above the capitol building at the center of the main government compound. By 1400, the opposition in front of 3/5 broke entirely, and Taplett's men, exhausted and exultant, swept into the corridors of the capitol.

Just after 1500, the Stars and Stripes replaced the North Korean flag atop the building. Only the mopping up remained—and the victory ceremony, in which MacArthur (in one of his rare visits to Korea) turned over the newly liberated capital to South Korean president Syngman Rhee. Smith, long disgusted with Almond's overriding personal ambition, patronizing attitude, and tactical recklessness, refused to pull his battalion commanders away from their units to go over plans for the ceremony, in which the Marines were to provide honor guards to line the streets. The Marines had suffered about seven hundred casualties in the three days of street fighting in Seoul.

The Inchon-Seoul campaign certainly enhanced the Marines' reputation among both decision makers and the American public as an organization peopled by tough fighters who would not quit until the job was done. For its efforts, the 1st Marine Division suffered 415 deaths, 2,029 wounded, and 6 men missing in action. X Corps estimated it had inflicted some 14,000 deaths on the NKPA. The number, like most such estimates prepared by victors, is probably too high. Whatever the truth, the vast majority of the North Koreans who had died in the campaign had been killed by U.S. Marines.

MacArthur, in one of his many spellbinding orations, had in July 1950 promised to land at Inchon and crush the enemy. He had made good on his proclamation. The United Nations' victory was also one of the most stunningly successful campaigns in all of American military history. And it was a victory with resounding implications for the cold war.

SIX

THE KOREAN WAR

From the Chosin Reservoir to the Armistice, July 1953

The stunning success of the Inchon-Seoul campaign broke the back of the NKPA as an effective fighting force, destroying many of its regiments outright and sending the remnants of other units into harried retreat. The victory at Inchon and the Eighth Army's counteroffensive, though by no means entirely successful in smashing the retreating North Koreans against the anvil of X Corps, opened the door for the Truman administration to seek a more ambitious U.N. military objective than restoration of the status quo antebellum. Unfortunately, in their effort to exploit one of the most impressive victories in twentieth-century warfare, the U.N. forces and the American public would learn the wisdom of the old French proverb, "Nothing fails like success."

Given the euphoria in Washington and Tokyo in October 1950, the urge to inflict a devastating blow on the aggressors was almost irresistible. The critical question was whether the U.N. attack should cease at the 38th parallel or go on to unite all Korea.

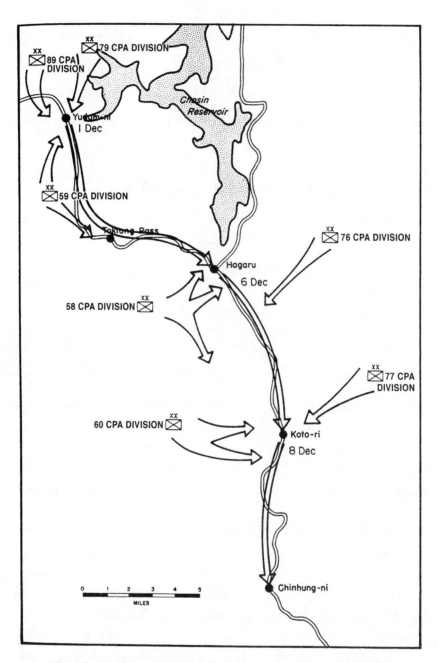

The Chosin Reservoir Campaign, November–December 1950

Adapted from Lynn Montross, *The Chosin Reservoir Campaign.* U.S. Marine
Operations in Korea, 1950–1953 series. Washington, D.C.: USMC, 1957.

Even before Inchon, President Truman announced publicly that the United States supported the right of all Koreans to be "free, independent and united under the guidance of the United Nations."[1] That objective had a magnanimous ring, but Truman, along with the policy-planning staff in the State Department, was deeply concerned that an invasion deep into North Korea would result in the direct intervention of Chinese or even Soviet forces into the conflict.

Both Communist giants had sent clear signals via Indian diplomatic channels that a U.N. drive across the border could bring about such an event. Thus, Truman's initial authorization for undertaking actions north of the 38th parallel came with an array of qualifications and caveats. In seeking to crush the NKPA, MacArthur was authorized

> to conduct military operations, including amphibious and airborne landings or ground operations north of the 38th Parallel . . . provided that at the time of such operations there has been no entry into North Korea by major Soviet or Chinese Communist Forces, no announcement of intended entry, nor a threat to counter our operations militarily in North Korea.[2]

Initially the Joint Chiefs of Staff ordered MacArthur to deploy only ROK army units for deep penetrations into North Korea, but the supremely confident American general scoffed at such timidity, and argued that it was militarily unsound to withhold stronger American units. The success of the Inchon-Seoul campaign, earned at comparatively low cost in casualties, appears to have convinced MacArthur that his forces were invincible, and destined to liberate all Korea, no matter the hand-wringing among the diplomats in Washington and London. The United Nations' public call on October 9 for MacArthur's forces to take "all appropriate steps" to ensure "the establishment of a unified, independent and democratic government in . . . Korea," buttressed the commander's belief in his own aims, and fueled public support for carrying the fight deep into North Korea.[3]

Neither Truman nor the JCS found it easy to challenge or countermand MacArthur. As an architect of victory over Japan, and its virtual viceroy, the West Pointer had often ignored directives that conflicted with his own schemes. When U.S. intelligence in October presented evidence that the Soviet Union was in the process of distancing itself from Kim Il Sung, MacArthur's critics were quieted. Sinologists in the State Department doubted that Mao would intervene without direct material help from—and the approval of—Stalin.

The consensus view turned out to be disastrously wrong. As British historian Max Hastings points out, American preoccupation with Stalin blinded them "to the nationalistic considerations at play."[4] When MacArthur's forces, prominent among them the vaunted 1st Marine Division, drove forward toward the Yalu River, where North Korea bordered China, they encountered a wealth of evidence that the Chinese People's Liberation Army had crossed the border in strong numbers. The evidence was ignored or rationalized away, and in late November, with the onset of a bitterly cold winter in the mountains of North Korea, a disciplined force of three hundred thousand PLA soldiers, many veterans of World War II and the postwar fight against the Chinese Nationalist army, entered the fray, putting an abrupt end to the U.N. drive, and to the widespread hope that the Americans would be home by Christmas. In the disastrous campaign that followed, the U.S. Army suffered its longest retreat in history and a stunning humiliation. The Marines, too, would be sent into retreat, but it was a very special kind of "retreat," as we shall see.

The Marine command in later years described that retreat as "an attack in a different direction," and they were right. In those dark hours of the Korean War, the American people's hopes focused intensely on each harrowing phase of the Marines' seventy-six-mile withdrawal from the Chosin Reservoir, down a tortuous two-lane road surrounded by hills and mountains, to the port of Hungnam, where they were evacuated.

Like General MacArthur's plan for Inchon, the concept of operations for the destruction of NKPA forces and occupation of North Korea was controversial, risky, and highly unorthodox, and the projected timetable put even more strain on the logistical capacities of the U.N. forces than Inchon had done. North Korea's rail and road network was primitive, with the vast majority of paved roads running along the valleys just east and west of the Taebeck Mountains. The JCS, Headquarters Marine Corps, and General Smith, in the field, were all skeptical of MacArthur's decision, in his rule as commander in chief of the Far East (CinCFE), to again split the attacking forces into two commands: X Corps, under General Almond, which would drive northeast of the Taebeck Mountains, and the Eighth Army, under General Walker, which would push up on the western side of the peninsula. Approximately eighty miles of mountains separated the two commands, making mutual reinforcement fiercely difficult if not impossible. But even the JCS—although above MacArthur in the official chain of command— did not feel comfortable vetoing the scheme of maneuver of the man many felt was the most brilliant strategist in the history of American arms.

The trajectory of the new plan went like this: once Walker's Eighth Army forces relieved the 1st Marine Division and the other ROK and U.S. Army units of X Corps from their responsibilities in and around newly liberated Seoul, the Marines would board transports at Inchon, sail around the Korean Peninsula, and conduct another amphibious assault at Wonsan, about 150 miles north of the 38th parallel—in the very heart of North Korea. Once again, the 7th Infantry Division would follow the Marines in trace into the port of Wonsan in preparation for the drive north, along with one ROK division.

The Eighth Army began its drive into North Korea on October 1, and, to the surprise of Walker and his staff, encountered tough resistance for only one week, after which the army infantry met with but scattered, desultory resistance. By October 27, Pyongyang, the North Korean capital, was in U.S. Army possession.

President Harry S. Truman, still very much concerned about the possible outbreak of World War III, arrived at Wake Island on October 15 to discuss the next phase of the war with his CinCFE. MacArthur resented being called away from the front during an offensive, and suspected the timing of the summons to be politically motivated. Truman would soon be running for reelection, MacArthur suggested to his aides, and wanted to bask in the glory of the humiliating defeat he had just inflicted on Communist North Korea.

General MacArthur met Truman as he disembarked from his plane. After failing to salute his commander in chief—an oversight not appreciated by the plain-speaking president from Missouri—MacArthur reassured the president and his entourage that they had nothing to worry about. He reportedly told Truman, "Now that we have bases for our air force in Korea, if the Chinese tried to get down to Pyongyang, there would be the utmost slaughter." [5]

On October 25, a serenely confident MacArthur issued a directive to all U.N. troops "to drive forward with all speed and with full utilization of all their force." [6] In other words, field commanders should feel free to ignore an earlier JCS directive to MacArthur's headquarters prohibiting U.S. forces from approaching the North Korean border with its two Communist allies to the north.

Meanwhile, the Wonsan assault initially slated for mid-October was postponed for some ten days. The entire 1st Marine Division, some twenty-six thousand officers and men, had to languish in ships just outside Wonsan harbor while the navy struggled to clear the port of mines. By the time the lead Marine forces disembarked from their transports on October 25 the planned assault had morphed into a simple administrative landing. ROK units had already occupied the port and, indeed, the entire city. The North Koreans had fled. Even Bob Hope and a coterie of USO performers had reached town ahead of the Marines, leading to a few well-meaning jokes at the amphibious troops' expense. Among the Marines, rumors were generally that the North Koreans had no fight left in them, and that the entire 1st Division might well find itself heading home to Camp Pendleton before the year was out. Generals Almond and MacArthur surely hoped the Marine scuttlebutt was correct.

While the Marines waited for the mine-clearance operation to conclude, X Corps staff was busy putting the finishing touches on an audacious plan of attack to crush the NKPA east of the Taebeck Mountains. Almond on October 25 issued General Smith orders outlining the Marines' mission for the next phase of the conflict. Their area of operations was fifty miles east to west, running from Wonsan, in the south, to Majon-ni, in the west, and no less than three hundred miles south to north, from Koto-ri up to the border with China.

The 1st Marine Regiment, under Colonel Chesty Puller, would remain in the southern part of the area of operations for the initial part of the offensive, in the Kojo–Majon-ni area, cutting off the remnants of NKPA units in retreat while the division's other two infantry regiments, the 5th and 7th Marines, displaced northward on the two-lane winding road through the mountains between Hamhung and the Chosin Reservoir, with Colonel Horner L. Litzenberg's 7th Marines in the vanguard and Murray's 5th Marine Regiment close behind.

Once elements of these units had pushed north and dispersed their sundry battalions and companies along the main supply route (MSR) up to the Chosin Reservoir area, General Smith was to prepare his forces for yet further advancement to the northern border of Korea, where he was to occupy the northeastern corner of North Korea.

In their motorized march north only the Taebeck Mountains covered the division's left flank; eighty miles lay between the advancing Marines and the Eighth Army's right flank. On the Marines' right flank other elements of X Corps, including the 7th U.S. Army Infantry Division and several ROK units, were deployed.

The first combat of the new campaign fell to Puller's Marines around the Majon-ni and Sudong areas, where several 1st Marine companies were ambushed between Majon-ni and Wonsan. The road between the two towns quickly earned the sobriquet "Ambush Alley." Nine Company H Marines were killed and three trucks lost on November 2. Captain Robert Barrow of Company A, who had distinguished himself so well in the Seoul campaign, resolved to get revenge against the Chinese the next day, and he succeeded beyond all expectations when he deployed several infantry platoons about eleven hundred yards north of a motorized column close to the scene of the successful NKPA ambush the previous day. Near a bend in the road, one of Barrow's platoons stealthily made its way toward about seventy NKPA soldiers in bivouac. The North Koreans had failed to place sentries around their perimeter, and the Marines immediately opened up with every small arm and heavy weapon at their disposal, killing no fewer than fifty-one enemy soldiers and taking three prisoner.

A retaliatory attack on the 1st Battalion that night found the Marines more vigilant than the hapless North Koreans earlier in the day, and the enemy force was beaten back into the mountains. Puller's Company E the following day suffered thirty-eight men wounded in action, including all five officers of the unit, and eight Marines died in a ferocious fight following an ambush at the head of Company E, moving forward in column.

While Puller's Marines battled to the west of Wonsan against North Koreans, Colonel Litzenberg's 7th Marines had the distinction of being the initial Marine regiment to engage elements of Mao's People's Liberation Army in the Sudong Valley, just to the south of Chinhung-ni, on the sole winding road that led north to Hagaru and the Chosin Reservoir. It fell to the 7th Marines to lead the seventy-eight-mile trek north to the Chosin Reservoir. ROK troops in the area had come under fire from the Chinese in this area already, so Litzenberg had a sense of the solemnity of the situation. He pulled no punches in addressing the Marines. It was important that the regiment prevail in its first encounter with Mao's volunteers—it was not yet clear that whole divisions had been ordered to cross the Yalu and enter the fray—for, as Litzenberg put it, "The results of the action will reverberate around the world, and we want to make sure that the outcome has an adverse effect on Moscow as well as Peking."[7]

The Corsairs of Marine Squadrons VMF-312 and VMF-513 effectively suppressed sporadic mortar fire from PLA units during the day of November 2. All was quiet as dusk faded into night. Then, at 2300,

Lieutenant Colonel Ray Davis's 1/7 found itself under a skillfully executed attack.

Despite taking very heavy casualties, the PLA forces broke through gaps into the Marine-held hills and swarmed over 1/7's heavy mortar section, making off with one of the tubes, and threatening by dawn to overrun both the 1st and 2nd Battalions CPs, as they scurried forward in small, uncoordinated attacks while under heavy fire from the Marine rifle companies above them in the hills and from supporting artillery.

It was a close-run thing, and a series of small-unit clashes continued in the area all day. More than six hundred PLA corpses were counted in 1/7's area alone by late in the afternoon. But the Marines prevailed in the end; the MSR was reopened within forty-eight hours, but not before the destruction of five North Korean tanks that had joined in support of the PLA infantry and more spirited infantry fighting.

One Marine battalion commander remarked that this initial engagement with the Chinese put the Marines "in a dickens of a mess," and, indeed, he was quite correct. The Chinese soldiers, in their mustard yellow and white uniforms of quilted cotton and their canvas and rubber boots, sporting a wide assortment of Russian and American rifles and machine guns, along with plentiful burp guns, were hardy and determined infantrymen. They were highly skilled with mortars, but lacked heavy supporting arms. Because they were masters of camouflage, ambushes were a favorite tactic. Invariably, the PLA sought to minimize U.N. superiority in supporting fires by assaulting at night, and they were devilishly hard to locate while moving into attack positions during the day. It took the Marines some time to adjust to their method of assault, neatly summarized by Marine historians Lynn Montross and Nicholas A. Canzona:

> Once engaged and under fire, the attackers hit the ground. Rising at any lull, they came on until engaged again; but when fully committed, they did not relinquish the attack even when riddled with casualties. Other Chinese came forward to take their places, and the buildup continued until a penetration was made, usually on the front of one or two

platoons. After consolidating the ground, the combat troops then crept or wriggled forward against the open flank of the next [enemy] platoon position. Each step of the assault was executed with practiced stealth and boldness, and the results of several such penetrations on a battalion front could be devastating.[8]

As the 7th Marines moved north of Chinhung-ni, the two-lane road rose into mountains about a mile above sea level, and twisted and turned like a serpent around Funchilin Pass, a one-lane artery bordered by a cliff on one side and a yawning chasm on the other. The pass stuck out like a finger pointing due east, and Hill 891, named How Hill by the Marines, offered a superb vantage point for direct-fire weapons to halt traffic coming through the pass. The Chinese put up a spirited defense at Funchilin, but by November 4, as the Marine infantry began to get its bearings on PLA tactics and with the help of excellent close air support, the Leathernecks broke through the narrow pass and pushed north toward the village of Koto-ri, some eight miles north of Chinhung-ni.

After the spirited fighting at Sudong, the PLA vanished into the snow-covered mountains. Organized resistance against the Marine advance ceased entirely for several days. Litzenberg's Devil Dogs made their way into Koto-ri in force on the Corps' birthday, November 10. Three more days of methodical progress found the vanguard regiment deeper into the mountains, at a town just below the Chosin Reservoir called Hagaru-ri. It was to serve as the forward base for offensive operations farther north.

Almond vented his frustration over the slow pace of the Marines' advance. Always an audacious officer, Almond was anxious for the Marines to gather their strength at Hagaru-ri and prepare to push toward the Yalu. He shared MacArthur's view that the air-interdiction campaign, Operation Strangle—in which Marine fighter squadrons participated—had stanched the flow of PLA troops and material into northern Korea. Smith's relations with Almond had been poor since the two first met, and they worsened in mid-November, as Smith's intelligence sources left him with a strong hunch that the days of heady progress ahead were numbered. He wrote on November 15 to Commandant Cates that "he did not like the prospect of stringing out a Marine division along a single mountain road for 120 air miles from Hamhung to the border."[9] Rather than push the 5th Marines and supporting forces to Hagaru-ri for further offensive operations, Smith focused the division's energies on buttressing the supply dumps at Hagaru-ri and Koto-ri. Puller's 1st Marines moved up the MSR, with the vast majority of troops setting up camp, along with most of the Marine tanks, at Koto-ri. The highly competent Lieutenant Colonel J. H. Partridge's 1st Engineer Battalion, accustomed to the fast pace of expeditionary logistical work, hacked out short airstrips; they also fortified the four-square-mile perimeter at Hagaru-ri.

Neither Litzenberg nor his commanding officer, General Smith, were pleased to learn on that day that Marine reconnaissance planes had multiple battalions of Chinese soldiers crossing the Yalu River heading into X Corps' area of operations. Meanwhile, the advance of the 7th Marines up to Hagaru-ri had proceeded virtually unmolested.

All the while, General Smith resisted constant pressure from the X Corps commander to move his division north at a faster pace, fearing that his units were too spread out to withstand a full-fledged assault by the PLA. Smith had felt from the outset that MacArthur's plan to drive into North Korea on both sides of the mountains was unsound. MacArthur and Almond remained supremely confident, though.

After an estimated 150,000 Chinese were detected north of the Eighth Army, the U.N. plan of attack was altered significantly in the third week of November, when MacArthur gave orders for the Eighth Army, in the west, to begin a massive attack on November 24. The 1st Marine Division would drive westward from Yudam-ni toward the Eighth Army on November 27, thus cutting into the Chinese supply lines and forming the eastern arm of what MacArthur called a "massive compressive envelopment."[10]

Elements of the 7th Marines under Lieutenant Colonel Raymond Davis pivoted to the west and seized Yudam-ni on November 25. Two days later they were joined by Murray's 5th Marines. The road west from

Hagaru-ri is initially flat and then, as the official Marine history describes it, "winds its way up to 4,000-foot Toktong pass. Descending through gloomy gorges, [the road] finally reaches Yudam-ni, where roads break off to the north, west and south from a western arm of the reservoir." [11]

The two Marine regiments conducted a joint attack to the west beginning at 0800 on November 27. Company G, 7th Marines pushed twelve hundred yards to its first objective, before coming under heavy PLA machine-gun fire. By 0930, spotter planes reported PLA units all across the front of the advance route. Murray and Litzenberg realized by early afternoon that they were in a precarious situation. Indeed, the attackers, having made marginal gains of some fourteen hundred yards in one day, were about to be counterattacked by elements of at least three Chinese divisions.

On the night of November 27, every Marine company deployed on the five ridges surrounding Yudam-ni was hit with furious infantry assaults, as were those security forces that remained in the town. The MSR by early morning had been cut up into four segments. Facing elements of three Chinese divisions, the two regiments of Marines had no choice but to surrender some of the high ground. The main enemy effort that night came from the northwest against the Marines west of Yudam-ni. The artillery of the 3rd Battalion, 11th Marines could not dig in because bulldozers were useless against the eight-inch-thick–frozen ground; first mortar fire threatened the unit, then direct-fire weapons added to the unwelcome chorus.

A secondary series of attacks against the troops along the MSR between Yudam-ni and Hagaru-ri by the Chinese 59th Division also put several companies in danger of utter destruction. After aiding Company B of the 7th Marines, one of the units along the MSR, to withdraw under fire to Yudam-ni, Captain John F. Morris's Charlie Company of the 7th Marines deployed its two rifle platoons and 60mm mortars in a crescent on the lower slopes of Hill 1419, to the east of the MSR. At 0230, a strong Chinese force of at least a company bent back the left flank. Reinforcements from the headquarters section reached that flank just in time to prevent its destruction. Then the Chinese assaulted the right flank. The Marines barely held on throughout a nightlong fire-fight. Artillery fire from Yudam-ni at dawn finally drove the attackers back up into the hills, but as the official Marine history of the operation has it, Company C "remained pinned down by enemy fire from every direction, including the crest of Hill 1419 directly above. The Chinese were in absolute control of the MSR to the south, toward Toktong Pass, and to the north, in the direction of Yudam-ni."[12]

Other elements of the 59th Division threatened to wipe out Captain William Barber's Fox Company, 2/5, which had the unenviable and exceedingly lonely job of protecting Toktong Pass. That twisting stretch of road was a critical choke point along the MSR, and if the Chinese could seize it, Marine officers knew the prospects for extrication of the 5th and 7th Regiments would be very poor indeed. At 0230 on November 28, Barber's men defending the pass were attacked from three directions. Two squads were immediately wiped out. For the next fourteen hours Fox Company endured repeated assaults. They held their ground, however, sustaining twenty dead and fifty-four wounded.

To the east of the reservoir, the Chinese were in the process of destroying the 7th Infantry Division, X Corps' other American division. Soldiers left their heavy weapons and broke southward toward Hagaru-ri. More than a thousand men stumbled into the Marine perimeter in groups of two or three, sometimes half a shocked and broken platoon, with horrific tales of entire units being swallowed up by hordes of Chinese infantry.

Hagaru-ri itself was surrounded by hills and mountains, and had only one infantry battalion as a security force. General Smith, sensing the seriousness of the situation, spent most of November 28 placing cooks, supply troops, army stragglers, and green ROK troops around the perimeter. Disaster loomed when PLA troops overran American positions on a hill to the east of the base. The defenders had never trained together, and the terrain greatly favored the attackers. "So cut up into ridges and ravines was this great hill mass that the troops seldom knew whether they were advancing in defilade or exposing themselves to the fire of hidden adversaries. Thus the attack became a lethal game of hide-and-seek in which a step to the right or left might make the difference between life and death."[13]

Only well-aimed howitzer fire kept the Chinese from exploiting the gaps in the perimeter and overrunning the camp from the east, and a mixed group of soldiers and Marines managed to regain the military crest of East Hill by morning. But with two of its three infantry regiments extended west around Yudam-ni—and with the entire division surrounded by elements of an estimated seven divisions of Chinese— even the most hardened Marine veterans found it difficult to be sanguine about the division's fate. Colonel Alpha Bowser, the division operations officer, was to say in an interview years later:

> I really thought we'd had it. We did not know the details of what was happening to the Eighth Army, but we knew that there was only eighty miles of open flank on our left. We knew the size of the Chinese against us—and we didn't at the time understand their shortcomings. I would not have given a nickel for our chances of making it. Fortunately, a lot of people down the line could not see the overall situation as I could and they continued to conduct themselves as if they were going to get out.[14]

General Smith, under fire from the Chinese and his own commander, remained unflappable in the midst of growing crisis. Enemy forces had set up well-defended roadblocks cutting off Yudam-ni, Hagaru-ri, Toktong Pass, and Koto-ri from one another. He knew he had to concentrate his forces to prevent the units of the division from being attacked in detail and decimated by the Chinese. To attack the Marine units one at a time and destroy them was precisely what the PLA planned on accomplishing.

The 5th and 7th Marines would thus have to reverse course while under heavy attack from several directions. The division had roughly three days' worth of fuel, food, and ammunition. There was a very worrisome shortage of artillery ammunition, and it was clear to every senior

Marine that for Hagaru-ri to remain in Marine hands—and it had to remain so if the 5th and 7th Marines were to have a chance of surviving—it needed reinforcements from the 1st Marines. Puller's men were by this point themselves precariously deployed at Koto-ri eleven miles south along the MSR.

Smith ordered Colonel Puller to send reinforcements from Koto-ri and knock out the PLA roadblocks along the way. The first effort failed entirely. Chesty Puller ordered Company D, 1st Marines north under cover of mortar fire. That unit was turned back after a fierce firefight one mile to the north. A reinforced company alone would never drive through the Chinese, because of their remarkable proficiency with mortars.

Then Puller sent a nine-hundred-man force, including the highly regarded Royal Marines 41 Commando—about two hundred British marines—supported by twenty-nine Marine tanks, to try to break through on the afternoon of November 30. The column was ambushed and cut into four segments. Only about three hundred men of Task Force Drysdale (named for Lieutenant Colonel Douglas B. Drysdale, who commanded the Royal Marines) made it to Hagaru-ri, but they were joined by seventeen of the twenty-nine tanks that had left Koto-ri. Several hundred more Marines straggled back to the Koto-ri perimeter. The remainder of the task force were killed or taken prisoner by the PLA.

While Puller and Smith worked to button down Marine positions in the southern area of operations, Murray and Litzenberg, under extreme time pressure, put together a solid plan for the fighting withdrawal of their regiments. The 5th Marines would lead the attack out while the 7th Regiment would conduct the tricky disengagement from Yudam-ni.

At 0800 on December 1, Lieutenant Colonel Taplett's 3/5 passed through 3/7 and seized the high ground on both sides of the MSR, facing east. Taplett's Marines now had to execute the tactically difficult disengagement from Hill 1282, on the ridge north of Yudam-ni. The problem was solved by withdrawing the Marine rifle companies just as Corsairs pounded the Chinese on the reverse slope of the ridge with bombs and machine-gun fire. By 1500, 3/5's companies were leapfrogging one another on the shoulders of the hills, methodically eliminating the PLA infantry as they resisted the withdrawal. As the infantry exhausted itself in the cold and brutal combat in the hills, eight thousand Marines, along with their trucks, howitzers, dead, and wounded, crept along the two-lane road below. Only the dead and seriously wounded rode in the vehicles; the rest of the Leathernecks marched alongside the column, fending off periodic assaults from both sides by PLA units. The main train of vehicles and men moved only about fifteen hundred yards before buttoning up for a cold night in the mountains.

In the early morning of December 2, Company I, 5th Marines, under Captain Harold O. Schrier, was driven back off the slopes of Hill 1520. By the next morning, three hundred Chinese corpses littered the area, but Company I was all but destroyed in the maelstrom. Only twenty of its Marines were able to continue the drive toward Toktong Pass and Hagaru-ri.

Lieutenant Colonel Harold Roise's 2/5 had the unenviable task of protecting the rear of the column after they burned as much of the supplies as they could at the Yudam-ni base. The infantry platoons fell back, one covering another, all the while supported by Marine close air support. The Chinese conducted a vicious series of attacks on 2/5's companies. As the official after-action report of the battalion makes clear, the PLA's infantry were well practiced and disciplined. The Chinese

> use fire and movement to excellent advantage. They would direct a frontal attack against our position while other elements of their attacking force moved in to Company flanks in an attempt at a double envelopment. Then in turn the force on both flanks would attack while the forces directly to our front would move closer. [Thus, they] were able to maneuver their forces to within hand grenade range of our positions.[15]

Just before noon on December 2, the Marines in the vanguard near Hill 1520 spied a discouraging sight: the PLA had blown a bridge the road crossed. With temperatures approaching zero, the engineers were called forward to build a bypass strong enough to support the heavy trucks. This they accomplished just before nightfall. Another frigid night followed, with most Marines struggling to gain two or three hours' sleep. The column moved on at dawn.

The glacial pace of the long column's progression on the first several days of the withdrawal made it clear that Barber's thinned and tired Marines at critical Toktong Pass would likely succumb unless they could be reached by their brothers in arms from a direction far afield from the MSR. The unit designated to come to the rescue was Lieutenant Colonel Raymond Davis's reinforced 1st Battalion, 7th Marines.

Late in the afternoon of December 1, Davis's men broke through the Chinese defensive positions on Hill 1419. The wounded and dead from that tough fight were brought back to the main column. Davis and his five hundred remaining men, each carrying extra ammo and supplies, and with several heavy mortar, began their lonely and treacherous march through the mountainous wilderness, moving southwest toward Toktong Pass. White phosphorous shells lit their path for the first several miles of the eight-mile trek, and then Davis steered the column by the positions of the stars. Because of the wide assortment of defiles, ridges, and draws, the Marine column at several points had to halt, take compass readings, and redirect itself. In the eerie darkness and subzero temperatures, exhausted men stumbled into one another, fell on slick, packed snow, and rolled off the trail, only to have to expend precious energy rejoining the column above. NCOs and officers had to prod and kick at those who fell, urging them to get up quickly, to resist the natural temptation to rest—or, even worse—to fall asleep and risk dying of hypothermia.

Lieutenant Joseph Owen of Company B, heading up the column, recalled in his searing memoir of the frigid march by 1/7, soon known throughout the Marine Corps as the "Ridgerunners of Toktong Pass," that "our bodies sweated with the strain, but our hands and feet were frozen numb. The wind-borne cold attacked with terrible fury." [16]

Increasingly miserable and numb, few of the Marines had slept for more than an hour or two in the three days preceding the night march through the wilderness. At some points, the Marines of Company B trudged through knee-deep snow. Lieutenant Colonel Davis, a soft-spoken, iron-tough Marine from Georgia, recalled in an interview:

> Up on the ridge we were exposed to the wind, and the cold was just plain numbing. I would hunch down in an abandoned Chinese foxhole to check my compass. When I was sure of my direction I would . . . stand up. I would be dazed by the cold. Two or three people standing around would say something. By the time I'd answered them, I'd forgotten what I'd done with the compass and map and repeat the entire process. We were absolutely numb with cold. It was hard to believe.[17]

Well after midnight, after some seventeen hours of fighting and marching with no significant rest in subzero temperatures, the Marines of 1/7 came up against a much surprised unit of Chinese infantry. Companies B and C formed into columns and attacked the Chinese on Hill 1520, killing some and driving off the rest at the cost of but a few wounded Marines.

At 0300 on December 2 Davis finally let his men rest for several hours. At dawn they rose, a mile and a half from Fox Company, and got the better of their adversaries in a series of short-lived firefights. As bad as the Marines had it, the Chinese suffered even more from the cold. Many were clad only in canvas boots with rubber soles. Many lacked adequate gloves.

Under cover of effective close air support, 1/7 secured its final objective four hundred yards north of Barber's company perimeter. The reinforced battalion that now registered its 81mm mortars and heavy machine guns' fields of fire on the vulnerable approaches to the pass made clearance of the division train through Toktong all but a certainty.

William Barber's Fox Company had turned in one of the most steadfast and heroic performances in battle of a U.S. Marine unit in history. Barber and his Marines held on to the pass for five days and nights, at the cost of 118 casualties, including 5 of the 6 officers. Almost every

Marine who had not been pierced by an enemy bullet or shell fragment suffered from serious frostbite. Barber's stalwart defense earned him a Medal of Honor; Davis's daring eight-mile march across trackless mountain ridges and three valleys to rescue Fox Company earned him the same.

With the defense of Toktong Pass, the worst of the Yudam-ni breakout—the most precarious leg of the campaign's retrograde drive to the sea—was behind the Marines. Pressing ahead against sporadic resistance in the shoulders of the hills, Marine infantry, closely coordinated with howitzers firing from the main column on the MSR, entered the friendly confines of Hagaru-ri at 1630 on December 3.

Hagaru-ri looked like an old Klondike mining camp to at least one Marine as he approached the tightly packed dwellings, tents, reinforced bunkers, and hastily assembled low-lying buildings. Now Smith and his regimental commanders' task was to disengage from the heavy pressure of the Chinese to the east and north, and send the infantry once more into the hills to drive off the inevitable Chinese assaults on the main column winding its way to Koto-ri. The force gathered in the crowded perimeter numbered just over ten thousand U.S. Marines and four thousand U.S. Army, ROK, and British troops. While the 5th and 7th Marines caught up on sleep and hot food, the airstrip bustled with transports skidding along the short runway. The wounded were evacuated to the rear; ammunition was replenished and five hundred reinforcements joined the force, largely trained infantrymen.

A fierce and sustained attack by rested PLA forces on East Hill as the withdrawal began on December 6 was beaten back by elements of the 5th Marines with attached army units, some of which had been thrown together only the day before. The 7th Marines' infantry units resumed the exhausting clearance operations in the hills. Litzenberg's infantry companies leapfrogged ahead doggedly, as one platoon provided covering fire while another maneuvered forward against snipers and small groups of harassing soldiers. As the tail end of the column struggled forward in biting winds just south of the perimeter, everything that would burn was set alight within the confines of the abandoned base. The troops on the MSR suffered harassing attacks and sniper fire. At one point during an attack, one hundred PLA prisoners attempted to break for the hills. A few of the Chinese found their way back to friendly units, but most were killed. Just south of Hagaru-ri, a well-executed assault fell on the 3rd Battalion, 11th Marines, and the unit's howitzers were used as direct-fire weapons, blasting fléchette rounds at Chinese soldiers as close as forty yards away for more than two hours. At Hellfire Alley, scene of the infamous Chinese defeat of Task Force Drysdale as it attempted to make its way north to reinforce Hagaru-ri, a frostbitten but very much alive British marine was discovered, apparently having escaped the swarming Chinese by playing dead.

Onward they marched, faces lashed by wind and blowing snow. The only way for the men to keep their canned rations from freezing was to carry them in their armpits. Corpsmen kept morphine syrettes for the wounded in their mouths to keep the precious drug from freezing. In makeshift operating tents, hastily set up along the side of the road, navy surgeons had to don woolen gloves while operating.

The vanguard of the column warily made its way to the northern perimeter of Koto-ri thirty-eight hours after the breakout commenced. The ferocity and number of attacks from the hills diminished. Many of the battle-weary troops were beginning to believe that they might escape destruction and make it to Hungnam and the waiting armada of amphibious ships. But potential disaster still loomed: three and a half miles south of Koto-ri the PLA had blasted a twenty-four-foot gap in the single-lane road near Funchilin Pass. The ingenuity of Lieutenant Colonel John H. Partridge's engineers met its last and most dramatic test. Partridge arranged for the air force to drop a number of steel bridge sections into Koto-ri and had them driven up to the gap. The 1st Battalion of the 1st Marines marched north to attack entrenched Chinese positions blocking the passage of the column, taking 50 percent casualties for its efforts. Then Partridge's men hurriedly assembled a makeshift bridge strong enough to withstand the weight of the column's tanks. On went the 1st Marine Division to Chinhung-ni. Colonel Partridge, in an interview more than fifteen years after the event, recalled:

> The sensation [on the night of December 9–10, the first night after the bridge was constructed] was extremely eerie. There seemed to be a glow over everything. There was no illumination and yet you seemed to see quite well; there was . . . the sound of many artillery pieces being discharged; there was the crunching of the many feet and many vehicles on the crisp snow. There were many North Korean refugees walking on one side of the column. . . . Every once in a while, there would be a baby wailing. There were cattle on the road. Everything added to the general sensation of relief, or expected relief, and was about as eerie as anything I experienced in my life.[18]

The weary column made its way into the Chinhung-ni early on the morning of December 10. The drive from Koto-ri cost the 1st Marine Division 75 dead, 256 wounded, and 16 missing.

At the beginning of December, military analysts had come to some grim conclusions about the fate of the 1st Marine Division. Elements of seven divisions of the PLA's Ninth Army Group swarmed into the flanks of Marine units stretched out along the seventy-eight-mile route from Yudam-ni to Hungnam. Their mission was plain: separate the units and destroy the Marines. The 1st Marine Division's withdrawal—and it was indeed just that, despite General Smith's famous remark to reporters that his Marines were "attacking in a different direction"—was an extreme trial for the Leathernecks, but in subzero weather the Marines fought their way out, bringing not only their guns, but also the vast majority of their vehicles and all but about one hundred of the dead. Those men were buried in a mass grave at Koto-ri. What made Chosin an atypical withdrawal was that throughout the campaign the division had retained tactical integrity and inflicted devastating blows against the PLA. Those troops suffered even more than their American adversaries from the horrors of the Korean winter, as indicated by PLA records released after the war.

The fate of the Marines as they trekked south became a national fixation in the news media during a very dark time. When word came of their successful departure from Hungnam, there was much relief and rejoicing. Amid talk of bugouts and the possibility of a full-scale evacuation from the peninsula, a division of Leathernecks had punched their way through what the newspapers of the day referred to as "unconquerable Chinese hordes."

Total Marine casualties for the Chosin campaign, from October 26 through December 15, 1950, were reported by the division as 604 killed in action, 114 dead of wounds, 192 missing in action, and 3,508 wounded. More than seven thousand Marines who hadn't been wounded in combat suffered from frostbite. Estimates of enemy dead, which are inevitably exaggerated by Marines as they are by every other army in combat, were placed at fifteen thousand killed by ground-force action and another ten thousand by Marine Corps airpower. Whatever the correct numbers, it is clear that many of Mao's companies and battalions sustained so many casualties that they ceased to function as effective combat units.

Marine and navy airpower had played an indispensable role in helping the infantry inflict so much damage. Indeed, the campaign has been correctly heralded as a vindication of the Corps' air-ground team concept, and its underlying belief that infantry success often depends on effective and timely close air support.

The close air support was indeed steady and effective, and Marine pilots often flew in horrendous conditions to help their brothers on the ground. When mountains prevented forward air controllers on the ground from calling in close air support, for the first time in Marine history fixed-wing aircraft were used to direct supporting fire. The tail end of the Chosin campaign also witnessed the first appearance of Marine fighter jets in combat. The temptation to compare the dramatic fighting withdrawal of the Marines to that of the ten thousand Greeks surrounded by the Persian army in 401 B.C. is an irresistible one, for as Xenophon wrote in *The Anabasis of Cyrus:*

> The enemy, by keeping up a continuous battle and occupying in advance every narrow place, obstructed passage after passage. Accordingly,

whenever the van was obstructed, Xenophon, from behind, made a dash up the hills and broke the barricade, and freed the vanguard by endeavoring to get above the obstructing enemy. Whenever the rear point was attacked, Cherisophus, in the same way, made a detour, and by endeavoring to mount higher than the barricades, freed the passage for the rear rank; and in this way, turn and turn about, they rescued each other, and paid unflinching attention to their mutual needs.[19]

***

X Corps had successfully extricated itself from Hungnam by Christmas, but, unfortunately, the agonies of the Eighth Army continued well into January. Seoul fell again, this time to the Chinese. The enemy crossed the critical Han River in strength. The demoralized commander of Eighth Army, General Walton H. Walker, was killed in a car accident two days before Christmas.

The crushing defeat of U.N. forces in North Korea placed the Korean War in a delicate political context. The Joint Chiefs debated the options, which were sobering. Fear that Korea was simply the trip wire for a wider Communist assault on the West persisted. On January 12, the JCS recommended attacking China with air and naval forces in the event of attacks on any U.S. forces outside Korea. MacArthur, shocked and embarrassed by the Chinese "treachery," recommended immediate attacks on supply centers and military installations in southern China. The JCS even reviewed plans for the use of nuclear weapons, much to the horror of America's European allies.

But as January wore on, it was clear the Communist offensive was running out of gas, and for all their great numbers, the Chinese lacked the supporting arms or secure supply lines to drive the United Nations from South Korea. A groundswell of American outrage lent strong support for General MacArthur's "no substitute for victory" notion, yet such talk alienated America's European allies, particularly the British. They feared that an attack on China would lead to a Soviet attack against Western Europe, where newly formed NATO forces wouldn't have stood the slightest chance of halting a conventional thrust by Soviet armored columns. Cooler heads prevailed—at least within the Truman administration. The American president became increasingly frustrated with MacArthur's bellicose pronouncements. The self-proclaimed greatest American soldier of the twentieth century was urging U.S. foreign-policy goals at odds with those of the administration he served.

In early February, a cooler head arrived on the shoulders of the new commander of the Eighth Army, a handsome fifty-six-year-old paratrooper, Lieutenant General Matthew Ridgway. Ridgway had had a brilliant combat record with the 82nd Airborne in World War II, and was known to be a highly effective staff officer who emphasized teamwork, discipline, and spirit. He stood ramrod straight, and, when in the field, he sported a hand grenade prominently affixed to his field jacket. His most striking feature, however, wrote historian Clay Blair, "was the aura of force and determination he radiated."[20] The Marines loved him.

Arriving in Korea on Christmas Day, he immediately visited every major unit in his command, taking their measure. He diagnosed the Eighth Army's problems, both moral and tactical, in a hurry. The army needed to get off the roads, train harder, and fight as the Marines had fought at Chosin: by sending the infantry up onto the high ground, by protecting flanks, and, most of all, by believing in themselves and their ability to handle the Chinese onslaught. The U.N. forces would use airpower and ever-increasing quantities of artillery to check the Communist advance, and then they would drive the Chinese and North Koreans back across the 38th parallel. Incompetent combat leaders would be fired and replaced with people who could get the job done.

Ridgway hired thirty thousand South Korean laborers to work with the army, building two massive defensive belts across the peninsula, one north and one south of the Han River. The handsome paratrooper made it clear that after regrouping and reequipping—it had lost an astonishing number of its vehicles, tanks, and big guns—the Eighth Army would go on the offensive. The new commander envisaged important roles for the unit he once called the most powerful in Korea: the 1st Marine Division.

The Marines thawed out in the same bean patch near Mansan in which Ed Craig's 1st Marine Provisional Brigade had bivouacked after throwing back three North Korean attacks on the Pusan perimeter. First, the division took on much-needed replacements and got some sorely needed rest. Its first post-Chosin mission consisted of limited anti-guerrilla operations in the Pohang area against NKPA troops harassing the rear area from mid-January to mid-February. Then in February it took its place along the east-central portion of the MLR—the main line of resistance—for the limited U.N. counteroffensives meant to push the PLA back across the 38th parallel in February and March.

The third phase found the Marines stepping into the breach when major Communist counteroffensives threatened not only to reverse the territorial gains of early spring, but also to annihilate several ROK units and one U.S. Army division by breaking through the MLR entirely and investing the U.N. rear support areas. After a short hiatus in fighting in June and July amid talk of peace, the Marines found themselves in horrific offensive actions north and east of a large gash in the earth called the Punchbowl, a terrain feature surrounded by spurs and ridges and heavily defended by Chinese artillery wheeled in during the abortive truce talks. On September 21, after an intense and costly eleven-day battle for a series of hills north of the Punchbowl, the Marines concluded their last offensive drive of the war and settled down into twenty-one months of World War I–style war of position, the grim characteristics of which were intense artillery duels—thousands of rounds traded for days and nights on end—punctuated by battalion, company, and platoon attacks on key terrain features. In Ridgway's first limited offensives, Operations Killer and Ripper, the Marine division recaptured Hoengsong, a major enemy supply center held by one PLA division, and advanced through wooded trackless country. After regrouping, the Marines had the pleasure of driving the PLA back across the 38th parallel as part of IX Corps, including an offensive that resulted in the recapture of Seoul. The 1st Marine Division then went on to push the Chinese out of the area around the Hwachon Reservoir, part of a system that provided power to the capital city.

In April 1951, Smith's Marines again proved their reliability in combat by closing off two powerful PLA counteroffensive break-throughs. The first occurred on the Marine left flank, when the ROK 6th Division collapsed at the end of April, resulting in a dangerous four-mile penetration that threatened to bring chaos to the rear areas supporting the U.N. front line. Yet the Marines held firm as the Chinese tried to swerve around their left. The 7th Marines' rifle battalions pulled back from the line, echeloned to the left in good order, and closed the vital Hwachon corridor. From April 23 through April 25, elements of the 1st and 7th Marines blunted ferocious attacks on Hill 902 near Horseshoe Ridge. Company B, 7th Marines found itself heavily engaged in hand-to-hand combat, as the Chinese used tactics employed by the American Indians in the nineteenth-century West: they lit bundles of straw, filling the air with smoke, and then attempted to envelop the Marine company with multiple assault waves. Private First Class Dan Koegel recalled in an interview with historian Donald Knox that "Baker Company withstood these swarming attacks [because of] the skill and guts of the artillery forward observer attached to the company. The FO, marking the [location of] the first rounds, walked succeeding volleys up the hill until they crashed into the front ranks of the attackers just yards below Baker's positions."[21]

April 26 marked the end of General Smith's term of command of the 1st Marine Division. He left with the abiding respect of his men and an impressive legacy of combat leadership. Smith's successor was General Gerald Thomas, winner of the Silver Star at Belleau Wood and a veteran of Guadalcanal. He was widely regarded as one of the best minds in the Corps, and had an impressive combat résumé as well.

In mid-May, after a limited U.N. drive had pushed the Chinese back across the 38th parallel, another Chinese counterattack broke the back of the ROK units to the east of the 7th Infantry Division, which was tied into the Marines' right flank. This time the enemy penetrated about thirty miles behind the lines, menacing the rear of the U.S. Army's 7th Infantry Regiment. Now the Marine battalions echeloned to the right, again containing the breach and plastering the PLA, send-ing them back to the northern ridge of the Punchbowl.

Peace negotiations in the summer of 1951 dragged on, making no substantial progress. There was a lull in the fighting, which the PLA and the North Koreans used to bring an impressive number of heavy ar-tillery tubes down to the MLR, in addition to building a formidable array of mutually reinforced outpost positions, minefields, and reverse-slope bunkers that would prove devilishly hard to knock out in the last full-scale U.N. offensive of the war (August to September 1951).

There was little sustained combat during the summer along the peninsula-wide front separating armies of about equal strength—six hundred thousand or so men on each side of the line, but with the Communists enjoying superior numbers of troops close to the front due to their comparatively low ratio of support troops to combat troops.

At the end of August, shortly after the Marine division returned to the line after a well-deserved respite, General Thomas proposed to the new Eighth Army commander, General James Van Fleet, that the Marines mount an amphibious landing on the east coast to turn the Communist flank and cut off their supply lines. The proposal was rejected. Korea would remain a war of two great armies slugging away at each other across the entire peninsula. Van Fleet had taken command in April, replacing Ridgway. Ridgway, in turn, became the commander in chief, Far East Forces, when President Truman, disgusted and appalled by MacArthur's critical public statements about the limited war aims, sacked the five-star general on April 11. Three-quarters of the American people disagreed with the decision. Given the enormous prestige of MacArthur and the broad trajectory of American military history—the United States had never engaged in a major conflict without achieving outright victory—the response was understandable. Yet the outrage over Truman's decision was naive. Nuclear weapons had transformed geopolitics and the nature of warfare. An American decision to bomb China would have upped the ante, threatening to turn a brutal and costly limited war into World War III. The president's decision was wise and prudent.

In the August offensive, the Marines found themselves back in the area of the Punchbowl, with the mission of taking a series of bleak ridge-lines and hills north of it. It was ideal country to defend, and in this phase of the war, the 1st Division's Devil Dogs found themselves up against well-equipped and trained units that belonged to two NKPA corps.

Supplying the two-regiment Marine attack would prove a major challenge because the broken country of hills, draws, and ridges had few roads. While it took about ten pounds of supplies a day to keep the North Korean or PLA soldier fed and supplied at the front, it took sixty pounds to supply and feed an American soldier or Marine.

The first of four major objectives assigned to the Marines lay just south of the series of hills that constituted Yoke Ridge. Land mines, some of them originally laid by U.N. forces, took their toll on the attack-ing Devil Dogs in the ghastly melee of the coming days, but by Septem-ber 3 the hills south of Yoke Ridge had been cleared.

The next objective, Kanmubong Ridge, lay fifty-five hundred yards to the north. It took six days to get the beans, bullets, and fuel up to the line of departure before the assault could begin. Mud and rain rendered many of the roads leading from the supply depots in the south all but impassable. NKPA units took advantage of the delay to reinforce their positions. The attack recommenced on September 9, with the objec-tives being Hill 673 and Hill 749. North Korean soldiers, fighting from well-prepared bunkers, blunted the initial Marine daytime assaults on Hill 673. But under cover of darkness on September 11, two Marine platoons managed to position themselves behind the NKPA bunkers that lay halfway between Yoke and Kanmubong ridges. The Marines' attack on Hill 673 on September 12 was a rousing success.

Before the Marines could press the attack on Hill 749 in earnest, they needed to be resupplied. For the first time in military history, the resupply of an infantry battalion in the midst of an assault would be car-ried out exclusively by helicopter. The task fell to Marine Transport He-licopter Squadron 161. The pilots of the HRS-1 birds flew twenty-eight flights in two and a half hours, delivering a total of 18,848 pounds of supplies into the assembly area of the 2nd Battalion, 1st Marines. These same helicopter pilots removed seventy-eight battle casualties as well. Two days later the squadron conducted the first large-scale lift of infantry into a combat zone. The HRS-1 helos were sturdy enough, but their lift capacity was very limited. They could carry only four to six combat Marines or three to five casualties.

Along the ridgeline between Hills 673 and 749, a group of stubborn NKPA soldiers found themselves in an untenable position, caught between the guns of the 1st and 2nd Battalions of the 7th Marines. Still, not a prisoner was taken; the enemy fought until the last man was killed. Marine casualties for September 11 and 12 were 22 dead and 245 wounded.

The next phase of the fighting centered around Hill 749, where the 2nd Battalion, 1st Marines at 1500 on September 14 finally reached the summit, thanks to the help of two companies of the 7th Marines attacking the reverse slope. Their first assault had failed, and there was little time to celebrate the success of the second effort, since their ownership of the high ground did nothing to silence firing from several well-placed bunkers hidden among the trees on the slopes. Dispatching those positions took until dusk. Tanks in support fired more than seven hundred 90mm rounds, neutralizing six enemy bunkers on and around the hill. This was costly fighting: on September 14 alone 39 Marines were killed in action and 463 wounded.

September 15 was eerily quiet. The NKPA had apparently spent themselves in the ghastly ridge fighting of the previous day. And then, at precisely 1201 on September 16, the North Koreans unleashed a thunderous counterattack on Hill 749, as hundreds of shells—105mm and 122mm howitzer rounds supplemented by mortar rounds—rained down on the Marines. No one can accurately recall how many waves of infantry attacked during the next four hours of mayhem. Several Marine units emplaced on the slopes had to give ground and narrowly avoided being overrun. The 1st Marine Division Historical Diary of September 1951 records that the artillery barrage leveled against Hill

749 "reached an intensity that was estimated to surpass that of any barrage yet encountered by the 1st Marine Division in Korea."[22] Not until 1800 on September 16 was Hill 749 firmly in the hands of the 1st Battalion. The enemy attack was estimated to have been of regimental size. Every yard was contested in fighting that reminded the Pacific war veterans of Iwo and Okinawa.

The last phase of the offensive was carried forward by the most decorated Marine regiment in history—the 5th Marines. Against stiff resistance they conquered, lost, and conquered again an ugly terrain feature called the Rock. On September 21 the Eighth Army called a halt to offensive actions all along the front. The war of maneuver in Korea had come to an end. The Korean War had reached its final, longest phase.

From October 1951 until July 1953, the two great armies would sit in stalemate. The Marines, in effect, became one more infantry division under army control in a conventional land campaign. Until March 1952, the Marines remained along the east-central section of the main line of resistance, where they had conducted their final offensive in the fall of 1951. Here, under the direction of the engineers, they built hundreds of bunkers on the reverse slopes of hills, and observation posts anywhere from a few hundred to a few thousand yards to the front of the bunkers, with networks of interconnected trenches. In March 1952 the Marines were relieved by the 2nd Infantry Division. The twenty-eight-thousand-strong 1st Marine Division was then redeployed to a critical thirty-five-mile sector in western Korea, protecting the South Korean capital from attack by Communist forces.

In between launching and fending off minor assaults, Marines found themselves conducting night raids and ambushes launched from their tenuously held outposts a few hundred yards in front of the MLR, frequently in terrain studded with land mines and booby traps. The Marine war in Korea became a platoon leader's conflict, and small-unit night action was a constant feature. Outposts with names like Berlin and those named after Nevada cities—Vegas, Carson City, and Reno—became the scenes of savage hand-to-hand fighting. Marines caught defending such outposts against superior enemy numbers often had no choice but to call in artillery attacks on their own positions. This technique is known as "box me in" fire. The defenders call in artillery, and then quickly hunker down and hope for the best.

For the infantry, it was a frustrating war of digging, digging, and more digging; of taking one's turn lugging water and ammunition into outposts unreachable by Jeep or truck; of hours of boredom looking northward for signs of attack, punctuated by moments of sheer terror and savage close-in fighting. Units along the line had to be relieved every three months because of the frustrations that came with seeing one's comrades fight and die for seemingly meaningless hills and outposts that had no strategic bearing on the conflict as a whole.

A typical action of this phase of the Marines' war, the battle of Bunker Hill, began around daylight on August 9, when a reinforced PLA platoon assaulted one of the vulnerable forward outposts in the 1st Marine Regiment's sector about a quarter mile north of the MLR. The outpost on Hill 58A was manned by a single Marine squad. These Marines wisely retreated to the MLR as soon as they detected the strength of the enemy attack. The first attempt by a reinforced Marine platoon to retake the outpost crumbled under heavy fire from Chinese mortars and artillery. Marine jets then worked Hill 58A over with napalm and air force fighters dropped thousand-pound bombs. Marine artillery punished the Chinese defenders, and then another Marine infantry assault carried the day. At 1103 Hill 58A was back in the hands of Company E, 1st Marines. Yet the two platoons that held the position were subjected to such a massive pummeling by Chinese artillery that they suffered 75 percent casualties, and were once again forced to retreat. "Siberia," as Hill 58A had been christened, had changed hands twice in less than a full day. The PLA had fired around five thousand rounds of artillery in attempting to hold one hill.

Twice in the course of the "positional phase" of the war (October 1951 to July 1953), the Marine Corps pressed higher command to use the 1st Marine Division in an amphibious end run. Twice the commander of the Far East forces demurred. The U.N. strategy remained a conservative one of static defense. Meanwhile, U.N. and Communist delegations met periodically in the grim North Korean town of Panmunjom just north of Seoul, but the negotiations repeatedly stalled. A major stumbling block to bringing a conclusion to the war concerned the fate of prisoners of war. Thousands of captured Chinese and North Koreans had no wish to return to the repression and poverty of their homelands. The United Nations was adamant in respecting their wishes. For their part, the Communists were steadfastly committed to the proposition that all their soldiers should be repatriated in any exchange.

By war's end, of the 137,000 Americans killed, wounded, or missing, the Marine Corps suffered 30,544 casualties. During the western deployment, total Marine casualties were 13,087, according to the official history of operations. Just over 39 percent—1,586 men—of the Marine ground forces killed in the conflict lost their lives along the western end of the MLR.

The casualty figures might have been lower had the Marines on the MLR possessed their enemy's skills and dedication at digging in and building defensive fortifications. In the wake of the heavy casualties, Lieutenant General Franklin A. Hart, commander of Fleet Marine Force in the Pacific, visited the battleground. While proud of the guts and determination of the 7th Marines in the fight, he criticized the regiment for their lack of attention to such bunker complexes. Other military authorities noted that Chinese defensive fortifications were invariably superior in strength to those of the Marines. No doubt there was some truth to the criticism, as the Marine Corps was—and remains—an essentially offensive-minded organization.

Another cause of high casualties, and one that was the source of great bitterness to the Marine Corps' senior officers, was the detachment of the 1st Marine Air Wing from support of Marine ground forces after the conclusion of the Chosin campaign. The main result of this decision was a precipitous decline in the quality and quantity of close air support. Against strident protests from senior Marine leaders in Korea and Washington, the Corps' air assets were put under the control of the air force and used largely in the ineffective campaign to interdict the flow of supplies and men to the MLR area of operations. This same problem would arise in Vietnam, and once again, the Marine Corps lost the battle to keep its air-ground team together as a single fighting entity.

The Korean War came to a long-overdue conclusion with the signing of an armistice on July 27, 1953. A cease-fire commenced that night at 2200, and has remained in effect through the present day. The 1st Marine Division stayed on in Korea for more than a year, taking its place along a heavily fortified DMZ. Ultimately it returned to its home at Camp Pendleton, in Southern California, replaced in Korea by U.S. Army forces. The army still maintains forces to this day along the DMZ between North and South Korea.

The prisoner issue was ultimately resolved when the opposing sides agreed to turn over the Communist soldiers who did not wish to be repatriated to a neutral party—in this case a supervisory commission run by India.

By any measure, the Marine Corps' performance in Korea was exemplary. The speed with which the 1st Provisional Marine Brigade was assembled, and its victories against previously undefeated NKPA forces in the first months of the war, confirmed the value of America's seaborne force in readiness. The steadfast performance of a hastily assembled, undertrained 1st Marine Division in the Inchon-Seoul campaign rebuked General Bradley's claim that the amphibious landing was anachronistic in the atomic age. When disaster struck in late November as the Eighth Army and X Corps drove north in widely separated columns, the 1st Division demonstrated in their fighting withdrawal the soundness of Marine Corps training techniques. What accounted for the success of the Marines in the end was, of course, not only their organizational doctrine and enduring belief that all Marines, regardless of occupational specialty, must be trained as riflemen. Their victory had also been a moral one: it was Marine esprit, that centered self-confidence that, being Marines, they would find a way out, no matter the odds. Quitting was no more an option than leaving behind the dead or heavy weapons. The code—the creed—would not be forsaken. The American people took great pride and solace in the Marines' breakout from the Chosin Reservoir, and rightly so.

The concluding volume of the Marine Corps' official history asserts that "the performance of the Marine Corps was . . . responsible, in part, for changing post–Korean War military doctrine from total reliance on new tactics and weaponry to a more balanced concept that combined both sophisticated innovations, and viable, established procedures."[23] In other words, future conflicts involving the U.S. military would not be determined by tactical nuclear weapons or airpower alone. The well-trained foot soldier remained relevant in the cold war era. Events of the next four decades proved this analysis to be astute. Far from making conventional forces obsolete, the nuclear standoff between East and West dictated that future conflicts would of necessity be limited, carefully calibrated ones, where well-trained, versatile forces like the Marines would prove indispensable.

The Corps emerged from the Korean War with heightened prestige, for it had clearly demonstrated versatility, aggressiveness, and imagination in the face of difficult circumstances. The Marine Corps—not the U.S. Army—developed the doctrine for the use of helicopters in resupply, command and control, combat assault, and medical evacuation missions. In Korea, it put its doctrine into practice for the first time. It was the Marine Corps, too, that took the lead developing the first body armor. The Marine flak vest made its initial appearance on the battlefield in 1951 and immediately proved effective in preventing casualties from shrapnel and some small-arms fire. The first thermal boots used by the U.S. military were also developed by the Marines.

The Leathernecks' performance on the battlefield received a great deal of favorable press coverage, which brought increased public prestige, which in turn led to the passing of a new federal law, PL416, signed by President Truman on June 28, 1952, which at last guaranteed a powerful, combat-ready Marine Corps of three divisions and three air wings during peacetime. The new legislation also confirmed the status of the Corps as a separate military service within the Department of the Navy, and secured for the commandant a place on the Joint Chiefs of Staff whenever matters of direct concern to the Marine Corps were on the agenda. The *New York Times* spoke for a great many Americans when it opined that the legislative action anticipating PL416 "is a direct reaction to (1) the magnificent record on the ground and in the air of the Marines in Korea; and (2) the persistent attacks upon the Marine Corps by high officials inside and outside the Pentagon during and since the 'unification' fight."[24] The public prestige of the Corps was enhanced even further after the war when studies showed that Marines had consistently performed with great valor and spirit as POWs. Of the 227 Marines captured, only two succumbed to intensive enemy indoctrination and were charged with collaborating with the enemy. A higher percentage of Marines survived the horrors of the POW experience than those from any other service—in large part, according to the official reports—because they continued to maintain military order, discipline, and leadership among themselves even after capture.

Now, with the Korean conflict concluded, the Marines could set about building up their base and force structure to meet the challenge of serving at the tip of the spear in a cold war waged by a United States with global interests and responsibilities. Although the Corps was never seen as playing anything but a tangential role in direct conflict with the Soviet Union, the Marines needed to structure themselves to be a self-sustaining expeditionary force, with enough speed to get to crisis spots quickly, and enough punch to get the job done once they arrived. By the time of their entry into the next war, the Marine Corps was without question the most capable expeditionary force in world military history.

SEVEN

BETWEEN TWO WARS, 1953 TO 1965

After Korea, the Marines could weigh in on Department of Defense policies, budgets, and programs, particularly in the thorny area of service roles and missions, and get the results they wanted with greater frequency than ever before. Not long after the war, the Department of the Navy resolved a long-standing bone of contention between the navy and Marines by issuing unambiguous directives confirming that the commandant stood on an equal footing with the chief of naval operations. He could now speak for the Corps' interests in the upper reaches of government. The department also established the commandant's control over Marine Corps operating and support forces not specifically attached to the fleet at sea or under the navy chain of command as security forces at naval bases.

But the Marines in this era also faced considerable doctrinal and budgetary challenges. They knew they might find themselves up against regular forces or insurgents or both. Chances were good that either type of force might be supplied by the Soviet Union or China, with a formidable selection of small arms and heavier weapons. The Corps had to be able to land forces on hostile shores throughout Asia, the Middle East, the Caribbean, or northern Africa. The Corps had to be ready to do just about anything soldiers do short of conducting an independent major land campaign against the Soviets on the plains of Western Europe. That meant they needed money. To meet these threat scenarios, the reinforced battalions and attached squadrons of aircraft that constituted the Marine combat units had to jettison much of their World War II–Korean War vintage equipment, from rifles to machine guns to aircraft, both fixed-wing and rotary.

The costliest items on the wish list were more specialized amphibious ships. The Inchon style of amphibious assault was a thing of the past. In effect, the Marine Corps had to reinvent amphibious warfare.

A critical element in the new amphibious doctrine was vertical envelopment. Nuclear weaponry and advances in conventional weaponry meant that ships bringing the Marines to the fight had to be widely dispersed. The faculty at the Marine Corps schools in Quantico, where all research and development efforts were centered, realized that vertical envelopment—assault by helicopter—was critical to solving the central doctrinal problem of the new amphibious assault.

Undaunted, Commandant Lemuel Shepherd put together an advanced research group (ARG) of sixteen colonels and lieutenant colonels to study the problems of future amphibious operations. In the spring of 1954, the ARG produced two reports, which had radical implications for the structure of the Corps. The board concluded that the Corps must shape doctrine and equipment with a view to landing an entire division as far inland as 110 miles, and up to 50 miles in width. The Sikorsky HR2S helicopter, then under development, would need to lift 12,500 pounds of payload—allowing for the transport of heavy trucks and 155mm howitzers. The navy would have to supply sixteen amphibious assault ships, and these forces would have to be protected by fixed-wing jets of the navy and Marines.

In 1955, the ARG's concept was formally approved by the chief of naval operations, Admiral Arleigh A. Burke, and General Shepherd. Yet it was soon very clear that, though the navy had approved the concept in principle, it had no intention of funding anything remotely like a fleet of sixteen helicopter assault ships. What's more, the HR2S transport helicopter engineers at Sikorsky were struggling in their efforts to meet the lift requirements.

These technological and budgetary obstacles, along with the navy's tepid response to the new vertical envelopment concept, were very much front and center in the deliberations of a new board assembled in 1956 under Major General Robert Hogaboom. Its task was ambitious: to reevaluate the structure and organization of the entire FMF. The board's work set in motion monumental changes in force structure and organization. Indeed, the Hogaboom board provided the underlying rationale for the Marine Corps structure that remains in place today. The board took issue with the core assumption of the ARG's "all helicopter" concept:

> The Board believes that this line of thinking has perhaps obscured the continuing importance of crossing the beach operations. . . . We believe that for the foreseeable future a substantial portion of men and material required in effecting a lodgment on a hostile shore must still cross the beach in a "conventional" fashion. . . . Reduced to its simplest terms the Board visualized an operation wherein the flexibility of the helicopter-borne assault forces would be exploited to uncover and secure the beaches and to seize critical areas which will be required to enable us to phase in the additional means to maintain the momentum of the assault and secure the objective area. The Board considers that helicopters will be employed initially to displace the assault elements of the landing force from ships at sea to attack positions ashore from which they can seize the critical terrain features. In subsequent operations ashore helicopters will be employed to maneuver disengaged units into attack positions from which they can launch an attack against critical objectives at a decisive time.[1]

The importance of the Hogaboom board is hard to overestimate. Limiting its study to problems and solutions that could be implemented within six to eight years, the board called for radical changes in the structure of the Marine Corps division. The projected division of the early 1960s, argued the board, had to be able to execute an amphibious assault faster and more efficiently than those of the Pacific islands, and do so from a widely scattered fleet over the horizon. It should be structured to ensure the rapid formation of temporary air-ground task forces of various levels of strength, ranging in size from a battalion landing team, to a full regiment, to a full division and air wing. No matter what the size of the core infantry force, the unit needed to be flexible enough to integrate specialized units not organic to the division itself—intelligence, engineers, photo processing, motor transport, logistics, and security forces—depending on the nature of the mission and adversary.

The equipment of the entire division had to be air transportable, for the board recognized that the paucity of amphibious shipping would wreak havoc on a division so heavy that it could be transported to an area of operations by sea power alone. The board called for a stripped-down headquarters battalion for each division, featuring an expanded number of aircraft observers attached to each of the division's nine infantry battalions.

Within each battalion—the battalion being the basic tactical unit of the Marine Corps—the headquarters company would take on functions previously furnished by an independent service company, thus integrating a larger number of support and command functions under one command.

The infantry battalions were stripped of their heaviest organic weapons. The 81mm mortars and recoilless rifle sections moved from organic battalion command to independent headquarters and service companies. They would be attached to a given battalion only when a commander could make a compelling case for his unit's carrying the extra weight. A fourth rifle company was added to each infantry battalion, thus making it possible for commanders to plan two- or even three-company assaults while using the fourth rifle company as a reserve or to provide security in the rear of the combat operations area, where the headquarters and service company would be located.

By reducing the size of each company commander's headquarters section and machine-gun sections, the size of the rifle company dropped from 7 officers and 231 enlisted men to 6 officers and 197 enlisted men.

Most dramatically, the division's tank battalion was removed from the division's table of organization and given to an entirely separate organization called force troops. Force troops consisted of specialized units that could be attached in various combinations to any one of the Corps' three infantry divisions as needed. To compensate for the lack of organic armor, each division received forty-five Ontos vehicles. These were very fast, lightly armored tracked vehicles, each of which mounted six 106mm recoilless rifles. The Ontos were designed to provide close support for infantry. Trouble was, they themselves—unlike tanks—were extremely vulnerable to heavy-machine-gun fire.

There were many other changes of import: without tanks, it was possible to diminish the size of the heavy engineering element attached to each division. The number of artillery tubes per battalion was sharply reduced, and all the heavy artillery joined the tanks as part of the force troops, thereby greatly lightening the division.

The Hogaboom board examined the division's service-support structure closely as well, and found it wanting. The logistical units organic to the division had to become lighter if the division was to become more mobile. What was more, there were simply too many echelons (i.e., levels of organization such as companies and battalions and, in the case of artillery, batteries) in the chain of command. In the end, the service regiments became battalions, and many functions previously handled within the division chain of command were transferred to force troops.

The new service battalion consisted of seventy-four officers and fourteen hundred enlisted men. It contained three highly mobile light support companies designed to operate independently in support of a single infantry battalion on the front lines. The light support companies, unlike the traditional service companies, could be lifted into the zone of operations by helicopter without the aid of ground transport. "Readiness" has been a mantra in the Corps for over a hundred years,. but never in its

180-year history had the requirements for readiness been so rigorous, so demanding. The cold war of the mid-1950s held out the possibility of simultaneous Marine deployments in brushfire conflicts, peacekeeping operations, and rescue missions.

The Marine Corps' most likely deployments were heavily weighted toward the Pacific in the 1950s and early 1960s. The disposition of forces reflected this fact, with the 1st Marine Division not returning to Camp Pendleton in California from Korea until 1955, the 3rd Marines Air Wing and 3rd Marine Division were stationed and trained together in Japan, and the 1st Marine Air Wing headed west from Florida to El Toro in Southern California. The East Coast force in the Carolinas consisted of the 2nd Marine Division and the 2nd Marine Air Wing. Their beat was typically the Mediterranean and the Caribbean as part of the Second and Sixth Fleets.

President Dwight D. Eisenhower's New Look defense policy sought to keep defense spending at $40 billion a year in light of the sluggish domestic economy. A Soviet nuclear buildup led the administration to put most of its resources into strategic and tactical nuclear weapons. As a result, conventional forces suffered.

Headquarters Marine Corps had to lobby strenuously in Congress to maintain what it saw as the minimum number of people it needed to perform its duties. In 1954, the Corps' active forces consisted of about 225,000 people. Ike and his planners made it plain that they wanted to downsize from 215,000 in fiscal year 1955 to 193,000 in 1956. Congress blocked the cut, but the administration impounded funds from the budget and forced the Corps to reduce to about 200,000. In 1955, the Corps' budget slipped below $1 billion. In fiscal year 1958, it dropped to $942 million, and by fiscal year 1961 it was only $902 million. By June 1960, there were only 170,000 Marines under arms. In 1959, six BLTs were deactivated along with six air-wing squadrons.

Another manpower problem concerned the officer corps. The Marines' enhanced status within the Department of the Navy meant that for the first time Marine officers would take up staff positions in Washington in support of the JCS's planning process. The insatiable need for information and studies siphoned off many of the Corps' most thoughtful and innovative officers from field and staff billets within the operating forces. In sum, the Marine Corps of the mid- and late 1950s was stretched very thin indeed.

The changes resulting from the Hogaboom board's recommendations were implemented gradually in the latter half of the 1950s, during the commandancy of General Randolph McCall Pate. Pate, unlike his three predecessors, lacked a distinguished combat pedigree, having spent most of his career in staff positions. Nor did he seem as comfortable as his predecessors in pushing forward the Corps' agenda within the Department of Defense. He did not like politics, and shunned the Washington party scene and the congressional armed services committees. In short, he was not an effective advocate for the Marines at precisely the time when the Eisenhower administration's cuts put great pressure on the Corps.

It was in the late 1950s that much of the equipment that would fight in Vietnam was selected and purchased. The procurement budget increased from $135 million to $190 million in the last three years of the decade. The Corps joined with the navy in buying the Chance-Vought F-8 Crusader as an air superiority fighter with limited close air support potential. The gull-winged Corsairs were retired in favor of the Douglas A-4 Skyhawk for most of the Corps' increasingly important close air support work. (Since there were fewer artillery tubes attached to each battalion, airpower had to fill the gap.) The Hawk antiaircraft missile made its debut in the FMF in 1960, and extensive experimentation was done with antitank missiles around the turn of the decade.

A critically important innovation was the easily transportable short tactical airfield. Made of high strength, lightweight aluminum, it could be brought ashore and assembled with astonishing rapidity, provided the infantry could seize several thousand yards of reasonably level terrain. If the engineers had to create such terrain it would take a little longer.

Perhaps the most important procurement concern in the late 1950s, though, was for modern amphibious shipping. The navy didn't have enough modern transports or specialized amphibious shipping to move more than a single Marine division and air wing to a theater of operations rapidly enough to suit HQMC. The Corps wanted a commitment to build twelve specially designed helicopter-bearing amphibious assault ships. Initially the navy offered up just a handful of converted World War II–era escort carriers, which were quickly declared unsatisfactory. Between 1959 and 1961, three larger Essex-class carriers were converted for Marine use. In 1961, the navy commissioned the first of seven ships built from the heel up for amphibious assault—the LPH, or Landing Platform Helicopter, class. Each of these ships could carry a full helicopter squadron and the lion's share of a battalion landing team.

While Marine BLTs cruised the seas, a tragedy unfolded at the Marines' legendary recruit-training depot at Parris Island. Just after 2000 on the moonless Sunday night of April 8, 1956, an inexperienced drill instructor, Staff Sergeant Matthew McKeon, strutted into the barracks of his recruit platoon. He called on his charges to fall out in two minutes. It had not been a good day for Platoon 71. Twice the seventy-four recruits had been punished for lackluster discipline. Staff Sergeant McKeon had become furious when he found several recruits lying down in the grass during a smoking break. The entire platoon had been ordered to conduct two "field days"—Marine slang for scrubbing down every inch of their barracks with creosote and yellow soap—that Sunday. Now, in the darkness, McKeon marched the platoon into the "butts," an area behind the island's rifle ranges, and into the chilly waters of a tidal estuary called Ribbon Creek. It was a common, albeit not officially sanctioned punishment designed to instill greater discipline into wayward platoons. The waters of Ribbon Creek run in serpentine fashion through a thousand-yard-long marsh, and were from four to twelve feet in depth.

The recruits struggled to maintain some sense of order as they splashed through the unfamiliar terrain on the edge of the creek. Shortly before 2030 hours, a group of recruits stumbled into deep water with a strong current. Within seconds, pandemonium reigned. Amid anguished screams and cries for help, McKeon acted quickly, ordering all recruits out of the water and attempting, with the help of several good swimmers, to come to the aid of those in danger. In spite of their efforts, six recruits drowned.

Within a few hours, the recruit depot commander had contacted headquarters in Washington. The Ribbon Creek affair captured national headlines for the next several months, and was a major stain on the Corps' reputation. Many Americans concluded that recruit training was out of control, and that the Corps had crossed the line from tough training into sadism and abuse. The incident threatened to strip the Marines of the power to train its people as it saw fit, without interference from the Department of Defense and Congress. Ribbon Creek also pitted Marine against Marine in the ensuing controversy over how the Corps' training regimen should be reformed. Senior Marine officers, of course, knew what every graduate of Parris Island and San Diego knew—drill instructors did occasionally cross the line between demanding training and outright abuse. Not all DIs were innocent of inflicting humiliations and even serious physical injury on their charges.

To make matters worse, the Marine Corps' initial handling of the incident was a PR disaster. At first the commander of Parris Island stonewalled, offering up precious little information to the local media in South Carolina. Headquarters' press release, when it finally appeared, failed to identify the platoon, causing unnecessary alarm among the thousands of families with Marines stationed on the island. When General Pate, the commandant, insisted on briefing the media himself, he stumbled badly by appearing to convict McKeon before the Corps had conducted even a preliminary investigation. Then the unfortunate recruit depot base commander, Major General Joseph C. Burger, who had assumed command only at the beginning of January 1956, caused further embarrassment by appearing to deny that the recruit-training regimen was in need of any reform whatsoever. More astute officers at HQMC had already decided that the Corps' best hope to limit damage was to deal forthrightly and tactfully first with the families of the lost recruits, and then with Congress and the nation as a whole, by admitting that the training program had developed serious problems, and by fixing them.

It was essential, of course, that boot camp remain physically and emotionally stressful. Yet certain abuses were unnecessary and counterproductive. Recruits who committed disciplinary infractions at least since the 1930s had been subjected to a gauntlet called the "belt line," in which, wrote one Parris Island recruit, "The platoon was formed into two ranks facing inward. . . . Grasping the buckle end of [his] belt, each man had to swing and hit the man being punished as he ran through. Whoever missed and was spotted by a DI also had to run through the line. Often, the DIs made us run through the line for no reason at all." [2] Other punishments were less harsh, and arguably useful. Slow recruits were subjected to torrents of verbal abuse and threats. The unfortunate recruit who dared to slap one of the ubiquitous sand fleas that attacked any exposed flesh during drill might be forced to do fifty push-ups. Other minor offenses brought such punishments as carrying buckets of sand for extended periods of time, or pushing a wheelbarrow full of sand along the beach, or raising and lowering a rifle several hundred times at a rapid pace.

With the great expansion of the Corps in World War II, abuses clearly increased, in part because of the strains on the system that put increasing numbers of inexperienced Marines in charge of recruit platoons. The writer William Manchester recalled that "it was quite common to see a DI bloody a man's nose, and some boots were gravely injured." [3] While the training establishment shrank after World War II, many of the hazing techniques remained. Some men were forced to smoke six cigarettes with a bucket placed on their heads; others were kicked in the rear end or whacked with swagger sticks.

In the aftermath of the Korean War, the Corps found itself with far more noncommissioned officers than it needed. Many of these men had been temporary officers during the war, and they resented their loss of status. Too many of them became drill instructors in the mid-1950s. Some platoons, conversely, lacked the requisite number of DIs. This meant that each DI had to put in huge numbers of hours, which in turn placed great strain on his family life. According to the most reliable historian of the Ribbon Creek incident, Parris Island also became something of a repository for officers who lacked drive and ambition in the mid-1950s. The result was a lack of supervision of the DIs under their command. "An inertia, an inability or lack of desire to correct fundamental problems . . . crept into the training system."[4]

When Major General Burger assumed command of Parris Island in January 1956, mistreatment had reached a deeply disturbing level. Brigadier General Wallace Greene, a highly sophisticated and intelligent Vermont native and future commandant, arrived at the training depot in the immediate aftermath of the incident. It took him no time at all to see that Parris Island had a problem. He found no fewer than ten recruits in the sick bay with broken jaws. Greene witnessed one DI breaking the jaw of a recruit who was forced to stand at attention as his instructor punched him repeatedly. When the recruit fell to the ground, the DI began to kick him. Marine training had always sought to duplicate real combat conditions as closely as possible, but this was beyond the pale.

Staff Sergeant McKeon was charged by the military equivalent of a grand jury with manslaughter, recruit abuse, and drinking while on duty. His court-martial lasted three weeks, and because McKeon had an exemplary service record, including combat duty in Korea, and was a good family man, his trial became the Marine Corps' trial.

McKeon's civilian attorney, New Yorker Emile Berman, kept the Marine prosecution team off balance, frustrating their attempt to show the illegality of McKeon's ordering his men into the creek. Berman presented ample evidence to confirm that night marches through Ribbon Creek, if not officially sanctioned, were nonetheless a condoned custom of recruit training and either encouraged or ignored by officers in charge of training at several echelons of command. Berman was able to put both Commandant Pate and the Corps' legendary icon Chesty Puller on the stand to testify. The trial became something of a circus, with McKeon appearing as a scapegoat for a training system gone awry. Puller's testimony fueled public sympathy for Staff Sergeant McKeon. The retired lieutenant general testified that night marches through creeks were effective in creating discipline, and discipline made Marines great fighters.

McKeon was acquitted of manslaughter on August 4, but convicted of negligent homicide and drinking on duty. (It was widely believed that McKeon had had several glasses of vodka earlier in the day, though the exact number remains unclear.) He was sentenced to a bad conduct discharge, required to forfeit $30 a month for nine months while confined to hard labor, and reduced in rank to private. The sentence was seen as too harsh by Marine traditionalists, and too lenient by the families of the dead.

Two months later the secretary of the navy reduced the sentence on the recommendation of HQMC. McKeon's misconduct discharge was reversed; the hard labor charge was reduced to time served in the brig; and he remained an active-duty Marine until 1959, when he was medically discharged as a corporal.

Even before the trial had finished, HQMC had begun an impressive PR campaign that minimized the long-term damage of the incident. The Corps' leadership sought guidance from Representative Carl Vinson, a longtime Corps admirer and chairman of the powerful House Armed Services Committee, and Massachusetts senator Leverett Saltonstall. A full congressional investigation was averted, but only when it was clearly established that the Marines themselves would take a hard look at the problems, and more important, take steps to fix a system that had broken down.

General Pate appointed two highly regarded brigadier generals as commanders of independent training commands at Parris Island and San Diego. General David Shoup, a hard-driving Medal of Honor winner, would oversee those commands as inspector general of recruit training. Shoup insisted on increasing officer supervision of the DIs, and he prohibited the striking of recruits and even the use of profanity. He also took the pressure off the boot camp instructors by decreasing the number of hours each had to spend with their platoons. The Corps enhanced the DIs' prestige in subtle but nonetheless tangible ways, such as providing free laundry and reintroducing the distinctive "Smokey the Bear" campaign hats that are today synonymous with the Marine DI image. The formation of a special training unit for over-weight and understrength recruits—the people who tended to drag down unit performance and thus add considerable pressure on the drill instructors—alone improved morale and performance immeasurably among instructors and recruits alike. In addition, the training cycle was extended from ten to twelve weeks.

Time has proven these changes to have been enlightened, to say the least. Undertaken by the Marines themselves without direct, formal su-pervision by Congress, they were initially controversial, and nowhere more so than within the family of the "Green Machine" itself. Many former Marines thought the changes cut into the heart of the boot camp experience, and thus threatened the mystical, transformative process of making Marines. One newspaper reporter overheard two old-school DIs lamenting the new developments. "We've had the Old Corps, the New Corps, and now we have this fouled-up thing." The other DI sighed and said wistfully, "We get more like the army every day."[5]

While the Corps worked to repair the damage done to its good name, its BLTs continued their regular cycle of training with three or four navy ships for about six months, and then deploying on "floats" with those same ships as part of amphibious ready groups. As the pro-curement budget jumped, training budgets had to be squeezed. Few senior officers were happy with the numbers of major training exercises. In 1959, only one division-sized and six regimental-level exercises were held, while another eighteen BLT landings took place at Marine bases.

Real-world operations were few in the years between 1953 and 1965.

In addition to Suez, Taiwan, and other routine deployments, in July 1958, Marine units of the Sixth Fleet landed in the Middle East to help defuse a political crisis.

At 0930 on July 14, 1958, Chief of Naval Operations Arleigh A. Burke sent a terse communiqué to Admiral James L. Holloway, commander in chief of naval forces, Eastern Atlantic and Mediterranean Sea, informing him of the possibility of a Marine intervention in Lebanon within forty-eight hours. Lebanon, with a mix of Christian and Muslim peoples and a pro-Western government, was long a banking and commerce center for the region. About the size of Connecticut, this small nation-state was besieged by civil strife. Lebanon also faced the very real threat of invasion by pro-Soviet Egypt and Syria, two countries that were decidedly antithetical to the government of President Camille Chamoun.

Politics in Lebanon in 1958 was wracked by tensions between Muslim and Christian factions within the government. Lebanon had become an independent nation only in the wake of World War II. A degree of stability followed, thanks to dividing power between the two factions.

By the summer of 1958, Muslims in Lebanon had become increasingly disaffected with their president for failing to break off relations with Great Britain and France during the Suez crisis. Violence erupted when Chamoun announced that he would seek a second term as president despite a constitutional prohibition, and an anti-Chamoun newspaper editor was assassinated. Riots broke out in Tripoli and the Basta, the section of Beirut peopled by Muslims.

When army officers in pro-Western Iraq staged a successful coup on July 14, King Hussein of Jordan, another pro-Western state, expressed fear that his regime was in serious danger as well. Eisenhower and the Washington foreign-policy establishment were deeply alarmed. The Lebanese army showed little inclination to quell the rioting, and it was feared that the army might splinter into Christian and Muslim factions. President Chamoun formally requested U.S. assistance, and Ike ordered the Marines to land in Beirut within thirteen hours. The objective of the intervention was not to keep Chamoun in office by force of arms, but simply to preserve some semblance of order and to deter adventurism on the part of Syria or Egypt.

The landing force of the Sixth Fleet was designated the 2nd Provisional Marine Force and was under the command of Brigadier General Sidney S. Wade. Although General Wade had in his possession quite detailed plans for a joint landing with British amphibious forces in both Lebanon and Jordan, Ike's order to hit the beaches not later than 1500 on July 15 required the fast sorting out of a tremendous amount of planning details. Only the 2nd Battalion, 2nd Marines, under Lieutenant Colonel Harry Hadd, was close enough to Beirut to conduct the landing by the deadline. The 2/2 was a very light battalion, for the landing ship, carrying its critical shore party battalion, its underwater demolition team, and two of its five tanks were sailing to Malta for repairs.

Until the moment of their arrival on the beach in full combat gear, Hadd's Marines had no idea whether or not the Muslim irregulars challenging Chamoun's government would resist their landing. Saeb Salam, the leader of the Muslim militia in Beirut, had been rumored to say that he would attack the Marines if they landed. U.S. intelligence sources discounted the remark—if indeed it had been made—as bluster, for although the Muslim forces in the area may have numbered ten thousand men, they were neither well organized nor well trained.

As the Marine LVTPs made their way toward shore on that sunny afternoon, the scene was a tranquil one. Lebanese soft drink vendors lined the beach, and a diverse lot of men, women, and children were swimming or playing in the surf. Far from being alarmed at the arrival of these American soldiers of the sea, they greeted the Marines with warmth and smiles. Children even attempted to help the Americans bring their equipment ashore in the light surf. "The scene on the beach," writes historian Jack Shulimson, "was perhaps one of the most colorful in the long history of Marine landings."[6]

Within twenty minutes, 2/2's four rifle companies were on the beach, heading for the airport. One company took up positions in and around the main terminal; another cleared the beach and prepared it to receive the heavy equipment and ammo; and the remaining two companies spread out along the perimeter of the airport and began to dig defensive positions. Not a single shot was fired.

Even before all of 2/2's units had begun their ship-to-shore movement, however, the complexities of Middle Eastern politics began to show. When informed of the Marines' impending arrival at the airport, General Faud Chehab, commander of the Lebanese army, told the U.S. ambassador in Beirut that the Marines' landing might split his army in two. A somewhat frantic Ambassador Robert McClintock attempted to call a halt to the landing with just ninety minutes to spare. Unable to communicate directly with the amphibious task force off the coast, he sent his naval attaché to the landing beach. The landing force commander, Captain Victor B. McCrea, flatly refused. Ambassador Mc-Clintock, meanwhile, and quite contradictorily, conveyed another request through his naval attaché: Could Captain McCrea send one hundred Marines at once to the Presidential Palace in downtown Beirut? He had heard rumors that an assassination attempt against President Chamoun was in the offing. Lieutenant Colonel Hadd protested. He could not spare so many men, as his battalion was already too widely dispersed for his taste at the airport. Nonetheless, Hadd was initially ordered to saddle up a motorized force, but the order was immediately reversed. Hadd could keep his Marines at the airport; the Lebanese army would guarantee the president's safety. It was just as well, because 2/2 was having its share of problems transporting its vehicles and equipment to shore due to the absence of its shore party and the bridging equipment used to link the vehicle-bearing LSTs to the shore. Hadd would later comment that it was most fortunate that the landing hadn't met resistance, as "the delay in the beaching of the causeway and the unloading of the LSTs would have been disastrous if the landing had been opposed."[7]

By the morning of July 16, 3/6 began to land on the same stretch of beach where 2/2 had come ashore. The new BLT took up 2/2's defensive positions, and Hadd's men saddled up and moved toward the city. Now word came from the embassy that General Chehab requested that the Marines refrain from entering Beirut. A Lebanese army roadblock one mile from the airport halted 2/2. The Lebanese commander refused to let the Marines pass. A potentially explosive situation was defused only when Ambassador McClintock, Admiral Holloway, Brigadier General Wade, and General Chehab hastily assembled for a roadside conference. When the Americans assured the commander of the Lebanese army that they were not there to interfere in the internal political process of Lebanon (by ensuring that Chamoun would remain in power), Chehab ordered his men to let the Marines move into the city.

Chehab himself, of course, had personal political ambitions, and had the Americans failed to clarify their mission, violence might very well have broken out on the road to Beirut. For their part, the Americans consented to alter their original route to avoid entering the Basta.

That night Muslim militiamen fired a few desultory rounds into the Marine positions south of the airport, and the Marines fired back. No casualties resulted. The next day, two Marines accidentally entered the Basta, the Muslim area of the city, and were seized at gunpoint. After being treated to a harangue on the injustice of U.S. imperialist intervention, they were released unharmed.

On July 18, a third BLT arrived off the Lebanese coast and came ashore four miles north of Beirut. The battalion took up blocking positions in the event the Syrians opted for a thrust toward the city. A fourth Marine battalion, 2/8, embarked from the Corps' air station at Cherry Point, North Carolina, on July 15. It took the eight-hundred-man unit just fifty-four hours to land in Beirut, a tribute to the logistical efficiency of the staff officers at Camp Lejeune. There they were joined by the U.S. Army 24th Airborne Brigade.

Much to the disappointment of the Marines, a U.S. Army major general, Paul Adams, was given command of all U.S. forces in Lebanon. The Marines remained in Beirut through August 1958. Foot patrols in their area of operations took sporadic small-arms fire, though not a single Muslim insurgent's bullet found its mark. American aircraft took fire as they approached the airport, and a firefight broke out among rebels, plainclothes Lebanese police, and Marines. A single policeman was wounded, but the Marines emerged unscathed.

Soon Marine motorized patrols of amtracs and tanks rumbled through the streets of Beirut and its eastern suburbs, with helicopter air support at the ready. Ultimately, army and Marine forces established a twenty-mile defense perimeter around the city, deterring any foreign ground attacks.

The civilians welcomed the infantry patrols warmly as they sauntered through the narrow streets, but only Lebanese government forces operated in the Basta area. Meanwhile, the diplomats, ably assisted by retired Marine colonel William Eddy, who knew the complexities of Lebanese politics well, assured all parties that the sole purpose of the U.S. intervention was to ensure the security of the country until Lebanese political factions could see their way clear to a peaceful solution obtained through a legitimate election process.

On the last day of July, the rival factions had agreed on the broad principles for a new election. General Chehab, who was Christian, was elected president, and he, in turn, selected a Muslim prime minister. The Marines began their withdrawal, and on August 14, their positions and patrol routes were taken up by U.S. Army units. The last soldiers departed by the end of October. The only Marine deaths in the operation — there were but two — resulted from friendly fire.

The American forces had been successful in stabilizing the country until the Lebanese could sort out their grievances. Marine units displayed admirable discipline in adhering to the rules of engagement, which permitted return fire only when a clear target was in view. Once again, the Corps had proven its value as a ready expeditionary force, capable of undertaking "such missions as the President may direct." Indeed, the landing of a BLT that had heavier weapons than an army airborne unit, and that could sustain itself for a protracted period, had lent credence to the Marines' assertion that seaborne infantry had critical capabilities that airborne troops did not possess. However, the operation also showed the limitations of a naval expeditionary force in sustaining themselves for ground operations lasting more than a few weeks. Ultimately the Marines became dependent on army transport and supply.

In the words of the Marine Corps' official monograph detailing the Lebanon intervention, "The Marine landings . . . vividly demonstrated the close interplay between American military preparedness and the success of U.S. diplomacy."[8]

The dawn of a new decade found the nation at peace, and the Marine Corps with a new commandant. Tired of what they saw as excessive service partisanship among the small cadre of Marine lieutenant generals, the Eisenhower administration appointed Major General David Shoup as commandant. Shoup was correctly perceived as more of a team player than Lieutenant General Merrill Twining, the favored man for the job among the senior Marine lieutenant generals, and a man who had made tremendous contributions to the Corps' development for more than two decades. Virtually every lieutenant general in the Marines—some seventeen men—retired in protest. That was fine with both Ike and David Shoup.

Shoup was intense, hard driving, and utterly determined to improve the Corps' efficiency in long-range planning, budgetary management, and the tenor of its relationship to the Department of Defense. The Marines lagged behind the larger services in administration procedures, and Ike and Shoup wanted to fix the problem. The new commandant did not suffer fools gladly; he was demanding. This native of Indiana was not exactly adored by the senior officer corps or the Marine enlisted ranks. He was respected, however, and Shoup proved to be an exceptionally effective leader, placing renewed emphasis on realistic combat training and heightened physical fitness standards. He insisted that the best Marine officers do stints on the planning staff of the JCS, thereby better integrating the Marines into the Department of

Defense. The assistant commandant under Shoup was the sophisticated Vermont native Wallace Greene. Green had an extraordinary record of achievement as a staff officer and planner, and he had many good friends in high positions in Washington circles. His relations in the capital city paid subtle but important dividends in the effort to secure a navy commitment to a robust amphibious shipbuilding program, and funds to ensure the replacement of Marine aircraft, which were rapidly becoming obsolete.

By 1965, the year the first Marine ground forces landed in Vietnam, the Corps was in superb shape. Indeed, contends historian Allan Millett, the Corps of 1965 was more capable of performing its missions than at any other peacetime juncture in the history of the United States.

Shoup's leadership was not the only factor in explaining this happy development. In November 1960, John F. Kennedy, a navy war hero with a fondness for the Marines' "can do" mind-set, was elected president. In his stirring inaugural address, Kennedy famously remarked that "the torch has been passed to a new generation of Americans," and that the United States "was prepared to pay any price, bear any burden, meet any hardship, support any friend, oppose any foe to assure the survival and success of liberty."

JFK and his team of foreign-policy advisers made it plain that they had plans for an active U.S. foreign policy. They would seek to expand the boundaries of the free world without hesitation or hand-wringing. In foreign policy, America would act with resolve and "vigor," a word that Kennedy used often.

The Kennedy administration would not be intimidated by Soviet premier Nikita Khrushchev's publicly stated goal of supporting "wars of national liberation." Kennedy rejected the previous administration's strategic focus on nuclear weapons as a deterrent to Communist adventurism for many reasons, not the least of which was a firmly held belief that cold-war conflict was likely to be played out in third-world countries in Asia, Latin America, Africa, and the Middle East. Nuclear forces weren't appropriate or effective in these situations. The nation needed to be able to respond to varied levels of Communist threats symmetrically. Kennedy's flexible-response doctrine required a strong intervention force, and he was generous with the Marines, giving them the funding and moral support to buy new aircraft and more capable landing craft and amphibious shipping.

It wasn't until a year and a half after Kennedy's death that the Marine Corps was again called upon to intervene in a foreign crisis. Their intervention in the Dominican Republic had its origins in the Monroe Doctrine, the revolution of rising expectations in Latin America, and Kennedy's and Johnson's fears of Fidel Castro's ability to foment Communist revolutions in the banana republics. The Monroe Doctrine of 1823 established the principle that no European power could intervene in or exert excessive political or economic influence in the Western Hemisphere. Since that time, and particularly since 1900, the United States has dominated the nations of the hemisphere indirectly, "usually by alliance with the wealthy landowning governing class. . . . Invested American capital spoke louder than guns. . . ."[9] Guns, however, were often required to prop up one dictatorial regime or another, or to quell anarchy and civil strife when Latin American strongmen took up arms against one another or against the persecuted peasantry, which typically composed 95 percent of the populace of such island nations as Haiti, the Dominican Republic, and Cuba. When guns were needed, American presidents had invariably turned to the Marines rather than the army. Political instability and economic decline prompted the U.S. government to establish a military government in the Dominican Republic from 1916 until 1924, to cite but one example. The Corps trained a new Dominican police force in addition to performing other basic functions of governance.

In 1961, the U.S.-installed Dominican Republic strongman Rafael Trujillo was assassinated. Dominican politics entered a four-year period of intrigue, chaos, and violence. A critical reason for the turbulence was "the revolution in expectations" throughout the third world—a broad

movement on the part of the poor and exploited masses for better economic opportunities and self-determination. These ideas, ironically,
were largely inspired by the history of the United States. Not surprisingly, it was a "revolution" that became one more battleground in the
cold war. The Kennedy administration's response to this movement, the
Alliance for Progress, was well intentioned. It encouraged popular sov-
ereignty and land reform throughout the hemisphere, but it was often
opposed by American business interests and the fear that behind every
Latin American reform party was a cadre of Cuban Communists. When
a left-leaning Juan Bosch won election as president of the Dominican
Republic in 1962, the United States extended support, but Bosch was
soon overthrown by a military coup that enjoyed the support of the
landowning class. The United States withheld recognition of the regime
and called for free and fair elections by 1965. In spring 1965, a pro-
Bosch faction within the army joined a loose coalition of liberal parties
to oust Reid Cabral, the titular head of the military junta. The lion's
share of the country's armed forces, however, remained under the control of Brigadier General Wessin y Wessin. The general ordered the
armed forces to crush the largely irregular forces of the pro-Bosch faction. After the presidential palace was strafed by Wessin's P-51s, pro-
Bosch forces broke into an armory and distributed weapons to swelling
crowds of civilian supporters. The armed mob proceeded to conduct
random attacks on the homes of the Cabral regime's supporters.

In the wake of the Cuban missile crisis of October 1962, the administration of President Lyndon B. Johnson read the popular revolt as
Communist-inspired. In fact, though there were Communists and Communist sympathizers in the ranks of the insurgency, they were a small
minority. Johnson ordered a ready amphibious task group sailing in the
Caribbean Sea to the coast of the Dominican Republic. Its landing
force was the 6th Marine Expeditionary Unit, a reinforced BLT with a
squadron of helicopters attached. The Marines began to evacuate American civilians and foreign nationals on April 27, 1965, amid shooting
and widespread looting in Santo Domingo.

The evacuation was carried out with good discipline and professionalism. Six hundred civilians were evacuated by LSTs and the helos of HMM-264 (Marine Medium Helicopter Squadron 264), which operated from a hastily established LZ (landing zone) near the Ambajador Hotel.

The next day, the U.S. embassy encouraged General Wessin to form a provisional junta to challenge the pro-Bosch faction, which was thought to be infected with Communists. He did so, and promptly requested the landing of U.S. Marines to oust the "rebels" from the business district of downtown Santo Domingo, where they had begun to set up defensive positions. He uttered the magic words to the U.S. State Department: he feared that if the pro-Bosch forces were victorious, they would soon be subverted from within by the small Communist faction in their midst.

The JCS ordered the 3rd Battalion, 6th Marines into Santo Domingo, along with elements of the 82nd Airborne. The paratroopers seized the airport, and the Marines deployed to establish an international security zone. The Marine companies were supported by Ontos vehicles, which sported recoilless rifles and were excellent for punching holes in the walls of city buildings and the hulls of tanks. Company I, in moving past the old Santo Domingo airport, drew steady small-arms fire from the rebel forces. One Marine platoon was pinned down, and suffered four men wounded in action. A second platoon, using standard fire-and-maneuver tactics, methodically advanced toward the rebel shooters, killing two men and forcing the remaining irregulars to flee with their wounded.

By nightfall, after taking small-arms and sniper fire, the Marines had linked up with units of the 82nd Airborne and established a strong perimeter around a safety zone on the western side of the city. Two U.S. soldiers were killed in the day's action, and two were wounded.

While U.S. diplomats worked furiously with the Organization of American States and the warring factions in the Dominican Republic, two more battalions came ashore from Camp Lejeune. A cease-fire was brokered on May 1, but it was ineffective. Fights between the rebels and the military junta broke out all over the city, and when the U.S. embassy took fire, the Marines had to extend the boundary of their security zone four blocks to the east. As the company assigned to the mission crossed the line of departure, its Marines came under fire from rebel automatic weapons. The Marines took no casualties themselves, but they killed two of the rebel riflemen. That same day, May 2, two Marine trucks came under a torrent of rebel fire when they accidentally strayed into rebel territory, killing one Marine and wounding two.

The Marine contingent in the troubled country peaked at seventy-nine hundred men. As they patrolled their zone and buttoned down each evening, the odd round would come their way, but there were no sustained firefights. In June, after the establishment of a tentative peace plan, the Marines boarded their ships and left Hispaniola Island to the 82nd Airborne.

They had performed with strict discipline and professionalism under trying circumstances in a country wracked with civil strife. Yet if historian Allan Millett is correct in saying that the Corps was at its peacetime zenith in 1965, it would not last. The Marines were about to fight their longest war.

EIGHT

TRAGEDY IN THE MAKING

The Marines in Vietnam, 1965 to 1967

At 0600 on March 8, 1965, Rear Admiral Don W. Wulzen, commander of U.S. Navy Task Force 76, barked out an order from the bridge of the USS *Mt. McKinley* that would have been familiar to any Marine of World War II or Korean War vintage: "Land the Landing Force!" The Leathernecks aboard the four ships of the task force formed the vanguard of the 9th Marine Expeditionary Brigade (MEB) under Brigadier General Frederick Karch. They were four thousand yards off the coast of Red Beach, Da Nang, a prominent port city of the southeast Asian peninsula known as Indochina. It was drizzling, and an eight-knot breeze from the northwest roiled the seas so much that the Marines had to abandon the plan to come ashore in their amphibious tractors in favor of larger, World War II–era landing craft. Just after 0920, the first assault wave reached the shore.

It was an uneventful landing. Not a single shot was fired by the guerrilla forces that regularly harassed the big Da Nang air base, which was used by the American and South Vietnamese air forces. Young Vietnamese girls greeted the infantrymen, placing yellow and gold leis

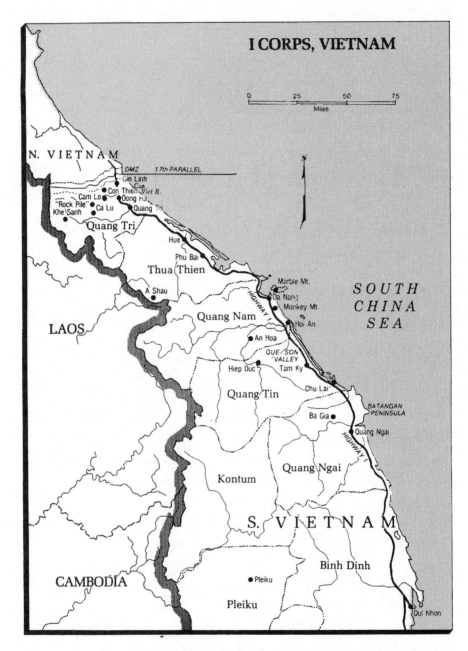

I Corps: Area of U.S. Marine Operations in the Vietnam War

Source: Allan R. Millett, *Semper Fidelis: The History of the United States Marine Corps*, revised and expanded edition. New York: The Free Press, 1991.

around the necks of the newcomers as they made their way to the trucks that would carry them to the air base. There, other Marines in helicopter squadrons and Hawk antiaircraft missile batteries awaited them. The first Marine support units had arrived in 1962, and the Corps had had a small presence in Vietnam since then.

The generals and colonels at HQMC in Washington did not realize at the time that the Corps was about to begin its second major war since the defeat of the Japanese in the Pacific. Vietnam is a beautiful country that stretches along the eastern edge of the Indochinese Peninsula. Its two-thousand-year history has been shaped by a tropical climate; tortuous relations with the colossus to the north, China; and a long series of wars among various political factions and against foreign interlopers such as the Japanese and the French. Vietnam was colonized by the French from the 1850s until 1954, when they were defeated by a Communist-led nationalist movement under the guiding hand of one of the great anticolonial figures of the twentieth century, Ho Chi Minh.

Many Americans in 1965 couldn't place Vietnam on a map, despite their government's having spent $3 billion in an effort to restore the French to power after World War II. Even after the Communist victory, Washington used its considerable diplomatic and military power at the Geneva conference of 1954 to keep the southern half of Vietnam—the territory below the 17th parallel—from Ho Chi Minh's control. Thus, Ho became president of the Democratic Republic of Vietnam, or North Vietnam, with its capital at Hanoi, and with the supreme objective of unifying the entire country under his government. Ho and his followers always saw the southern half of their nation as an American puppet state.

South Vietnam, officially the Republic of Vietnam, was governed first by Emperor Bao Dai, and then, beginning in 1955, by an imperious, white-suited Roman Catholic with a firm commitment to enhancing the power and prestige of his family and political minions: Ngo Dinh Diem. Within a year after the Geneva conference, the South Vietnamese were fighting in a low-intensity conflict against Ho's guerrillas and political cadres, many of whom had been left behind in the South to continue the struggle after the country was split in two.

The mission of Karch's Marine unit was widely advertised in Washington as a defensive one. His two reinforced battalion landing teams, deployed to contend with an estimated twelve Vietcong guerrilla battalions that were within striking range of the crowded air base, impeded further VC harassment of air operations by use of tactics that ranged from support of the Army of the Republic of Vietnam (ARVN) ground operations to deep strikes by fighter-bombers against North Vietnam itself.

Yet the arrival of the 9th MEB marked a critical change in America's participation in the war between the two Vietnams. The Marine BLTs were the first American ground-combat units to deploy to South Vietnam. The twenty-three thousand American military personnel already in-country at the time of the Marines' arrival were either advisers to the South Vietnamese army or combat support personnel. The landing on Red Beach would mark the beginning of the longest continuous overseas deployment of U.S. combat forces in a war in history.

In one way, the arrival of the 9th MEB was similar to many other Marine landings on strife-torn shores. American foreign policy makers were facing a potentially humiliating defeat, so the Marines were summoned to step into the breach. South Vietnam was on the brink of collapse. The National Liberation Front took its marching orders from Ho Chi Minh. The Vietcong, whether organized as regular battalions, small bands of local guerrillas, or members of the National Liberation Front, were disciplined, ruthless, resourceful, and indefatigable.

In 1960, Ho ordered the Vietcong to shift strategic emphasis from political to armed struggle. The insurgency found itself by March 1965 on the brink of victory against a corrupt and ineffective regime in Saigon that had squandered millions of dollars in U.S. economic and military aid and shown indifference to the peasants it was meant to serve.

The decision to intervene with Marines was reached only after a prolonged period of debate in Washington. In the fall of 1963, three thousand ARVN soldiers had suffered an ominous defeat at Ap Bac at the hands of about three hundred Vietcong, despite the presence of U.S. helicopters and armored cars. At one point in the battle the South Vietnamese army officer running the fight appeared to allow some trapped VC infantry to escape, refusing to order his men to chase the fleeing enemy. U.S. Army adviser John Paul Vann, who knew as much about the war's dynamics as any American, would later say of the battle in which he participated: "It was a miserable damn performance. These people won't listen. They make the same goddam mistakes over and over again."[1] Ap Bac was a harbinger of many defeats to come in the next twelve years. Then in January 1965 came a serious Buddhist uprising against the South Vietnamese government. The regime was largely peopled by the minority Catholic population, and the Buddhists were an oppressed group. Soon after, in early February, the Vietcong launched a bold attack on the American air base at Pleiku, damaging more than one hundred aircraft. Three days later, guerrillas killed twenty-three Americans at another base at Qui Nhon.

President Lyndon B. Johnson sent National Security Adviser McGeorge Bundy to Vietnam to evaluate the situation in early 1965. Bundy minced no words. Without new U.S. action, defeat appeared inevitable. The Johnson administration faced a dilemma: the president felt bound by containment policy and domestic political pressure to defend South Vietnam, yet he did not want the United States fully engaged in another land war in Southeast Asia, for fear of provoking a wider conflict with China, the Soviet Union, or both.

These fears led President Johnson to escalate U.S. troop strength and aid to the South Vietnamese army in a slow, methodical fashion over the next three years, a policy that has been widely criticized as providing enough troops to stave off defeat but not enough to defeat the insurgency. American military strength in South Vietnam would peak at 540,000 people in 1969. It began in early March 1965 when Johnson deployed the Marines.

Over the next six years, two reinforced Marine divisions and a reinforced air wing—more than two-thirds of the combat power of the U.S. Marine Corps—would find itself deeply enmeshed in the most divisive conflict in twentieth-century American history. The conflict soon turned into a test case of American resolve in the cold war. It didn't seem to matter that the United States had no vital interest in the fate of Vietnam per se, for under the widely accepted "domino theory," if South Vietnam fell, so, too, would other Asian states in its wake. When South Vietnam was finally conquered by the People's Army of Vietnam (PAVN) in April 1975, about four million Vietnamese on both sides were dead, along with more than fifty-eight thousand Americans.

The Vietnam War, along with the Watergate scandal, triggered a downward spiral in the American people's faith in their governmental institutions, especially the armed services. It also contributed to a serious decline in the economy. As George Ball, one of Johnson's more prescient foreign-policy advisers, put it, Vietnam was "a defeat for our political authority and moral influence abroad, and for our sense of mission and cohesion at home."[2] For the people of the United States and Vietnam, writes historian Stanley Karnow, the "war was a tragedy of epic dimensions."[3]

The war in Vietnam, as constructed by the decision makers of the Kennedy, Johnson, and Nixon administrations, was grotesquely misconceived at the strategic level. Washington placed far too much stock in the American military's awesome weaponry and technology. Policy makers couldn't imagine that a tiny nation like North Vietnam might support an insurgency and endure against the massive destructive firepower the United States could bring to bear.

Indeed, most serious scholars today believe the United States consistently focused on chimeras. The big-unit battles on the ground—those involving battalions or larger units—were invariably won by the Americans. But these "victories" were less important strategically than the battle for the allegiance of the people in the villages, and for the enormous and closely related task of building a viable, independent South Vietnamese government.

The U.S. military had to play a role in the process, but it could not play the key role or solve the underlying political and social problems that plagued the South Vietnamese regime. Above all, American policy makers turned a blind eye to the crushing vulnerabilities and incompetency of the South Vietnamese government. Starting with President Diem, and continuing with a series of juntas and individual strongmen, the South Vietnamese regimes were marred by an attitude of indifference and even hostility toward their people, a penchant for political intrigue, and corruption at all levels.

With the exception of a few elite units such as the Vietnamese Marines and the Rangers, the South Vietnamese army was poorly motivated and lacking in fighting spirit. The army was also riddled with Vietcong sympathizers. Marine officers learned early on that if the South Vietnamese knew about an American operation in advance, the chances were all but certain that the operation would be compromised. For three years following the deployment of the 9th MEB, Washington and Military Assistance Command, Vietnam assessed the war through the rose-colored glasses of body counts. In so doing they violated the basic principles of fighting wars that the Marine Corps had lived and died by for more than 190 years: war is ultimately a test of wills, in which the human and moral dimensions are far more vital than the technological and administrative ones.

The Marines, in the first year of the war at least, challenged the strategic approach of the top field commander in Vietnam, U.S. Army General William C. Westmoreland. Early in the war, the Marines had the wiggle room to pursue their own strategy, focused on slowly developing security in a series of enclaves, but only to a very limited degree. In the broad scheme of things, the Marines' considered views on the conflict, their "inkblot" strategy, was shunted aside in favor of an attrition strategy focused on destroying the armed forces of the enemy.

Vietnam proved to be a searing experience for the U.S. Marine Corps. The conflict made a lasting imprint on the officer corps and, thus, on the shape and trajectory of Marine history ever since. The Vietnam War damaged the Corps' reputation among the American people as an elite and spirited fighting force. It created deep racial and social rifts in the ranks, and severely damaged the Corps' capacity to take on many of its missions. Deployment to Vietnam forced the Corps to expand from 190,000 to 314,000 men, placing an enormous strain on the training establishment, and turning the 2nd Marine Division—the only division not deployed to Vietnam—into a shell of its former self.

The enormous expansion couldn't be met by relying on volunteers as the Corps always had. In the end, the Marines took in large numbers of draftees—nineteen thousand in 1967 alone—and the quality of its recruits suffered dearly as a result.

By the end of 1967, the Corps had sustained more casualties in Vietnam than in any other war save World War II. And by the time the last maneuver battalions departed from Southeast Asia, the Marines had sustained more battle casualties there than they did in World War II, though fewer Marines died. In Vietnam, the Corps suffered 101,574 killed and wounded, about 4,000 more total casualties than in World War II, though 19,733 Marines died in World War II, as compared to 13,574 in Vietnam.

In the sparsely populated western border areas, Marines faced rain forest and triple-canopy jungle amid rugged mountains and isolated plateaus. The mountains gave way to gentle hills in the east, and then to rice country—with many river deltas and acre upon acre of rice paddies and dikes. The soil here consisted of a muddy, shifting red clay called laterite, which made for tough going for armored vehicles and even Jeeps. Finally, along the coast lay flat, sandy lowlands and lovely beaches. Here are located most of the important cities of the region, including Da Nang, Hue, and Quang Tri city, in the province of the same name.

The Marines of the 9th MEB began immediately to construct a wide variety of defensive positions around the airport, and in the hills to the west of the air base. Constant foot patrols of squad and platoon size commenced. Soon the Marines found themselves the object of sniper fire, the odd mortar round, and an occasional short-lived firefight against "Charlie," who from the outset showed a marked preference for "hit and run" over "stand and fight" engagements. The overall defense of the Da Nang area remained under the control of a South Vietnamese general, but as the Marines grew in numbers, they exerted increasing influence on the war in their zone, patrolling an increasingly large area of operations. Their desire to conduct more aggressive patrolling over a wider area was fueled by the realization that ARVN forces were more anxious to avoid the Vietcong than to engage them in combat or seek to break their stranglehold on the village life after sunset.

After establishing a cordon sanitaire around the base proper, it took the Marines months to negotiate with South Vietnamese authorities to clear out the ragtag semipermanent dwellings of some seven thousand Vietnamese who lived within about four hundred yards of the base perimeter. Hundreds of thousands more Vietnamese would become refugees as the American war expanded over the next three years.

By April 1, President Johnson approved the deployment to Vietnam of about twenty thousand more soldiers and Marines. Two more BLTs joined the five-thousand-man brigade. Johnson also granted the Marines authority, in consultation with the secretaries of state and defense, to conduct limited offensive operations outside the defensive perimeter around the Da Nang air base. The first such operations against the estimated fifty thousand Vietcong in I Corps, the Marines' principle area of operations in Vietnam, took place about a mile south of Da Nang near the Cam Do River, long an epicenter of VC political and military activity. BLTs 2/3 and 3/4 were deployed in the vicinity of the Phu Bai airfield in mid-April—the second of three enclaves the Marines would establish in the early months of the war along the coast.

The third enclave was located fifty-five miles south of Da Nang at Chu Lai. The 3rd Marine Amphibious Brigade (MAB)—the word "Expeditionary" was changed to "Amphibious" because the former evoked the idea of a colonized power—took up residence there on May 7, supported by a helicopter squadron and engineers. Chu Lai lacked an air-field, so Marine engineers brought with them a portable tactical air-field, replete with aircraft carrier–style catapults and a short, lightweight runway, and set it up on top of the shifting soil. By early June, fighter-bombers were stationed at Chu Lai along with infantry, providing much needed relief for the overtaxed Da Nang air base.

With all three enclaves up and running, a corps-level headquarters, III Marine Amphibious Force (III MAF), was established under Major General William R. Collins, whose Far East tour would soon end. Major General Lewis W. Walt, a Marine's Marine, commanded III MAF for the critical first two years of the war beginning in May 1965. His influence on the conduct of the Marine war was enormous, and he became for the American people the face of the Marines in Vietnam. A college football star with a brilliant combat record in both World War II and Korea, Walt was widely respected by the Marines who served under him for his integrity and personal bravery. He cared deeply about his Marines. Walt, along with General Wallace Greene, the commandant, and Lieutenant General Victor Krulak, the commander of the Fleet Marine Force Pacific, who was responsible for providing III MAF with logistical and administrative support, were the chief formulators of the Marines' strategy in Vietnam.

In short, the Marines believed that the U.S. and South Vietnamese forces—the army, police, and local security forces—should work under one command and focus most of their combat forces and resources in breaking the Vietcong's stranglehold on village life and gradually estab-lishing stability and control over more and more of the country's four-teen thousand village hamlets, thereby denying the Vietcong access to the main source of food and funds. In other words, the Marines empha-sized "pacification" over seeking out and destroying the enemy's regular infantry units in traditional battles. Pacification came down to establish-ing responsive local government to provide for the basic needs of the people. It was at one and the same time a military, political, and eco-nomic process.

Joe Rosenthal's famous photograph of the second flag-raising on Mount Suribachi is also, memorably, an image of teamwork between five Marines and a navy corpsman. It remains a powerful symbol of American victory and resolution, and it crystallizes the spirit of the Marine Corps itself. *Courtesy Associated Press*

General Lewis B. "Chesty" Puller, with one of his many shotguns, pictured in his retirement. This legendary Marine always led from the front, and was awarded an astonishing five Navy Crosses for valor. *Courtesy USMC*

Marines on northern Iwo Jima dig in. While the battle raged, an entire city was being built behind the front line. *Courtesy USMC*

Infantrymen of the 28th Marines blast away at Mount Suribachi.
Courtesy USMC

A demolitions team supported by tanks goes to work against a Japanese cave on Iwo Jima.
Courtesy USMC

Forward artillery observers take advantage of the excellent visibility afforded the Marines on Mount Suribachi's crest. *Courtesy USMC*

Generals Harry Schmidt, Holland Smith, and Clifton Cates compare notes late in the battle for Iwo Jima. *Courtesy USMC*

Men of the 22nd Marines take a break after a long night of fighting in Naha on Okinawa. *Courtesy USMC*

Marines under fire in Death Valley in Okinawa in early May 1945. The Marines took well over 100 casualties in eight hours while trying to cross this draw. *Courtesy USMC*

General Douglas MacArthur, commander in chief of UN forces in Korea, listens to General Lemuel Shepherd, USMC, aboard the USS *Mt. McKinley*, flagship for the invasion of Inchon, Korea. MacArthur's relations with the Corps were uneasy in World War II, but at Inchon he nevertheless demanded to have the 1st Marine Division in the vanguard. *Courtesy USMC*

North Koreans surrender to wary Marine infantry on the way to Seoul, a few days after the successful Inchon assault. *Courtesy USMC*

The campaign at the Chosin Reservoir was among the bitterest and most dramatic engagements in Marine Corps history. *Courtesy USMC*

Corporal Charles Price sounds taps over the graves of
Marines who died during the Chosin Reservoir campaign.
Courtesy USMC

The 1st Marine Division redeploys from Korea,
with no regrets. *Courtesy USMC*

A Marine reconnaissance patrol in Lebanon, 1958, one of the few Marine deployments of the decade following the end of the Korean War in 1953. *Courtesy USMC*

Less than a month after the fall of Vietnam on April 30, 1975, Marines were sent to the rescue when Cambodian Communists inexplicably took the crew of the SS *Mayaguez* prisoner. Here, Marines board the ship only to find it deserted. *Courtesy USMC*

The most important Marine operations of the early 1980s occurred amid the byzantine political intrigues of Lebanon. *Courtesy USMC*

At Camp Lejeune, North Carolina, a Marine looks for the name of a buddy on the memorial honoring the 241 Marines who died in Beirut on October 23, 1983, when a truck bomb blew up at the headquarters of 1st Battalion, 8th Marines. *Courtesy USMC*

General Raymond Davis, USMC, one of the most respected and highly decorated Marines of the 20th century, was awarded the Medal of Honor for his leadership at the Chosin Reservoir campaign. He ably commanded the 3rd Marine Division in Vietnam in 1969. *Courtesy USMC*

During the bloody fighting in Hue during the Tet Offensive of 1968, members of the 2nd Battalion, 5th Marines carry their wounded to safety. *Courtesy USMC*

Marines patrol the streets of once-beautiful Hue
City, February 1968. *Courtesy USMC*

A patrol from 3rd Battalion, 9th Marines in action during
Operation Dewey Canyon, 1969. *Courtesy USMC*

Members of E Company, 2nd Battalion, 4th Marines advance across a
rice paddy toward Vietcong positions near Chu Lai. *Courtesy USMC*

Members of 3rd Battalion, 26th Marines take a break during a
search-and-clear operation in Vietnam, where tropical weather and
jungle terrain took a serious toll on the feet of Marine infantrymen.
Courtesy USMC

An American nun, along with South Vietnamese refugees, exits a Marine helicopter aboard a U.S. Navy ship during the evacuation of Saigon, April 29-30, 1975. *Courtesy USMC*

Marines fire their weapons from the fantail of the USS *Hancock* in preparation for Operation Frequent Wind, the final evacuation of Saigon. *Courtesy USMC*

The Marines have always served in small detachments aboard navy ships. Here Lance Corporal Michael LeMarte stands watch by an M2 .50-caliber machine gun aboard the USS *Wisconsin* during the Gulf War of 1990–91. *Courtesy USMC*

First Lieutenant D. S. Schultz cleans his M16 rifle in the Kuwaiti desert during Operation Desert Storm, 1991. *Courtesy USMC*

A Marine examines a T-55 main battle tank abandoned by the Iraqis on Highway 60 during Operation Desert Storm. *Courtesy USMC*

Iraqi civilians assist Air Force personnel and Marines of Marine Wing Support Squadron 371 with the removal of Iraqi heavy mortar rounds near An Nasariyah, Iraq, during Operation Iraqi Freedom, spring 2003. *Courtesy USMC*

Three Marines examine a display of Iraqi weapons captured during Operation Iraqi Freedom. *Courtesy USMC*

Armored assault amphibian vehicles of the 1st Marine Division halt for a rest while in a convoy driving toward Baghdad on Highway 80 during Operation Iraqi Freedom. *Courtesy USMC*

A lone Marine of Regimental Combat Team 5, 1st Marine Division, watches the smoke from a nearby explosion in a Baghdad suburb. *Courtesy USMC*

Major General Fred E. Haynes, retired, talks about fighting the Japanese in the caves of Iwo Jima with a young Marine, spring 2003. *Courtesy Fred E. Haynes*

Pictured here in his own days as a young Marine, Captain Fred E. Haynes takes a break during the 28th Regiment's assault on Hill 362A, a critical strongpoint in the Japanese defense system on northern Iwo Jima. *Courtesy Fred E. Haynes*

The ambiguous chain of command and the Marine Corps' control of "Marineland," as I Corps was often called, gave Lew Walt and his III MAF headquarters staff room for experimentation. Walt's commander was army general William C. Westmoreland, but Westmoreland reported to Admiral U. S. Grant Sharp, commander of the Joint Pacific Command. Sharp strongly supported the Marines' strategy, thanks in no small measure to the energetic persuasiveness of Lieutenant General Brute Krulak.

The Marines responded to the challenges of Vietnam with a number of innovative tactics, units, and types of operations. Taken together, these operations were costly and frustrating to the Vietcong and their PAVN (People's Army of Vietnam) brothers. Ironically, the amphibious specialists known as disciplined and aggressive shock troops soon became the foremost advocates of a strategy emphasizing population control. This won the Marines no friends at MACV (Military Assistance Command, Vietnam) in Saigon, for Westmoreland was unabashedly committed to a strategy of attrition. He felt the South Vietnamese ought to be left to the business of pacification. Broadly speaking, pacification required breaking the stranglehold of the Vietcong political infrastructure on the life and work of the peasantry. Generals Greene, Krulak, and Walt felt it was essential that American troops take up a wide range of pacification duties, from tackling civic-action projects like building markets, irrigation systems, and schoolhouses, to providing security against the Vietcong, who regularly intimidated and often killed village officials as a "persuasive" technique. Marines tried to identify and neutralize VC tax collectors and education/indoctrination cells who force-fed the peasants a steady diet of Communist propaganda.

As General Greene wrote, "The real target in Vietnam [was] not the VC and the North Vietnamese but the Vietnamese people."[4] The Marines' thinking reflected their extensive experience with third-world insurgencies in the Caribbean and Central America in the first third of the twentieth century, which put a premium on doing a great many things with comparatively few troops. The Marines, by the summer of

1965, learned to train and arm local security forces just as they had in Nicaragua and Haiti. The Vietcong did not represent the enemy's "center of gravity"; Marine reaction forces were to be ready to take on North Vietnamese army and Vietcong units when they assembled in the jungles and mountains to move eastward toward the population centers, but that was to be only one type of operation in a "balanced strategy." Lieutenant General Krulak put it this way:

> The Marines' view of how to fight the war . . . could be articulated in three convergent declarations:
>
> (1) Put the primary emphasis on pacifying the highly populated South Vietnamese coastal plain. In conjunction with South Vietnamese forces, protect the people from the guerrillas so they will not be forced to provide the enemy with rice, intelligence and sanctuary. Expand the pacified areas as rapidly as possible, but only as fast as they are secure, tranquil and effectively policed by Vietnamese . . . forces.
> (2) Degrade the North Vietnamese ability to fight by cutting off their military substance before it ever leaves North Vietnam ports of entry.
> (3) In coordination with South Vietnamese forces, move out of our protected . . . areas when a clear opportunity exists to engage the VC Mainforce or North Vietnamese units on terms favorable to ourselves.[5]

By emphasizing pacification over attrition, the Marines hoped to engender a close, mutually beneficial working relationship with the South Vietnamese army, and the Popular Forces and Regional Forces, local militia units known by the Marines as "Ruff Puffs," neither of which had received sufficient weapons or training. Morale was at a decidedly low ebb among these units, and desertion rates were high. The Marines' heavier weaponry, mobility, and excellent small-unit infantry skills would nicely complement the South Vietnamese knowledge of the terrain and of the rhythms of everyday life.

Marine pacification ideas were first employed eight miles north of the Da Nang airfield in the village of Le My. Le My was indisputably "Indian country." Two VC platoons had lived in the village for years.

They had developed an impressive cave, tunnel, and fortification system; conducted regular indoctrination sessions for the villagers; and recruited many young men and women of the village. The Le My chief would follow a typical routine for a minor government official: he slept in Da Nang, fearing VC assassination if he remained overnight in his own hamlet. The South Vietnamese army made occasional sweeps through the village in force, searching halfheartedly for weapons and VC suspects, but these sweeps invariably came to nothing. The local ARVN commander seemed indifferent as well to the Marines' notion of providing the village with sustained relief from the Vietcong predations. So after interviewing the district chief, another low-level GVN (Global Volunteer Network) official, and the village elders, Lieutenant Colonel David A. Clement's 2/3 conducted an aggressive sweep through the village, ousting the Vietcong. Villagers helped the Marines remove booby traps and close tunnel entrances, breaking down the cleverly camouflaged VC fighting holes and reinforced positions. After ensuring the village was clear, Clement's men began rudimentary infantry and security training of the local militia.

Navy corpsmen attached to 2/3 set up aid stations and tended to a host of minor ailments and wounds. Engineers worked with a group of village boys and men to repair two bridges leading out of town into the countryside. Within a couple of weeks, Le My was a village transformed. It stayed free of VC domination for the next five years. The Marines did not remain, but they guaranteed that any attack by enemy troops would be met by a fierce reaction. It was this sort of pacification process that the Marines hoped to bring to a growing number of villages in close proximity to their three major base areas of Phu Bai, Da Nang, and Chu Lai. The Marine concept became known around the Pentagon and in Washington as the "spreading inkblot strategy."

Among the innovations supporting the inkblot strategy and aimed at disrupting the Vietcong's dominance along the coast in I Corps was the "County Fair" concept of operations. These were joint ARVN–U.S. Marine affairs. One or two Marine companies would cordon off a VC-controlled village at night to prevent reinforcement. Early in the morning an ARVN infantry force would enter the village's hamlets and flush out the Vietcong from their hiding places in tunnels and camouflaged pits under the floors of the villagers' modest thatch-roofed homes. Once the village was deemed secure, the entire population would be ordered to assemble at a central point, where a census was taken and identity cards either issued or checked. While the locals' paperwork was processed, the Marines would provide simple medical and dental care, in addition to food and sometimes even a bit of entertainment.

County Fairs were conducted in all three enclaves. Another pacification innovation made its debut during the rice harvest in September and October in the Hoa Vang district of Quang Nam Province, south of Da Nang. Here the 9th Marine Regiment conducted "Golden Fleece" operations, saturating the villages and rice paddies with small-unit patrols, night ambushes, and cordon-and-search operations, thereby frustrating the enemy's efforts to extract rice from local farmers. Marines, often reinforced with recoilless rifles, tanks, and amtracs, helped the farmers transport the main staple of the Vietnamese diet from the fields to the market. It was very much a hands-on approach, and it worked well — provided, of course, that the Marines were able to secure the trust and cooperation of the village and district officials and elders. The 9th Marines ran into concerted resistance from a main-force enemy unit only once, and those Vietcong broke off the engagement as dark settled in. Walt was quite pleased with the results. Lieutenant Colonel Clement, detached from 2/3 and serving on III MAF's headquarters staff, conducted a study based on interviews with village chiefs. It concluded that Golden Fleece operations had denied more than five hundred thousand pounds of threshed rice to the enemy. He commented that "at the accepted rate of 1.5 pounds per person per day, this could have subsisted [sic] 1,900 VC for the six months until next harvest."[6] As a result of this success, Walt ordered his planning staff to prepare to repeat the Golden Fleece operations during the spring harvest.

Beyond these "inkblots," the Marines developed Combined Action

Platoons (CAPs) to connect with individual hamlets. Even General Westmoreland, despite writing in his book *A Soldier Reports* that the Corps' inkblot strategy left the Vietcong free to come and go throughout I Corps, admitted that the Marines' CAP program was one of the best military innovations developed in South Vietnam.

The CAP Marine's missions and experiences in-country were altogether different from those of the majority of American troops who manned the maneuver battalions in the army and Marine Corps. It fell to the CAP Marines, who from 1969 to 1970 comprised only about two thousand men divided into some 114 platoons, to live, work, fight, and sleep within the confines of a single Vietnamese village. Their chief objectives, as put forward by General Lewis Walt, were to train the lightly armed local units, such as the Popular Forces (PF), in static defense, infantry patrol tactics, and the use of small arms to a point where they could function as a local security force independent of the Marines; to instill in the local militia a strong sense of discipline and confidence; in conjunction with the PF, to provide security for the people of the village and to obtain intelligence about local VC intentions and operations with a view to destroying Communist efforts to expand their infrastructure in the countryside; and, finally, to help the village authorities implement civic improvement projects ranging from the creation of health clinics, the establishment of electrical power, and the building of schools, bridges, and small government buildings, to improved irrigation techniques.

The relation between the Marine squad, the PF, and the other villagers was largely one of reciprocity and cooperation, almost completely unhindered by formal command relationships. With the exception of the Marine squad leaders who led the very first CAP units formed in the summer of 1965, American Marines were not officially in command of the PF soldiers. That role fell to the *trung si,* or PF platoon sergeant. The *trung si* and his *nghia quan* (Popular Force soldiers) took their orders from the South Vietnamese government district chief and his representative on the local level, the village chief, and it was with those officials that the Marines had to work out the details of CAP organization and deployments.

In practice, the CAP Marines even enjoyed a large degree of independence from the traditional Marine chain of command. From 1965 through early 1967, the program drew personnel directly from regular Marine battalions in the specific area of operation where the CAP was to be deployed. Early deployments were ordered directly by III MAF after consultation with the district Vietnamese officials and regular-unit commanders. In 1967, General Walt established a separate chain of command and table of organization and equipment for the program—testifying to its success in the eyes of the Corps' leadership—but even with a more formal command structure, most of the decisions affecting individual platoons were made within the confines of the village by Marine noncommissioned officers. Like the American war effort as a whole, the CAP program escalated at a methodical pace.

And then there were the big-unit engagements. The first multibattalion Marine offensive engagement of the war was fought between August 18 and 24, 1965. The objective of Operation Starlite was the destruction of the 1st Vietcong Regiment, which had inflicted heavy casualties on an ARVN garrison at Ba Gia village, near Chu Lai. The scheme of maneuver called for the 3rd Battalion of the 3rd Marine Regiment to land two companies, along with eight tanks, at Green Beach, about two miles south of Van Tuong, the suspected command post of the VC force, and to block that unit's escape to the south. Company M of the 7th Marines would come down from Chu Lai and set up blocking positions north of the area of operations. The 2nd Battalion of the 4th Marine Regiment would be helilifted to three landing zones about a mile inland and sweep northeast through a series of VC-held hamlets, driving the enemy toward the sea.

The amphibious landing went off on schedule at 0630 against light resistance. At one landing zone, however, the Marines deployed right on top of the 60th Vietcong Battalion, and fierce fighting ensued throughout the day. It was particularly difficult for the Marines to drive through the fortified village of An Cuong, which had camouflaged trench lines connected by tunnels. A Huey helicopter gunship was downed, and a Marine supply column of amtracs was ambushed by the Vietcong, who possessed recoilless rifles, mortars, machine guns, and small arms. Thanks to supporting fire from Marine jets and two destroyers, the Leathernecks were able to push the VC toward the coast and inflict heavy casualties on them in the process. Most of the heavy fighting was over by nightfall, and the remnants of organized resistance were eliminated by noon on August 19. From August 19 to 24, the Marines systematically cleaned out the tunnels, which still contained a few stragglers from the 1st VC Regiment. Vietcong losses totaled 614 killed in the action. The Marines lost 45 men killed in action and 203 wounded.

Operation Starlite was typical of hundreds of offensive sweeps run by the Marines between 1965 and 1968 against the VC guerrillas. Superior mobility and firepower were put to work effectively only when intelligence had a firm fix on the enemy's location. Blocking forces were put in place, and then a powerful ground assault would sweep across the enemy's position, driving them toward the blocking force. Like a great many of the operations in the war's first three years, Starlight involved the simultaneous deployment of an amphibious landing force and an assault force brought to the battle by transport helicopters, with close air and artillery support on call. Most of the combat engagements fought by Marine infantry against the Vietcong took place at the company, platoon, or squad level rather than at battalion or regimental level. The actions tended to be brief, intensely violent firefights with small arms. These fights were often the result of an ambush, or were caused by the unexpected collision of small groups of soldiers at fairly close range. The Vietcong preferred hit and run tactics because they lacked the supporting arms and tactical mobility to bring a conclusive amount of firepower to bear on their adversaries.

Infantry fighting in a modern war zone is never a picnic, but in Vietnam it was an exceptionally grueling business, both terrifying and exhausting. The emphasis on population control meant that Marine line companies faced endless patrolling in search of an elusive enemy, often on the same ground week after week. The VC guerrillas' ethnicity and appearance was identical to that of the general civilian population. The guerrillas knew the local trails and terrain features; they often seemed able to melt into thin air. They could vanish into a nearby village and quickly hide weapons, or hide in tunnel networks that contained kitchens, dispensaries, weapons-repair rooms, and sleeping quarters. Many of the tunnel complexes proved to be hard to destroy. Even when Marines made substantial efforts to blow them up with gasoline or C-4 explosives, the end result was typically only limited damage to a small section of a network. The Vietcong were masters of homemade booby traps, most of which were designed to wound rather than kill, on the sound theory that a wound caused a greater diminution in enemy combat strength than death (since they required care). It was the Vietcong, not the Marines, who chose the time and place of most small-unit combat in I Corps in the first three years of the American ground war. Vietnam was a conflict without fronts. Once a particular area had been cleared of regular Communist units, the Marines would depart. A few months later, the Vietcong and North Vietnamese army would have a new or reconstructed regiment back in precisely the same area. As the thirteen months of the typical Marine's tour moved toward completion, the war took on the aura of a Sisyphian task.

As 1965 came to a close, III MAF and MACV were cautiously optimistic about the Marine war and the American war in general. U.S. intervention had taken the pressure off the South Vietnamese army. Starlite and other large operations had shown that the Marines were able to defeat main-force VC units in combat. Generals Walt and Krulak had reason to be pleased with the pacification techniques and programs aimed at decimating the enemy's infrastructure.

In January 1966, the entire 1st Marine Division was earmarked for deployment to Vietnam along with additional air assets. Over the first few months of 1966, the division deployed to the Chu Lai area under Major General Lewis J. Fields, and took up responsibilities for operations in the southernmost provinces of I Corps: Quang Tin and Quang Ngai. In early March, elements of the division were engaged in Operation Utah along with ARVN forces. Battalions 1/7, 2/7, and 3/1, along with ARVN units, deftly attacked the 36th PAVN Regiment about three miles northwest of Quang Ngai from the north and south, badly mauling the enemy force. The Marines claimed 358 killed between March 3 and 6. Utah marked the first major engagement in which PAVN units squared off against the Marines.

By early 1967, the war against the North Vietnamese eclipsed the fight against the Vietcong in I Corps. Fought mostly in Quang Tri Province near the DMZ, the combat against the North Vietnamese regular army involved larger units than the guerrilla war, and was far more intense and costly. The 1st Marine Division's maneuver battalions conducted many battalion-sized operations west of the Chu Lai TAOR (tactical area of responsibility), but made precious little contact in 1966. Most of their efforts were in pacification operations, clearing out Vietcong, or providing security and reaction forces in the event the enemy decided to return in force.

In early June, General Walt received some intelligence indicating a formidable number of PAVN troops in the Que Son Valley, near the border of Quang Nam and Quang Tin provinces. The valley ran about twenty-four miles east to west, and was among the most fertile rice-growing regions in of all Vietnam. With sixty thousand inhabitants, it was thought by the ARVN leadership to be a key piece of terrain in the Corps area. Walt deployed seven reconnaissance teams to the valley by parachute and helicopter in so-called Stingray operations. Their objective was to set up camouflaged observation posts in the hills and collect intelligence on enemy dispositions. If they spotted large clusters of PAVN or VC main-force troops, the reconnaissance battalion commander could call in jets, artillery, or an infantry helicopter assault.

One such team was led by Sergeant Jimmie Ray Howard, a former football star and Korean War veteran. Howard's twenty-man team set up on the crest of a fifteen-hundred-foot hill called Nui Vu, twenty-five

miles west of Chu Lai, on June 13. For two days it called in one successful fire mission after another on PAVN units. On the night of June 15, a
clearly well-trained and disciplined battalion of enemy troops attacked
Howard's small perimeter on a rock-strewn knoll atop the hill. Thus
began one of the great small-unit actions of the Vietnam War.

As luck would have it, a Green Beret patrol that was also in the area
was able to see the PAVN unit prepare for the assault, and had relayed a
warning to Howard. The initial multicompany assault against the Marines' perimeter was repulsed, thanks to good Marine marksmanship,
Howard's expert defensive preparations, and a bit of luck. After regrouping, the North Vietnamese tried again. Once more the Marines pre-
served the integrity of their small perimeter, but after the second
onslaught, every one of the twenty Leathernecks was either killed or
wounded. A rifle round had ricocheted into Howard's back, but he refused morphine and continued to encourage his men. In an inspiring
display of grace under pressure, the sergeant called in a welter of supporting fires from jets and helicopter gunships under the eerie light of
flares. Private First Class Joseph Kosoglow, one of the survivors, recalled
the scene at about 0100 on June 16: "There were so many [enemy
troops] it was like an anthill ripped apart. They were all over the place."[7]

More attacks followed, but they diminished in intensity as a result of
the fire from the gunships. At 0300, the North Vietnamese turned back a
couple of H-34 transport helos with machine-gun fire, but Howard, now
temporarily paralyzed, continued to direct the movement of his men,
while calling in air strikes. When their ammo ran low, Howard ordered
his Marines to toss rocks, and to fire single rounds at any PAVN soldier
who exposed himself in the act of firing in the direction of the noise
caused by the rock as it landed. This technique worked to great effect.

By noon the next day, a rescue force had pummeled the remaining
PAVN troops, and the battle of Howard's Hill was over. Howard was
awarded his fourth Purple Heart and the Medal of Honor. Most of the
survivors received the Silver Star. One helo pilot recalled Howard's performance with admiration. "He'd say, 'You gotta get this guy because

he's hurting my boys.' He was really impressive. His whole concern was for his men."[8]

It happened that the multibattalion operation that was meant to follow the reconnaissance operations in mid-June came to an abrupt end just after it commenced, as a major political crisis, the Struggle Movement, erupted in Hue when a popular and effective ARVN general was relieved by the country's governing council. Fighting broke out among various factions within the South Vietnamese army, and General Walt was instrumental in restoring order. He had to threaten the use of force to do so. It was just as well that Operation Kansas was halted. For in late June, the commandant of the North Vietnamese army, General Vo Nguyen Giap, apparently attempting to take advantage of the Struggle Movement crisis, began to move forces into Quang Tri Province in alarmingly large numbers. III MAF moved up reinforcements for the 4th Marines, whose command post was near the DMZ at Dong Ha. Between July 4 and 14, reconnaissance patrols in the vicinity of the Rockpile, a seven-hundred-foot hill sixteen miles west of Dong Ha, found hundreds of PAVN fighting holes dug into the earth. A series of reconnaissance units had to be extracted under fire from PAVN units that were well equipped with AK-47 rifles and full combat gear.

All of this activity led General Walt to initiate Operation Hastings, the first major encounter between sizable Marine and North Vietnamese army units in Quang Tri. Hastings initially involved four maneuver battalions, organized as Task Force Delta, under Brigadier General Lowell English. Hastings got off to a rough start. The scheme of maneuver called for the 3rd Battalion, 4th Marines to set up blocking positions at the southwest end of the Ngan Valley, while three miles to the northwest 2/4 would helo assault into the valley's mouth, then sweep southwest, driving the enemy forces in the valley toward the 3rd Battalion, 4th Marines. Both battalions landed against light resistance, but two CH-46 transport helos collided and crashed as they approached one LZ. Another hit a tree and crashed. Then the PAVN shot down a fourth Sea Knight, killing thirteen Marines. So it was that the Ngan Valley was christened "Helicopter Valley."

The 2nd Battalion, 4th Marines advanced at a snail's pace toward 3/4. The terrain was worse than the enemy, for the vegetation was so thick that the Marines couldn't see beyond a couple of feet, and had to rely on compass readings. It was a steaming day, with no breeze and close to 100 percent humidity. The 3rd Battalion ran into a numerically superior enemy force and fought an intense battle for three full hours in defense before the PAVN broke off. One Marine died and five were evacuated with wounds. Another thirty or so sustained minor wounds and stayed with the battalion. The PAVN lost the engagement; seventy-nine of their troops were killed.

The next day, General English shifted the direction of the sweep to the northeast. Company K was charged with destroying the downed helos in the valley. As his Marines did so, they sustained a multiwave enemy infantry assault preceded by a mortar barrage. Close to a thousand enemy troops swarmed into the Marines' line. A tough staff sergeant from Boston, John J. McGinty, recalled the intensity of the action: "We just couldn't kill them fast enough."[9] Captain Robert Modrzejewski made a Herculean effort to bring the fire of his other two platoons to bear on the attackers. Well-placed napalm from fighter-bombers killed twenty enemy soldiers in a matter of seconds. Then forty more were killed when another fiery bomb hit its mark. The fighting went on for four hours unabated, until Company L, 3/4 could position itself on the high ground and drive off the attacking enemy. Captain Modrzejewski won the Medal of Honor for his superb leadership that day. So did Staff Sergeant McGinty. His citation for America's highest award for valor in combat tells the story:

> With each successive human wave which assaulted the 32-man platoon during the four-hour battle, . . . McGinty rallied his men to beat off the enemy. In one bitter assault two of the squads became separated from the remainder of the platoon. With complete disregard for his safety, . . . McGinty charged through intense automatic-weapons and mortar fire

to their position. . . . Finding 20 men wounded and the medical man killed, he quickly reloaded . . . magazines and weapons for the wounded men and directed their fire. . . . Although he was painfully wounded as he moved to care for the disabled men, he continued to . . . direct their fire. . . . When the enemy tried to outflank his position, he killed five of them at point-blank range with his pistol. When they again seemed on the verge of overrunning the small force, he skillfully adjusted artillery and air strikes within 50 yards of his position. This destructive power routed the enemy, who left an estimated 500 bodies on the battlefield.[10]

Casualties from this fight were heavy. Company K lost fourteen dead and forty-nine wounded; McGinty's trapped platoon alone lost eight dead and fourteen wounded.

Hastings continued through August 3, with intense fighting—some of it carried out under heavy artillery fire from the enemy's excellent Chinese howitzers, but the worst of it was over by July 26. Marine intelligence wasn't sure whether the North Vietnamese army's 324B Division had retreated back north or slipped into the remote jungle to the west. One thing was clear: the Marines faced, in effect, a new war for control of the DMZ. In Hastings, for the first time in Marine history, entire battalions had been moved in and out of battle exclusively by helicopter. And it also meant that new strategic conundrums existed. Documents on PAVN dead suggested that the ultimate objective of the 324B Division had been to penetrate corridors northeast and northwest of the Rockpile and then to invest several cities on the coast. Should the Marines reinforce their strongpoints at Dong Ha and Cam Lo and try to crush the PAVN ambitions in Quang Tri, or conduct defensive operations against those units while it focused on the pacification war along the coast? MACV in Saigon, for its part, put pressure on III MAF to build up strength in Quang Tri, as it had indications that two more full PAVN divisions were about to infiltrate.

The pressure from MACV resulted in the continuation of Hastings by a different name. Operation Prairie began on August 3 and continued unabated until January 31, 1967. Most of the fighting happened on the same ground as Hastings—around the Rockpile. At its height, it involved seven of the III MAF's eighteen infantry battalions. The first major action involved a recon team and a platoon from 2/4. As they attempted a helicopter withdrawal, about three hundred PAVN troops assaulted the thirty-two-man Marine force. The enemy got in so close that no artillery support was possible. A relief force from Dong Ha saved the day. Five Marines had died; fifty-three enemy bodies were counted. Nine days later, on August 17, 2/4 ran into a bunker complex west of Cam Lo and killed ninety-three North Vietnamese. Tanks proved indispensable in blowing the concrete bunkers. When Prairie was over, the enemy body count totaled 824.

The Marines came to respect the professionalism of the North Vietnamese army that came down the trail looking for a fight. They were disciplined, well equipped, and well trained. A Marine rifleman named John Muir recounted a savage attack his company endured near Dong Ha in July 1966:

> They put artillery up above us and were shooting down right on top of us. Rockets, machine-gun fire, rifle fire, everything you want. It was all point-blank.
>
> Helicopters kept resupplying us. They would take a quick low pass at the top of the hill and zoom by there, throwing out water and ammunition, grabbing as many wounded as they could. . . . We really didn't think about the future. I had no expectation of getting out of there alive. . . . I had written us off. People were too tired to cry. . . . Sometimes [the NVA would] come on a dead run hollering and screaming. Usually they came in a well-organized, well-controlled assault. We knew we were up against professionals; we knew we were up against some good ones.[11]

By mid-October 1966, the Marine presence in I Corps had grown to sixty thousand. The three enclave TAORs consisted of eighteen hundred square miles. About 950,000 Vietnamese lived inside their protective rings. Since deploying in March 1965, the Marines had conducted 150 operations of battalion size or greater. Smaller units had conducted two hundred thousand patrols and ambush operations. III MAF claimed four thousand guerrillas and seventy-three hundred PAVN and main-force Vietcong killed. President Johnson remarked at this time that he saw "a light at the end of what had been a long and lonely tunnel."[12] Yet the enemy's will was undiminished, and he was more than able to replenish his losses with fresh troops from the North. The interdiction campaign to halt the flow of supplies into the South through the Ho Chi Minh Trail was failing. Along the trail, the resilience and resourcefulness of PAVN logistics specialists triumphed over high-tech sensors, highly destructive ordnance, and superb air force and navy pilots. Furthermore, some of the early gains in the pacified villages were lost, as more and more Marines were drawn away from village patrolling to fight regular enemy units in the jungles and mountains to the west of the coastal plains.

In short, the war was being neither lost nor won. It was only expanding, growing in intensity. No one knew how long the enemy could match American resources, yet a naive confidence prevailed in Saigon and Washington. The North had to crack, or so it was hoped.

In mid-April 1967, the field commander reported haughtily, "We'll just go on bleeding them until Hanoi wakes up to the fact that they have bled their country to the point of national disaster for generations. Then they will have to reassess their position."[13] There was more than a little irony in the statement. Within a year, it was the United States that had done the reassessment: victory over Communism in South Vietnam was no longer the goal. From April 1968 on, Washington sought a reduction in military operations while avoiding outright defeat. By that point, a great deal more blood had been spilled. Under enormous pressure from an increasingly strident antiwar movement, President Johnson decided that too much of that blood had been American. And a very high percentage of that blood was shed by U.S. Marines.

In 1967, the war in I Corps would become the big show, and more Americans would die there than in any of the other three tactical zones of South Vietnam. The Vietcong continued to contest Marine occupation of the An Hoa basin in Quang Nam, rich in rice and coal production. Near the DMZ, MACV intelligence reported fresh regiments poised to strike. Having lost a thousand men killed in Hastings, the North Vietnamese army came back in force early in 1967 to the same battleground. By the end of Hastings II on March 18, another 690 had been killed, and 20 taken prisoner. Marine losses in the forty-six-day operation were 93 dead and 483 wounded.

Down south in Quang Nam's An Hoa basin, a three-day battle ending on March 22 cost the Vietcong 118 dead. The 2nd Battalion, 5th Marines lost 5 Marines, with another 55 wounded. The kill ratio was always much better in the war in the South, where there was no enemy artillery to fear, and most combat was at the platoon or company level. Yet it was here in the endless patrolling under the merciless tropical sun that so many Marine infantrymen lost their illusions about war and their respect for the strange and mysterious people they were supposed to be saving. "I knew we were in big trouble," said Fred Haynes, a high-ranking III MAF staff officer in mid-1967, "when I had to preside over the courts-martial of two young Marines who had lost control of themselves and vented their frustration by killing two Vietnamese civilians and were trying to cover it up." According to Haynes, both young Marines had done very well in high school and in the Corps. They had no previous disciplinary problems and had, in fact, been leaders among their peers. Ultimately, they were convicted of murder.[14]

The small-unit pacification war placed extraordinary pressures on infantry soldiers. Many became depressed and angry, a condition thought by the French to be unique to the Vietnamese bush—*le cafard*, it was called—the cockroach. Marine lieutenant Philip Caputo suffered from its effects. He recalled in *Rumor of War* the type of combat that brought out *le cafard*: "There was no pattern to these patrols and operations. Without a front, flanks or rear, we fought a formless war against a formless enemy who evaporated like the morning jungle mists, only to materialize in some unexpected place. . . . most of the time nothing happened, but when something did, it happened instantaneously and without warning."[15]

In early 1967, the Marines met the North Vietnamese in force on a remote plateau in the northwestern corner of South Vietnam called Khe Sanh. For months, Westmoreland had pressed Walt to protect the small base used by U.S. Special Forces and GVN regional forces and defended by one Marine battalion. The base lay astride the main east-west artery from the mountains to the sea in northern Quang Tri Province. Just four miles from Laos and fourteen from the DMZ, MACV saw it as the ideal jumping-off point for operations into Laos to cut off troop infiltration. The trouble was, Washington was yet to permit ground combat in that "neutral" country. It was nonetheless important for recon operations to the west. And it just might be the place to lure the enemy into a multidivision conventional battle.

Walt and HQMC were reluctant to deploy a big force so far west permanently, and resisted Westmoreland's pressure. They favored mobile reaction forces in the area. In any case, the North Vietnamese moved into the region in strength in mid-March, triggering a series of fights for the hills surrounding the base. A platoon of Company E, 2nd Battalion, 9th Marines was ambushed while on patrol on March 16. A relief effort came under intense fire from well-camouflaged PAVN troops. Nineteen Marines died and fifty-nine were wounded. The 3rd Marine Division HQ responded to increased enemy pressure by bringing in tanks and Ontos vehicles, with their six 106mm recoilless rifles, to the base via Route 9. On April 24, a small Marine force was decimated when it attempted to reach the crest of Hill 861—a place thought to be clear of enemy troops. Then a two-platoon reaction force was pinned down and had to fight it out through a hellish night. Supporting artillery fire from the base saved the day. From April 25 until May 11, several Marine battalions bloodied themselves in costly assaults on Hills 861 and 881S. The latter hill was particularly formidable, as each of its two knolls had an independent, well-fortified strongpoint connected by linear defenses between the knolls. There were six mortar pits linked by communications wire with the main command post. In the initial assault 43 Marines were killed. It took almost four days to wrest the hill from the enemy. By the end of the fight, 155 Marines had died, and 425 were wounded. Enemy casualties were estimated at 940.

Responding to the increased activity of the enemy, Westmoreland ordered army units into southern I Corps. The idea was to free up the Marines' entire 3rd Division to battle the North Vietnamese regular army units near the DMZ. The 1st Marine Division would concentrate its operations in Thua Thien and Quang Nam provinces. The 196th Brigade, under U.S. Army brigadier general Richard Knowles, arrived in Chu Lai on April 9. Other army units followed. On April 26, Task Force Oregon took over responsibility for the entire Chu Lai area, albeit under III MAF command.

Meanwhile, the 5th Marines of the 1st Division conducted operations in April in the last remaining stronghold between Chu Lai and Da Nang—the Que Son Valley, just south of the ridge that forms the border between Quang Nam and Quang Tin provinces. After about a month of fighting, the 5th Marines claimed 282 confirmed enemy killed; 290 probably killed, and 34 taken prisoner. The enemy appeared to have left the area. But appearances in Vietnam were deceptive. The Marines had punished main-force VC and guerrilla units there in Operations Harvest Moon (December 1966) and Colorado (August 1966).

Toward the end of spring, Lieutenant General Robert Cushman succeeded Lieutenant General Walt as commander of III MAF. Walt then became assistant commandant. Under Cushman's able watch, the Marines would fight their most prominent engagements of the Vietnam War, the battle of Khe Sanh and the horrific street battle for Hue in February 1968. And they would begin to draw down the size of their commitment in a stalemated conflict that had already begun to have corrosive effects on Marine worldwide readiness and long-range modernization programs.

Soon after Cushman assumed command, his attention was drawn to increased enemy activity near the eastern end of the DMZ, where the construction of "McNamara's Wall"—or the Strongpoint Obstacle System, as it was officially known—was well under way. The wall, a source of major friction between III MAF and MACV, was actually an elaborate defensive barrier system of manned strongpoints connected by barbed wire, minefields, watchtowers, and thousands of electronic sensors designed to protect against infiltration. The 11th Engineers had begun this monster construction project in early spring of 1967. By the end of June, it had absorbed ten thousand man-hours and five thousand tractor-hours. The project also siphoned off hundreds of combat troops to provide security and build individual bunkers out of logs, sandbags, and concrete along a 650-yard-wide "firebreak" cleared of vegetation.

McNamara's Wall was despised by the Marines as the Vietnam equivalent of the Maginot Line. As one Marine officer put it, "With these bastards, you'd have to build the [wall] all the way to India, and it would take the whole Marine Corps and half the army to guard it. Even then, they'd probably burrow under it."[16] The engineers and security troops who built the wall were a favorite target of enemy artillery. "Building the wall was an immense waste of time, money and lives. We thought it was nuts," remarked Fred Haynes, who, in 1967, as General Cushman's operations officer, had met and discussed the wall, and Marine strategy in general, with Westmoreland several times.[17] The McNamara Wall was the subject of a very private briefing one Sunday morning in late summer 1967. Lieutenant General Robert Cushman invited General Westmoreland to the III MAF command post in Da Nang. Cushman and Colonel Fred Haynes calmly laid out sobering casualty projections for the building of the barriers between strongpoints. It seemed a great waste, Cushman explained. The enemy was, after all, already on both sides of the barrier: the Vietcong on one side, the North Vietnamese on the other. What's more, the North Vietnamese army's 122mm artillery would punish the troops building the barrier. Westmoreland listened intently, and, in a few days, work on the barrier was quietly terminated.

As the 11th Engineers worked stoically, an undetermined number of PAVN battalions were swarming into the area around the small Marine base at Con Thien. It was called the Hill of Angels by the locals, but Con Thien was no blessed place in the summer and fall of 1967. Located fourteen miles inland and just two miles from the DMZ, this lonely Marine outpost, large enough to hold just a single battalion, lay astride a key infiltration route. In summer and early fall, PAVN battalions clashed with the defenders with great frequency in their efforts to either close in on the small redoubt and take it from the Marines or while in transit toward other Marine installations that formed the area known as "Leatherneck Square": the four corners of the square formed by Gio Linh, in the northeast; Dong Ha, in the southeast; Cam Lo, in the southwest; and Con Thien, in the northwest. The official campaign names for these operations were Operations Buffalo and Kingfisher.

One of the earliest of the Con Thien fights occurred on July 2 when two companies of Lieutenant Colonel Richard Schenny's 1st Battalion, 9th Marines were conducting sweeps north of the base along a dirt road bordered by hedges. Suddenly the Marines came under heavy small-arms fire from both flanks and their front. Then came devastating PAVN artillery rounds. A rescue force sent out from Con Thien, with tanks, proved insufficient against a North Vietnamese force estimated at two battalions. By late afternoon, all of 1/9's combat assets were engaged, along with three companies from the 3rd Battalion, 9th Marines. The 3rd Battalion's firepower finally forced the PAVN unit to retreat, while two companies of 1/9 hustled back to the base, anticipating an assault. It had been a bad day for Company B. Only 27 of about 200 men were left unscathed by the attack. The 1st Battalion, 9th Marines suffered no less than 84 killed and 150 wounded.

The enemy continued to prowl around the base for the next week. On July 5, a full PAVN battalion was spotted in motion 3,300 yards northeast of the base. An artillery strike left two hundred bodies for the Marines to count. Just after 1600 the next day, four hundred PAVN troops were spotted crossing the Ben Hai River, heading toward 3/9 and 1/3, which were in the process of conducting yet another sweep of the area around the base. Suddenly, these Marines were in the midst of an artillery bombardment. Unfortunately for the North Vietnamese infantry, Company A, 9th Marines was covering the left flank of 3/9, and had gone undetected. When the attacking PAVN troops got to within about 160 yards of Company A, the Marines opened up with hundreds of rounds of rifle and machine-gun fire. Scores of men in the North Vietnamese army fell within seconds. When it was over, 154 NVA bodies lay on the battlefield in front of Company A's positions.

Meanwhile, the 90th PAVN Regiment assaulted the two Marine battalions. A harrowing and bloody night of combat followed. Again, the Marines got the better of the fight, thanks in large measure to accurate helicopter gunship support, and naval and field artillery barrages. The morning revealed a landscape littered with about eight hundred dead North Vietnamese.

By the time Operation Buffalo was concluded on July 14, the butcher's bill totaled 1,290 PAVN troops killed; Marine losses were 159 killed and 345 wounded. Yet there was much more intense fighting ahead. In the first week of September, there was a sharp increase in the number of small-unit contacts. On September 4 and 7 Marines clashed in sustained firefights with enemy companies three to four miles south of the base. Then, on September 10, the 3rd Battalion, 26th Marines engaged a unit estimated at regiment size three and a half miles southwest of the base. After tough combat lasting four hours, the enemy withdrew, leaving 140 bodies. An attack directly on the base, preceded by a heavy artillery barrage, was repulsed early on the morning of September 13. Then the NVA began to shell Con Thien at a brisk pace—from September 18 through September 24, the base received no less than twenty-four barrages. On September 25, more than one thousand enemy artillery rounds were counted in the Con Thien area. As the month ended, once again the enemy's pressure slackened, and Marine patrols met little or no contact. Brigadier General Louis Metzger told the press what every grunt in the vicinity already knew: the North Vietnamese were "there in strength and our firepower isn't going to drive them away."[18] The general was correct: about four full divisions faced off against the Marines in northern Quang Tri, and they had sanctuaries in Laos and North Vietnam where they could rest and refit.

Some of the momentum in the pacification war lost in 1966 had been regained, in no small measure because in May 1967, the entire American pacification effort, involving thousands of civilian and military personnel from disparate organizations, was streamlined into one chain of command under Robert Komer, a MACV civilian who headed up the Civil Operations and Rural Development Support (CORDS). The year saw clear improvements in security for many South Vietnamese villagers. Election participation increased, and the number of assassinations of village officials tailed off, reflecting a general trend toward more freedom of movement.

Yet the center of gravity of the Marines' war was the big-unit fighting in Quang Tri. Beginning in 1966, Hanoi had begun to refer to the conflict against the South as a "regular-force war." III MAF would have concurred, surely.

As the year ended, III MAF had 103,000 people in its ranks, including about 73,000 U.S. Marines. About 27,500 U.S. Army soldiers were under Marine command, mostly in the lower two provinces. For the entire year, enemy losses tallied up at 25,452 confirmed dead and 23,363 probably killed—14,000 more enemy killed than in 1966.

In September, General Westmoreland returned to Washington to meet with the president and to address Congress. He put in a request for more troops—and Johnson approved it. Soon 525,000 American troops would be in-country. Westmoreland told Congress that great progress had been made. Indeed, he claimed, "We have reached an important point where the end begins to come into view." [19]

Far less publicized was a speech by retired general Wallace Greene in September 1967:

> In the Marines' area alone we have 1,282,000 people inside our security screen. We must double that number. This will take time—and fighting men on the ground. We have 2,000 square miles of territory inside the same screen. . . . But we need a total of 3,000 square miles. Again, it will take time—and fighting men on the ground to do this. I cite these figures to give you some idea of the problems in the Marine area alone. [20]

General Greene did not mention other disturbing developments that challenged Westmoreland's upbeat assessment. In 1967 alone, according to MACV, some 90,000 men came down the Ho Chi Minh Trail. In 1965, the figure was put at 35,000. This went far toward explaining journalist Malcolm Browne's comment: Each American attack on the enemy's mainforce units was "like a sledgehammer on a floating cork. Somehow the cork refused to stay down." [21]

What's more, the immense firepower of American forces had created more than 500,000 refugees throughout Vietnam. Most lived in hovels on the outskirts of American bases or in Vietnam's coastal cities. The South Vietnamese government was as corrupt as ever. Marine and army infantry grew disdainful of their ARVN allies.

When Westmoreland returned to Vietnam, his intelligence people had accumulated a vast amount of evidence that the enemy was planning a major operation for early in the new year. As he pondered the maps and assessments, the most likely place for an attack seemed to be the base he described as the western anchor of the American defense in Quang Tri: Khe Sanh. The enemy had something on a different scale in mind, though Khe Sanh was to play a big role in their plans.

N I N E

FROM TET TO THE FALL
OF SAIGON, 1968 TO 1975

In mid-January, Westmoreland's attention was riveted on Khe Sanh. The general was convinced that the enemy was planning something big; signs pointed to a multidivision attack on the isolated base, which was manned by five Marine battalions of the 26th Regiment and one ARVN Ranger battalion. If the North Vietnamese could overrun the base, it would be a devastating blow, perhaps enough to break the will of the Americans to keep fighting. A team from the 3rd Reconnaissance Battalion had been patrolling north of Khe Sanh combat base, the westernmost U.S. Marine outpost along the DMZ separating North and South Vietnam. On January 17, 1968, the recon team was moving slowly and quietly along one of the many gnarled ridges that made up Hill 881 North when they were ambushed by soldiers of the North Vietnamese army.

Within just a few seconds, the team commander and his radio operator were dead. The six other Americans, all wounded, pulled back from the NVA firing positions as fast as they could and called the commanding officer of India Company, 3rd Battalion, 26th Marine Regiment, Captain Bill Dabney, whose command post was on Hill 881 South. The team was in big trouble. Captain Dabney had a platoon from his company based on the hill, and it was quickly dispatched to attempt a rescue. With the help of helicopters from the combat base, Lieutenant Thomas Brindley's 3rd Platoon managed to pull off the rescue, but in the excitement of the action, the rescuers left behind a radio and the sheets of radio codes called shackle cards.

The cards were considered important—Dabney didn't want them in NVA hands, so he sent out another platoon to collect the gear. This platoon, too, came under attack from an estimated twenty-five North Vietnamese soldiers. Lieutenant Harry Fromme's Marines withdrew under the steady cover of mortar fire. It was the second time the NVA had engaged the Marines on the same terrain, which was unusual. Since November, signs of increased enemy activity—fighting holes, bunker complexes, widened trails, even newly created, paved roads—were uncovered on a regular basis uncomfortably close to the Khe Sanh combat base and in the surrounding hills that protected the approaches to it. Recon teams spotted NVA soldiers brazenly marching out in the open. Often the enemy soldiers were wearing new uniforms and carrying new AK-47 assault rifles. Meanwhile, the U.S. Army Green Berets at Lang Vei, seven miles to the west of Khe Sanh, were also discovering ominous signs of an enemy buildup in their deep patrols into Laos. A vast array of electronically gathered intelligence, from both the air and the ground, confirmed these reports. There were more than ten thousand enemy soldiers in the area, and more en route.

Perhaps the most dramatic evidence of the buildup came in the form of a group of NVA officers who had been shot on January 2 while attempting to gather intelligence just a few hundred yards from the eastern perimeter of Khe Sanh. Walt Rostow, the U.S. national security adviser, told President Johnson that in the estimation of Westmoreland, the NVA "were massing for another major offensive in this area, perhaps targeted this time around Khe Sanh."[1]

On January 11, a gravely concerned General Earle Wheeler, chairman of the Joint Chiefs of Staff, cabled the field commander in Saigon, asking for contingency plans in the event of an attack and asking also if such an attack might be forestalled by a Marine withdrawal to the east. The next night, after conferring with the III MAF commander, Lieutenant General Robert Cushman, Westmoreland cabled back his answer: two Marine battalions could be on the scene in twelve hours if needed. He had already alerted an army brigade to be prepared to go north to fill the Marines' shoes. And Westmoreland vigorously rejected the withdrawal option:

> This area is critical to us from a tactical standpoint as a launch base for SOG [Special Operations Group, a Saigon-based joint CIA-military command] teams and as flank security for the Strongpoint Obstacle System [the series of manned outposts and unmanned barriers stretching across much of the DMZ]. It is even more critical from a psychological viewpoint. To relinquish this area would be a major propaganda victory for the enemy. Its loss would seriously affect Vietnamese and U.S. morale. In short, withdrawal would be a tremendous step backwards.[2]

Recalling the situation on the eve of the battle, artillery aerial observer Major Jim Stanton "saw literally hundreds of North Vietnamese soldiers in their bright green, easy-to-see uniforms. They were in large numbers, they were bivouacking in the open, they were doing things that made it very difficult to patrol. I could go out and recon areas by fire and *always* get North Vietnamese to scatter."[3]

It was against this backdrop that Captain Bill Dabney asked his battalion commander for clearance to conduct a reconnaissance in force on the morning of January 20. He would use most of India Company's infantry to determine just what the enemy was up to in the area of Hill 881N.

The first several hours of the patrol were slow going. Progress was hampered by fog—it was the tail end of the monsoon season—and by waist-high elephant grass and the hilly terrain. As the Marines advanced toward Hill 881N along two ridgelines, NVA infantry opened fire from fortified positions on four small hills.

Within thirty seconds, twenty Marines were dead or wounded. Lieutenant Brindley's platoon, leading the right column, was stopped cold and went to ground in the folds of the hillside. Firing and maneuvering continued for several hours. In the course of the engagement, the NVA shot down a CH-46 chopper sent in to retrieve the wounded. Brindley called in artillery fire on the NVA positions, momentarily silencing their guns. Once the artillery barrage lifted, the lieutenant rose to lead his men in a frontal assault on the NVA positions.

It worked. The NVA broke and fled their positions, as the Americans continued to pour small-arms, mortar, and artillery fire after them. But Thomas Brindley was killed at the moment he reached the summit of the NVA stronghold, and a recon team that had joined in the assault had been overrun and shot up by the fleeing NVA troops. The immediate objective for the Marines was to retrieve that team, all of whom were wounded or dead. This, too, was accomplished, but several more Marines fell in the process.

It was now late in the afternoon. Captain Dabney could see that the NVA were preparing to counterattack, and he acted fast: he called in air strikes on the enemy positions and then pulled his weary Marines off the hill. By the order of Colonel David Lownds, who commanded the entire 26th Regiment, they were to return to their own real estate on Hill 881S.

Although they couldn't have known it at the time, Dabney's Marines had just concluded the first fight in the longest and most dramatic battle of America's longest war. Within weeks, an apprehensive American public was transfixed by the developments around Khe Sanh, and they remained so even as the war's great turning point, the Tet Offensive, came and went. From late January through March, stark and striking images of an isolated garrison of some six thousand American troops (and one battalion of South Vietnamese Rangers) locked in combat against an estimated twenty thousand NVA soldiers were transmitted via nightly newscasts, newspapers, and magazines.

It seemed to many Americans, including quite a number of military strategists, to be a deadly gambit. The Marine outpost was totally surrounded. The only road connecting the base to the string of other U.S. strongpoints along the DMZ, Route 9, had been under enemy control since August 1967, when the Marines determined that too many men were required to protect the "Rough Rider" truck convoys that brought food, ammunition, and desperately needed construction supplies to Khe Sahn. This meant that the 150 tons of supplies a day it took to keep the Marines in fighting shape had to be transported by air.

President Lyndon B. Johnson, the man who had first committed combat troops to Vietnam in March 1965, became obsessed with the fate of the Marines and the dynamics of the battle, by its dangers, and by its potential to alter the whole calculus of a mystifying and frustrating war against a third-rate power. On many nights during the siege, Johnson could be found in the basement of the White House in his bathrobe, poring over the latest strategic assessments from Westmoreland in Saigon, and the reports from III MAF, which exercised command over the 3rd Marine Division, and thus the battalions of the 26th and 9th Marine Regiments and the 37th Ranger Battalion of the Army of the Republic of Vietnam that manned the base.

Indeed, Johnson was delighted when his staff provided him with an exact model of the combat base and surrounding environs so that he could better acquaint himself with each day's developments. "No single battle of the Vietnam War has held Washington and the nation in such complete thrall as has the impending struggle for Khe Sanh," observed *Time* magazine in mid-February.

No one was more focused on the impending battle than its chief architect, William Westmoreland, who had for more than a year pressured and cajoled the Marine command in Da Nang first to keep Khe Sanh operational, then to expand the size of its garrison. Westmoreland had moved a number of army battalions north to I Corps in preparation for what he plainly conceived of as the war's big battle.

General Lew Walt, who commanded all the Marine units in Vietnam from June 1965 through May 1967, and his successor, General Robert Cushman, couldn't see the wisdom of holding the line so far to the west of South Vietnam's highly populous coastal plains. Vietnam was, at least in the Marine command's estimation, a war for the villages. The area around Khe Sanh, less than twenty miles from Laos, was thickly jungled, mountainous terrain, populated largely by isolated pockets of Bru Montagnard tribesmen. To the Marines, Khe Sanh seemed a distraction from the main theater. As Marine Corps brigadier general Lowell English put it, "When you're at Khe Sanh, you're not really anywhere. . . . You could lose it and you haven't lost a damn thing."[4]

So why did Westmoreland persist in the showdown at Khe Sanh? Both during and after the battle the army general was never at a loss for reasons. He described the base as the crucial anchor of defense along the demilitarized zone. He argued that the base was crucial for cutting off infiltration into South Vietnam from the Ho Chi Minh Trail. Westmoreland also told his senior officers in Saigon that the base would be necessary for his ambitious plan to launch a devastating thrust into Laos, designed to destroy the enemy's base camps. (In 1967 and 1968, of course, such an invasion was not a live option; Washington had ruled out any combat actions in either Cambodia or Laos. Hence Westmoreland's plan rested on the assumption that he could convince his bosses to jettison that restriction.)

The overriding reason for Westmoreland's ardent desire to fight at Khe Sanh may not have been rooted in any particular tactical equation. Rather, he saw the impending battle in the context of a larger canvas: if he did not react to Hanoi's movement of two elite divisions into the area, he would be letting the Communists gain a key psychological edge in a war where psychology and perceptions played a defining role.

What's more, if the enemy could be lured into a fight in large concentrations, Westmoreland could inflict shatteringly high casualties from the air, with his hundreds of tactical aircraft and even B-52 strategic bombers. It was a force capable of destructive power the likes of which had never been deployed against ground troops in the history of warfare. It might very well force the Communists to recognize that their effort to conquer South Vietnam was destined to fail. "In a war that frustrated traditional analysis or easy measurement," commented historian Robert Pisor in *The End of the Line*, "Khe Sanh would be the single, dramatic blow that would cripple the North Vietnamese beyond any question or doubt. It would be the definitive victory, the perfect finishing stroke for [Westmoreland's] generalship in Vietnam, and he had prepared for it painstakingly."[5]

Adding to the drama, and very much on Westmoreland's mind on January 20, as Dabney's Marines made their way back to comparative safety, was a bit of history. In April 1954, a French garrison in a remote fortress at Dien Bien Phu, in northern Vietnam, considerably larger than that of the Marines at Khe Sanh, found itself under a choking siege by the Vietminh, as Ho Chi Minh's army was called during the French Indochina War (1946–54). Displaying great patience, sacrifice, and resilience, the Vietnamese troops under General Vo Nguyen Giap (who now led the entire People's Army of Vietnam and had a direct hand in shaping strategy for the siege of Khe Sanh) hauled large artillery pieces through the jungle and pummeled the French positions out of existence one at a time. More than ten thousand of France's finest troops surrendered; only seventy-three members of the fifteen-thousand-man garrison escaped the grasp of the Vietminh. With the humiliation of the fall of Dien Bien Phu, the war in Indochina ended for France.

The big question in January 1968 was whether the NVA could turn in a performance similar to that of its predecessors, or whether the Americans—with far greater firepower and air support than the French could even have imagined, and with their unrivaled intelligence-gathering technology—could accomplish a "Dien Bien Phu in reverse." Throughout the siege at Khe Sanh, Bernard Fall's book about the French disaster, *Hell in a Very Small Place*, was read by Marine officers and by the increasingly large army of reporters drawn to the siege.

Surely Dien Bien Phu was on the mind of Colonel David Lownds of the 26th Marines on January 20, when he learned that a low-ranking NVA officer had defected, turning himself in to Marines at the base and revealing that an attack was imminent within twenty-four hours. The officer, Lieutenant La Thanh Tonc, told Marine intelligence interrogators that Hill 861, about three miles to the northwest of the base, was to be attacked and overrun that very night. Once that key hill outpost was in North Vietnamese hands, said the NVA officer, a regimental-sized attack on the base would commence. Colonel Lownds and his boss, General Ravthon Tompkins, commander of the 3rd Marine Division, decided that there was nothing to lose by assuming the information was accurate. That night all units were put on 50 percent alert. Sure enough, at 0030 on January 21, well over two hundred NVA soldiers assaulted the Hill 861 minifortress, blowing holes in the Marines' perimeter wire with bangalore torpedoes and satchel charges. The company commander was wounded three times, and his gunnery sergeant was killed. Within a few minutes, a helicopter landing pad was in enemy hands, and NVA soldiers were running all around the firing positions of the Marines, who were forced to withdraw to a smaller, higher position on the hill.

With the help of expert mortar support from Dabney's India Company Marines on a nearby hill, the Company K Marines regrouped and counterattacked, inflicting heavy punishment on the NVA with knives and rifle butts as well as small-arms fire. By 0515, the only North Vietnamese on Hill 861 were dead.

But Lownds and his Marines had little time to celebrate. Just a few minutes after the fighting had stopped, the Khe Sanh base itself came under rocket attack from the NVA positions on Hill 881N. One of the first hits occurred in the eastern sector of the base perimeter, landing directly in the main ammunition dump and setting off, in Robert Pisor's words, "a colossal explosion that bathed the Khe Sanh plateau in a glaring white light of apocalypse."[6] To some of the Marines near the explosion, it must indeed have seemed like the world was about to end, as helicopters tumbled over and clouds of tear gas enveloped the landscape. All sorts of artillery ammunition, some white hot, was scattered about the base, and fires burned within the Marine positions for two days.

At 0630, the North Vietnamese mounted their assault—but not on the main base as the NVA defector had predicted. Instead, their target was the village of Khe Sanh, the seat of the regional South Vietnamese government. There, a small contingent of Civic Action Marines was stationed. They led poorly armed local security forces in the defense of the village. To the surprise of many, the small contingent repulsed two attacks with minimal casualties. After the second attack, and one thousand rounds of artillery fire support, Lownds decided that he couldn't defend a position so far from his main outpost, so he ordered helicopters to retrieve the Marines in the village. The local forces would have to walk back.

The effect of the first (of many) NVA bombardments of the base was devastating. More than 90 percent of the Marines' ammunition had gone up in smoke. Most of the aboveground bunkers had been severely damaged or destroyed. The airstrip had also been damaged: only two thousand feet of the three-thousand-foot aluminum runway were usable. That meant smaller transport planes had to be used to replenish desperately needed ammunition. The situation, Lownds remarked, "was critical, to say the least."

The hill fights and the artillery barrage on January 21 set the pattern for the battle of Khe Sanh—a struggle that lasted two and a half months. Almost every day the base would take fire from rockets, mortars, and large-caliber artillery. Meanwhile, navy, air force, and Marine airpower dropped many tons of high-explosive ordnance and napalm on suspected troop and headquarters positions of the two crack enemy divisions in the area. As the Marines busied themselves each day digging deeper into their cloud-shrouded plateau, reinforcing their bunkers, revetments, and minefields along suspected routes of approach, they were sporadically probed by NVA sappers and snipers. "Thus," writes

Marine Corps historian Captain Moyers Shore II, "the two adversaries faced each other like boxers in a championship bout; one danced around nimbly throwing jabs while the second stood fast waiting to score the counter punch that would end the fight."

What happened on the last day of January—or rather, what did not happen—added another element of mystery. Hanoi on this day launched its biggest offensive of the war. Combined Vietcong–North Vietnamese forces struck ferociously at district capitals, military installations, and all of South Vietnam's major cities, including Saigon, where a VC sapper team made its way into the U.S. embassy compound. Khe Sanh received not even a single probe. It was the Tet Offensive. Most of the Tet attacks resulted in disastrous casualties for the Communists, and they were quickly repulsed. Hanoi did succeed, however, in greatly discrediting the American military's rosy predictions that the end of the war was coming into view in early 1968.

The Tet Offensive ratcheted up concern over the enemy's intentions regarding Khe Sanh: did the flurry of attacks on January 31 foreshadow a big assault on the isolated Marine garrison? General Westmoreland even considered the possibility of using "a few small nuclear weapons" at Khe Sanh—the first time that option had been seriously weighed by an American general since the Korean War.

If the North Vietnamese army were going to overrun the base, however, they would have to neutralize the company of Marines dug in on Hill 861A, northeast of Hill 861 and about two and a half miles northwest of the base. Private First Class Mike Delaney of Echo Company, 2nd Battalion, 26th Marines remembered that "there was nothing but double- and triple-canopy jungle on the hill [861A] when we got there. It was heavy growth, and we saw a lot of wildlife. . . . It was super hot. It was like a smothering heat. Very little wind. The vegetation held the heat close to the ground. It was . . . constantly humid. The fog would roll up from the valley . . . that was scary because we couldn't see anything below us."[7]

What lay below the Marines on the night of February 4 was a battalion of NVA assault troops. At 0305, the next morning, the Americans on the hill were hit by a mortar barrage that led to one of the most ferocious engagements of the entire siege. A battalion-strength unit of NVA troops overran Echo Company's First Platoon. Captain Earle Breeding's troops quickly mounted a counterassault with bayonets, small arms, and bare hands. The company commander remembered that one Marine knocked an enemy soldier unconscious with a roundhouse punch, and then finished him off with a knife. "It was uncontrolled pandemonium," Breeding recalled. The engagement lasted for more than three hours. Bill Dabney's India Company on Hill 881S was kept busy, firing around eleven hundred mortar rounds. Air strikes were called in and may very well have broken up the enemy's reserve battalion. The North Vietnamese left 109 bodies on the battlefield that night. Seven Marines died; thirty-five had to be evacuated from the hill with serious wounds.

On Hill 861A, the Marines prevailed. An extraordinary five Navy Crosses were awarded for heroism in action that night. On February 7, however, it was the NVA's turn: the Special Forces camp seven miles west of Khe Sanh was overrun—and for the first time in the Vietnam War, the enemy used tanks on the battlefield. Ten of the twenty-five Green Berets at Lang Vei that night were killed in the fighting, and as many as several hundred of the Civilian Irregular Defense Group (CIDG) members who were stationed in the Special Forces compound were lost to enemy fire as well.

The fall of Lang Vei greatly increased the rancor between the Special Forces and the Marines, largely because Colonel Lownds had refused to mount an infantry relief force, fearing that it would face an ambush. It also brought to the front gate of the Khe Sanh combat base more than six thousand Bru and Laotian refugees seeking refuge from the increasingly intense artillery and aerial barrages that were turning the once-lush landscape around Khe Sanh into a wasteland of charred earth and blasted trees. The arrival of the civilians unnerved the Marines, who feared the NVA might try to use them as a human screen behind which to mount an attack. Lownds was sympathetic to the locals, most of whom had family members fighting with the Americans, and he managed to evacuate the Laotians and some Vietnamese, but the Bru Montagnards, who had fought bravely and with great loyalty, were denied the right to evacuate to the lowlands by the Vietnamese government and had to fend for themselves in a hazardous combat zone.

Lang Vei emboldened the NVA—or so it seemed, for at 0445 on the morning of February 8, they attacked painfully close to the perimeter, this time against the reinforced Marine platoon on Hill 64, very near a rock quarry just to the west of the combat base. Within fifteen minutes a force of sixty-five Marines was reduced to around twenty—everyone else was dead or too seriously wounded to carry on. The fight raged for hours, with the Marines barely hanging on to a small portion of their original perimeter until reinforcements combined with airpower at around 0830, driving off the attacking force. On one of the 150 NVA corpses was found a map of Khe Sanh showing that, as one veteran recalled, "almost to a bunker, they knew where almost everything we had was, including the positions of our underground ammo bunkers. If they had hit [in an assault on the main combat base], I'm sure an initial wave of RPG [rocket-propelled grenade] men . . . would have decimated many of these positions."[8] The official tally has it that twenty-four Americans were killed in action, and twenty-nine were wounded that night on Hill 64. In fact, the total was probably somewhat higher—many veterans hold firm to the belief that all U.S. casualty figures at Khe Sanh were deliberately set far below the real totals.

By the second week in February, Johnson and the Joint Chiefs of Staff were worried. The Marines were taking a daily pounding from gun positions that could not, apparently, be knocked out by artillery or airpower. The U.S. troops were unable to patrol more than a few hundred yards from their base, and even then faced ambushes. Thoughtful military men, even Westmoreland's protégé, the scholar-soldier General Maxwell Taylor, were beginning to have grave reservations over the rationale for holding on to so remote an outpost. There was vigorous debate over whether the United States should risk using Marines as bait to lure NVA infantry units into the open, to be crushed in a bombing campaign. It was a new kind of tactic. Who knew if it would work?

In a provocative memo to the president dated February 14, Taylor, at this point serving as the chief executive's personal military adviser, argued for an alternative to holding on to Khe Sanh. He felt that Westmoreland's own cables and statements revealed that the rationale for holding the base was faulty:

> *He* [Westmoreland] *concedes that Khe Sanh has not had much effect on infiltration from Laos, and it is not clear whether he regards the role of blocking the Quang Tri approach as of current or past importance* [Taylor's emphasis]. Thus, General Westmoreland does not appear to argue strongly for the defense of Khe Sanh because of its present value. . . . *Whatever the past value of the position, it is a positive liability now.* We are allowing the enemy to arrange at his leisure a set-piece attack on ground and in weather favorable to him and under conditions which will allow us little opportunity to punish him except by our air power.[9]

The tremors of doubt only caused Westmoreland to redouble his determination. He worked furiously at Military Assistance Command, Vietnam to preserve a unified front among the senior staff, insisting that there was no room for negativism and defeatism, and that "there are no advantages of military significance [accruing] from abandoning Khe Sanh if it is indeed our purpose to eject or destroy the invading NVA forces."[10]

While the president and the JCS doubted and debated, the NVA infantry entered a quiet phase. For two weeks, no major attack was attempted on either the hill strongpoints or the base. But the steady shelling went on and on. Often more than five hundred rounds a day struck inside the base, and the Marines grew ever more weary of waiting for a big assault, eating K rations, and getting by (very often) on less than a canteen of drinking water a day.

Keeping the base in food and ammunition proved a daily struggle. A big KC-130 transport was hit by incoming fire and exploded on the runway on February 10, killing six people. Khe Sanh's airstrip, dreaded by fliers all over Vietnam, was a favorite target of NVA artillery. So hazardous was the airstrip that the air force stopped landing its star transport, the big, vulnerable C-130, and began to drop supplies out of the back hatch of both the C-130s and the smaller C-123s. The so-called Low Altitude Parachute Extraction System (LAPES) required steady nerves and a strong heart, as pilots had to bring their planes to within five feet of the tarmac and then pull up hard, as parachutes dragged the cargo pallets out of the rear. In March and February alone, eight transports were lost to NVA antiaircraft fire. Hundreds more were hit by small-arms and machine-gun fire.

While the Marine defenders struggled, an astonishing array of combat, transport, and intelligence-gathering aircraft crisscrossed the skies over the plateau. Marine and navy A-6 Intruders and A-4 Skyhawks, and air force F-4 Phantoms and F-105s—indeed, planes from all over South Vietnam, Thailand, and even aircraft stationed on carriers in the South China Sea—were ready for action should they be called on by either the Tactical Air Direction Center of the 1st Marine Air Wing or the 7th Air Force's Airborne Command and Control Center, both of which orchestrated the air war (not without friction) during the siege.

And then, of course, there were the B-52 bombers. During the course of the battle these behemoths dropped sixty thousand tons of ordnance on NVA positions. Along with the forty thousand tons dropped by the tactical aircraft, five tons of bombs were dropped for each of the twenty thousand NVA soldiers suspected of being in the general area. NVA veterans still speak today with a mixture of terror and awe at the thunder that rained down on them. Some have said the B-52 strikes, coming as they did without any warning, were by far the worst aspect of a very rough campaign. Yet they failed to win the battle.

And what of the Marines' morale? It remained, by most accounts, surprisingly high, especially considering the rapidly deteriorating conditions. Sleep was a hard commodity to come by amid the sporadic shelling, and it was not unusual for Marines to sleep standing up in their fighting holes. The condition of the base, and the Marines' rough-edged, "up the middle" approach to war, horrified U.S. Army officers who visited during the weeks of the siege. Major General John J. Tolson, commander of the 1st Cavalry Division, the outfit that ultimately relieved the Marines at Khe Sanh in April, recalled that the base was "the most depressing and demoralizing place I ever visited. It was a very distressing sight, completely unpoliced, strewn with rubble, duds, and damaged equipment, and with the troops living a life more similar to rats than human beings."[11]

There was constant digging and preparing. Lives depended on it, and nowhere so much as on the isolated hill positions. Lance Corporal Phil Torres of India Company, 3rd Battalion, 26th Marine Regiment, remembered:

> We lived like moles, never leaving the trenches or bunkers. We were constantly digging—it never stopped—day and night, filling sandbags, digging trenches, carrying food. We were always laying German tape concertina wire, which was very dangerous to work with because it was covered with razor blades. . . . There was about a hundred meters of clearance between the concertina and the trenches. We built home-made bombs from 106mm recoilless-rifle shell canisters filled with C-4 plastic explosive, machine-gun links, expended M-16 cartridges, anything we could find.[12]

Rats, artillery rounds, cold food, bad weather, snipers, mortar fire—the catalog of irritants was large, and those reporters who made the dangerous trip to the base were struck by the peculiar horrors of the place. Michael Herr, whose reflections on Khe Sanh take up a good part of his masterpiece, *Dispatches*, recalled:

> Nothing like youth ever lasted in their faces for very long. It was the eyes: because they were always either strained or blazed-out or simply blank, they never had anything to do with what the rest of the face was doing, and gave everyone the look of extreme fatigue or even a glancing madness.[13]

The last week in February brought an unnerving revelation. On February 23, the shelling of the base reached an all-time high: 1,307 rounds landed within the perimeter. Two days later, NVA trenches approaching the base were detected for the first time. Hanoi's daily newspaper, *Nhan Dan*, turned up the volume on the propaganda, claiming that the actions in Quang Tri Province had "shown the aggressors that they cannot avoid not only one but many Dien Bien Phus."[14]

One of the newly discovered trenches ran due north, only about twenty-five yards from the base perimeter. The Americans saturated the trench areas with fire from AC-47 Spooky gunships and jet strikes.

For the Marines, February 25 was the darkest day of the siege. Increasing enemy pressure called for a response, and a large reconnaissance patrol of forty-seven men was mounted to locate a mortar that had been particularly troublesome. About an hour into the patrol, the reinforced squads stumbled into an NVA ambush; when another group of Marines tried to come to the rescue, it, too, was caught in ferocious fire, and most of the men were killed outright. The toll for venturing beyond the confines of the base was great: twenty-eight dead and more than twenty wounded.

The appearance of trenches, the high level of shelling, the "lost patrol" of February 25—all of these deepened the apprehension and foreboding of Colonel Lownds and his troops. Meanwhile, the acoustic and seismic sensors that had been dropped along all the approaches to the base indicated ever-increasing levels of activity just hundreds of yards from the Marine positions. On February 29, Lownds, thinking "this might well be the main attack," called in B-52 strikes on suspected NVA positions just a thousand yards or so from the base. The results, recalled the Marine colonel, "were devastating . . . those strikes caught at least two battalions."[15] Later that night, the enemy assaulted the perimeter where the sole ARVN battalion of the battle was in place, and was repulsed handily.

Was the February 29 attack meant to be the main one? Records of NVA radio traffic that night indicate that a big assault may well have been brewing, but like so much about the battle, the truth remains a mystery, in large part because we don't yet know when and why the NVA decided to scale down the number of combat units in the area of Khe Sanh.

We do know, however, that the attack on the ARVN Rangers' positions that followed the B-52 attacks that night was the last serious probe by a large force of infantry. In effect, the siege was lifted—but the United States could not be sure.

On March 8, a front-page story in the *New York Times* offered a sobering comparison of Khe Sanh and Dien Bien Phu. It was around that day, ironically, that CIA and Marine intelligence sources began to report a sharp diminution of enemy activity in the immediate area. The heavy shelling, however, continued. On March 30, Company B of the 1st Battalion, 26th Regiment fought a three-hour battle in close proximity to where their comrades had fallen during the lost patrol on February 25. Once the guns were silent, 115 NVA bodies were counted on the battlefield, as compared to 9 Marines killed in action. It was the last big firefight of the battle.

The great ground assault that the Marines had long awaited simply never came. By the end of the month, Marines were running patrols farther and farther from the confines of the base perimeter. By the end of March, major combat was finished. The North Vietnamese army remained in the area and proved more than prepared for a good fight on occasion, but the clashes of the next months had none of the strategic overtones of those in January, February, and March.

Operation Pegasus, the relief of Khe Sanh, began on April 1, as the U.S. Army's 1st Cavalry Division pushed westward at high speed along the DMZ, meeting little resistance. The four battalions of the 26th Marines Regiment, under David Lownds, the men who'd done most of the fighting—and the waiting—at Khe Sanh, began to be airlifted out of the area on April 18. They would never return as a unit.

Even before Lownds's troops left the base, the controversy over Khe Sanh's meaning began. Westmoreland felt that the siege would be remembered as "a classic example of how to defeat a numerically superior besieging force by coordinated application of firepower." Indeed, "Khe Sanh [was] one of the most damaging one-sided defeats among many that the North Vietnamese [have] incurred, and the myth of General Giap's military genius was discredited." [16]

Giap and his fellow Vietnamese soldiers have naturally disagreed, arguing that they prevailed by manipulating Westmoreland, by causing him to focus his attention and his precious combat troops in the remote northwestern corner of Quang Tri Province, far from where the real battle was—in the cities and towns to the east. A number of respected American historians have accepted this view, including Stanley Karnow and Neil Sheehan, who writes in *A Bright Shining Lie:* "Khe Sanh was the biggest lure of the war. The Vietnamese Communists had no intention of attempting to stage a second Dien Bien Phu there. The objective of the siege was William Westmoreland, not the Marine garrison. The siege was a ruse to distract Westmoreland while the real blow [the Tet Offensive] was prepared." [17]

Yet Tet was a failure, too. Of course, if Giap ever did have a plan to try to seize the base, he did not reveal it after the fact. Giap, it would seem, paid for his "ruse" at Khe Sanh with the lives of at least ten thousand men, and he got precious little for it. Khe Sanh was a tactical victory for the United States. The Americans prevailed in all the major hill attacks, and U.S. artillery and airpower undoubtedly broke up many NVA assaults before they happened. The diaries of North Vietnamese soldiers confirm the grim hardships of the campaign and the atrocious casualties caused by incessant aerial bombardment. The Americans suffered greatly, but their casualties were almost certainly less than one-tenth of the enemy's. (The official Marine tally is 205 killed in action. It doesn't include more than fifty servicemen who lost their lives in the dangerous airspace above the base, and the Green Berets who lost their lives at Lang Vei.)

The irony of Khe Sanh, as with Tet, is that the tactical victory was irrelevant. General Westmoreland, the Joint Chiefs of Staff, and the president had envisioned the confrontation as a great turning point in a mystifying and complex war. American military power was meant to crush two divisions of NVA infantry and, in the process, break Hanoi's will to carry on the fight against so powerful a foe. That did not happen. The Vietnamese will to carry on the fight was just as strong after Khe Sanh as it was before.

Khe Sanh, the battle without a proper last act, demonstrated the futility of the American way of war in Vietnam. Westmoreland, like many of the nation's military and political leaders, focused on kill ratios and advanced weapons, but his lower-tech adversary would not give in. In June 1968, a few days after General Westmoreland surrendered command of MACV to General Creighton Abrams, Marines began to dismantle the runway and raze the Khe Sanh combat base with bulldozers and explosives. Nothing was to be left for propaganda photos by the enemy. When the story reached the press, it set off a furor in the United States. MACV, aware of the PR problem that came with abandoning a base described several months earlier as "the anchor of our defense" along the DMZ, issued a communiqué explaining that with greater numbers of army troops in Quang Tri Province facing fewer NVA units, it no longer made sense to hold on to so remote an outpost. Holding "specific terrain" was no longer necessary. The base was given up after all.

Giap's intentions in launching the great Tet Offensive are quite clear. The former history teacher turned defense minister sought to bring the war to a dramatic conclusion with one great stroke. More than eighty thousand troops attacked all the major cities in the South and most of the provincial capitals. This general offensive was to spark a general uprising in which the people of South Vietnam would turn against the Saigon regime and join the PAVN and Vietcong to complete the liberation of their country from American domination.

Historian David Zabecki has written that the "buildup and the staging for the Tet Offensive was a masterpiece of deception." [18] So it was, yet in the offensive itself, Communist casualties exceeded 50 percent of the force. No general uprising materialized, and the South Vietnamese army did not break and run, as Giap had hoped. Caught by surprise, the Americans and the Army of the Republic of Vietnam exhibited steadfastness and guts amid confusion and general panic among the civilian population. Within a week, virtually every attack had been crushed, and order restored.

The Communists, however, hung on tenaciously to Hue, South Vietnam's most elegant and cultured city. It fell to the U.S. Marines to enter the city and take it back while the army sought to isolate Hue and cut off reinforcements and resupply.

The North Vietnamese army's assault on Hue was brilliantly executed by an estimated fourteen battalions. Enemy troops invested the old imperial capital, seizing control of the city by 0800 on January 31. VC sappers and political cadres in civilian clothes had slipped into the city streets two days in advance of the attack, and prepared the way for the invasion. They brushed aside what little resistance they met with ease.

The American and ARVN troops hung on to two small islands within the city limits: the 1st ARVN Division held the northern half of the "city within the city"—the imposing Citadel. Built at the turn of the nineteenth century, the Citadel had three-yard-high brick walls that in some places were thirty-five feet thick, reinforced with earth. Across the Perfume River to the south, in the new part of the city, two hundred Americans and a few Australian advisers repulsed several direct assaults, even though the enemy got into their compound grounds. Urgent pleas for reinforcements went up the chain of command from both beleaguered groups.

So began Tet's most vicious and sustained battle. For the next twenty-five days, ARVN troops and U.S. Marines hammered away at the enemy at point-blank range, fighting block by block, taking out one reinforced defensive position after another, often at great cost.

The fighting in Hue had a vastly different rhythm and required different small-unit tactics than the fighting the Marines were accustomed to in Vietnam's jungles, mountains, and coastal plains. The last time the Corps had fought in a city was Seoul in September 1950—and only a handful of Marines among the senior noncoms and officers in Vietnam had seen that action. Combat in Hue was often hand-to-hand inside houses. At times, company commanders had to call in artillery fire from miles in front of—as opposed to behind—their lines, a risky procedure. Captain Ron Christmas of 2/5 was later to say that "street fighting is the dirtiest type of fighting I know."[19] Christmas, who retired a lieutenant general, knew a great deal about fighting.

In many ways, the battle of Hue was a metaphor for the useless suffering of the war as a whole. Until Tet, an unwritten agreement spared the city from combat. With its elegant mix of French and native architecture, tree-lined boulevards, and fascinating city within a city at the Citadel, it was the most cosmopolitan city in Vietnam, and the home of the nation's greatest university. When the war was over, the city lay in smoking ruins. Among its 140,000 residents, almost 116,000 were left homeless.

The most horrific event of the battle wasn't known among the Marines until after the enemy had been driven from the city. The bodies of about 6,000 intellectuals, priests, and GVN sympathizers were uncovered in shallow graves or never seen again. The local VC cadres—not the North Vietnamese troops—had butchered them en masse. Many had been bludgeoned to death with clubs or shovels. Strangely, world and American opinion seemed indifferent to this sad development.

Hue was a charnel house. Yet it must be said: this terrible battle showcased the guts, adaptability, and steadfastness of the U.S. Marines. The three battalions of infantry that fought there—1/5, 2/5, and 1/1— were tasked with clearing out the southern half of the town, the New City, with its large government buildings, university, and hospital. That took close to a week. Then the Marines crossed the river by boat, and doggedly fought their way up the southeast side of the Citadel, reducing scores of enemy strongpoints in the narrow, tightly packed streets.

The Marines fought with stubborn gallantry and selflessness under severe disadvantages: initially by order of the South Vietnamese government, no large-caliber weapons, artillery, or air strikes were permitted. By

February 12, that restriction was lifted out of dire necessity. But there were other problems. The Marines had never trained for urban warfare. Their tactical intelligence was awful. Commanders deployed insufficient forces in the fight. The first company sent from Phu Bai when the call came in for help was decimated. Once the fight began in earnest, in many cases the attackers were far less numerous than the defenders—a violation of a fundamental principle of offensive warfare. Nor were there adequate maps. And the weather was ominous—cold, cloudy, and often raining.

The lack of urban training was a real deficit during the first week. The Marines made some costly mistakes because they didn't yet have a sense of how to maneuver when under fire from rooftops and windows from every direction. Americans were horrified to see televised images of dead and wounded Marines lying in the street. Their comrades, filthy from days of relentless combat, often hungry, and with hollow eyes, couldn't attempt to rescue them until all resistance had been cleared on a given field of fire.

Tear gas was misused by the Marines during the first days, and often the gas blew back into Marine lines. In the end, though, the inspiring leadership provided by such excellent officers as Lieutenant Colonel Ernest Cheatham, commander of 2/5, Major Robert Thompson, leading 1/5, and Captains Myron Harrington and Ron Christmas, combined with the "can do" attitude among the Marine infantry, compensated for the lack of urban combat experience. By battle's end, the Marines were highly competent urban fighters.

It all began in the midst of massive chaos and confusion. As Tet commenced, the 3rd Marine Division was in the process of moving its HQ from Phu Bai to Dong Ha; the 1st Marine Division and the army's 1st Cavalry Division were also in transit. Thus Highway 1 and the rest of the underdeveloped road network along the coast was overburdened with military vehicles and civilians fleeing in panic.

The staff at III MAF seriously underestimated the strength of the enemy force in Hue, and since Phu Bai and Dong Ha were both being shelled, General Cushman was reluctant to commit his reserves to the increasingly desperate situation in the old imperial capital. Army units of the 101st Airborne Division deployed to the west of Hue to cut off the enemy's supply line, but resistance was fierce, and it took several weeks for the army to isolate the battlefield.

No wonder word spread like wildfire among the forces in Hue that a major disaster was about to unfold. Lieutenant Colonel Cheatham, who played a pivotal role in clearing out the New City in the first week of combat, along with the other battalion commanders, had to make his operations plans on the fly with inadequately detailed maps and precious little time for preparation. When "Big Ernie" Cheatham asked Colonel Stanley Hughes, a mustang Navy Cross winner who, as leader of the 1st Marines, commanded all Marine ground forces in Hue, for his marching orders, Hughes offered up this gem, according to Cheatham: "I want you to move up to the Hue University building, and your right flank is the Perfume River and you're going to have an exposed left flank. . . . Attack through the city and clean the NVA out." Cheatham waited for clarification from his boss, but all Hughes said was, "If you're looking for any more, you aren't going to get it. Move out!" He then added in a softer tone: "You do it any way you want to, and you get any heat from above, I'll take care of that." [20]

After experimenting with different clearing techniques, the Marines fell upon the idea of an eight-man team: two riflemen would lay down suppressive fire; two Marines would rush forward with satchel charges or grenades, and the four remaining riflemen would cover the exits, waiting for the enemy to escape. "We hope to kill them inside," said 2/5's commander Ernie Cheatham, a former professional football player, "or flush them out the back for the four men covering the exits. Then taking the next building, two other men rush the front. It sounds simple, but the timing has to be as good as a football play." [21] For 2/5 and 1/1, the grim business of clearing the New City finally came to an end on February 10.

Then eyes focused on the Citadel across the river to the north. The 1st Battalion, 5th Marines became the center of attention on February 11, after being airlifted into the combat zone, when it commenced fighting on the edge of the Citadel, attacking along the northeast wall. Intelligence told Major Robert Thompson, 1/5's new commander, that two PAVN battalions were inside the Citadel, while one more battalion protected the supply route in the west. But as Companies A and B of 1/5 moved toward what they were told was the ARVN's line, they learned the truth: the South Vietnamese units had picked up their gear and left, and the North Vietnamese forces were well dug in and initially not detected. Thompson recalled that from the outset of movement to contact, "[within] fifteen minutes all hell broke loose. There was no airborne unit in the area [as he had expected] and Company A was up to their armpits in NVA."[22] Under fire from rockets, mortars, and AK-47s, A Company lost thirty-five men in less than five minutes.

Companies B and C, supported by two tanks, took up where A had left off. They advanced three hundred yards before a torrent of fire from a tower atop an archway on the eastern wall stopped them. The enemy had tunneled under the tower and was well dug in, impervious to direct fire. So long as they held the Dong Ba tower, they could bring reinforcements inside the Citadel.

For the next two days, the Marines hurled themselves toward the defenders. Even with the help of artillery, tanks, and A-4 jets dropping napalm and five-hundred-pound bombs that turned the tower into rubble, the NVA hung on. When Captain Myron Harrington's Company D finally captured the tower on February 15, the North Vietnamese retook it in a furious counterattack that night. Finally, Harrington himself led a counterattack that drove off the enemy for good.

Myron "Mike" Harrington was in the center of the storm. Years after the fight, he told Stanley Karnow,

> as a Marine, I had to admire the courage and discipline of the North Vietnamese and the Vietcong, but no more than I did my own men. We were both in a face-to-face, eyeball-to-eyeball confrontation. Sometimes they were only twenty yards from us, and once we killed a sniper only ten yards away. After a while survival was the name of the game as you sat there in the semidarkness, with the firing going on con-

stantly . . . and the horrible smell. You tasted it as you ate your rations, as if you were eating death. It permeated your clothes, which you couldn't wash because water was very scarce. . . . You went through the full range of emotions, seeing your buddies being hit, but you couldn't feel sorry for them because you have the others to think about. It was dreary, and still we weren't depressed. We were doing our job—successfully.[23]

For the next week or more, the Marines fought on wearily, taking out hundreds of mutually reinforcing positions in row after row of thick-walled, single-story houses, often fighting with their flanks exposed. There was no other way. The pattern of combat in the Old City was as follows: tanks would race forward toward an enemy position, covered by suppressive fire, pump a few 90mm rounds into the position, quickly shift into reverse, and retreat at top speed while the infantry dashed forward to take out whomever was left alive. It finally came to an end when ARVN forces assaulted the Imperial Palace grounds in the heart of the city. The Marine casualties at Hue were 142 dead and 1,100 wounded. Another 70 U.S. soldiers of other services died. PAVN casualties are not known, but estimated at 2,500 to 5,000 troops killed.

More than thirty years after the event "Big Ernie" Cheatham was interviewed for a documentary by CBS Productions on the Tet Offensive. The retired lieutenant general recalled the experiences of his battalion with the same wry, clipped, unsentimental voice he must have used in addressing the Marines of 2/5 as the fight for Hue dragged on. At the very end of the film, Cheatham appears one last time to offer some personal reflections. His voice cracks slightly, and his eyes betray emotion. "I don't ever remember seeing people with that kind of commitment. They were wounded once, twice, sometimes three times, but they would not leave their squad. . . . These guys were real heroes."[24]

From a distance of nearly four decades, it is ironic that Tet proved a PR defeat. The American and South Vietnamese forces responded with great speed and ferocity to the nationwide attacks, and defeated the enemy soundly everywhere except Hue within ten days. About half the enemy's force of eighty thousand were killed or wounded, and the VC units, which had spearheaded the attacks, were utterly decimated.

Yet Tet resulted in a fundamental shift in American goals. Washington abandoned the quest for conventional victory. The very fact that the enemy could marshal an eighty-thousand-troop assault against so many targets on the same night put the lie to Westmoreland's upbeat assessments, and suddenly Americans decided the war was unwinnable.

A *Wall Street Journal* editorial published just as the North Vietnamese were about to be driven from Hue put it simply: "The American people should be getting ready to accept . . . the prospect that the whole Vietnam effort might be doomed."[25]

In the wake of Tet, Westmoreland and JCS chairman Earle Wheeler requested the deployment of an additional two hundred thousand troops and the relaxation of restrictions on operations in Cambodia, Laos, and North Vietnam. A number of internal government studies of the situation, including an influential memorandum by Assistant Secretary of Defense Paul Warnke, expressed skepticism that those two hundred thousand additional troops would allies be sufficient to reach the long-sought "crossover point," where the enemy would be unable to replace his losses on the battlefield. Warnke and other well-placed civilian defense analysts raised difficult questions about the overarching strategy—questions for which the army and Westmoreland had no good answers. Why hadn't more emphasis been placed on expanding the ARVN's combat role? How could the war be won if the South Vietnamese themselves turned in such lackluster performances? The Warnke memo argued for reconsideration of a pacification-based counterinsurgency strategy and the abandonment of attrition. This time, unlike 1965 when the Marines had argued for just such a strategy, Washington listened. By the summer of 1968, pacification was once again a key concern of American military planners, and of the grunts. The Warnke memo had a tremendous impact on the new secretary of defense, the able and highly polished Washington insider Clark Clifford, who, in turn, had great sway over President Johnson's thinking about foreign affairs. Speaking of the bankruptcy of the attrition strategy, Clifford would later write, "All we had was the advice from the military that if we continued to pour troops in at some unknown rate and possible in an unlimited number for an unknown period of time that ultimately . . . the enemy would have suffered that degree of attrition that would force [him] . . . to sue for some kind of peace." [26]

The coup de grace to attrition as a guiding strategy came in March, when the so-called Wise Men, a group of more than a dozen foreign-policy experts including W. Averell Harriman, McGeorge Bundy, Generals Matthew Ridgway and Omar Bradley, and others, recommended turning down the request for additional troops, seeking negotiations with Hanoi, and beginning to draw down the level of American military commitment. President Johnson not only accepted their recommendations, he announced on March 31 that he would neither seek nor accept the nomination of the Democratic Party to run for president in the 1968 election.

The enemy persisted in multiregimental offensives against American units in the spring and summer of 1968. In April and May, a new series of attacks came in I Corps and farther south. The army fought a major action in the A Shau Valley, besting the North Vietnamese, and the Marine 3rd Division found itself in heavy, sustained combat around the base at Dong Ha against the 320th PAVN Division.

Then, for the entire month of May, the Marines fought a major engagement in eastern Quang Tri, in the vicinity of the hamlet of Dai Doa on the Bo Dieu River. That river was a main tributary of the vital Cua Viet River, which was a main supply artery for the 3rd Marine Division. The enemy's aim was to sever—or at least disrupt—the flow of material. In the heavy fighting in this area, the Marines lost 327 people, with about 1,200 wounded; enemy losses were put at 3,600 killed.

The early summer of 1968 saw a sharp diminution in the intensity of combat until August, when the last Communist offensive of the year was fought. Again, PAVN forces took very heavy casualties. Brigadier General Edwin Simmons, who commanded the 9th Marines early in the

Vietnam War and went on to write many gripping histories of the Marines in battle in Vietnam and elsewhere, has observed that the intensity of combat in the first half of 1968 was roughly double that of the second half. The statistics certainly bear out the general's comment. In the first six months of 1968, the Marines claimed 40,144 enemy killed in action. In the second half of the year the figure was 22,093. The number of weapons seized was 14,744 through June, but only 7,207 from July through December. Marine deaths numbered 3,057 through June, and 1,561 thereafter. By the turn of the new year, General Creighton Abrams of the army had been running the show for almost six months. The Marines shared the opinion of many old Vietnam hands in Saigon that Abrams was a highly intelligent and committed officer with a subtle grasp of the political complexities of this strange war. Indeed, Abrams's performance over the next two agonizing years of fighting in Vietnam would be truly impressive.

Although both the Johnson and Nixon administrations were committed to extricating the United States from Vietnam and leaving in its place creditable South Vietnamese armed forces, American forces continued to lead the war for the next two years. There were notable, if short-lived successes. Pacification made remarkable strides both in I Corps and farther south. The enemy's political and military infrastructure were considerably degraded. The campaign plan for 1969 correctly assumed that the enemy's objective had shifted from defeating the American and South Vietnamese forces on the battlefield to a "fight and talk" strategy. Since Tet had exposed the soft underbelly of the American war effort—public will to carry on the fight was waning—Hanoi aimed at gaining increased political leverage at the bargaining table. Marine planners assumed that the enemy would attempt to draw U.S. forces away from the populated coastal area, and that their attacking forces would rely on such tactics as assassination, rocket and mortar attacks on key installations, and direct assaults on isolated units. Hanoi would seek to demoralize allied forces, discredit the South Vietnamese government, and disrupt the pacification effort.

The war was now down to territorial control. A key III MAF document described the new plan as follows:

The campaign to provide sustained territorial security in the countryside and concurrently to introduce political, economic and social reforms which will establish conditions favorable for further growth . . . is just as important as anti-aggression operations. Operations to annihilate the enemy, while essential to pacification, are by themselves inadequate. The people must be separated and won over from the enemy.[27]

It was not to be. Conflict continued, and "hearts and minds" were not won.

The 1st Marine Air Wing reached the height of its professionalism and combat prowess in 1968, and continued to perform well in 1969. Even the army infantry officers had high praise for the close air support provided by the Marine Air Wing. It was in 1969 that the highly effective Cobra helicopter gunship joined the Marines in Vietnam. Throughout the year Marine fixed-wing aircraft flew 64,900 sorties, and the helos— CH-46 Sea Knights, heavy transport CH-53 Sea Stallions, Cobras, and Hueys—flew no less than 548,000 sorties and transported 895,000 troops. Combined, the fixed-wing and rotary craft delivered 100,000 tons of ordnance.

On the ground, the lion's share of the combat engagements occurred in Quang Nam and Quang Ngai provinces. By year's end, the statisticians claimed 30,000 enemy killed or captured in I Corps. Marine losses were tallied at 2,259 killed and 16,567 wounded.

July 1969 marked a turning point: the 9th Marines became the first of the Marine Corps' regiments to pack its colors up and leave for home. As the year drew to a close, the Marine presence dropped from an all-time high of just over 80,000 to 55,000 service members.

When it became clear that the Corps' days of large unit combat were numbered, few tears were shed over the prospect of departing a war in which victory in any meaningful military sense was declared to be beyond reach. The active leadership of the Marines, along with a highly influential cadre of retired Marine officers who retained an abiding interest in the institution's health, breathed a collective sigh of relief. The Marines were proud of their sacrifice and bravery in the jungles and rice paddies, but five years of ceaseless combat and the requisite expansion in ranks had a deleterious effect on Marine standards. Nonetheless, the redeployment of significant numbers of Marines lay in the future. Still, the Corps continued to innovate. Major General Ray Davis, the tough 3rd Marine Division commander and Medal of Honor recipient for his daring "march through the mountains" during the Chosin Reservoir campaign, decided to conduct an ambitious regimental-sized chopper assault. Davis had spent time in 1968 attached to the First Team — the U.S. Army's elite 1st Cavalry Division — and had come to admire their advanced helicopter tactics and professionalism. He wanted to adapt that high-mobility style of warfare to Marine operations in Quang Tri. Davis planned to send the 9th Marines into Laos in regimental strength and destroy the ample supply stockpiles in the Da Krong Valley. Those stores were thought to be very safe by the enemy because of the ban on deploying ground troops into Laos set by Washington. But now, the ban would be temporarily lifted.

One of the Corps' most distinguished officers of the twentieth century, Robert Barrow, led the 9th Marines in the operation known as Dewey Canyon. Barrow's infantry companies leapfrogged by helicopter into the Laotian jungle hinterlands, and established a string of fire bases to provide artillery and logistical support. PAVN convoys had long come down Route 922 to feed this base area — a location from which they could easily attack eastward into the A Shau Valley. Operation Dewey Canyon resulted in the destruction of twenty tons of foodstuffs and several 122mm field guns, and one successful ambush of a supply convoy on Route 922. Not surprisingly, the raid, which had been cleared all the way up to General Abrams, resulted in a formal protest from the Laotians to the American ambassador, and, no other conventional Marine or army units officially entered Laos from Quang Tri for the rest of the war. The Marines nonetheless learned the value of such a fast, mobile operation.

For the 1st Marine Division 1969 was a year of continuous small-unit operations, interspersed with the odd multibattalion sweep. Two factors explain this pattern: First, the enemy's strategy dictated less-intense combat. Second, both the army and Marines were under pressure from Washington to keep casualties down to a minimum. An increasingly high percentage of contacts made by Marines unfolded in Quang Nam Province, and most of those were within a hundred-mile radius of Da Nang itself.

Commanded by Major General Ormond Simpson, a Texan, the 1st Marine Division deployed its four regiments—the 1st, 5th, 7th, and 26th—in a series of radiating belts to the north and west of Da Nang. To the north the 26th Marines covered the Hai Van Pass and Highway 1; the 7th covered the mountainous jungles and scrub-covered piedmont to the west; and to the southwest, the most decorated regiment in the Corps, the 5th Marines, saw the most activity between the Thu Bon and Vu Gia rivers. The 1st Marines were south of Da Nang, in the Dodge City and Go Noi Island region. Here, too, the enemy would be routinely trounced in combat only to reappear, phoenixlike, after a short hiatus. Colonel Robert Barrow, who would play a key role in rebuilding the Corps as commandant in the early 1980s, said in an interview about this period:

> Those Marines went out day after day conducting . . . combat patrols, almost knowing that somewhere on their route of movement, they were going to have some sort of surprise visited on them, either an ambush or explosive device. . . . I think that is the worst kind of warfare, not being able to see the enemy. You can't shoot back at him. You are kind of helpless. It is easy to become fatalistic, as indeed a lot of our young men did.[28]

Conducting these sorts of operations in a war for which victory was not an option—and which did not enjoy the support of the American people—had terrible effects on combat performance. While "elite within the elite" units, such as the reconnaissance units and many combined action platoons, maintained excellent discipline and outclassed the VC and NVA in combat in most engagements, there is little reason to doubt historian Allan Millett's assertion that "the regular infantry showed signs of slackened enthusiasm and professionalism. Marine operations, therefore, showed striking contrasts between very good and very bad."[29]

A constellation of factors led to decreased combat performance and even a rise in criminal behavior. Not the least of these was the upheaval caused by the gradual drawdown of Marine forces, in which men in units slated for redeployment out of Vietnam who had yet to complete their thirteen-month tour were shuttled from one unit to another. As one Marine general on the scene put it, "As units folded up and left Vietnam a young fellow would go from the 7th Marines . . . to the 5th Marines; then, as one of their outfits would leave, they'd shift him to a different outfit and finally [he] ended up in the 1st Marines. . . . In a period of six months, he might have been in seven organizations."[30] As the war dragged on into the 1970s, the Corps found itself with severe shortages of experienced NCOs and technical specialists. Sergeant Major Edgar R. Huff, who had the distinction of being the highest-ranking enlisted Marine during his two tours in Southeast Asia, explained the source of these problems succinctly: "If I were to sum up the 'Marine Experience' in Vietnam, I would say that the Corps grew too fast and that this growth had a devastating impact on our leadership training and combat effectiveness."[31]

In 1970 and 1971, Marines were fewer in number in Southeast Asia, but the number of atrocities against civilians, friendly-fire incidents, and the fragging of officers increased.

On February 19, 1970—twenty-five years to the day since the Marines landed at Iwo Jima—a five-man "killer team" designed to lay down ambushes from the 1st Battalion, 7th Marines entered one of the hamlets of Son Thang in the Que Son Valley area of Quang Nam, after some Marines in the area had been gunned down by a VC ambush. They executed five women and eleven children. One member of the team was convicted of premeditated murder and sentenced to one to five years of hard labor. This was not the only such incident.

No problem struck at the heart of Marine identity and culture more severely than fragging. Defined in a 1st Marine Division information notebook as "a deliberate, covert assault by throwing or setting off a grenade or other explosive device . . . with the intention of harming or intimidating another," fragging made a mockery of the Marines' abiding commitment to brotherhood and loyalty to the Corps.[32] Forty-seven such incidents occurred in the 1st Division alone in 1970. Only one Marine died, but forty-seven were wounded. Many of these incidents were aimed at NCOs and low-level officers, often by inexperienced enlisted men. Personality disorders brought on by stress and morale problems were all too common.

Investigators found two other social problems swirling around the fragging incidents: drug dealing and racial tensions. The Corps responded quickly and effectively to the increase in fragging with morale-building measures and tough responses. By the last quarter of 1970, investigators were catching a much higher percentage of perpetrators than they had in late 1969 or early 1970.

Racial incidents were on the rise as the Marines pulled out of Vietnam. Blacks were well aware of racism within an institution dominated by white southern males. Thirteen percent of the Corps' personnel were black, compared to only 1.2 percent of the officers. While violent racial incidents were much more common in the army than the Marines, there were some very ugly incidents in the Corps as well. Claims of discrimination increased markedly, and fighting broke out with depressing frequency in Vietnam and at Marine outposts around the globe. The Corps made some concessions that were more than cosmetic to blacks, including relaxation of strict regulations about hair length and style, and the creation of multiracial leadership councils to deal with their resentments. Nonetheless, black-white relations in the Corps remained strained.

Marine regiments and various support and air groups departed from Da Nang and other Vietnamese port cities at a steady pace from mid-1969 through mid-1971. After that date, Marines continued to serve in staff positions at MACV, as advisers to the Vietnamese Marine Corps, and, of course, as guards at the U.S. embassy and other important installations.

For all intents and purposes, the Marine ground war came to an end when the 1st Marine Regiment stood down in Da Nang on April 13, 1971, at which point the regimental headquarters company was already en route to Camp Pendleton. It was elements of the 1st Regiment that had first gone to war in Vietnam in 1965. One battalion from the regiment had landed at each of the Marines' three enclaves—Da Nang, Chu Lai, and Phu Bai. Over the next six years, the regiment fought in fifty major operations, including the battle for Hue and Operation Meade River in late 1969, one of the Marines' largest helicopter assaults in Vietnam, in which Marines captured three hundred enemy troops and left more than one thousand enemy dead. The last American combat units left Vietnam by the end of March 1973, in accordance with the Paris Peace Accords, which included a cease-fire and prisoner exchange. Its fatal weakness was that the North Vietnamese were allowed to stay wherever they controlled terrain within South Vietnam.

In the spring of 1975, reckoning correctly that there would be no American military response, the North Vietnamese launched the final offensive of the Vietnam War: a multipronged armored invasion of more than twenty divisions slammed into South Vietnam from the north. They poured through the Central Highlands and Quang Tri, led by Vo Nguyen Giap's protégé General Van Tien Dung. With the exception of a courageous two-week stand at Xuan Loc, the South Vietnamese army broke and ran in panic.

In the desperation and chaos that swirled around the conquest of South Vietnam, the U.S. Marines returned for their last act: the evacuation of Saigon. Operation Frequent Wind was the largest helicopter evacuation in history. A country was coming apart, and tens of thousands of desperate people were trying to escape death and imprisonment. They were in no mood for orderly queuing. An air of desperation and terror hung over the evacuation.

The Marines of Brigadier General Richard Carey's 9th Marine Brigade had rehearsed a number of evacuation scenarios throughout the spring. Nothing they had rehearsed much resembled the event that unfolded in the last hours of South Vietnam's life as a nation. The evacuation order was issued more than a day later than it should have been, and then the fixed-wing evacuation, planned to take place from Tan Son Nhut Air Base, fell apart when North Vietnamese rockets destroyed a C-130 transport at 1600 on April 29 and the base had to be closed to planes. Two Marines guarding the Defense Attaché's Office adjacent to the air base were killed by artillery fire. Corporal Charles McMahon of Woburn, Massachusetts, and Lance Corporal Darwin Judge of Marshalltown, Iowa, were the last Marines killed in the Vietnam War.

Just after noon on April 29, Colonel Al Gray of the 4th Marines presided over the complicated ballet of moving 2/4's Marines to their assigned ships for the flights into Tan Son Nhut. Twenty-three CH-53 Sea Stallions took part in the operation. Once the battalion had landed and fanned out to protect the perimeter, these choppers, along with smaller CH-46 Sea Knights, supported by Cobra gunships, evacuated 335 Americans and 4,435 Vietnamese in nine hours. Just an hour and a half into the operation, Gray and Carey received the unwelcome news that two thousand people were in need of rescue in the Saigon embassy compound. By 1415 that afternoon, one CH-53 and one CH-46 was landing every ten minutes. It was a mad rush to the ships of the Seventh Fleet off the coast. At 0558 on April 30, the few Americans left in the compound with hundreds of shocked and angry Vietnamese could sense doom. The Marines at the embassy had to barricade the door to the roof and beat away grasping hands trying to break through windows to gain access. Small-arms fire issued from the crowd.

At around 0750 on April 30, the last group of Marines struggled to fend off the panic-stricken Vietnamese as the CH-46 came into view. In a few minutes it was all over as the Marines dropped tear gas to keep the

Vietnamese at bay. A few shots whined by the Sea Knight as it made its way toward the sea. As they departed the tear gas blew back up into their air space, blinding a number of the Marines temporarily.

For America, the Vietnam War was at last part of history. In a few hours, the North Vietnamese were rejoicing in the Presidential Palace in Saigon.

TEN

FROM ABYSS TO
RESURRECTION, 1975 TO 1991

The next fifteen years were largely ones of reform and rebuilding in the Corps. The late 1970s were not a happy time for any of the services, particularly the Marines. Just two weeks after Operation Frequent Wind, the Marines found themselves in the midst of another crisis in Southeast Asia. The crew of an American containership, the *Mayaguez*, was seized for no apparent reason by forces of Cambodia's Communist Khmer Rouge on May 12 in the Gulf of Thailand. Since the ship was clearly sailing in international waters—and since American honor had been so recently wounded with the collapse of Vietnam—President Gerald Ford insisted on a rapid military reaction. As it happened, the response was all too rapid, as Ford and the Joint Chiefs of Staff in Washington intruded excessively into command and control of an operation halfway around the world. The U.S. Marine Corps ground-assault force charged with undertaking the assault was flown into battle by air force chopper pilots they'd met just a few hours before the mission commenced. What was worse, the ground commander wasn't given the available intelligence on the Khmer force it was attacking. The results were not surprising: the assault was badly botched.

A joint service operational plan involving air force Special Operations pilots flying CH-53 rescue helicopters, and a ground assault force consisting of infantry companies the 4th and 9th Marines from Okinawa, was put together over the course of two tension-packed days under a tight deadline set by the president. The attack was launched on May 15 against the suspected location of the captive crew: Koh Tang Island. Koh Tang was a tiny speck of land, three and a half nautical miles long by two and a half nautical miles wide, shaped like a crucifix, just off the Cambodian coast. Although the thirty-man crew was released by the Khmer Rouge unharmed, inexplicable gaffes in providing intelligence on Cambodian forces and the inability of the Marines and air force to communicate with each other effectively led to a violent daylong battle in which 240 Marines found themselves fighting well-armed Cambodians in three separate perimeters. Only superb leadership and a number of individual acts of great courage prevented the Marines from being overrun. Moments before boarding the choppers that would take them on the 190-mile flight from Thailand to Koh Tang, Captain James Davis, commanding Company G, 9th Marines, and his gunnery sergeant, Lester McNamar, were handed a batch of aerial reconnaissance photos of the island they were about to assault. What they saw was deeply disturbing: a barracks circled by unmistakable signs of well-prepared defensive bunkers perilously close to the designated landing zones. And there were antiaircraft-gun pits as well—many gun pits. "It was then," said the gunny, "that we knew were going into shit."[1]

The first wave of eight helos that attempted to land simultaneously in two groups on the east and west coasts of the northern tip of the island were hit hard. Three helos were shot down, resulting in heavy casualties and deep confusion. The initial plan of attack had called for the two groups of Marines to link up, but that plan now had to be abandoned. Within just a few minutes, three isolated groups of Marines were under a concerted and disciplined attack, their backs against the sea. The three groups had to fight for several hours before they could link up and form a tight perimeter.

On the east beach, the scene of the main effort, the forward aircraft spotter team had crashed in one of the downed CH-53s. One member of the team, however, found an emergency radio and called in A-7 fighter-bombers while swimming in the sea awaiting rescue by U.S. Navy craft. But because of the thick jungle and the dispersion of the Marines into three groups, the jets were unable to pinpoint locations of friendly and hostile units and suppress the heavy enemy fire.

As the battle raged on, a Marine boarding party raided the *Mayaguez* itself, only to find the ship deserted. During the afternoon, while the fight on Koh Tang rolled on, the Cambodians released the crew for reasons that remain obscure to this day. The men were picked up by a navy destroyer. A second wave of Marines landed—increasing the force to 240 men, and none too soon. As dusk began to fall, and amid a series of confusing orders and counterorders, the Marines completed a hair-raising extraction, but so intense was the fighting that two dead Marines had to be left behind.

The cost of the mission was high: fourteen Marines killed in action, two navy corpsmen killed in action, forty-one Marines wounded, and twenty-three airmen killed. There was a great deal of bitterness and finger pointing. The Marine Corps was livid when it learned that the Defense Information Agency had excellent intelligence on the numbers of Khmer Rouge troops and their crew-served weapons and yet that information hadn't been given to the planning groups in Thailand. An air force C-130 had reported taking fire from heavy weapons while flying near the island in advance of the assault, and yet this information, too, failed to make its way to the ground force commander. This sorry episode confirmed the need for a crisis response team that trained extensively together before deployment. Indeed, it was seen by many in Washington as another indication that the Marine Corps was fouled up, and had become only marginally useful as an arm of U.S. military and foreign policy.

The senior officer corps hardly disputed that the Marine Corps in 1975 was in bad shape. It stood out among the services for its rates of desertion, drug and alcohol abuse, and imprisonment. It was clear that in the new era of the all-volunteer military, the Marines were not able to attract enough quality recruits. It was meeting its numbers, but only by taking in thousands of underqualified young men. Twenty percent of the recruits in 1972 had been Category IV mental types—meaning of borderline intelligence—and by 1975, almost half of the recruits hadn't finished high school. Just under half the enlisted recruits who joined the Marines between 1972 and 1975 washed out before completing their first enlistment. It was not only a numbers problem, but a critical identity problem: the Corps was losing its reputation as an elite force. In both world wars, in Korea, and even in the early years of Vietnam, large numbers of physically fit and motivated young men had wanted to be Marines. Now the Corps couldn't find enough quality people to sustain a force of two hundred thousand.

The Vietnam War had delayed the Corps' modernization programs for far too long. It needed new planes, particularly an effective vertical takeoff and landing jet that could fly off the decks of amphibious assault vessels and provide close air support from very close range—by taking off and landing from roads or portable landing strips. A new generation of amphibious assault ships and amtracs was overdue, and a new air superiority and ground attack fighter was also on the want list at headquarters. Yet the possibility of obtaining funds for modernization was small in the late 1970s. The only monies Congress was willing to lay out for new long-range programs, as opposed to funds for training or personnel, were for conventional forces that had a pivotal role to play in a NATO war against the Soviet Union on the plains of Europe. That pretty much left out the Marines, as they had only a minor role to play in Europe. Although some senior Marine officers thought the Corps should "bulk up" its forces so it could take part in ground-force fighting against the Soviets, most recognized that such a shift posed a fundamental threat to the core identity of the Marines as a "go anywhere and go there first" organization. Armor was heavy. It slowed down deployments. An armor-heavy force was by definition not an expeditionary force. And if the Marines began to resemble the army, why would there be a need for a Corps at all?

Ronald Wilson Reagan's victory over Jimmy Carter in 1980 was a godsend to the Marine Corps. Reagan, the former movie star, carried himself with an infectious self-assurance. He was determined to rid the country of the post-Vietnam malaise that Carter had talked about but never solved. The old actor did indeed restore hope and confidence to the American people. He was an avid cold warrior, providing aid to no less than six different anti-Communist insurgencies—in Afghanistan, Angola, Cambodia, Ethiopia, Nicaragua, and Mozambique. He went on a major defense spending spree; much of it on nuclear weapons, but conventional forces also benefited greatly. The Marine Corps on Reagan's watch received ample funding to modernize its major weapons systems. Reagan loved the Marines. As he put it, "Some people wonder if they have made a difference in the world. The Marines don't have that problem."[2]

Between 1978 and 1986, the Corps' budget jumped from $4.6 billion to $14.8 billion. Much of the money was spent on rebuilding and modernizing major weapons systems. By 1984, the Marines had an approved program in place to acquire the McDonnell-Douglas AV-8B Harrier, a much faster and more deadly version of a British plane, to replace all its light-attack A-4 squadrons. This was no easy feat, as the Harrier AV-8A jump jet had made a bad public impression with more than fifty crashes during 1979 alone.

On the logistics front, the Marines' supply lines were improved by bringing to shore much of the sea-based logistical system. This meant acquiring two new army vehicles: the M-939 five-ton truck, and a logistical vehicle system designed to transport twelve tons of supplies over very rough terrain. The venerable but aging Jeep soon bit the dust, and a new High Mobility Multipurpose Wheeled Vehicle—known as the "Humvee"—replaced the most recognized military vehicle in the world. The Humvee was vastly more powerful than the Jeep, and it had a wider and higher wheelbase, meaning it could go over all sorts of terrain that a Jeep could not.

Perhaps the most promising new piece of equipment was the Light Armored Vehicle (LAV). This rugged eight-wheel armored car was fast, maneuverable, and amphibious. It could be outfitted to carry antitank weapons, as a mobile command post, or with one of the most deadly weapons ever fired by Marine infantrymen: the 25mm Chain Gun, which had an effective range of three thousand yards.

In 1985, the Marines made another big decision—to start using the army's M1-A1 Abrams tank with its superbly accurate 120mm gun. The Abrams, the new M-198 155mm howitzer, and the LAV bumped up the Marine's mobility and firepower exponentially.

By the end of Reagan's term, Marine infantry had acquired many new tools of the trade, most of which remain in service today. A new Belgian-made 5.56mm Squad Automatic Weapon (known throughout the Marines as the SAW) put a light machine gun in the hands of every infantry fire team. Sturdier versions of the M-16 and the M-60 machine gun joined the inventory. The Marines also procured several new antiarmor weapons, the Dragon antitank missiles and TOW, and more lethal mortars in both the 60mm and 81mm variety.

Much progress was made on the amphibious-lift front. The navy agreed to provide the Marines with a new class of highly capable all-purpose assault ships—the *Wasp*-class multipurpose amphibious assault ship. Construction of the USS *Wasp* commenced in 1985, and she was commissioned in 1988. Four other ships of this class would eventually join the fleet. In 1985, the USS *Whidbey Island*, a new class of LSD (Landing Ship Dock), entered the navy's amphibious ship inventory. It could carry within its hull several assault hovercraft, each capable of ferrying sixty tons of vehicles and men across the ocean at an astonishing fifty knots. It was a major boost in amphibious capability, as the landing craft in use prior to its arrival had proceeded at a mere eight to ten knots.

A set of prepositioned ships carrying a full package of equipment for a Marine brigade was initiated in 1980 by Secretary of Defense Harold

Brown and embraced with tremendous enthusiasm by the Marines and the navy. Seventeen logistical ships carrying a full load of ammo, supplies, and vehicles for a Marine brigade were docked in a protected anchorage at the tiny island of Diego Garcia in the Indian Ocean. A Marine brigade, carrying only their personal gear and weapons, could be flown to a port near a crisis point in the Persian Gulf or elsewhere while the ships sailed from Diego Garcia to meet them.

By the end of 1986, two other sets of ships were added to the Maritime Prepositioning System (MPS)—one in the eastern Atlantic and one in the western Pacific. The event that prompted Brown and Marine and navy planners to develop the program happened on Carter's watch: the Iranian hostage crisis, followed by the disastrous failed rescue attempt in which several Marine CH-53 pilots died when one helo collided with an air force transport in the Iranian desert.

Even before the golden days of the mid- and late 1980s, with their MPS and brilliantly effective new weapons, the Marine leadership put enormous effort into sorting out their considerable personnel problems. Critics pointed to two sets of problems, one geopolitical, the other organizational and tactical. On the geopolitical front, U.S. forces were highly unlikely to deploy anywhere soon, except possibly to the Middle East to halt a Soviet attempt to staunch the West's oil supply. The days of military adventurism of the 1950s and 1960s, the pundits, the defense analysts, and the American public agreed, were gone. So recruiters faced a motivational problem.

On the organizational and tactical front, the Corps lacked the armored muscle and the mobility to fight in Europe, or even in the Middle East, given the attrition rates of both Israeli and Arab armored and air forces in the Yom Kippur War of 1973. What's more, thanks to the rapid evolution of antiaircraft weaponry in the late 1960s and early 1970s, it seemed doubtful that a Marine amphibious assault could be brought off even if the United States decided it needed to launch one. Marine heliborne infantry, the argument went, would never make it ashore, and unless an air assault could reach behind the main enemy beach defenses, it seemed quite clear even to the most optimistic Marines that the surface attack from ship to shore was doomed, because the accuracy of modern antiship weapons was too much to bear. Nor did the Corps' detractors think the Marines' largely sea-based logistical system was capable of supporting a division-sized force in sustained combat, given the demands for jet and ground-vehicle fuel, and the projected attrition rate, particularly for tanks.

These were tough problems, and the Corps needed an inspired leader to face them. The general who led the Marines out of the wilderness and well on its way to becoming the supremely confident and capable amphibious force that turned in such a magnificent performance in the Gulf War of 1991 was Louis A. Wilson. Wilson was chosen to lead the Corps over Commandant Robert Cushman's favored successor, General Earl Anderson, for a number of reasons. Cushman had been personally unpopular among Marine general officers. His sizable waistline was something of an embarrassment to an organization that prized physical fitness like no service. His man Anderson was seen by influential insiders as more interested in technology and systems than people. The Corps, of course, has always been more about people and spirit than technology. A Mississippian by birth, Louis Wilson had performed exceptionally well in both staff and combat billets throughout his long career. One hellish night on Fonte Hill during the battle for Guam, in the Marianas, Captain Wilson held his company together under the most dire circumstances, organized the defense against repeated Japanese assaults, and provided steady inspiration and reassurance to his Marines in both action and words. Although he sustained three wounds, the lanky southerner repeatedly refused medical evacuation. His unit held the perimeter throughout the night. Then, in the morning, Wilson led a charge to secure a critical piece of high ground. Again, he and his men prevailed, despite ferocious resistance and heavy Marine casualties. Wilson earned the Medal of Honor for his work that night. Even by Medal of Honor standards, Fonte Hill was a magnificent piece of soldiering.

Major General Fred Haynes, who had survived some punishing combat himself on Iwo Jima and in Vietnam, commanded the 3rd Marine Division on Okinawa during Wilson's tenure as commandant. Haynes remembered his old commander with fondness and deep respect almost thirty years after both men had retired:

> He was a very tall, spare individual. There was no hint of any excess of any kind in his appearance. He had a very even temperament. He could however, show anger . . . but usually he was simply very forceful and quiet. . . . He was very dignified. Lou Wilson had the manners of a southern gentleman. He had a square jaw and a very fine intellect—he was able to handle any of our issues before Congress with ease. He could express himself very well, but I have to say, he could be at times very stubborn, and I expect that quality made its appearance that night on Guam at Fonte Hill. He was highly respected, particularly by those of us who worked closely with him.[3]

Wilson appointed Haynes to lead a highly influential study group of senior officers charged with undertaking a general review of the Corps' post-Vietnam missions, structure, and personnel policies. The Haynes board, which issued a summary of its findings in late 1975, noted that the personnel problems were serious: "In the past four years, overall quality of first term enlisted Marines fell below the high level desired." It located the main cause of the problem not in broad social trends, or in the steady increase in numbers of blacks, whom certain racist white Marines blamed for high rates of desertion and drug abuse. Rather, "inadequate emphasis was placed on the importance of recruiting high school graduates to maintain a quality force." That's it. They needed graduates, not dropouts. Statistical evidence suggested that a high school diploma, more than natural mental ability as measured in standardized tests, was a better index of a person's ability to withstand the rigors of Marine training and the discipline of life in the Corps.[4]

The Haynes board went on to present goals for the Corps' recruiting, principally to increase the percentage of high school graduates over several years. By 1983, 90 percent of all Marine recruits held diplomas. Three years later, the number reached 97 percent. It helped that postwar demand for new recruits was shrinking. In the mid-1970s the Corps needed to recruit fifty thousand new Marines a year; by 1986, the figure had decreased to thirty-seven thousand. That was good news, for it meant that more and more young Marines were reenlisting; thus, the Corps gained a higher percentage of experienced troops. General P. X. Kelley, the spirited Bostonian who served as the twenty-eighth Marine commandant, from 1983 to 1987, said toward the end of his tenure that "you need quality people, and we now have the highest quality in the history of the Corps. I cannot keep all the kids that want to stay."[5]

The board also recommended, and Wilson approved, that all retention goals—meaning the percentage of recruits who remained Marines for their first enlistment period—be abolished, with a view to cleaning out the dead wood, and that an "expeditious discharge program for marginal and substandard performers be initiated."[6]

General Haynes recalled in an interview that in one day he supervised the discharge of more than 150 substandard Marines from the 3rd Division in Okinawa. "Most of these men were malingerers of one sort or another who moaned chronically about how much their feet hurt from marching, and often sought relief through sick call. Others were active in gangs that were really hurting our cohesion and spirit."[7]

As demand shrunk, supply expanded, thanks in part to the steady increase in female Marines. On the Corps' two hundredth birthday in 1975, there were only three thousand women Marines. By the end of the 1980s, there were more than ten thousand. Other changes that helped the Corps move back toward its elite status took place at the recruit depots. In 1975, one Marine was killed in a pugil stick incident and another was shot and seriously wounded by a drill instructor, causing a national uproar similar to that of Ribbon Creek. Again, officer supervision of drill instructors was increased. To help recruiters meet the challenge of finding better men, a sophisticated publicity campaign was crafted by senior Marines and the J. Walter Thompson advertising agency. One of its key slogans was "We Never Promised You a Rose Garden." By the end of 1976, wrote then brigadier general Bernard Trainor, "it was clear that the Corps was well along the way in its quest for quality. All the indices of performance reflected improved health. Recruit attrition was down; physical and mental categories and high school graduates were up. . . . In the field, expeditious discharges began to taper down . . . desertion and crime went down dramatically. A sense of spiritual rejuvenation was evident throughout the Corps."[8]

The Haynes board's recommendations for changes in force structure were limited but nonetheless significant. It took the view that the force structure should continue to be a balanced one—that is, it should not be tailored to meet a specific theater's requirement, such as the Middle East or North Asia (Korea). Nor should it increase greatly its number of tanks, despite the Corps' having recently won the new mission of protecting airfields in Denmark and Norway to support U.S. reinforcements in a war with the Soviets. The board put through other initiatives, all of which were approved by Wilson, and supported in later years by his successor, Robert Barrow. These included the establishment of a combined-arms training center at Twentynine Palms in the Mojave Desert in California. For the first time the Marines would train with all supporting arms at brigade and even division level.

The tank battalion structure and location were changed to allow extensive combined-arms training. Two additional tank companies were added to the Marine inventory. Each regiment was given far more TOW and Dragon antiarmor weapons. The TOW was vehicle mounted and had a range of three thousand yards, while the dragon was shoulder-fired and had a range of one thousand yards. These weapons made the prospect of going up against a heavy armored force far more certain of success.

As for aviation, the board recommended that the Corps hold off buying the very expensive F-14 Tomcat as a dual-purpose fighter-bomber and wait until the far less expensive F-18 Hornet became available.

General Wilson confirmed the Marine Corps' identity and purpose in a letter of December 31, 1975, to Senate Armed Services Committee chairman Sam Nunn:

> As you know, there have been some who have criticized Marine forces as being structured for only one role, for having too much tactical air, for being too light, for not having enough armor, etc. Because it is so often characterized as an amphibious force, the Marine Corps' full versatility and flexibility, as clearly demonstrated by its performance in the past thirty years, are frequently neglected. Based on that performance as a proof of broad capabilities, the corps should be more accurately described as a ready, mobile general purpose force with amphibious expertise. . . . Marine air remains an essential component of that force, providing unique capabilities. Its structure is solidly based on combat experience and exists primarily to provide close air support for Marines when they are employed in ground combat. It is the only air arm with a truly expeditionary capability, designed to operate in the immediate area of the troops. Its operations are integrated with those of the ground units it supports. This total integration, a pioneering and fundamental Marine Corps practice for decades, represents the finest in air/ground cooperation.[9]

Ronald Reagan's activist foreign policy was shaped and supported by no less than three key former Marine officers: George Schultz, secretary of state; James Baker, chief of staff; and Robert "Bud" MacFarlane, national security adviser. In the global struggle against Communism, Reagan and his men were more than willing to match tough rhetoric with action, even illegally. When Congress prohibited the administration from funding anti-Sandinista insurgents in Nicaragua, Reagan stealthily funneled money to the "Contras" anyway. The money had its origins in illegal arms sales to Iran. A highly decorated Vietnam veteran, Marine lieutenant colonel Oliver North, ran the operation. North's abuse of the system was an embarrassment that fueled the perception of Marines as political extremists. Yet some in the Marine community took pride in his defiance of a Congress they thought lame on national security issues.

When a Marxist government in the tiny Caribbean country of Grenada in 1983 invited Cuba to help it build a ten-thousand-foot runway and started to build up its indigenous military forces, neighboring island states grew uneasy. When Grenadian insurgents of the Revolutionary Military Council kidnapped and murdered the prime minister of the country and riots broke out, the Reagan administration hurriedly put together an invasion plan to take control of the situation—ostensibly to remove American medical students and foreign nationals. The six-day operation (October 25 to 31) succeeded in ousting the Marxist regime and rescuing the medical students. The 22nd Marine Amphibious Unit performed very well indeed, despite having some difficulties communicating with U.S. Army forces on the islands. The major military mission of the Reagan years, and the most controversial, was in the Middle East—in Lebanon. The Marines, of course, had been there before. In 1982, Lebanon was once again highly unstable. It was exactly what a U.S. government report called it: "a country beset with virtually every unresolved dispute affecting the peoples of the Middle East."[10] Syria was exerting pressure; Muslims and Christians were descending into civil war, and neighboring Israel was threatened. In September 1982, Marines came ashore, joining the Italians and the French in a multinational peacekeeping force. The fighting had turned bitter between various Christian and Muslim factions in Beirut. The Israeli army had invaded Lebanon on the grounds that it was a haven for Palestine Liberation Organization (PLO) terrorists in June 1982. This first deployment tested Marine discipline in the extreme, as they were assigned port security duties and the evacuation of several thousand PLO troops, including Yasser Arafat.

A second and far more significant deployment followed, as Lou Cannon, author of *President Reagan*, points out, "in behalf of changing and ill defined goals and in defiance of the recommendations of [Reagan's] military advisors. The result was catastrophe." The Marines were ostensibly there to keep the peace, but they came to be seen as active combatants in support of the weak Christian government by the Syrians and indigenous Muslim militias. After months of enduring sporadic sniper and artillery fire, and more than four thousand recorded threats of car bombings, on October 23, 1983, a lone, young Muslim suicide bomber drove a yellow Mercedes truck full of explosives through a public parking lot, past the sentry posts guarding a three-story concrete building at Beirut International Airport—the headquarters of the 1st Battalion, 8th Marines—and blew the building to smithereens. The explosion had the force of twelve hundred pounds of TNT, and was at the time the largest nonnuclear explosion in history. As the official report put it, "the force of the explosion ripped the building from its foundations. The building then imploded upon itself. Almost all the occupants were crushed or trapped inside the wreckage."[11] Two hundred and forty-one Marines died in the blast. Not since Iwo Jima had so many Leathernecks perished in a single day.

This second Lebanon deployment had begun more than a year earlier. On September 29, 1982, the 32nd Marine Amphibious Unit landed in response to two events: the assassination by Muslim extremists of president-elect Bashir Gemayel on September 14 and the massacre two days later of Palestinian refugees in the camps at Sabra and Shatila in West Beirut by Christians, which had almost surely been carried out with Israeli complicity. It fell to U.S. special ambassador Philip Habib to sort out the mess. The mission of the Marines, as defined by the State Department, did not call for the completion of concrete military objectives. Rather, the Marine unit, under the command of Colonel James Mead, was to provide "a presence in Beirut that would establish the stability necessary for the Lebanese government to regain control of the capital."[12] As the official Marine history points out, "The American mission of presence was repeatedly discussed and analyzed by Col. Mead and his staff. The concept of 'presence,' as such, was not taught in any of the military schools Marines have attended."[13]

Marine infantry hunkered down in defensive positions around Beirut International Airport. Their mission was hopelessly naive. They sought to bring order and stability amid entrenched factionalism born of centuries of religious and cultural resentment. It was a classic no-win situation. It was necessary for Colonel Mead and his successors with the 22nd and 24th Marine Amphibious Units—in essence the same small air-ground task force that today is called a Marine expeditionary unit—to balance unit security and safety against visibility in a highly charged and dangerous atmosphere. Mead had to play a dual role, as warrior and diplomat. The Marine colonel had his normal duties of managing Marine motorized and foot patrols, seeing to it that defensive positions were well maintained, developing small-scale civic-action programs to benefit the distressed locals, and training the fledgling Lebanese army, while at the same time participating in daily negotiations with French and Italian units as well as the Israeli army, which was none too keen about being reined in by the multinational peacekeepers. In short, the commander of the MAU was pulled in different directions. He was responsible for the safety of his Marines, yet he was not permitted to secure the high ground to the east of the airport. His entire unit remained vulnerable to mortar, sniper, and artillery attacks that wounded and killed Marines on a regular basis.

Most ominously, the Marines had to work with a dearth of accurate human intelligence, and their position near a vital Israeli supply line gave the impression to many hostile Muslim militiamen that they were in Beirut to buttress the Israeli presence. This was decidedly not their purpose, but perception mattered far more than reality.

In the spring of 1983, the 22nd MAU's BLT commander, Lieutenant Colonel Donald F. Anderson, aptly summed up just one of a constellation of problems he and his Marines faced:

> My 2 [intelligence officer] can't tell me what's going on in the Bekaa Valley [a vitally important area tactically given the Marines' disposition] and he can't tell me what's going on in Tripoli, and he can't tell me what's going on in this, that and the other. We have no foggy idea of what's going on right outside our gate. We have no capability of tapping that and understanding how those people out there are feeling about us, if there's anything going on. That's one of my biggest problems and that is one of the things I don't know exactly how we solve.[14]

In Beirut, political considerations trumped sound military judgment whenever the two converged. Colonel Tim Geraghty, commander of the 24th MAU and the doomed 1st Battalion, 8th Marines, was from the outset deeply troubled by the "permissive" quality of his unit's disposition. More than thirty commercial flights came in and out of the airport each day. He had no real control over his perimeter. Repeated requests to "button up" his defensive positions were systematically turned down either by higher elements of a Byzantine chain of command, or even by Reagan's foreign-policy team in the White House. It was utterly bizarre, as historian Eric Hammel makes clear in his riveting account of the Marines ill-fated deployment, *The Root:* "Frankly, everyone in authority—both military and political—appears to have known precisely what was going on, and everyone was kept abreast of what might happen. But political considerations—some domestic, some foreign—prevented the MAU commander from taking many prudent steps that might have saved American and Lebanese lives or, indeed, kept the lid on the Beirut International Airport and its immediate environs." [15]

In March 1983, after a period of sporadic violence and Muslim militia shelling around the airport, and a lull in the diplomatic negotiations to bring peace, Colonel Mead reported up the chain of command that the terrorist threat to his unit "increases as the diplomatic situation stagnates." [16] New PLO units were known to be entering Beirut, and the Syrians, having recovered from earlier Israeli attacks, were being reinforced and rearmed with better weapons, thanks to the Soviets. Life was more and more dangerous for the MNF (multinational force). An Italian soldier was killed on March 15, and nine others were wounded in an ambush by the Syrians. The next day an assailant dropped a grenade out of an apartment window into a Marine foot patrol. In late March, amid rising tensions, the Marines finally began to patrol with loaded magazines. The rules of engagement hadn't up to that point permitted the grunts to load their rifles! Even then, rounds were not to be chambered for fear of an accidental discharge.

Patrolling the narrow streets of Beirut at this time tested the nerves of the saltiest Marines. Lebanese kids as young as eight teased the Americans and baited them, tossing soda cans and stones in their path. Some boys pointed toy guns at the Leathernecks, and yet Marine discipline was such that no shootings occurred.

The gravity of the situation was brought home to all Americans when a terrorist drove a van loaded with explosives past a sleeping Lebanese guard into the American embassy, killing sixty-three people, seventeen of whom were American. For weeks afterward, the Marines got little sleep as they helped in rescue and cleanup operations in addition to running a full load of patrols. Early May brought a new round of artillery duels between Christian and Muslim militias, and the odd shell would drop inside Marine lines.

On May 30, Colonel Tim Geraghty's 24th MAU relieved Mead's 22nd MAU, and things were relatively peaceful through the summer months, but in August came a pivotal development. The Israelis agreed to withdraw from the Chouf region near Beirut under a deal worked out in large measure by U.S. envoy Philip Habib. But the Israeli withdrawal was predicated on a simultaneous withdrawal from Muslim West Beirut by the PLO and Syrians. Neither of these parties had been part of the negotiations and neither had any intention of withdrawing. The Israeli army in the Chouf region had acted as a deterrent to violence between Muslims and Christians. With the Israeli Defense Force gone from this critical location, the Muslims stepped up attacks on the hapless Lebanese army, with a view to embarrassing the shaky Christian-led government forces. On August 28, after a number of days in which shells had fallen at odd intervals into the Marine lines, and Muslim militiamen had taunted Marines, pointing their fingers at the Leathernecks as if they were aiming a rifle and shouting, "Bang! bang!," a ninety-minute small-arms fight erupted. The next day, an artillery round killed two Marines and wounded twenty-eight, bringing the casualty figures to six killed and forty-two wounded since September 1982. By mid-September, the Marines found themselves in the midst of a true civil war in which they were more and more widely perceived as combatants and targets.

Democrats in Congress attempted to invoke the War Powers Act of

1973 in order to get Reagan to withdraw the Marines. Political cartoonists captured widespread sentiments. One cartoon by Vern Thompson in the *Lawton (Virginia) Constitution* depicted two Marines in a foxhole at night looking out wearily at exploding shells illuminating the sky. One of them says to the other, "Wonder how much longer we'll be [here] 'keepin the peace'?" Paul Conrad of the *Los Angeles Times* replaced the Eagle atop the Marines' famous emblem with a sitting duck. Syndicated cartoonist Steve Kelley drew two U.S. Marines in combat gear seen through the crosshairs of a sniper's rifle scope. The caption read, "How are U.S. Marines viewed in Lebanon?"

Meanwhile, the negotiations continued. An agreement seemed tantalizingly close in mid-October, but then came the horrific attack of October 23. A Marine lieutenant colonel, Harold W. Slacum, recalled the devastation:

> I'm walking through debris that's about midcalf deep, and I just didn't even notice it. It's just one of those surrealistic scenes where things are . . . so grotesque and so odd that your mind doesn't comprehend, you're still in somewhat of a little bit of shock and I just didn't notice the stuff until I got to the steps of the building and I looked and the thing that struck me is that it was deathly silent. . . . And there was a gray dust over everything you could see, as far as you could see. . . . I first looked around and there's when [I saw] the first bodies, and went to check those that I could see in front of me and then realized the magnitude of the problem. I heard no one, I saw no one.[17]

In the months that followed, a congressional investigation would lay partial blame at the doorstep of many Marines, including Colonel Geraghty and Lieutenant Colonel Howard Gerlach. The committee found that inadequate security measures had been taken to protect the Marines from the full spectrum of threats. Geraghty was found to have made serious errors in judgment in failing to provide better protection for his troops. His immediate superior, Commodore Morgan France, U.S. Navy, was charged with the same errors. The investigation's findings, though, clearly took into account the Marine Corps' position that the entire security situation had been shaped and conditioned by political and diplomatic considerations. There were inherent security compromises in the Reagan administration's policy. High visibility inevitably meant greater-than-necessary security risks.

MacFarlane's insistence that the Marines call in naval gunfire, against the wishes of Geraghty, had reinforced the perception that the MAU was not a peacekeeping unit but an active combatant operating in support of the pro-Christian government.

The dead were shipped home. Finally, in February 1984, President Reagan pulled the Marines out of Beirut for the last time.

Lebanon was a tragedy for the Corps, but it did not derail the Marines' institutional rebirth. Indeed, just two days after that disaster, they performed well in the twenty-four-hour invasion of Grenada. Not even Ollie North's infamy later in Reagan's second term could stop them from reclaiming their elite status. More embarrassing news for the entire Marine Corps community surfaced when scandal erupted in April 1987, involving two Marine security guards at the U.S. embassy in Moscow who had given secrets to female Soviet agents in return for sexual favors.

In July 1987, a tough whirlwind of a general named Alfred Gray took over the reins from General Kelley. The twenty-ninth commandant was a fifty-seven-year-old mustang who'd first seen combat in Korea. He distinguished himself on the battlefield there, and in several critical billets during the Vietnam War. Gray commanded the ground force for Operation Frequent Wind, the evacuation of Saigon in 1975. The new commandant looked and acted like a Marine's Marine. Gruff, intensely energetic, he had a marked preference for field as opposed to staff operations.

Al Gray was a man with preoccupations. He wanted to reinvigorate the warrior ethos, opting for forced marches in combat gear over workouts in Nikes and shorts in the gym. He favored Marine officers with a passionate interest in combat tactics and strategy over those who preferred Pentagon politics or who championed new technological systems. Gray abhorred the intrusion of the Pentagon's bureaucracy on the real work of the Marine officer and corps: leading Marines in tough training and in battle.

Al Gray was constantly calling on Marines to remember that they were above all else warriors. And being a warrior required not only action, but study. He instituted a mandatory reading list and put his personal prestige behind the new educational programs and the creation of a Marine Corps University out of the diverse set of schools that had grown up at Quantico since its inception in 1917.

A lifelong student of military history, Gray demanded that his officers and NCOs study the great military campaigns of the past. His own study of warfare and his view of the complexities of the contemporary battlefield, in which conventional combat between well-armed, mobile national armies was likely to be more the exception than the rule, led to the writing of an enormously influential official publication: Fleet Marine Force Manual Number 1, *Warfighting*. Written by Captain John Schmitt and lightly revised under the direction of General Charles C. Krulak, *Warfighting* is a highly readable primer of four short chapters: "The Nature of War," "The Theory of War," "Preparing for War," and "The Conduct of War." The book doesn't provide a series of black-and-white answers to typical tactical questions. Rather, it "articulates our operational philosophy and the authoritative basis for how we fight. It provides not just guidance for combat actions, but more importantly a way of thinking about combat in general."[18] *Warfighting* is a brilliant distillation of the lessons the Marines have learned from their diverse combat experiences over more than two centuries. It describes "maneuver warfare." It places great emphasis on guile, speed, audacity, and rapid, decentralized decision making by all Marines, from corporal to general. It advocates striking at the enemy's most vulnerable point rather than attempting to destroy his forces through a slug fest, as General Westmoreland attempted with his attrition strategy in Vietnam. The key objective is to keep the enemy off balance by creating friction, uncertainty, and disorder in both his mind and his plans.

Decentralized decision making in war is essential, says *Warfighting*, because "a military action is not the monolithic execution of a single decision by a single entity but necessarily involves near-countless independent but interrelated decisions and actions being taken simultaneously throughout the organization. Efforts to fully centralize military operations and to exert complete control by single decision maker are inconsistent with the intrinsically complex and distributed nature of war." [19]

Warfighting encapsulates the human-centered view of war to which Marines have subscribed for decades:

> War is an extreme trial of moral and physical strength and stamina. Any view of the nature of war would hardly be accurate or complete without consideration of the effects of danger, fear, exhaustion and privation on those who must do the fighting. However, these effects vary greatly from case to case. Individuals and peoples react differently to the stress of war; an act that may break the will of one enemy may only serve to stiffen the resolve of another. Human will, instilled through leadership, is the driving force of all action in war. . . . No degree of technological development or scientific calculation will diminish the human dimension in war. Any doctrine which attempts to reduce warfare to ratios of forces, weapons, and equipment neglects the impact of the human will on the conduct of war and is therefore inherently flawed. [20]

Al Gray instituted some changes in the organization of the Corps' ground units, too. A fourth maneuver company was added to each infantry battalion to provide the battalion commander with added flexibility. Reconnaissance and engineer battalions also received an additional company. More civil affairs and psychological operations units were attached to deployed MEUs to cope with the type of operations the Corps expected: low- and medium-intensity combat operations against irregular forces. Gray also saw to it that each deployed Marine force had additional intelligence personnel.

The first combat deployment of the Gray era was strictly limited in scope. Operation Just Cause, the December 20, 1989, invasion of

Panama, had as its objective the elimination of the corrupt and repressive regime of Manuel Noriega. Noriega himself was to be brought to justice for extensive involvement in drug dealing and extortion.

The operation to bring down the regime of the former CIA informer was largely an army show, but some seven hundred Marines, including a special Marine Corps security force—trained security guards—and the 2nd Light Armored Infantry (LAI) Battalion played an important secondary role in protecting a major U.S. air base and a fuel-storage depot. These Marines also secured the Bridge of the Americas, which crosses the Panama Canal and provides a likely avenue of approach from the west. The 2nd LAI Battalion conducted a number of sweeps through Panamanian towns and ports, engaging in several short firefights. For about eight months before the U.S. invasion, Panamanian defense forces had harassed elements of the 3rd Battalion, 4th Marines and several other Marine units deployed to Panama in the wake of Noriega's refusal to abide by election results. Noriega had been defeated in an election of May 7, 1989, but he refused to accept the result, and attacked his political rivals. When diplomacy failed to persuade the dictator, the U.S. military was sent in to crush his regime. Ultimately, he surrendered to American officials and was convicted of drug smuggling and other crimes. He is now serving an extended sentence in a federal penitentiary.

For the Marines, however, Panama was little more than a warm-up exercise for their new, agile style. It wasn't until 1991, in Kuwait and Iraq, that they were able to show themselves off to the world.

ELEVEN

THE GULF WAR TO SOMALIA

In November 1989, the Berlin wall came tumbling down, and the cold war ended with a whimper. There was talk of the "end" of history, and of a "peace dividend" that was sure to come as the great military establishment built to fight the Soviets was laid to rest in favor of a much smaller force. In the new world order, the United States had no great enemy. Armed conflict between nations would no longer dominate world politics.

These happy thoughts were brought up short on August 2, 1990, when the brutally repressive dictator of Iraq, Saddam Hussein, sent his formidable army, the fourth largest in the world, into the tiny oil-rich state of Kuwait, which lay due south of Iraq. Saddam had long coveted his wealthy neighbor. He had borrowed $15 billion from the Kuwaitis to finance his war against Iran in the 1980s, and had never repaid the loans. With Kuwait annexed as the nineteenth province of Iraq, he would have control over almost 20 percent of the world's known oil reserves. With a very well-equipped army of more than 500,000 men, he could easily dominate the Gulf region.

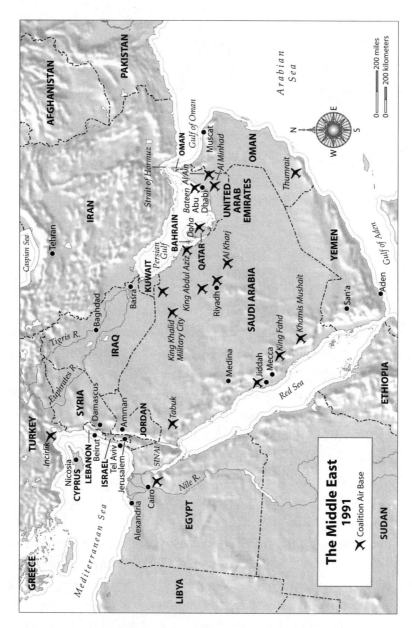

Overview of the Gulf War Region, 1991

Adapted from Michael R. Gordon and General Bernard E. Trainor, *The Generals' War.*
Boston: Little, Brown, & Co., 1995.

The reaction to his brazen act of piracy—the seizure by force of an independent nation-state without provocation—was virtually universal condemnation. The United Nations officially condemned the attack on August 2. President George Bush, who had been reading about Europe's failure to challenge Hitler's aggression in the late 1930s in a newly published history of World War II, wrote in his diary, "I had decided in my own mind in the first hours that the Iraqi aggression could not be tolerated."[1]

Bush, ably assisted by JCS chairman Colin Powell, a U.S. Army general, and his secretary of defense, Dick Cheney, put together a large international coalition, including the majority of the Arab states, to force Saddam out of Kuwait. After several months of diplomacy failed to persuade Saddam to withdraw voluntarily—while coalition forces massed in Saudi Arabia—Operation Desert Storm began on January 17, 1991.

A monthlong air campaign, Operation Desert Shield, preceded a ground assault initiated on February 24. The air campaign was so successful at destroying Saddam's command and control and degrading his armed forces that the ground war lasted only a hundred hours. By the time of the cease-fire, Coalition forces had liberated Kuwait and destroyed about half of Iraq's military capability. Saddam, however, remained in power. The decision not to press forward and remove him would haunt the United States and eventually lead to a second Gulf war.

The Marine Corps played a critical and distinguished role in the first Persian Gulf War. Almost half of the active duty strength of the Corps, eighty-four thousand Marines, was in the area of operations when Desert Storm began, and the Marine pilots and their supporting units had already performed with great skill in Desert Shield. The main elements of the Marine force were the 1st Marine Expeditionary Force, including the 1st and 2nd Divisions and the much-reinforced 3rd Air Wing. Afloat in the Persian Gulf, the 4th and 5th Marine Expeditionary Brigades posed a credible amphibious invasion threat, thereby keeping several divisions of Saddam's best troops facing the sea and unable to challenge the Marine ground assaults. Those assaults punched through two defensive belts in southern Kuwait, enabling the army XVIII Corps' "left hook" drive from western Saudi Arabia to the Euphrates River and on to cut off Highway 8, the route of retreat the Iraqi army was expected to take.

Marine airpower performed well in both Desert Shield and Desert Storm, attacking strategic targets such as electric plants and command and control centers, and supporting Coalition (primarily Marine) forces on the ground. The 1st and 2nd Marine Divisions fought their way straight through two elaborate Iraqi fortification lines, seized the Kuwait City airport, and inflicted severe punishment on Iraq's armored and mechanized divisions in Kuwait, forcing those forces to withdraw a mere fifty-four hours after their initial attack. Indeed, the Marines' performance won them high praise from Army general H. Norman Schwarzkopf, who was the overall commander of Coalition forces in the conflict:

> I can't say enough about the two Marine divisions. If I use words like brilliant, it would really be an underdescription of the absolutely superb job that they did in breaching the so-called impenetrable barrier. It was a classic, absolutely classic military breaching of a very tough minefield, barbed wire, fire trenches type barrier. They went through the first barrier like it was water. They went across into the second barrier, even though they were under artillery fire at the time. They continued to open up the breach. . . . Absolutely superb operation, a textbook, and I think it'll be studied for many years to come as the way to do it. . . . [2]

In the aftermath of the war, however, the Marines were more critical of their performance than Schwarzkopf had been. They needed better mine-detecting equipment and techniques. They also needed better night-fighting equipment. Nor were they happy with the speed at which they'd been able to get their forces to the desert, despite the fact that they had managed to get a heavily armed brigade in place, ready to take on Saddam in the event of an attack on Saudi Arabia, well ahead of any U.S. Army unit. Senior Marines, General Gray included, were unhappy with the state of amphibious shipping. They felt the navy had again undervalued this asset. But then again, the Marine Corps had been singing that song since the lean years following World War II.

Despite the self-criticism, the Persian Gulf War was largely a triumph for the Marine Corps. It vindicated the key decisions made by Generals Wilson, Barrow, Gray, and others about both doctrine and new weapons and transport systems, most notably the Maritime-Prepositioning System, which married Marines with their equipment near a designated area of operations, but also the Light Armored Vehicles that provided critical mobility on the desert battlefield and the selection of the FA-18 Hornet as the fixed-wing fighter for the service. The war was something of a logistical miracle: the Marines had been able to get almost ninety thousand people and their equipment to the Gulf in a matter of several weeks, and then conduct a powerful, rapidly moving assault deep into the desert. The Vietnam War had tarnished the Marines' reputation, but the Gulf War restored the Corps' reputation as an elite, highly adaptable organization of first-class warriors. Only a tiny percentage of the ground force that broke into Kuwait had had any combat experience, and yet the Marines performed like old salts. More than anything else, perhaps, the Persian Gulf War confirmed the excellence of Marine Corps training and the Marine mind-set.

The Marines were not the first U.S. troops rushed to Saudi Arabia in the wake of President Bush's decision to challenge Saddam. That honor fell to the troopers of the army's 82nd Airborne Division. However, the 82nd's arrival was mainly symbolic. They did not have sufficient combat power in terms of tanks and artillery to defend against an Iraqi armored attack. The 7th Marine Expeditionary Unit, which flew into Saudi Arabia and linked up with three ships' worth of equipment, was the first U.S. ground force with sufficient strength to withstand an Iraqi attack. By late August, it was in place, ready to defend the vital port of Jubayl as well as the island emirate state of Bahrain. Other units followed in a steady flow, prompting the burly commandant of the Marine Corps, Al Gray, to remark: "There are four kinds of Marines: those in Saudi

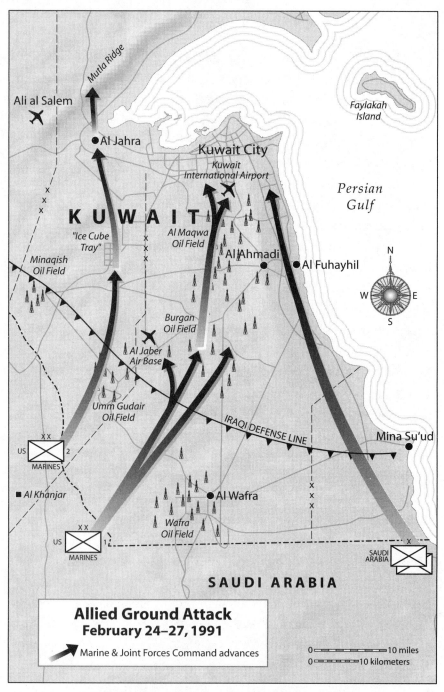

The Marine Attack into Kuwait, February 1991

Adapted from Michael R. Gordon and General Bernard E. Trainor,
The Generals' War. Boston: Little, Brown & Co., 1995.

Arabia, those going to Saudi Arabia, those who want to go to Saudi Arabia, and those who don't want to go to Saudi Arabia but are going anyway."[3]

The field commander of the Marines in the Gulf War was a soft-spoken lieutenant general from the tidewater region of North Carolina, Walter Boomer. He looked more like a farmer or a professor than a professional Marine, but his looks were deceiving: Boomer had won two Silver Stars in Vietnam, a medal the Marines do not give out easily. He had also taught at the Naval Academy, was a lifelong outdoorsman who loved to hunt, and was known to be highly intelligent. Boomer had enjoyed excellent relations with the media during a stint as a senior public-affairs officer. He would get on well with the media during the Gulf War, too.

Ironically, the initial planning staff for the ground war, conducted in the late summer and early fall of 1990 in Riyadh, Saudi Arabia, included no Marines whatsoever. Schwarzkopf's handpicked planning staff, known as the Jedis, worked out a detailed strategy for an attack from western Saudi Arabia in which the Marines would "break down the door"—that is, they would breach the initial obstacles and forces opposing the Coalition attack—but the army's heavy armored divisions would then score the coup de grace, annihilating Saddam's forces. Worse, the Jedis wanted to detach the 3rd Marine Air Wing from the 1st MEF and use it in support of the army's drive north.

In early November, Boomer was finally invited to a major planning meeting. He fervently objected to the plan, arguing that the Marines were by definition an air-ground team, and that they shouldn't be used as a mere adjunct to the army. They should have their own attack plan, albeit in support of the main effort. A debate, with Schwarzkopf as moderator, followed. Schwarzkopf sided with Boomer. "Stop screwing with the Marines!" he snapped. They should be allowed to come up with their own attack, and they should be allowed to operate in the east—near the Gulf, as their logistical base was tied into the navy.

Now the Marines would get to use their new doctrine of maneuver warfare, which emphasized keeping the enemy off balance, attacking his command and control, and outthinking him, rather than pounding his forces into rubble with superior numbers of tanks and artillery pieces. A key thought of Boomer's that proved entirely accurate was that the grim statistical comparison between his forces and the Iraqi forces in southern Kuwait painted a false picture. "As I study the Iraqi soldier to the best of my ability, I believe we have a rather hollow army facing us, despite the amount of equipment they possess. I never underestimate my enemy," Boomer wrote before the ground war, "but these guys are not in our league except in total amount of equipment. My gut feeling is they are very shaky."[4] Boomer wasn't kidding about the equipment statistics. His 41,000 1st and 2nd Division Marines were attacking about 120,000 Iraqis. Those enemy troops possessed 1,400 tanks and more than 1,000 armored personnel carriers. The Marines had a grand total of 247 tanks and 521 APCs.

The plan of attack Boomer developed with his own staff as well as that of 1st Marine Division commander Major General Mike Myatt and 2nd Division commander Major General Bill Keys, both decorated Vietnam War vets, was as follows: Keys's division would be the main effort in the Marine attack. The 2nd Division would breach the Saddam Line, as the first belt of defenses was called by the Americans, near the southwestern border of Kuwait and Saudi Arabia, just to the south of the Al Minisha oil field. Keys's Marines would then drive past the oil field, heading due north for Al Jahra, a town less than ten miles west of Kuwait City. His left flank, which consisted of the most powerful unit controlled by Boomer, the U.S. Army's tank-rich Tiger Brigade, would press forward to the heights of Mutla Ridge, cutting off any enemy forces that attempted to retreat out of Kuwait City into Iraq. Major General Myatt's 1st Division would breach both defensive lines, and drive northeast between the Burqan and Wafra oil fields. Myatt would cover the 2nd Division's advance by seizing the Al Jabar airfield, which intelligence had determined held the lion's share of Iraq's artillery facing the Marines as well as a general headquarters.

The 1st MEF area of operations was located just south of the Kuwait-

Saudi border and west of the Wafra oil fields. The eastern border of the Marines' area of responsibility was roughly twenty-five miles from the waters of the Persian Gulf. To the east of the Marines was a corps of Arab units, mainly Saudis. The Marines had placed lightly manned forward outposts just south of the border to detect Iraqi probes or thrusts into Saudi Arabia. These forces were backed by Light Armored Vehicle (LAV) units, which were highly mobile and capable of providing quick support if the outposts got into trouble.

On January 29, one of the most competent of Saddam's generals, Salah Aboud Mahmoud, launched a multibrigade attack from the Wafra area into the Saudi town of Khafji. Mahmoud had managed to move his forces up near the border undetected by satellite, perhaps knowing when the satellites were passing overhead. According to *The General's War*, a superb history of the conflict by Michael Gordon and retired Marine lieutenant general Bernard Trainor, Saddam had personally approved the plan. After having taken two weeks of punishment from Coalition bombers, he wanted a ground victory with U.S. casualties early in the game, perhaps sparking an antiwar movement among the American public. Saddam has long been cognizant of the Americans' Achilles' heel: casualties. Body bags landing at U.S. air bases were likely to bring public support for the war crashing down precipitously.

The initial attack occurred about sixty miles north of the 2nd Marine Division's main base in the desert. A Marine reconnaissance team manning an old police border outpost was attacked by a mechanized force of APCs and tanks. The team leader, Lieutenant Stephen Ross, vainly attempted to call in an air strike before hopping in the team's Humvee and heading south in a hurry—the standard procedure for a recon unit. The Iraqis had jammed the frequency he tried to use to call in the air strike. Finally Ross was able to get word back to an LAV company, which drove forward at top speed to challenge the attack. Meanwhile, Ross managed to hook up with the air strike dispatchers and several jets appeared just in time. The LAV force and the air strikes together sent the Iraqis into retreat, but not before a couple of hours of combat. Eleven Marines were killed in the confusion by friendly fire from air force A-10 tank killers.

Later that morning, the Iraqis attacked again with tanks, this time farther to the west, near another observation post. Again, Marine LAV forces maneuvered their way into range without a single incoming round finding its mark and, with the help of Coalition jets, blunted the attack. Once again, there were no follow-on armored forces once the initial attack had been stopped. The Marines had destroyed thirty tanks and taken nine prisoners.

Yet a third Iraqi armor attack to the east broke through a light Saudi force and surrounded the town of Khafji. At the time, two Marine recon teams were on rooftops in the city. Rather than attempt to exit, these brave souls remained hidden and called in effective Marine air strikes and artillery fire during several assaults by Saudi and Qatari forces. By February 2, Iraqi forces had retreated back into Kuwait. Their multi-pronged attacks had cost them ninety tanks and armored personnel carriers. One hundred dead Iraqi soldiers were counted after one Saudi attack north of the town, and about a hundred prisoners had been taken.

The Marines who had fought in these border assaults emerged from the experience with a low opinion of their adversary. One young Marine put it this way: "Get in the first shot at him and the rest will run away."[5] General Boomer's prewar instinct that the Iraqi army was "hollow" seemed to be confirmed.

The ground assault was slated to begin early on the morning of February 24. Marine task forces from both divisions—largely highly mobile units with LAVs—were engaged in reconnaissance operations inside the Saddam Line two days beforehand. An LAV company from the 2nd Division under Lieutenant Colonel Keith Holcomb threaded its way undetected through the line and engaged Iraqi forces in heavy combat, knocking out twenty tanks and taking three hundred prisoners. Task Force Grizzly from the 1st Division, under Colonel Jim Fulks, cleared a lane through berms, wire, and trenches on February 23, and several thousand troops from the 1st Division then poured through, including a regimental headquarters, and were well inside the line when Boomer got the order to launch the general assault at 0400 on February 24.

The main assault began on a wet, cold Sunday morning. Fog and smoke from the burning oil fields—the Iraqis had set them alight to diminish the effectiveness of the Coalition's attack—threatened to choke off air support, but the wind changed in the Marines' favor, blowing smoke back toward the defenders. Loudspeakers from a psychological operations unit blared the Marines' Hymn as the Marines pushed toward the obstacle belts.

The 1st Division hit the first obstacle belt at 0615. Engineers worked with great precision, shooting live charges across minefields and blowing clear lanes for tanks and other vehicles. No antitank trenches were detected in the 1st Division area. Between the first and second defensive belts there was nothing but dummy tanks and abandoned fighting positions. The defenders had fled. The extensive bombing had crushed their fighting spirit—such as it was. A great many of the troops in these frontline positions turned out to be conscripts with no stomach for fighting.

Only after 1130 on Sunday, after penetrating the second belt, did the Marines encounter any serious resistance. They took artillery fire and sporadic small-arms fire. The Marines made effective use of counter-battery radar to detect the location of enemy artillery and call in their own strikes. By 1730 forces on the right flank of the 1st Division had isolated the Al Jabar airfield, taking the surrender of hundreds of Iraqis stationed there. The 1st Division's tally for the day was twenty-one tanks eliminated and four thousand prisoners taken at the cost of one Marine killed and nine wounded. Even that single death had been the result of friendly fire. Myatt set up his mobile command post southwest of the Burqan oil field.

The 2nd Division faced a very tough minefield, consisting of sophisticated British mines that were difficult to detect, so it took their engineers a full seven hours to clear six lanes. An enemy column coming toward the Marines from Kuwait City was detected, causing elements of the 2nd Division to consolidate their positions, but the column was decimated by artillery and air attacks, and it never reached the Marine infantry. By end of day the 2nd Division, in its first combat as a division since World War II, had knocked out thirty-five T-55 tanks and taken five thousand enemy prisoners. It fell to Myatt's troops to fend off the only serious ground counterattack of the entire war. This attack was led by the wily commander of the Iraqi attacks on Khafji, Salah Aboud Mahmoud. General Myatt had positioned his command post quite close to the burning oil wells at Burqan, thinking that the fires would protect his force from an attack from the east. At 0100 on February 25, after the Marines had dug in for the night, Myatt got word from a prisoner that Iraqi forces were in and around the Burqan oil field and were planning an attack. Myatt called up several LAV units to cover his front and his command post. At 0817, on Myatt's orders, the 11th Marines initiated an artillery barrage into the suspected enemy assembly area. It hit a large force of enemy tanks and armored personnel carriers from the Iraqi 3rd Armored Brigade and 8th Mechanized Brigade. Antitank missiles flew through the air from the Marine positions, many hitting their mark. The bark of the LAVs' 25mm Chain Guns—that extremely effective weapon with a range of up to three thousand yards—could be heard across the entire battlefield. The Iraqis retreated, regrouped, and attacked again. By that point, Cobra gunships had entered the fray. At least one Cobra began to drop spent shell casings right on top of Myatt's CP; at one point, Iraqi tanks were only four hundred yards away.

Still another attack boiled up, this time against the Marines' right flank, hitting the thirty-five-hundred-man Task Force Papa Bear, under Colonel Richard Hodory. Suddenly Iraqi antiaircraft guns were firing on Cobras and Harriers. A Marine OV-10 observation plane was shot down, its crew lost. A Harrier was hit by a heat-seeking missile. It crashed, but the pilot was rescued by an intrepid Marine driving a Humvee. Iraqi artillery fired rockets, and killed one Marine and wounded twelve. The Marines thought about using tear gas to drive the remaining enemy out of the oil fields, but then thought better of it, because such a move might have prompted the Iraqis to use chemical weapons. As it was, a shift in the wind brought smoke and the smell of chemicals from the oil refinery that set off one alarm after another. It began to rain. The fight was called off and the 1st Marine Division hunkered down in their protective suits and tried to catch a bit of sleep. Few succeeded, despite their exhaustion.

At 0400 on the morning of February 25, the 4th Marine Expeditionary Brigade launched a successful and highly dangerous deception. Ten helos were launched from ships in the Gulf with electronic equipment designed to make it seem like a full-scale attack was en route, and the big guns of the battleship *Missouri* opened up on suspected Iraqi defensive positions. The Iraqis responded to these deception maneuvers by launching two Silkworm missiles at the U.S. ships, but these were shot down before they made their way to the navy amphibious task force.

Boomer ordered the main ground attack to resume at 0400 on February 26. He felt he had the full measure of the enemy by this point, and that the vast majority of the Iraqis weren't anxious for a fight. He anticipated serious resistance now at only two points: in the vicinity of the Kuwait City airport, and at the town of Al Jahrah, at the head of the Gulf of Kuwait. Iraqi forces seeking to escape the Marines' drive northward would have to cut through the town or along its outskirts to retreat back into Iraq. Large numbers of troops were already reported by Marine intelligence sources to be leaving Kuwait City. Indeed, a mere fifty-four hours after the main attack commenced, Saddam Hussein ordered his forces in Kuwait to retreat northward in hope that they would escape destruction. Apparently they weren't anxious to greet the U.S. Marines.

The main obstacle to carrying out a successful attack in the early morning of February 26 was the oily blackness that hung over the entire battlefield due to the oil fires. It was, in effect, a night battlefield in the daytime. The Marines' Cobras lacked the army's excellent forward-looking infrared night-vision systems. The only flying they could do at night required optimum conditions. Once again, the Marine penchant for using what was on hand to solve an unexpected problem showed itself. A helicopter pilot, Lieutenant Colonel Michael Kurth, had a father-in-law who worked for a defense contractor that made a FLIR system, and he'd given the colonel one for his Huey chopper. Kurth would earn the Navy Cross by leading Cobras through the black night, sometimes flying under electrical wires, to the front, where the Cobras were able to knock out many enemy tanks with their Hellfire missiles once Kurth had put his laser designator on the targets. Between the Cobra attacks and the ground attacks by elements of Task Forces Shepherd and Taro, the 1st Marine Division destroyed some three hundred tanks in the approaches to the Kuwait City airport.

Meanwhile, the 2nd Division got into a serious donnybrook at 0230 on February 26 when the Iraqis attacked a road intersection held by the 4th Tank Battalion and Company B, 8th Marines. In the ninety-minute fight, the Iraqis closed to within a hundred yards of the Marine positions before they were beaten back by highly accurate firing by the artillery of the 10th Marines. Later that morning, planes from Marine Air Groups 11 and 33 discovered a gigantic traffic jam on the six-lane highway leading north out of Al Jahrah. For six hours Marine pilots pounded the fleeing forces on the highway. It was a horrific scene, dubbed the "Highway to Hell" by the Marines. That afternoon, Army colonel John Sylvester's Tiger Brigade swung into Al Jahrah and went on to the high ground north of the city—Mutla Ridge. There they found a great retreating column of Iraqi tanks and began to destroy them with their Abrams tank's 120mm main guns. The brigade destroyed 166 tanks that day, with a bit of help from elements of the 6th and 8th Marine Regiments of the 2nd Division.

On Tuesday night, twelve Marines from the 1st Platoon, 2nd Force Reconnaissance Company entered the compound of the U.S. embassy in Kuwait City, directed to that locale by three carloads of Kuwaiti resistance fighters wearing red armbands. The Marines found the city looted and essentially gutted. Strangely, the embassy itself remained locked and undisturbed. The next day, the Marines, joined by U.S. Army Special Forces, raised a U.S. flag that, on a forty-foot fireman's ladder, had flown in Vietnam.

Early on Wednesday, the 1st LAV Battalion secured the deserted Kuwait City airport. For the Marines the fight for Kuwait was essentially over. By this point, the great left hook had punched into the heart of the Iraqi army in Iraq, crushing most of the forces Saddam had held back to defend his home turf.

The Marines from the outset had been instructed to let the Arab forces enter Kuwait City first. The Marines' job was not so much to destroy every tank and fortified bunker as to sow confusion and panic in Saddam's ranks through rapid, tightly focused mechanized assault; to destroy his command and control; and to overwhelm the enemy by making quick, sensible decentralized decisions. It was warfare according to the principles Al Gray had inspired. "We changed plans while on the move," said Colonel Ron Richard, a key planner for Bill Keys's 2nd Division. "We were mapping things out in the sand."[6] Major General Myatt made a more general observation along these lines. "This was not the old classic frontal assault. We wanted to create chaos for them. If we were there to destroy every artillery piece and every soldier, we'd still be there."[7] Deception played a big role in the success as the senior Marines saw it. For two weeks before the ground assault commenced, the Marines' Task Force Troy, numbering a mere 460 people, used loudspeakers and electronic equipment to mimic the traffic of a full Marine division to the west of where the real Marine divisions were emplaced. To the east, the 4th and 5th Brigades' efforts to mimic amphibious assaults clearly worked to good effect.

Early on Thursday, February 28, fearing the negative publicity of the Highway to Hell turkey shoot, President Bush ordered a cease-fire to take effect at 0800 Gulf time on February 28. The decision saved the lives of tens of thousands of Iraqi soldiers on the highways heading north. It also flabbergasted some of the field commanders. Aside from the decision to leave Saddam in power, many still wanted to degrade his military to a shadow of its former self. White House realists, however, were trying to balance public opinion with a vision of Iraq as a stable counterweight to Iran.

The Marines' attack had certainly succeeded in its major objective: the liberation of Kuwait. In retrospect, General Boomer was immensely proud of his Marines, but his candor and modesty were much in evidence when he remarked shortly after the end of the war that only about 25 percent of the forces faced by the 1st MEF were ready to stand and fight; most preferred to surrender or flee. A great many who'd chosen the latter course had been killed by Marine airpower and artillery.

Marine casualties were extraordinarily light: twenty-four killed in action, ninety-two wounded. Iraqi losses resulting directly from the Marine attack were estimated to be one hundred thousand military and civilian casualties.

Back at Camp Pendleton on April 24, the Marines of 1st MEF received a heroes' parade. General Boomer presented the Silver Star for exceptional heroism to five Marines that day, including Staff Sergeant Michael Kur of Michigan, of the 8th Engineer Support Battalion, who dug out antipersonnel mines by hand while under mortar fire and carried them out of the minefield. Later, as he guided a bulldozer through a minefield, it was hit by antitank fire, knocking the staff sergeant over. He got up, dusted himself off, and continued to clear mines. Another Silver Star was presented to Sergeant Gordon T. Gregory of Ohio, a reconnaissance platoon leader. On the first day of the ground war, he led his team through a minefield under intense enemy fire, halted friendly fire in his lines before any casualties occurred, and rescued two Marines trapped in a live minefield.

No group of Marines was happier to see the war end than the men and women of the 3rd Air Wing, commanded by Major General Royal N. Moore. For forty-three straight days, this remarkable group of people had worked, with admirable dedication and spirit, to keep more than forty squadrons of aircraft flying at a breakneck pace. Marines played a key role

in defeating the Iraqi air force in the first week of the war; in the air
force–controlled interdiction campaign designed to knock out Saddam's
major communications sites and military formations; and, of course, in
providing close air support during the hundred-hour ground war.

The 3rd Air Wing flew no less than eighteen thousand sorties, and
were based at six airfields throughout the theater. Many of the MAW's
A-6 Intruders, AV-10 Broncos, CH-46s and CH-53 Sea Stallions were as
old or even older than the men who flew them. Their aging frames had
flown in Vietnam, and the extra demands of keeping these birds in the
air in a desert environment kept many ground crews working well over
sixteen hours a day. Most Marine pilots flew every day, and virtually
every pilot in the wing flew more than one sortie a day most of the time
during both Desert Shield and Desert Storm.

By the end of the Gulf War, defense intellectuals inside the Beltway,
professors in the nation's senior war colleges, and foreign-policy experts
were charting a sea change in American foreign policy that had huge
ramifications for American military policy and culture. The end of the
cold war had not brought a halcyon age of peace and prosperity. Quite
the reverse: more and more serious observers spoke of the "new world
disorder." Ethnic and tribal resentments bubbled to the surface in the
Balkans, in Africa, and in Central Asia. In Somalia, Rwanda, and in
parts of Russia and Yugoslavia, civil order gave way to anarchy and in-
trastate violence. American armed forces would range far beyond
America's borders. Aside from the Gulf War, they would bomb Serbian
troops in Bosnia; overthrow Manuel Noriega in Panama; and stabilize
Haiti. Most memorably, they would also try to stabilize Somalia.

Low-intensity conflicts, peacekeeping and peacemaking, small wars,
operations other than war—in short, military operations where objectives, military means or both are strictly limited in scope—have loomed
larger in the past decade in American military planning than at any
other time in American history. The plethora of small wars and ethnic
and religious factionalism bordering on war in Central Asia, Africa,

South America, and the Middle East; the decline of the long-standing international principle of nonintervention by foreign powers in the internal affairs of sovereign states; heightened political expectations among repressed minorities and ethnic groups—all have placed extraordinary pressures on the United Nations and the world's major powers, particularly, of course, the United States.

Since the early 1990s, the Marines and other American military services have been engaged in a delicate balancing act, adapting doctrines and training regimens to meet the pressing requirements of operations other than war while attempting to maintain the capability to fight *major* regional wars against regularly constituted armies.

The impact of the new strategic environment on the military was—and is—everywhere in evidence. At the services' staff colleges, the curriculum now includes a hefty dose of courses on operations other than war, from "peace enforcement"—when soldiers are deployed to a locale where at least one hostile faction operates—to counterterrorism, humanitarian intervention, and drug-trafficking interdiction. While the total number of people on active duty in the services has declined from 2,170,000 in 1987 to about 1,400,000 in 1998, the number of deployments has moved in the opposite direction: between 1990 and 1997, U.S. forces were deployed thirty-six times compared to twenty-two between 1980 and 1989. The U.S. Marines have been the force of choice in the majority of these deployments.

Statements from the upper-echelon commanders in the navy and Marines in the mid- and late 1990s stressed their services' key role in suppressing nasty local crises before they could escalate into wars that threaten U.S. vital interests.

Amid so much uncertainty, the U.S. Marine Corps, because it is the smallest service and because it has always had to fight for its place at the table, has been better at adapting than its sister services. Like all the services, the Marines sustained some serious cuts in funding in these years. The first Bush administration entertained cutting the Marine Corps from about 194,000 active personnel to 159,000. Al Gray's successor as commandant, General Carl Mundy, argued that this diminution would cut into the bone, and that the Marines were going to be relied upon more than ever. When the Clinton administration concluded its "Bottom-Up Review" of the nation's national security needs, it made a far less painful cut in Marine personnel. Since the mid-1990s, the Marine Corps stands at about 174,000 active duty men and women.

Since the end of the cold war, the Marines have fought in two regional land wars, but the bulk of their deployments involve peace-keeping, humanitarian operations, antidrug trafficking, and rescues of Americans and foreign nationals from the world's trouble spots. Even before the first Gulf War, the Corps was proving its usefulness and skill in such operations amid anarchy in the horn of Africa—in Somalia—and in South Asia, when Bangladesh suffered a devastating typhoon that produced floods that took the lives of several hundred thousand individuals in a matter of hours.

In Operation Eastern Exit, the Corps conducted a brilliant evacuation of the U.S. embassy in strife-torn Mogadishu on January 5, 1991. Two amphibious ships, the *Guam* and the *Trenton*, were dispatched by Central Command at the request of U.S. Ambassador James Bishop. The ships carried a security evacuation force from the 1st Battalion, 2nd Marines, and long-range CH-53 helicopters to ferry them into the embassy compound. It was a hairy operation from the start. After Marine security guards exchanged gunfire with rebel forces outside the gates of the embassy compound, the plans for a daylight evacuation were scrubbed in favor of a night operation. "The messages from the Embassy gave the unmistakable impression they were being written from cover beneath a desk. . . . One message reported that a rocket-propelled grenade had slammed into the compound," wrote one Marine officer involved in the planning for the operation.[8]

In the early hours of January 5, a nine-man SEAL team and fifty Marines boarded two CH-53s and departed for the shores of Somalia from 466 nautical miles off the coast, successfully refueled twice in the air en route, and after landing reinforced the small garrison of Marine security guards at the U.S. embassy. After establishing a modicum of order in the compound and reassuring more than 280 U.S. citizens and foreign nationals, the Marines and SEALs conducted a successful evacuation.

The evacuation was conducted from an unusually long distance from the coast, and it was not without some heart-pumping moments. For one thing, the operation had to be mounted in such haste that the pilots had no clear, reliable maps indicating either the location or the layout of the compound. They had to do the night landings by eye, and it took more than ten minutes once the initial flights were over Mogadishu to find the compound. An AC-130 flying over the embassy to provide intelligence to the security force detected a SAM missile in the area of operations. The embassy received a call from one Somali warlord who ordered the evacuation to cease. His "order" was ignored. Shots were fired at Marine snipers by the unruly crowds, but no fire was returned.

Once the operation had been successfully completed, Ambassador Bishop had this to say: "Subsequent events made it clear that the Marines and SEALs came just in time. . . . We were very impressed by the professionalism of Eastern Exit. The Marines and SEALs appeared at all times to be masters of the situation. . . . The actions of those protecting the Embassy and evacuating the evacuees was indeed heroic."[9]

The Marines enjoy a reputation the world over as spirited, ferocious fighters. In Bangladesh, at least since 1991, the Corps is known for something else as well: for being agents of mercy and deliverance. Sixteen years to the day after the fall of Saigon—April 29, 1991—a powerful cyclone swept across Bangladesh's low-lying villages and farms, wreaking unimaginable devastation. On one night alone almost 140,000 human beings and 1 million cattle perished. The rice and jute crops over most of the country were completely destroyed. Tens of thousands more faced certain death unless help in the form of food and medical support and disaster management showed up, and fast.

Within twenty-four hours, help came in the form of a small planning staff of U.S. Marines and sailors under the command of Lieutenant General H. C. Stackpole. Only the U.S. Marines possessed the helicopters, ships, and organizational ability to undertake such a massive time-sensitive undertaking. Soon a seven-ship amphibious group was off the shores of Bangladesh, its people working at a breakneck pace to organize the efforts of a host of indigenous relief groups in addition to emergency rescue units from the United Kingdom, Pakistan, and Japan.

With cholera threatening because of thousands of floating corpses, the Marine planning staff "had to operate almost totally in the dark" because of the lack of information about topography, demographics, and the like. Yet by the second week of operations, the relief effort comprised thousands of U.S. Marines who distributed food and medicine in the hinterlands. Because floods had destroyed the road network, supplies made their way to the entire flood-stricken area by helo or landing craft designed to carry Marines to the beach for combat. In five weeks the Marines touched the lives of almost 2 million grateful people who had suffered great personal loss at the hands of one of the worst storms in the twentieth century.

Meanwhile, things went from bad to worse in the horn of Africa. Somalian society was self-destructing. Long an area where the superpowers vied for influence, the country was chock-full of small arms and the dreaded "technicals" — small four-wheel-drive pickups with machine antiaircraft guns secured in the bed. These tools of destruction were in the hands of roving bands of some fourteen different clans, under competing warlords. Little known to the United States, Al Qaeda had spread its tentacles to the country as well. Somalia by early 1992 was in chaos. The atmosphere and conditions that haunted it might have been dreamed up by some sadistic Marine planner for a training exercise, the objective of which was to develop a deep and enduring hatred of operations other than war among his charges. Marine lieutenant colonel T. A. Richards described it well: "Authority derived not from law but from influence, bribery, arms possession, intimidation and outright violence, including murder. . . . The situation had deteriorated so much [by June 1992] that people were starving from a fractured marketing and distribution system's inability to provide food equitably. Armed clansmen and thugs commandeered food from warehouse and convoy, then either sold it at extortionary prices or hoarded, according to their whims."[10]

Due to lack of political organization and the effects of a drought, more than three hundred thousand Somalis had starved between 1990 and 1992. Several million more were in danger of dying.

In August the Bush administration ordered 145,000 tons of food, medicine, and supplies to be sent to the country. The commander in chief of Central Command, General Joseph P. Hoar, USMC—General Norman Schwarzkopf's deputy commander during the first Gulf War—ordered a task force under Brigadier General Frank Libutti, also a Marine, to command Joint Task Force Relief, with 570 U.S. military personnel. The Joint Task Force used C-130s to deliver beans, rice, and cooking oil. The next month, five hundred Pakistani troops were flown in under the U.N. flag to help with the operation, but they proved too small a force to cope with the deteriorating situation on the ground. In Mogadishu, two warlords, Mohammed Aideed and Ali Mahdi, remained locked in a bitter power struggle, and the U.N. supplies were a prime commodity of plunder and influence. Food in effect became the currency of trade in a starving land, and as a result, roving bands of thugs hijacked food convoys. In November, the humanitarian relief effort all but collapsed, as Somali militiamen began firing small arms at ships trying to dock and unload in Mogadishu harbor.

President Bush then offered to send U.S. forces as part of Operation Restore Hope. Lieutenant General Robert B. Johnston, a Marine who had served as chief of staff to General Schwarzkopf during Desert Shield and Desert Storm, commanded the operation. Its mission was "to secure major air and sea ports, key installations and food distribution points in order to provide open and free passage of relief supplies; to provide security for convoys and relief organizations; and to assist U.N. nongovernment organizations in providing relief under U.N. auspices."[11] A U.N.

resolution clarified the objective of the operation further. The task force, which was staffed by members of all the services and formed at Camp Pendleton, was "to use all necessary means."

The 15th Marine Expeditionary Unit was moved to a position off Mogadishu. Then, early on the morning of December 9, a SEAL team followed by reconnaissance Marines in full combat gear came ashore in Mogadishu harbor, where they were greeted by a stable of print and TV journalists. The joint navy-Marine force made their way to the airfield to secure it for incoming flights. A particularly down-to-earth and knowledgeable State Department official, Ambassador Robert B. Oakley, had negotiated with the two warlords who controlled the city to allow the landing. Operation Restore Hope was conducted under U.N. auspices, but the notorious ponderousness of U.N. decision making ensured that General Johnston, commander of the multinational peacekeeping force, would make most of the critical decisions on the ground without seeking clearance from U.N. officials. His day-to-day job went beyond commanding the Marines and more than five thousand troops of other nations; he also had to serve as liaison between U.S. civilian agencies and local U.N. officials.

Operation Restore Hope was not without problems, and mistakes were made by leaders and wary Marines who patrolled the dingy alleys of Mogadishu and seized weapons from roving gangs of toughs. But knowledgeable observers have universally praised the execution of the operation and General Johnston's inspired leadership and professionalism.

Within forty-eight hours of setting up his headquarters, General Johnston's force of Marines, which ultimately expanded to include more than twenty thousand Marines of the 1st Marine Expeditionary force housed at Camp Pendleton, California, had secured both the port area in south Mogadishu and the airport. He and Ambassador Oakley—they worked well together—established a program of regular meetings with the nongovernmental organizations (NGOs) and the two main warlords, each of whom controlled roughly half the city. They secured an agreement to remove all technicals to depots outside the city, and to allow the

NGOs to create eight desperately needed relief centers for food and medicine distribution in the famine-plagued south and central areas of the country, many of which were up and running within a few weeks. A tentative cease-fire was put in place to facilitate the relief effort. A U.S. Army psychological operations unit attached to Johnston's force quickly established a newspaper and a radio station to facilitate communications and stanch the (grim) rumor mill that had come to pass for real information among the Somali population.

The twenty-eight thousand American military personnel, the vast majority from the Marines, worked security patrols and other duties with small numbers of forces from more than twenty nations. The trickiest job involved clearing "secure" areas of Mogadishu of weapons caches and removing large weapons from the possession of groups of clansmen. These procedures required an equal measure of quiet diplomacy and an ability to show command presence without prompting violent outbursts. By early January, the Marines estimated that they had collected some sixteen truckloads of these weapons. Their orders outside the secure areas were to disarm individual Somalis only if they felt themselves threatened. All told, about fifteen Somali men were killed when tense standoffs ended in gunfire. In early February about two hundred angry Somalis rioted near the port in Mogadishu, wrongly believing that Marines had killed six men who'd actually died in a clash between two rival militia factions attempting to gain control over several buildings. Marines arrived in force from helos and amtracs, with military police reinforcing them. After several hours of frustrating negotiations, the crowd dispersed without further bloodshed.

The riot underscored the extreme pressures placed on Marines who lived day and night in spartan conditions amid perpetual human suffering. All too many young children died despite the best efforts of relief agencies. Every U.S. Marine, no matter how worldly or tough, who observed the death of a four- or five-year-old child in the arms of a grieving, half-starved parent would carry the memory for the rest of his life.

Patrolling on foot or in food convoys was draining duty for both mind and body. Marine captain Mark Taol, who led an infantry company of the 24th MEU in sweeps through the town of Afmadow, in southern Somalia, waxed eloquently on the problems of applying "proportional force": "This New World Order stuff is putting a huge new responsibility on these kids—huge. It's hard enough for someone with a college education and years of experience to explain proportional force. But for a nineteen-year-old kid . . . in a high-stress situation where he's having rocks thrown at him and the guns are behind the rock throwers, what is 'proportional'?"[12]

As Marines patrolled the dusty streets in Mogadishu and in other towns, in temperatures that often exceeded a hundred degrees, young, half-starved children followed on their heels, hoping for a small handout of food, or a trinket such as a pen or one of the tiny USMC T-shirts that some Marines carried for the children. A lance corporal said, "You can't trust the kids. They make you feel sorry for them. During the day they beg for food, then at night they come at you with guns."[13]

As spring approached, the situation got worse. In February, another riot broke out on the rumor that Marines had aided the militia of the son of ousted dictator Said Barre. Even the strongest, most experienced Marines could take only so much of this duty before becoming disillusioned, cynical, or even cruel and resentful. Twenty-eight thousand troops were nowhere near enough to restore order everywhere, and convoys continued to be highjacked. One Marine officer who had reached his breaking point after several months growled, "A lot of Somalis just deserve to be killed." Although Oakley and Johnston kept up regular council meetings with both warlords, U.N. forces were regularly the targets of snipers and drive-by shootings. Luckily most of the Somali shooters, some of them mere teenage boys, were lousy shots. But not all of them; on January 20, 1993, Marine private first class Domingo Arroyo of Elizabeth, New Jersey, was killed in an ambush close to the airport. A fierce firefight ensued, but the Somali gunmen escaped. Before departing in May 1993, eight U.S. Marines were lost to small-arms fire.

After the Marines were gone, the United States sent in a contingent of U.S. Army Delta Force troops and Rangers to capture the best known of the armed militias. The tragic results have become famous through the book and film *Blackhawk Down*. Eighteen U.S. Rangers were killed in a ferocious all-night firefight. At least five hundred Somalis were killed by the Americans. The hunters had become the hunted, and the army troopers barely escaped complete destruction. From a tactical point of view, Marine analysts saw the main shortcoming of their experiences to be lack of on-the-ground intelligence and insufficient knowledge of the cultural mores of the local population. For Marines—or any other peacekeeping military force—it is important not only to appear formidable, but to acquire the respect of the locals. This lesson would fail to sink in, alas, in the current Iraq war.

TWELVE

Two Wars in a New Century

Afghanistan and the War in Iraq Through the Seizure of Baghdad

The horrific attacks of September 11, 2001, on New York's World Trade Center and the Pentagon in Washington, D.C., ushered in a new era in American history, national security, and world geopolitics. Within hours of these devastating assaults by a mere twenty-one Muslim terrorists, President George W. Bush had declared the United States to be at war against terrorism worldwide. That war, of course, continues as of this writing.

Since those attacks, American military and intelligence services have worked at a feverish pace to improve intelligence gathering and make U.S. forces lighter, more flexible, and more effective at fighting and winning "asymmetrical wars" against small widely scattered groups of unconventional warriors. The most prominent group—enemy number one—is Osama Bin Laden's Al Qaeda. That group and a host of others like it possess no end of resolve and a voluminous supply of recruits ready to go to war against the United States and, indeed, all West-

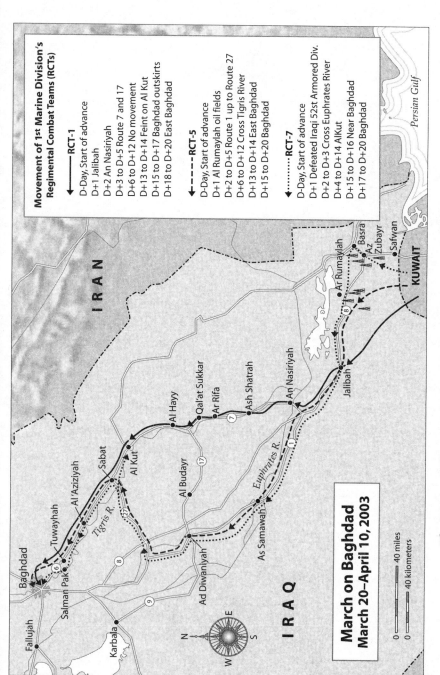

Movement of 1st Marine Division's Regimental Combat Teams (RCTs)

→ RCT-1
D-Day, Start of advance
D+1 Jalibah
D+2 An Nasiriyah
D+3 to D+5 Route 7 and 17
D+6 to D+12 No movement
D+13 to D+14 Feint on Al Kut
D+15 to D+17 Baghdad outskirts
D+18 to D+20 East Baghdad

– – – RCT-5
D-Day, Start of advance
D+1 Al Rumaylah oil fields
D+2 to D+5 Route 1 up to Route 27
D+6 to D+12 Cross Tigris River
D+13 to D+14 East Baghdad
D+15 to D+20 Baghdad

········ RCT-7
D-Day, Start of advance
D+1 Defeated Iraqi 52st Armored Div.
D+2 to D+3 Cross Euphrates River
D+4 to D+14 AlKut
D+15 to D+16 Near Baghdad
D+17 to D+20 Baghdad

IRAN

IRAQ

KUWAIT

Persian Gulf

Baghdad
Fallujah
Karbala
Salman Pak
Tuwayhah
Al'Aziziyah
Sabat
Al Kut
Al Hayy
Qal'at Sukkar
Ar Rifa
Ash Shatrah
Al Budayr
Ad Diwaniyah
As Samawah
An Nasiriyah
Jalibah
Ar Rumaylah
Az Zubayr
Basra
Safwan

Tigris R.
Euphrates R.

**March on Baghdad
March 20–April 10, 2003**

N
W   E
S

0 ___ 40 miles
0 ___ 40 kilometers

The Marine Offensive in Operation Iraqi Freedom, March–April 2003

Adapted from Bing West and Ray L. Smith, *The March Up: Taking Baghdad with the 1st Marine Division.* New York: Bantam Books, 2003.

ern institutions. No small number of these terrorists are prepared to die for their cause without hesitation. They are a formidable enemy.

The Marine Corps has a long and admirable tradition of anticipating emerging threats on the horizon and adapting to them effectively. This capacity goes far in explaining the Corps' remarkable institutional success in the twentieth century. The Marines continue to stay ahead of the curve. General Al Gray, commandant of the Corps in the late 1980s and early 1990s, didn't have Bin Laden in mind when he introduced maneuver-warfare doctrine to the Marines in 1989, but the mind-set and approach to war behind that doctrine are clearly conducive to combating terrorism. As we have seen, the Marines' current doctrine places extraordinary emphasis on outthinking the enemy, on keeping him off balance by striking at his weakest points and "playing with his head." Its emphasis on decentralized decision making and bold action, too, seems appropriate for taking on modern terrorist groups. The creation of "special operations capable" Marine expeditionary units—another Gray innovation—as well as a strong emphasis on urban combat training, and preparing Marines to fight the three-block war that General Chuck Krulak has championed (see Epilogue), also promise to put the Marines in good stead for confronting modern terror.

The first battle of the new war unfolded in Afghanistan in Operation Enduring Freedom. The ultra-fundamentalist Taliban regime there was very friendly to Al Qaeda. Bin Laden's major training bases, and the Taliban regime as a whole, were the targets. That war was conducted largely by U.S. Army Special Forces, who trained and led indigenous forces who were already deeply hostile to the Taliban, and it was largely successful in breaking the back of both Al Qaeda and the Taliban in that country.

The Marines played a critical role in the early days of the war, and as of this writing at least one battalion of Marine infantry and an unknown number of Marine Force Reconnaissance personnel remain in Afghanistan. In November 2001, it was Marine Task Force 58, a force drawn from two amphibious ready groups sailing in the North Arabian Sea off the coast of Pakistan, that established the first air bases from which American forces would prosecute the war.

Task Force 58, under the command of Brigadier General James N. Mattis, who would later lead the entire 1st Marine Division to war against Iraq, consisted of forces drawn from both the 15th and the 26th MEUs. On November 25, six CH-53 Sea Stallions flew about 150 combat-ready Marines 650 miles from the sea to a deserted airfield fifty-five miles southwest of the city of Kandahar. The helos had been re-fueled in the air by a KC-130.

Within hours of landing in a remote, mountainous region of Afghan-istan, a platoon of the 15th MEU's Force Reconnaisance Marines mounted their fast-attack vehicles—heavily armed, light, and very fast vehicles used by U.S. Special Forces—and set off on a long-range recon-naissance patrol. On December 6, the Force Recon team conducted a successful ambush of a Taliban convoy carrying rocket-propelled grenades and other weaponry intended to be used against U.S. forces. After taking out the lead vehicle in a short firefight, the team called in an air strike on the column of SUVs and trucks, resulting in its complete destruction.

In December 2002, eighty Marines secured the U.S. embassy in Kabul, which had been unoccupied for twelve years. Four days later, three hundred Marines from Camp Rhino secured Kandahar Interna-tional Airport. The area around the heavily damaged airport was stud-ded with minefields and debris. The Marines set up defensive positions, and over the next several months engaged in firefights with hostile forces attempting to shoot down U.S. aircraft as they took off or landed.

In April 2002, the Pentagon ordered virtually all naval and Marine forces to withdraw from the Afghan theater. Army troops replaced the Marines at Rhino and at Kandahar Airport.

Although the Marines played a secondary role in Afghanistan, their deployment there was not unimportant in terms of the Marine Corps of the future. According to Brigadier General Michael Innis, the director of intelligence at Headquarters Marine Corps, in establishing Camp

Rhino 658 miles inland, using forces and aircraft organic to two amphibious ready groups, Task Force 58 in effect "redefined the concept of an amphibious beachhead."[1] The speed and efficiency with which the Marines undertook operations so far from the sea proved that Marine forces could be effectively employed well beyond the range that official doctrine specified, that is, two hundred miles from the sea.

Cutting-edge intelligence and communications technology played a key role in the Marines' operations in Afghanistan. Mattis's troops were geographically isolated, and often widely separated. Nonetheless, they had at their disposal a remarkable range of intelligence assets. Even squad leaders had personal GPS devices for calling in fire support. Video teleconferencing between intelligence units in Afghanistan, Washington, D.C., Quantico, Virginia, and Tampa, Florida, where Central Command is headquartered, proved immensely valuable. General Innis explains:

> The intelligence Marines of TF 58 coordinated with Marine intelligence liaison officers at Navy [and Marine] Forces, Central Command [in Tampa, Florida] in order to voice their requirements. . . . Every evening representatives from each of these organizations would meet in a [video telephone conference] to discuss TF 58's current and future intelligence requirements—some of which were due in less than 24 hours. This allowed the requestors and producers of intelligence to meet in a collaborative environment and coordinate face to face. Priorities and deadlines would be established, and organizations would be assigned tasks. Marine Corps Intelligence Activity [in Quantico, Virginia], because of its dedicated team of topographic and imagery analysts working 24 hours a day, seven days a week, received the lion's share of [requests for] studies to support future operations. Studies ordered by TF 58 . . . were routinely turned around in less than 18 hours.[2]

The Marines' role in Afghanistan appears to be part of a larger trend: a deemphasis on amphibious operations per se and a movement toward using Marines both in special operations and in support of other special operations forces. The Marines signed an agreement with Special Operations Command in November 2001—the first month of the war—that calls for Marines to train under that command for the first time in history. It also stipulates that army Special Forces units will serve with all Marine expeditionary units afloat. That agreement was approved by then commandant James L. Jones, who later told the *Washington Post* that "for the foreseeable future, there's a requirement for more special operations–like forces. My argument is, if you already have a fair amount of those [in the Marines], don't reinvent the wheel. Use what you already have."[3]

The Marines' ability to move so far inland so quickly without any special packaging of forces specifically designed for the Afghanistan campaign was truly impressive. The Marines' capability to project power from the sea to the shore to "kick down the door" had been dramatically extended. A thoughtful analyst in the *Naval Institute Proceedings* was surely right:

Operational and geographic realities in the Afghan theater of war have shown the value of naval platforms in the new geopolitical environment. The USS *Kitty Hawk* [an aircraft carrier] and two amphibious ready groups with embarked Marines provided platforms for various missions ashore while denying the enemy an opportunity to strike back. In a world where missiles are proliferating and asymmetric tactics are most likely, such platforms will become increasingly valuable.[4]

His words were soon put to the test, in the next major conflict: war against Saddam Hussein's forces in Iraq. Hussein may not have had any connection to the events of September 11, but in the eyes of the Bush administration, he was a greater threat than ever in a world of cross-border terrorists who were itching to get their hands on weapons of mass destruction. This argument convinced a significant "coalition of the willing"—but not the U.N. Security Council—that Saddam's regime had to be overthrown.

Political decision making aside, the second Gulf War would prove to be a double-edged test of the Corps. An initial sweep across the country led to the fall of Baghdad and then a premature declaration that offensive operations were complete. Thereafter, American soldiers and Marines entered a long period of occupation, in which small-unit firefights and remotely detonated bombs were everyday events.

The three-week campaign to crush the regime of Saddam Hussein under the commander in chief of Central Command, U.S. Army general Tommy Franks, was one of rapid movement over vast distances. In the first Gulf War the press had complained vigorously about tight censorship of events on the battlefield. In Iraq in 2003, censorship hadn't disappeared, of course, but the Department of Defense made an extraordinary decision to place dozens of "embedded" reporters from print and television with units throughout the conflict. They were given training stateside to accompany Marines and soldiers in combat. The media would debate the merits of the program for years to come, but one thing was certain: because of the embedding technique and the advances in the global communication network, the public for the first time was allowed a clear window on combat as it happened. The result featured a lot of micro images, with overexcited journalists calling military operations in a style more befitting a sports announcer than a war reporter.

From the earliest planning stages, Franks's invasion plan had called for attacks into Iraq from both the north and south—with one division attacking from Turkey and a corps from the desert of northern Kuwait. Yet the Bush administration was unsuccessful in securing Turkish consent for deployment of Coalition forces, so Franks and his staff had to reconfigure their assault plan into something that bore a close resemblance to that developed in 1990 for Operation Desert Storm by General Schwarzkopf and his staff, with one critical difference. The main objective in the 2003 war was to "cut off the head"—Baghdad itself was to be seized, and Saddam hunted down. As in the first Gulf War, airpower played a pivotal role. Air strikes knocked out the Iraqi army's command and control, thus rendering Saddam's defensive network vulnerable to attack, and B-52 bombers softened up and demoralized the frontline defensive positions. This time around, there were far more precision-guided munitions, and an extensive use of unmanned aerial vehicles to gather intelligence and drop ordnance. A general consensus emerged in the Marines and among the other services that these technological marvels had a very bright future in the American military inventory.

The U.S. Army's V Corps conducted the main attack, a sweeping left hook in the west, where the defenses were expected to be lighter than they were in the east. It fell to the Marines of the 1st Marine Expeditionary Force, about eighty-five thousand people in all, under the command of Lieutenant General James Conway, to make the secondary attack east of the army's main effort.

The initial objectives of the 1st Marine Division's attack were the strategically vital Al Rumaylah oil fields and a key pumping station in the southern corner of Iraq. The fields contained more than 450 active wellheads. Then, the entire Marine attacking force would feint toward the city of Basrah, in an effort to convince the enemy that they planned to take the traditional invasion route up the Tigris River toward Baghdad.

Rather than driving up the roads that followed the river, however, the Marines pivoted west, and split the division's highly mechanized units between two roads that ran along a north-south axis: Highway 1, an unfinished four-lane road leading to Highway 6, which fed Baghdad from the southeast, and Highway 7, to the east of Highway 1, which also joined Highway 6 in the vicinity of Al Numaniyah.

The early feint toward Basrah worked. No less than five divisions of the Iraqi regular army were left sitting on their hands north of Basrah, as the Marines drove past them toward Baghdad. Had the division marched north along a single road, it would have stretched out more than 174 miles. Each day, according to *The March Up*, a account of the Marine war by two former Marines, Bing West and retired Major General Ray L. Smith, the Marine division consumed forty-five thousand to sixty-five thousand meals a day, drank thirty-five thousand gallons of water, and filled its eight thousand vehicles with two hundred thousand gallons of fuel.[5]

It would be an astonishingly fast march, despite the awful weather, and the periodic ambushes and fixed defensive stands by Iraqi soldiers and the Fedayeen, the irregular, poorly trained troops who were fanatically loyal to Saddam Hussein. The logistical forces attached to the Marine division waged their own private battle to keep up with the fighting end of the column. The Marines conducting this attack were both well trained and well led. All echelons of two of the three regimental combat teams (RCTs) doing the lion's share of the fighting, the 5th and 7th Marines, had trained as organic units for months before hostilities began. The third RCT, built around the 1st Marine Regiment, had been cobbled together in a hurry from all over the globe. Yet the 1st RCT displayed the same level of esprit and unit integrity as its sister regimental teams once the division pulled out of Kuwait.

The commanding general of the Marine division had the distinction of having commanded every infantry echelon from platoon through division. An intense, energetic Marine officer, Major General James N. Mattis is known for clear thinking and the ability to make decisions quickly. As far as Operation Iraqi Freedom was concerned, Mattis felt that speed was vital to the success of the overarching political objective: establishing a stable Iraq with democratic elections, law, and a market economy. It was also the best way to limit casualties. In December 2002, the general had assembled his commanders for a briefing on the upcoming war. "I know one thing," he said. "The president, the National Command Authority, and the American people need speed. The sooner we get it over with the better. Our overriding principle will be speed, speed, speed."[6]

Mattis, and everyone else, seemed to get their wish when Baghdad fell on April 9, just twenty days after the invasion began. It was the objective of the fastest-moving army in history. Yet as time went by, it became apparent that many of Saddam's fighters had melted away only to fight another day.

After Saddam's regime collapsed, the Americans and their allies found themselves in a protracted counterinsurgency conflict. Marines (and U.S. Army and foreign soldiers, most notably those of the United

Kingdom) were at once providing security forces to stanch anarchy and chaos; helping to rebuild a shattered infrastructure and build support for a fledgling Iraqi government beset with problems; and conducting continuous small-unit operations at the company and platoon level against an increasingly large and well-organized insurgency fueled by Muslim rage over the American occupation. Eventually there would be battalion-sized combat operations in the close quarters of insurgent strongholds such as Samarra and Fallujah.

The Marine drive on Baghdad commenced when the 1st Division's three regimental combat teams, the 1st, 5th, and 7th RCTs, crossed their lines of departure near the border of Iraq and Kuwait on March 20 and 21, 2003. The scheme of maneuver called for an attack along a southeast-to-northwest axis. It was a race all the way, though at a great many junctures, the vehicles at the front end of the Marines' columns would spill their most vital cargo—Marine infantrymen, ready and willing to take the fight forward, adding small-arms fire to the chorus of blasts from Abrams tanks and the LAVs' highly effective 25mm Chain Guns.

Almost without exception, the combatants faced by the Marines were not the regular forces of a deeply demoralized and outgunned Iraqi army, but rather thousands of irregulars, Ba'ath Party Fedayeen, kitted out with AK-47s, mortars, and a plethora of rocket-propelled grenade launchers of Russian and Chinese origin. Some proportion of the enemy who put up serious resistance—no one knows exactly what percentage—were not indigenous to Iraq but had been drawn to the conflict from Syria, Yemen, Saudi Arabia, and other Arab states by the chance to kill American infidels.

For more than half of the drive north, the most decorated regiment in the history of the Corps, the 5th Marines, conducted the main attack effort. A close look at the operation as experienced by elements of Colonel Joe Dunford's regimental combat team (RCT) reveals much about the trajectory of the campaign, the types of friction and challenges the Marines faced, and why the objective—wresting Baghdad from the clutches of Saddam and his Ba'ath Party loyalists—was achieved with re-markably low casualties. The 5th Marines' initial mission was to seize the southern Rumaylah oil fields. That attack commenced at 2030 on March 20, some nine hours in advance of the main attack. By 0100 on March 21, the regiment had overwhelmed the defenders of this strategi-cally invaluable piece of real estate at the cost of one Marine killed and one wounded in action.

By the evening of March 27, the 5th RCT had neutralized the de-fenders of the Hantush airfield. The Marines needed the airstrip so KC-130s could land and deposit fuel bladders to feed the advance, thus reducing the number of highly vulnerable giant fuel trucks Mattis needed to insert in the ground columns. Before the airstrip was opera-tional, though, the unwelcome word had come down from General Franks: all forces were to pause and shift from the offensive drive toward Baghdad to stabilizing operations along the increasingly lengthy supply lines. As the days and nights went by with no one sure of when the next engagement would come, few Marines were able to sleep due to the ca-cophony of hundreds of military vehicles, the crackle of radios, and barked commands of sergeants and officers. As night approached, the Marines broke stride and prepared night fighting and sleeping positions along the roads, with each vehicle pulling into its assigned night security position. Exhausted, sand-drenched enlisted Marines stood by to get word on the sentry schedules and layout of the machine-gun and mortar positions from their sergeants. A strict blackout was enforced—seven thousand Marines were encamped in the middle of Iraq each night, and not a single flashlight was visible.

The 5th RCT on March 31 defeated an armored Iraqi battalion in retaking the Hantush airfield—they had been forced to retreat a few days earlier when Washington feared that allied forces were overex-tended. In so doing, it played an important role in the division's decep-tion plan to make the enemy think the main attack would continue up Highway 1. The next day, the 5th RCT attacked in a northeasterly direc-tion along Route 27 and seized a bridge over the Saddam Canal.

Dawn on April 1 found Joe Dunford's 5th RCT on the line of departure for an important event: the crossing of the Tigris River and cutting of Highway 6, the main road connecting southern Iraq with the capital. The 1st Battalion, 5th Marines, under Lieutenant Colonel Fred Padilla, that day found itself heavily engaged in combat against a dug-in enemy battalion on the other side of the river. It took Padilla's Marines most of the day to reduce the enemy positions, but by the end of the day, most of the regiment was across the river and pushing north against light resistance, while the 7th RCT was attacking toward Al Kut.

By April 4 the 5th RCT was on the edges of Baghdad. The assault into Baghdad proper began for the unit on the night of April 8. The column plunged into a city in chaos, replete with looters and the continuous sound of small-arms fire. Colonel Dunford had orders to link up with the 3rd Infantry Division on the bridges on the west side of the city. While Lieutenant Colonel Padilla was orchestrating a series of company-level raids on several different objectives, word came down to Colonel Dunford that Division wanted the 5th RCT to take the Presidential Palace. It was a battalion-sized operation. Dunford gave it to Padilla's 1st Battalion, 5th Marines.

Padilla was dismayed to find out that he would have little tactical intelligence about the objective. Six hundred to eight hundred enemy troops were suspected to be in the vicinity of the palace. The maps Padilla's men had were 1:100,000 scale—useless for navigating narrow city streets.

Padilla put together a mechanized task force, leaving most of his soft-skinned vehicles behind. He was a disciple of Mattis: the byword to his men was "speed." Get in and get it done quickly. As they approached the heart of the city and the palace grounds, every street and alleyway came alive with small-arms and machine-gun fire, and rocket-propelled grenades. For the next nine hours, 1/5 fought what many observers believe to be the most intense and harrowing single-battalion action in the Marines' fight for Baghdad.

Events threatened early on to get out of hand. Shear chaos reigned when Alpha Company took a wrong turn and had to double back on itself. Traffic got snarled, as the alleyways and many streets were too narrow to accommodate more than one vehicle at a time. The incoming fire was inaccurate—the Fedayeen had a well-deserved reputation as lousy shots—but it was very steady and unnerving nonetheless.

In the midst of the fighting near the palace, Padilla received a message: Saddam Hussein himself had been spotted near the Abus Hanifah Mosque. A company from 1/5 was quickly dispatched. Soon, B Company pushed its way through the front gate of the palace, whose defenders had fled under intense fire. Padilla called in additional forces to consolidate the palace grounds, where he still had a fierce fight on his hands. Artillery was called in on enemy firing positions.

Company C was detached from the fight immediately around the palace to carry out yet a third battalion objective: a site where POWs had just been spotted. Captain Sean Blodgett's unit found itself under increasing fire as it approached the site. As it came up on an intersection, a Fedayeen militiaman on a rooftop let fly with a burst of AK-47 fire, the rounds impacting a mere six to eight inches from Blodgett's head. Several Marines returned fire, killing the enemy gunman.

Meanwhile, Alpha Company, under Captain Blair Sokol, had made its way to the mosque. It, too, was in the midst of a real brawl. Padilla had three companies engaged in independent fights. No reserves were available to assist any of his units should they get into trouble. Colonel Dunford then offered Padilla the RCT's quick reaction force. Padilla gladly accepted the offer. With additional men and air force and Marine air support, Padilla's Marines were soon getting the best of the enemy in all three fights. It was around the mosque that the fighting was the most concentrated since enemy troops kept challenging the Marines' tanks and infantry. The first attempt to take the mosque failed. A new breach point was established, and soon Marines were pouring into the building in good order, clearing one room at a time. Twenty enemy fighters surrendered inside the mosque, and fourteen RPGs were seized.

Fred Padilla was very surprised to learn that only twenty-two 1/5 Marines had been evacuated for medical treatment, given the intensity of the fighting. But in fact, a total of seventy-six Marines had been wounded in the fighting over the past nine hours or so, but most had refused medical evacuation. They wanted to stay and fight it out in support of their fellow Marines. Only one Marine from 1/5 had been killed in the fight.

Among the units attached to the 5th RCT for extended periods of time during the operation was the 3rd Light Armored Reconnaissance Battalion under Lieutenant Colonel Stacy Clardy. Indeed, Clardy's unit was at the tip of the 5th RCT spear for about half of its drive to Baghdad. Clardy's battalion of a thousand men and 125 LAVs, unique to the Marine Corps, was attached for five days to 5th RCT in the drive on Baghdad. However, for the remainder of the monthlong campaign, the 3rd LAR Battalion functioned as an independent battalion reporting directly to Major General Jim Mattis, commander of the 1st Marine Division.

For about 230 of the 500 miles of the march up from Kuwait, Clardy's Marines served as the eyes and ears of Mattis's entire force, blazing a high-speed path other units would ultimately follow. It was a campaign of rapid movement over varied terrain, with elements of the battalion often spread out over twenty-five miles. Neither Clardy nor anybody else in the four companies under his command got much sleep. Elements of the battalion encountered largely ineffective harassment by RPGs, mortars, machine guns, and small arms almost every day.

Lieutenant Colonel Clardy estimates that his unit moved about 3,100 miles in one month. In that short time, the men of the 3rd LAR Battalion had also engaged in fifteen firefights with the enemy of varying levels of intensity.

The most dramatic of the 3rd LAR Battalion's operations in Iraq unfolded on April 13. The unit had just completed an operation east of Samarra, and was preparing to attack north into Saddam Hussein's hometown of Tikrit, having been given but a few hours' notice of the time of departure. As the unit was saddling up in preparation for the march north at about 0700, an Iraqi civilian approached the battalion commander, claiming he knew of some American prisoners of war in Samarra under guard by Ba'ath Party members.

Clardy was initially skeptical. "We always had people walking up to us and saying they saw Saddam Hussein down the street or other such claims."[7] After a Marine human-intelligence exploitation team had interrogated the man, the Americans gained the impression that he might very well be telling the truth. Clardy attempted to contact his commander, Task Force Tripoli's Brigadier General John Kelly, for guidance, but communications failed, as they often did in Operation Iraqi Freedom. Clardy had to make the decision himself, and fast, because he was supposed to be heading toward Tikrit to link up with Task Force Tripoli.

"I couldn't just leave with the idea they might be there, so I said, 'Okay. Let's go get them.'" In making such a quick unilateral decision, Clardy was employing the Marines' war fighting philosophy that opts for making "intuitive decisions" fast, on the spot, with limited information, rather than "analytical decision making," which calls for more time and information before a decision is rendered.

Clardy knew that POW rescue was officially outside of his list of missions. In fact, such risky and sensitive tasks were typically carried out by special operation forces, like SEALs or Delta Force. But Clardy also knew his men and believed in them. Using a handwritten map — "even the house number designated as holding the prisoners was wrong" — Lieutenant Colonel Clardy's thirty-two Marines of the 3rd Platoon, Company D, 3rd LAR Battalion drove into a potential enemy stronghold, located the house where the Americans were held by identifying a POW in a window, and assaulted the house. The Ba'athist guards were overwhelmed and surrendered without a shot.

A little while later, the platoon returned with seven pajama-clad U.S. soldiers: two army Apache helicopter pilots, and five members of the 507th Maintenance Company who had been captured three weeks earlier. The prisoners emerged from the back doors of an LAV into the view of two hundred Marines. When the Marines realized who these

Americans were and the POWs realized they were safe, Clardy remembered, "There wasn't a dry eye in the house. We were a pretty happy bunch of Americans."

History will show the invasion to have been a textbook operation. Yet its very speed and success made things worse for the occupation that followed. There were too few troops available to provide security, and many hostile forces had deceptively melted away. Whether the occupation proves to be a success, only time will tell. Iraq was a major issue in the campaign for the presidency in 2004 between Democrat John Kerry and President George W. Bush. Bush's oh-so-narrow victory suggests that the American people remain deeply divided on the operation.

The performance of the 1st Marine Expeditionary Force, commanded by General James Conway, was in this writer's estimation even better than it had been in the first Gulf War. In the 1991 conflict, as General Boomer said, the enemy force was for the most part demoralized. On paper they constituted a formidable force, but in the event, most preferred to surrender than fight. In spring 2003, the Iraqi forces were outgunned and outfought, but they gave a better account of themselves on the ground, where close-in urban combat and the presence of thousands of civilians in the combat zones served to neutralize the considerable advantages enjoyed by the U.S. military as a result of technological sophistication and superior training. They were also fighting for their own land, not for Kuwait.

Operation Iraqi Freedom showcased the Marines' capacity to operate effectively in a land campaign in which a reinforced Marine division and air wing fought five hundred miles from the ships that ferried most of them to the fight and provided their core logistical capacity.

The Marine Corps' success over the period covered in this book is based in no small measure on its ingrained habit of engaging in self-reflection and criticism. The senior leadership openly and lavishly praised the dedication and courage of the young Marines who fought along the roads and in the cities, yet it recognized that there were a number of aspects of the operation that could have gone much better. For example, like the U.S. Army, the Marines recognized that they had not prepared sufficiently for the rapid shift from combat operations to peace enforcement and constabulary duties. Also, night operations were limited because not all units had the best night-vision equipment.

Although the American military is recognized the world over as having the most sophisticated intelligence gathering technology, a major criticism voiced by battalion commanders—including both Fred Padilla and Stacy Clardy, in interviews—was the dearth of tactical intelligence, particularly tactical intelligence obtained from human beings. A document prepared by the Marine Corps soon after Operation Iraqi Freedom highlighted this problem in no uncertain terms: "Generally, the state of the Marines Corps' tactical intelligence collection capability is well behind the state of the art. Maneuver units have limited ability to see over the next hill, around the next corner, or inside the next building. . . . The Marine Corps has a tremendous void in its intelligence collection capabilities at the echelon that needs it most."[8] The assessment went on to report that a "byzantine collections process inhibited our ability to get timely responses to combat requirements. . . ."[9]

Most of the 1st MEF's units pulled out of Iraq at the end of April 2003, turning over their areas of operations to the army, but the Marines were back in force a year later, and so they remain, fighting a stubborn amalgam of insurgent groups.

EPILOGUE

Taken together, the momentous changes in world geopolitics we have seen since the mid-1990s, including the horrendous events of September 11, 2001, seem to place the U.S. Marine Corps in a position of unprecedented importance and prestige as an instrument of American national security and foreign policy. Defense analysts, former military officers, and military historians generally agree that, among the branches of the armed services, the Marines have adapted to the radical changes in the security environment at least as well, if not better, than any other branch of the military. Indeed, the Marine Corps' leaders, from Louis Wilson to Charles Krulak to James Jones and Mike Hagee, have led their branch of the armed services not only with distinction but with uncanny vision and imagination.

These men and the senior Marines who served closely with them seemed to have guessed correctly about force structure, resource allocation, and training techniques. The Marines' performance in a host of operations, up to and including the current war in Iraq, has elevated its public esteem and trust. But the Marines can do only so much when it comes to politics. Since the navy issued its seminal white papers, "From the Sea" in 1992 and "Forward . . . from the Sea" in 1994, concise statements of the naval services' core missions and guides for all long-range planning, the Marine Corps has become for the first time in its history truly an equal partner with its larger sister service in fulfilling the nation's maritime military strategy. Ever since 1992, the Department of the Navy's main focus is no longer on fighting and winning major naval battles on the open ocean against the Soviet navy, but on littoral warfare—the projection of American military power from the sea to the coastal areas of the world, where more than 70 percent of the world's people reside. The navy and the Marines today do their work while "forward deployed." The critical jobs take place not on the high seas but within a couple of hundred miles of land.

When deployed in an operation, Marines are told to rely on themselves, their training, and the ideas and judgments of their brother Marines, regardless of rank. Candor between all Marines in the field and in the classroom is strongly encouraged. Sergeants in the Marines can, and frequently do, criticize the proposed plans of their commanding officers. At staff meetings, lieutenants and captains raise objections to projected schemes of maneuver worked up by majors and lieutenant colonels. Once a decision has been reached, though, everyone is expected to support the plan without further protest.

Marines on operations are also taught to engage with the local population continuously—to communicate with them when possible, to learn their manners and customs, and to make plans that take into account local conditions and sensibilities rather than imposing the Marine or "American" way on people who may find that approach disorienting or counter to their own. The Marine Corps encourages its people to accept that when forward deployed on any sort of operation, the situation is sure to be messy and complicated. Marines must accept—and cope with—a work environment where chaos and crisis are the rule, not the exception, where ambiguous orders from political authorities on the scene are to be expected, and where high stress and rapid change is constant. The Marines don't try to eliminate uncertainty, but to embrace and manage it through teamwork, constant communication, rigorous training, and self-criticism.

General Chuck Krulak, during his tenure as commandant, talked constantly about the need for solid moral character among deployed Marines who must navigate so often in places like Somalia or Liberia, where hope has all but died and religious and ethnic conflicts have fostered abiding distrust, and a great deal of cruelty, bloodshed, and hatred.

It was Krulak who popularized the notion of the three-block war to describe the peculiar parameters and challenges facing the American Marine and soldier today. In the three-block war scenario, General Krulak remarked in a speech to the National Press Club in 1997, Marines "in one moment of time . . . will be feeding and clothing the displaced refugees, providing humanitarian assistance. In the next moment, they will be holding two warring tribes apart—conducting peacekeeping operations—and finally, they will be fighting a highly lethal mid-intensity battle—all on the same day—all within three city blocks."[1]

General Krulak extended recruit training to include a formidable fifty-four-hour final exercise, on the theory that more complexity and confusion on the battlefield of today and tomorrow required more basic training. Thus, "the Crucible" is fifty-four hours of pure hell, in which recruits must work together to solve a baffling set of tactical problems while placed under extreme stress, with very little sleep and even less food.

The Crucible isn't enjoyed very much by the recruits. But it has been universally praised by old-salt Marines, by military training experts, as well as by the young Marines who make it through the ordeal, and in so doing ensure that they will wear the eagle, globe, and anchor. The Crucible appears to be an appropriate, even necessary, addition to a training regimen that was already second to none in the world for general-purpose troops.

In the wake of the tragic events of September 11, 2001, and two new wars in Asia, thousands of Marines would look back on their fifty-four hours of hell and thank God that General Krulak had instituted the Crucible—that final hurdle to becoming part of the great fraternity of American warriors—the United States Marines.

Notes

Introduction

1. Kuribayashi quoted in Joseph H. Alexander, *Closing In: Marines in the Seizure of Iwo Jima* (Washington, D.C.: History and Museums Division, Headquarters, U.S. Marine Corps, 1994), p. 11.
2. Quoted in Bill D. Ross, *Iwo Jima: Legacy of Valor* (New York: Vanguard Press, 1985), p. 57.
3. Quoted in ibid., p. 68.
4. Fred Haynes interview.

Chapter 1: "The Indefinable Inner Strength": Elements of Marine Corps Culture

1. Butler letter quoted in Max Boot, *The Savage Wars of Peace: Small Wars and the Rise of American Power* (New York: Basic Books, 2002), p. 342.
2. *United States Marine Corps Concepts and Issues,* 2003 (Washington, D.C.: Requirements and Programs Division, Headquarters, U.S. Marine Corps, 2003), p. 2.
3. *Warfighting* (Washington, D.C.: U.S. Marine Corps, 1997), pp. 13–14.
4. Ibid., p. 8.
5. Charles C. Krulak, "Cultivating Intuitive Decisionmaking," *Marine Corps Gazette,* May 1999.
6. Haynes interview.

7. Seth Haines interview.
8. Victor H. Krulak, *First to Fight: An Inside View of the U.S. Marine Corps* (Annapolis: Naval Institute Press, 1984), p. 159.
9. Zell Miller, *Corps Values: Everything You Need to Know I Learned in the Marines* (New York: Bantam Books, 1998), p. 5.
10. Chad Gill, comment to author during field training exercise, July 2003.
11. *Warfighting*, pp. 57–58.
12. Alberto Coll interview.
13. Zinni quoted in Marion F. Sturkey, *Warrior Culture of the U.S. Marines* (Plum Branch, S.C.: Heritage Books International, 2002), p. 27.
14. Gerald P. Averill, *Mustang* (Novato, Calif.: Presidio Press, 1987), p. 3.
15. James Webb interview.
16. Justin Wilson interview.
17. Lejeune quoted in Krulak, *First to Fight*, p. 157.
18. *Warfighting*, p. 19
19. James Webb interview.
20. Robert A. Wehrle interview.
21. Robert Barrow quoted in J. Robert Moskin, *The Marine Corps Story*, 3rd rev. ed. (Boston: Little, Brown), p. 712.
22. Holland M. Smith and Percy Finch, *Coral and Brass* (New York: Charles Scribner's Sons, 1947), p. 72.
23. Jeter A. Isley and Philip A. Crowl, *The U.S. Marines and Amphibious War: Its Theory and Its Practice in the Pacific* (Princeton: Princeton University Press, 1951), p. 582.
24. Charles C. Krulak, "A Farewell to the Corps," *Marine Corps Gazette*, April 1998.
25. *Small Wars Manual* (Washington, D.C.: U.S. Marine Corps, 1940), p. 2.
26. This phrase is from the Gospel of Luke. It was used by Robert Leckie, a former Marine, as the title of his fine combat history of the Marines in World War II.

Chapter 2: The Supreme Test: The Battle of Iwo Jima

1. Quoted in Karal Ann Marling and John Wetenhall, *Iwo Jima: Monuments, Memories, and the American Hero* (Cambridge: Harvard University Press, 1991), p. 21.
2. Holland Smith and Percy Finch, *Coral and Brass* (New York: Charles Scribner's Sons, 1947), p. 245.
3. Haynes interview.
4. Jeter A. Isley and Philip A. Crowl, *The U.S. Marines and Amphibious War: Its*

Theory and Its Practice in the Pacific War (Princeton: Princeton University Press, 1951), p. 43.

5. George C. Marshall, "Biennial Report of the Chief of Staff of the United States Army, 1 July 1943 to 30 June 1945, to the Secretary of War" in *The War Reports* (Philadelphia: J.P. Lippincott, 1947), p. 239.

6. Plans Committee report quoted in Whitman S. Bartley, *Iwo Jima: Amphibious Epic* (Washington, D.C.: Historical Branch Headquarters, U.S. Marine Corps, 1954), pp. 22–23.

7. Lardner quoted in Marling and Wetenhall, *Iwo Jima*, p. 29.

8. Smith quoted in Joseph H. Alexander, *Closing In: Marines in the Seizure of Iwo Jima* (Washington, D.C.: History and Museums Division, Headquarters, U.S. Marine Corps, 1994), p. 4.

9. Haynes interview.

10. Turner quoted in Marling and Wetenhall, *Iwo Jima*, p. 21.

11. Kuribayashi quoted in Bill D. Ross, *Iwo Jima: Legacy of Valor* (New York: Vanguard Press, 1985), p. 20.

12. Smith quoted in Joseph H. Alexander, *Closing In*, p. 6.

13. John P. Marquand, "Iwo Jima Before H Hour," *Harper's* (May 1945), p. 499.

14. Gallant quoted in ibid., p. 72.

15. Robert Leckie, *Strong Men Armed* (New York: Random House, 1962), p. 442.

16. Unnamed Marine quoted in Bill D. Ross, *Iwo Jima*, p. 105.

17. Sherrod quoted in Ross, *Iwo Jima*, p. 80.

18. George W. Garand and Truman R. Strobridge, *Western Pacific Operations*, vol. 4, History of U.S. Marine Corps Operations in World War II (Washington, D.C.: Historical Branch, Headquarters, U.S. Marine Corps, 1971), p. 53.

19. Richard Wheeler, *The Bloody Battle for Suribachi* (Annapolis: Naval Institute Press, 1994), p. 109.

20. Forrestal quoted in Alexander, *Closing In*, p. 27.

21. Quoted in Ross, *Iwo Jima*, p. 99.

22. Garand and Strobridge, *Western Pacific Operations*, p. 546.

23. Ibid., p. 548.

24. Ibid., p. 490.

25. Duplantis quoted in Ross, *Iwo Jima*, p. 168.

26. Stanton quoted in Wheeler, *Iwo* (New York: Lippincott & Crowell, 1980), pp. 195–96.

27. Erskine quoted in Garand and Strobridge, *Western Pacific Operations*, p. 562.

28. Ibid., p. 675.

29. Leckie, *Strong Men Armed*, p. 461.

30. Unidentified Marine quoted in ibid., p. 463.

31. Chuck Tatum interview in *Red Blood, Black Sand,* directed by Randy Bond (PBS documentary film, 1986).

32. Spruance quoted in Garand and Strobridge, *Western Pacific Operations,* p. 713.

33. Lewis W. Walt, *Strange War, Strange Strategy: A General's Report on Vietnam* (New York: Funk and Wagnalls, 1970), p. 27.

Chapter 3: The Final Struggle: Okinawa and the Legacies of the Pacific War

1. Quoted in Joseph H. Alexander, *The Final Campaign: Marines in the Victory on Okinawa* (Washington, D.C.: Marine Corps Historical Center, 1996), p. 12.

2. Jeter A. Isley and Philip A. Crowl, *The U.S. Marines and Amphibious War: Its Theory and Its Practice in the Pacific* (Princeton: Princeton University Press, 1951), pp. 539–40.

3. George McMillan et al., *Uncommon Valor: Marine Divisions in Action* (Washington, D.C.: Infantry Journal Press, 1946), p. 215.

4. Marine officer quoted in Benis M. Frank and Henry I. Shaw Jr., *Victory and Occupation* (Washington: Historical Branch, Headquarters, U.S. Marine Corps, 1968), p. 145.

5. Unidentified Marine quoted in George McMillan et al., *Uncommon Valor,* p. 217.

6. Alexander, *The Final Campaign: Marines in the Victory on Okinawa,* p. 19.

7. Charles Nichols and Henry I. Shaw Jr., *Okinawa: Victory in the Pacific* (Historical Branch, G-3 Division, Headquarters, U.S. Marine Corps, 1955).

8. After Action Report quoted in Charles Nichols and Henry Shaw Jr., *Okinawa,* p. 176.

9. William Manchester, *Goodbye, Darkness* (Boston: Little, Brown, 1979), pp. 378–80.

10. Pinnow quoted in James Belote, *Typhoon of Steel: The Battle for Okinawa* (New York: Bantam, 1984), p. 250.

11. E. B. Sledge, *With the Old Breed on Peleliu and Okinawa* (New York: Oxford University Press, 1990), pp. 243–45.

12. Nichols and Henry I. Shaw Jr., *Okinawa,* p. 277.

13. Owens quoted in Gerald Astor, *Operation Iceberg* (New York: Dell, 1995) pp. 485–89.

14. Vandegrift quoted in Robert Debs Heinl Jr., *Soldiers of the Sea: The United States Marine Corps, 1775–1962,* 2nd ed. (Baltimore: Nautical and Aviation Publishing Company of America, 1991), p. 591.

15. Lejeune quoted in Robert Lindsay, *This High Name: Public Relations and the U.S. Marine Corps* (Madison, Wis.: University of Wisconsin Press, 1956), p. 38.

Notes

Chapter 4: Transition and Challenge, 1945 to 1950

1. Statement by General A. A. Vandegrift to Senate Naval Affairs Committee, May 6, 1946.
2. McNarney quoted in Gordon W. Keiser, *The U.S. Marine Corps and Defense Unification 1944–47* (Baltimore: Nautical & Aviation Publishing Co. of America, 1996), p. 28.
3. Eisenhower quoted in Victor H. Krulak, *First to Fight: An Inside View of the U.S. Marine Corps* (Annapolis: Naval Institute Press, 1984), p. 34.
4. USMC memorandum quoted in Krulak, *First to Fight*, p. 35.
5. Clifford quoted in Keiser, p. 230.
6. Quoted in Allan R. Millett, *Semper Fidelis: The History of the United States Marine Corps*, rev. ed. (New York: Free Press, 1991), p. 463.
7. Vandegrift quoted in Richard Tregaskis, "The Marine Corps Fights for Its Life," *Saturday Evening Post*, February 5, 1949.
8. Cates quoted in Robert Debs Heinl Jr., *Soldiers of the Sea: The United States Marine Corps, 1775–1962*, 2nd ed. (Baltimore: Nautical and Aviation Publishing Company of America, 1991), p. 524.
9. Clifton B. Cates statement to the House Armed Services Committee, October 17, 1949.
10. Krulak, *First to Fight*.
11. Quoted in Charles R. Smith, *Securing the Surrender: Marines in the Occupation of Japan* (Washington, D.C.: History and Museums Division, Headquarters, U.S. Marine Corps, 1997), p. 28.
12. John Dower, *War Without Mercy: Race and Power in the Pacific War* (New York: Pantheon, 1986), p. 302.
13. MacArthur quoted in Smith, *Securing the Surrender*, p. 44.
14. Rockey quoted in Benis M. Frank and Henry I. Shaw Jr., *Victory and Occupation*, vol. 5, History of U.S. Marine Corps Operations in World War II (Washington, D.C.: Historical Branch, Headquarters, U.S. Marine Corps, 1968), p. 586.
15. Henry I. Shaw Jr., *The United States Marines in North China, 1945–1949* (Washington, D.C.: U.S. Marine Corps, 1962).

Chapter 5: The Korean War: From Pusan Through the Capture of Seoul

1. Day Jr. quoted in Donald Knox, *The Korean War, Pusan to Chosin: An Oral History* (San Diego: Harcourt Brace Jovanovich, 1985), pp. 23–24.
2. MacArthur quoted in Robert Debs Heinl Jr., *Soldiers of the Sea: The United States Marine Corps, 1775–1962*, 2nd ed. (Baltimore: Nautical and Aviation Publishing Company of America, 1991), p. 539.

3. Commander in Chief Far East dispatch to JCS, July 21, 1950.
4. Fenton quoted in Knox, *The Korean War*, p. 141.
5. Bohn quoted in ibid., p. 208.
6. Truman quoted in Heinl, *Soldiers of the Sea*, p. 546.
7. Capps quoted in Robert Debs Heinl, *Victory at High Tide: The Inchon-Seoul Campaign* (Baltimore: Nautical and Aviation Publishing Company of America, 1979), p. 68.
8. Douglas MacArthur, *Reminiscences* (New York: McGraw-Hill, 1964), pp. 349–50.
9. Quoted in Max Hastings, *The Korean War* (New York: Simon and Schuster, 1987), p. 105.
10. Brainard quoted in Joseph Alexander, *Battle of the Barricades* (Washington, D.C.: History and Museums Division, Headquarters, U.S. Marine Corps, 2000), p. 10.
11. Barrow quoted in ibid., p. 12.
12. Almond quoted in Heinl, *Victory at High Tide*, p. 231.
13. Ridge quoted in ibid., p. 236.
14. Ridge quoted in ibid., p. 238.
15. Bergee quoted in Knox, *The Korean War*, p. 299.

Chapter 6: The Korean War: From the Chosin Reservoir to the Armistice, July 1953

1. Truman quoted in Max Hastings, *The Korean War* (New York: Simon and Schuster, 1987), p. 117.
2. JCS message to MacArthur, quoted in Lynn Montross and Nicholas A. Canzona, *The Chosin Reservoir Campaign*, volume 3 of *U.S. Marine Operations in Korea* (Washington: Historical Branch, Headquarters, U.S. Marine Corps, 1957), p. 5.
3. U.N. communication quoted in ibid., p. 8.
4. Hastings, *The Korean War*, p. 122.
5. Ibid., p. 123.
6. Montross and Canzona, *The Chosin Reservoir Campaign*, p. 37.
7. Litzenberg quoted in ibid., p. 98.
8. Montross and Canzona, *The Chosin Reservoir Campaign*, p. 92.
9. Smith letter quoted in Robert Debs Heinl Jr., *Soldiers of the Sea* (Annapolis: Nautical and Aviation Publishing Company of America, 1962), p. 559.
10. Montross and Canzona, *The Chosin Reservoir Campaign*, p. 144.
11. Ibid., p. 96
12. Ibid., p. 179.
13. Ibid., p. 218.

14. Bowser quoted in Hastings, *The Korean War*, p. 157.
15. Report quoted in Montross and Canzona, *The Chosin Reservoir Campaign*, p. 265.
16. Joseph Owen, *Colder Than Hell: A Marine Rifle Company at Chosin Reservoir* (New York: Ivy Books, 1996), p. 233.
17. Davis interview.
18. Partridge quoted in Hastings, *The Korean War*.
19. Xenophon, *The Anabasis of Cyrus*, in F. R. B. Godolphin, *The Greek Historians*, vol. 2, trans. Henry C. Dakyns (New York: Random House, 1942), pp. 297–98.
20. Clay Blair, *The Forgotten War: America in Korea, 1950–53* (New York: Doubleday, 1987), p. 559.
21. Koegel quoted in Donald Knox, *The Korean War, Pusan to Chosin: An Oral History* (San Diego: Harcourt Brace Jovanovich, 1985), p. 164.
22. Diary quoted in Lynn Montross et al., *The East-Central Front*, volume 4 of *U.S. Marine Operations in Korea, 1950–1953* (Washington: Historical Branch, Headquarters, U.S. Marine Corps, 1962), p. 192.
23. Pat Mead and James M. Yingling, *Operations in West Korea*, vol. 5 of *U.S. Marine Operations in Korea, 1950–1953* (Washington: Historical Branch, Headquarters, U.S. Marine Corps, 1972), p. 483.
24. *New York Times*, June 28, 1951.

Chapter 7: Between Two Wars, 1953 to 1965

1. Eugene W. Rawlins, *Marines and Helicopters, 1946–1962* (Washington: History and Museums Divison, Headquarters, U.S. Marine Corps, 1976), p. 41.
2. Major Robert A. Smith, "First to Fight," *Marine Corps Gazette*, November 1976, p. 44.
3. William Manchester, *Goodbye, Darkness* (Boston: Little, Brown, 1979), p. 120.
4. Keith Fleming, *The U.S. Marine Corps in Crisis: Ribbon Creek and Recruit Training* (Columbia, S.C.: University of South Carolina Press, 1990), p. 25.
5. Ben Price, " 'Book' Is Sad Story to Marine Noncoms," *Washington Post*, May 27, 1956.
6. Jack Shulimson, *Marines in Lebanon, 1958*, rev. ed. (Washington, D.C.: History and Museums Division, Headquarters, U.S. Marine Corps, 1983), p. 12.
7. Ibid., p. 17.
8. Ibid., p. 36.
9. John Spanier, *American Foreign Policy Since World War II*, 12th ed. (Washington: Congressional Quarterly Press, 1992), p. 156.

Chapter 8: Tragedy in the Making: The Marines in Vietnam, 1965 to 1967

1. Vann quoted in Neil Sheehan, *Bright Shining Lie: John Paul Vann and America in Vietnam* (New York: Random House, 1988), p. 277.
2. Ball quoted in Charles Neu, ed., *After Vietnam: Legacies of a Lost War* (Baltimore: Johns Hopkins University Press).
3. Stanley Karnow, *Vietnam: A History* (New York: Viking, 1983), p. 11.
4. Greene quoted in Jack Shulimson and Major Charles M. Johnson, *U.S. Marines in Vietnam, 1965: The Landing and the Buildup* (Washington, D.C.: History and Museums Division, Headquarters, U.S. Marine Corps, 1978), p. 46.
5. Victor H. Krulak, *First to Fight: An Inside View of the U.S. Marine Corps* (Annapolis: Naval Institute Press, 1984), pp. 197–98.
6. Clement quoted in ibid., p. 141.
7. Kosoglow quoted in Francis J. West Jr., *Small Unit Action in Vietnam: Summer 1966* (Washington, D.C.: History and Museums Division, Headquarters, U.S. Marine Corps, 1967), p. 20.
8. Helicopter pilot quoted in ibid., p. 24.
9. McGinty quoted in Jack Shulimson, *U.S. Marines in Vietnam: An Expanding War, 1966* (Washington, D.C.: History and Museums Division, Headquarters, U.S. Marine Corps, 1982), p. 171.
10. McGinty citation quoted in George Lang et al., *Medal of Honor Recipients, 1863–1994*, volume 2 of *World War II to Somalia* (New York: Facts on File, 1995), pp. 717–18.
11. Muir quoted in Al Santoli, *Everything We Had: An Oral History of the Vietnam War by Thirty-three American Soldiers Who Fought It* (New York: Ballantine Books, 1981), pp. 28–29.
12. Johnson quoted in Edwin H. Simmons, "Marine Corps Operations in Vietnam, 1965–1966," in *The Marines in Vietnam, 1954–1973: An Anthology and Annotated Bibliography* (Washington, D.C.: History and Museums Division, Headquarters, U.S. Marine Corps, 1974), p. 58.
13. Westmoreland quoted in Simmons, "Marine Corps Operations in Vietnam, 1967," in ibid., p. 123.
14. Haynes interview.
15. Philip Caputo, *A Rumor of War* (New York: Ballantine Books, 1977), p. 89.
16. Marine officer quoted in Simmons, "Marine Corps Operations in Vietnam, 1967," in *The Marines in Vietnam, 1954–1973*, p. 82.
17. Haynes interview.
18. Metzger quoted in Simmons, "Marine Operations in Vietnam, 1967," in *The Marines in Vietnam, 1954–1973*, p. 82.
19. Westmoreland quoted in Stanley Karnow, *Vietnam*, p. 514.

20. Greene quoted in Simmons, "Marine Operations in Vietnam, 1967," in *The Marines in Vietnam, 1954–1973*, p. 238.
21. Malcolm Browne, *The New Face of War* (Indianapolis: Bobbs Merrill, 1968), p. ix.

Chapter 9: From Tet to the Fall of Saigon, 1968 to 1975

1. Westmoreland quoted in John Prados and Ray Stubbe, *Valley of Decision: The Siege of Khe Sanh* (Boston: Houghton Mifflin, 1991), p. 251.
2. Westmoreland quoted in ibid., p. 216.
3. Stanton quoted in Eric Hammel, *Khe Sanh: Siege in the Clouds* (New York: Crown Publishers, 1989), p. 39.
4. English quoted in Prados and Stubbe, *Valley of Decision*, p. 46.
5. Robert Pisor, *The End of the Line: The Siege of Khe Sahn* (New York: W. W. Norton, 1982), p. 36.
6. Ibid., p. 115.
7. Delaney quoted in Hammel, *Khe Sanh*, p. 178.
8. Marine quoted in Prados and Stubbe, *Valley of Decision*, p. 349.
9. Taylor quoted in ibid., p. 362.
10. Westmoreland quoted in ibid., p. 357.
11. Tolson quoted in Hammel, *Khe Sahn*, p. 484.
12. Torres quoted in ibid., p. 368.
13. Michael Herr, *Dispatches* (New York: Alfred A. Knopf, 1969), p .87.
14. Newspaper quoted in Prados and Stubbe, *Valley of Decision*, p. 395.
15. Lownds quoted in ibid., p. 409.
16. William Westmoreland, *A Soldier Reports* (Norwalk, Conn.: Easton Press, 1994), pp. 335–36.
17. Neil Sheehan, *A Bright Shining Lie: John Paul Vann and America in Vietnam* (New York: Random House, 1988), p. 71.
18. David T. Zabecki, "Tet Offensive: Overall Strategy," in *Encyclopedia of the Vietnam War*, Spencer C. Tucker, ed. (New York: Oxford University Press, 2000), p. 397.
19. Christmas quoted in Shulimson et al., *U.S. Marines in Vietnam: The Defining Year, 1968* (Washington, D.C.: History and Museums Division, Headquarters, U.S. Marine Corps, 1977), p. 185.
20. Cheatham quoted in ibid., pp. 179–80.
21. Ibid., p. 185.
22. Thompson quoted in ibid., p. 200.
23. Harrington quoted in Stanley Karnow, *Vietnam: A History* (New York: Viking, 1983), p. 532.

24. Cheatham interview in "Tet in Saigon and Hue: On the Frontline." Aired March 3, 2002.
25. *Wall Street Journal,* February 23, 1968, editorial page.
26. Andrew Krepinovich, *The Army and Vietnam* (Baltimore: Johns Hopkins University Press, 1988), p. 245.
27. III MAF campaign plan quoted in Charles R. Smith, *U.S. Marines in Vietnam: High Mobility and Standdown* (Washington, D.C.: History and Museums Division, Headquarters, U.S. Marine Corps, 1988), p. 13.
28. Barrow quoted in Smith, *U.S. Marines in Vietnam.*
29. Allan R. Millett, *Semper Fidelis: The History of the United States Marine Corps,* rev. ed. (New York: Free Press, 1991), p. 603.
30. Major General Alan J. Armstrong quoted in Graham Cosmas and Terrence P. Murray, *U.S. Marine Operations in Vietnam, 1970–1971* (Washington, D.C.: History and Museums Division, Headquarters, U.S. Marine Corps, 1986), p. 333.
31. Sergeant Major Edgar Huff quoted in ibid., p. 344.
32. Notebook quoted in ibid., p. 346.

Chapter 10: From Abyss to Resurrection, 1975 to 1991
1. John F. Guilmartin, *A Very Short War: The Mayaguez and the Battle of Koh Tang* (College Station, Tex.: Texas A&M University Press, 1995), p. 86.
2. *Operation Iraqi Freedom* (Washington, D.C.: 1st Marine Division Association, 2004), p. 28.
3. Haynes interview.
4. *Executive Summary of the Haynes Board* (Washington, D.C.: Marine Historical Center, page 2.
5. Kelley quoted in J. Robert Moskin, *The U.S. Marine Corps Story,* 3rd rev. ed. (Boston: Little, Brown, 1992), p. 758.
6. Ibid., p. 3.
7. Haynes interview.
8. Bernard Trainor, "The Personal Campaign Issue Is No Longer in Doubt," *Marine Corps Gazette,* January 1978, p. 27.
9. Wilson letter to Sam Nunn, December 31, 1975 (Washington, D.C.: History and Museums Division, Headquarters, U.S. Marine Corps).
10. Report quoted in Lou Cannon, *President Reagan: The Role of a Lifetime* (New York: Simon and Schuster, 1991), p. 389.
11. Ibid., p. 440.
12. Report quoted in Benis Frank, *U.S. Marines in Lebanon* (Washington: History and Museums Division, U.S. Marine Corps, 1987), pp. 82–84.
13. Ibid., p. 23.

14. Anderson quoted in Frank, *U.S. Marines in Lebanon*, p. 56.
15. Eric Hammel, *The Root: The Marines in Beirut* (San Diego: Harcourt Brace Jovanovich, 1985), p. 213.
16. Mead quoted in Frank, *U.S. Marines in Lebanon*, p. 57.
17. Slacum quoted in Ibid., p. 98.
18. Gray quoted in *Warfighting* (Washington, D.C.: Headquarters, U.S. Marines Corps, 1997), p. ii.
19. *Warfighting*, p. 13.
20. Ibid., pp. 13–14.

Chapter 11: The Gulf War to Somalia

1. Michael R. Gordon and Bernard E. Trainor, *The Generals' War: The Inside Story of the Conflict in the Gulf* (Boston: Little, Brown, 1995), p. 49.
2. Schwarzkopf quoted in Allan R. Millett, *Semper Fidelis: The History of the U.S. Marine Corps*, rev. ed. (New York: Free Press, 1991), p. 639.
3. Edwin H. Simmons, "Getting Marines to the Gulf," in *U.S. Marines in the Persian Gulf, 1990–1991* (Washington: History and Museums Division, U.S. Marine Corps, 1992), p. 14.
4. Boomer letter quoted in Gordon and Trainor, *The Generals' War*, p. 165.
5. Gordon and Trainor, *The Generals' War*, p. 288.
6. Molly Moore, "Allies Use a Variation of Trojan Horse Ploy," *Washington Post*, March 17, 1991.
7. Ibid.
8. Robert A. Doss, "Rescue from Mogadishu," in *Naval Institute Proceedings*, May 1992, p. 103.
9. Adam B. Siegel, "An American Entebbe," *Naval Institute Proceedings*, May 1992, p. 92.
10. Lieutenant Colonel T. A. Richards, "Marines in Somalia: 1992," in *Naval Institute Proceedings*, May 1993, p. 133.
11. "Marines 'Restore Hope' to Somalia," *Marine Corps Gazette*, January 1993, p. 3.
12. Taol quoted in David Bowne Wood, *A Sense of Values: American Warriors in an Uncertain World* (Kansas City: Andrews McMeel, 1994), p. 121.
13. Lance corporal quoted in ibid., p. 119.

Chapter 12: Two Wars in a New Century: Afghanistan and the War in Iraq

1. Michael E. Innis, "A New Operating Environment," *Marine Corps Gazette*, August 2002.

2. Ibid.
3. James L. Jones quoted in Bradley Graham, "Distancing Tradition, Marines Eye Role in Special Operations. Jones: Shed the Word 'Amphibious,'" *Washington Post*, November 17, 2002.
4. Frank G. Hoffman, "Early Lessons from Enduring Freedom," in *Naval Institute Proceedings*, April 2002.
5. Bing West and Ray L. Smith, *The March Up: Taking Baghdad with the 1st Marine Division* (New York: Bantam Books, 2003), p. 18.
6. Mattis quoted in West and Smith, *The March Up*, p. 5.
7. "'True Grit' in Iraq Earns Bronze Star for Marines," *Newport Navalog*, April 2, 2004, p. 12.
8. "Operation Iraqi Freedom: Lessons Learned" (Washington, D.C.: Headquarters, U.S. Marine Corps, 2004), p. 6.
9. Ibid., p. 4.

Epilogue

1. Krulak speech to National Press Club, October 10, 1997, transcript.

Selected Bibliography

Alexander, Joseph. *Closing In: Marines in the Seizure of Iwo Jima*. Washington, DC: USMC, 1994.

——. *The Final Campaign: Marines in the Victory on Okinawa*. Washington, DC: USMC, 1996.

——. *Sea Soldiers in the Cold War*. Annapolis, MD: Naval Institute Press, 1995.

Bartley, Lt. Col. Whitman S. *Iwo Jima: Amphibious Epic*. Washington, DC: USMC, 1961.

Blair, Clay. *The Forgotten War: America in Korea, 1950–1953*. New York: Times Books, 1987.

Boot, Max. *The Savage Wars of Peace: Small Wars and the Rise of American Power*. New York: Basic Books, 2002.

Cannon, Lou. *President Reagan: The Role of a Lifetime*. New York: Simon & Schuster, 1991.

Caputo, Philip. *A Rumor of War*. New York: Ballantine Books, 1977.

Corson, William R. *The Betrayal*. New York: W.W. Norton, 1968.

Davis, Burke. *Marine!* Boston: Little, Brown, 1962.

Feherbach, T. R. *This Kind of War*. Washington, DC: Brassey's, 1994.

Fleming, Keith. *The U.S. Marine Corps in Crisis: Ribbon Creek and Recruit Training*. Columbia: University of South Carolina Press, 1990.

Frank, Benis M. *U.S. Marines in Lebanon, 1982–1984*. Washington, DC: USMC, 1987.

Garand, George W., and Truman R. Strobridge. *Western Pacific Operations*. Vol. 4, History of U.S. Marine Corps Operations in World War II. Washington, DC: USMC, 1971.

Giap, Gen. Vo Nguyen. *Big Victory, Great Task*. New York: Praeger, 1968.

Selected Bibliography

Gordon, Michael R., and Gen. Bernard E. Trainor. *The Generals' War: The Inside Story of the Conflict in the Gulf.* Boston: Little, Brown, 1995.

Hammel, Eric. *The Root: The Marines in Beirut, August 1982–February 1984.* San Diego, CA: Harcourt Brace Jovanovich, 1985.

Heinl, Robert Debs, Jr. *Soldiers of the Sea: The United States Marine Corps 1775–1962.* Naval Institute Press, 1962.

——. *Victory at High Tide: The Inchon-Seoul Campaign.* Baltimore: Naval and Aviation Publishing Company of America, 1979. (Reprint of 1968 ed.)

Herr, Michael. *Dispatches.* New York: Knopf, 1977.

Hoffman, Jon T. *Chesty: The Story of Lieutenant General Lewis B. Puller, USMC.* New York: Random House, 2001.

Isley, Jeter A., and Philip A. Crowl. *The U.S. Marines and Amphibious War: Its Theory, and Its Practice in the Pacific.* Princeton, NJ: Princeton University Press, 1951.

Jacques, Sgt. Maj. Maurice J., and Maj. Bruce H. Norton. *Sergeant Major, USMC.* New York: Ivy Books, 1995.

Karnow, Stanley. *Vietnam: A History.* New York: Viking, 1983.

Krulak, Lt. Gen. Victor H. *First to Fight: An Inside View of the U.S. Marine Corps.* Annapolis, MD: Naval Institute Press, 1984.

Leckie, Robert. *Strong Men Armed.* New York: Random House, 1962.

Lehrack, Otto J., ed. *No Shining Armor: The Marines at War in Vietnam.* Lawrence: University of Kansas Press, 1992.

Lindsay, Robert. *This High Name: Public Relations and the U.S. Marine Corps.* Madison: University of Wisconsin Press, 1956.

Marling, Karal Ann and John Wetenhall. *Iwo Jima: Monuments, Memories, and the American Hero.* Cambridge: Harvard University Press, 1991.

McKean, Willam B. *Ribbon Creek.* New York: Dial Press, 1958.

Meid, Lt. Col. Pat, and Maj. James M. Yingling. *U.S. Marine Corps Operations in Korea: Operations in West Korea.* Washington, DC: USMC, 1972.

Melson, Maj. Charles D., USMC, et al., compilers. *U.S. Marines in the Persian Gulf, 1990–1991: An Anthology and Annotated Bibliography.* Washington, DC: USMC, 1992.

Mersky, Peter B. *U.S. Marine Corps Aviation: 1912 to the Present.* Baltimore: Nautical and Aviation Publishing Co. of America, 1983.

Millett, Allan R. *In Many a Strife: General Gerald C. Thomas and the U.S. Marine Corps 1917–1956.* Annapolis, MD: Naval Institute Press, 1993.

——. *Semper Fidelis: The History of the United States Marine Corps,* rev. and exp. ed. New York: The Free Press, 1991.

Montross, Lynn, and Capt. Nicholas A. Canzona, USMC. *U.S. Marine Operations in Korea: The Inchon-Seoul Operation.* Washington, DC: USMC, 1955.

Selected Bibliography

——. *U.S. Marine Operations in Korea: The Pusan Perimeter*. Washington, DC: USMC, 1954.

——. *U.S. Marine Operations in Korea: The Chosin Reservoir Campaign*. Washington, DC: USMC, 1957.

Montross, Lynn, Maj. Hubard D Kuokka, USMC, and Maj. Norman W. Hicks, USMC. *US Marine Operations in Korea: The East-Central Front*. Washington, DC: USMC, 1962.

Moskin, J. Robert. *The U.S. Marine Corps Story*, 3rd rev. ed. Boston: Little, Brown, 1992.

Nalty, Bernard C. *The Right to Fight: African-American Marines in World War II*. Washington, DC: USMC, 1995.

Newcomb, Richard F. *Iwo Jima*. New York: Holt, Rinehart and Winston, 1965.

Nichols, Maj. Charles S., Jr., and Henry I. Shaw, Jr. *Okinawa: Victory in the Pacific*. Washington, DC: USMC, 1955.

Nolan, Keith W. *Battle for Hue: Tet, 1968*. Novato, CA: Presidio Press, 1983.

Owen, Joseph R. *Colder Than Hell: A Marine Rifle Company at Chosin Reservoir*. Annapolis, MD: Naval Institute Press, 1996.

Parker, Capt. William D., USMCR. *A Concise History of the United States Marine Corps, 1775–1969*. Washington, DC: USMC, 1970.

Prados, John and Ray W. Stubbe. *Valley of Decision: The Siege of Khe Sanh*. Boston: Houghton Mifflin, 1991.

Puller, Lewis B., Jr. *Fortunate Son*. New York: Grove Weidenfeld, 1991.

Ricks, Thomas E. *Making the Corps*. New York: Simon & Schuster, 1998.

Ridgway, Gen. Matthew B. *Ridgway: The Memoirs of Matthew B. Ridgway*. New York: Harper Brothers, 1956.

Ross, Bill D. *Iwo Jima: Legacy of Valor*. New York: Vanguard Press, 1985.

Santoli, Al. *Everything We Had: An Oral History of the Vietnam War by Thirty-Three American Soldiers Who Fought It*. New York: Random House, 1981.

Shaw, Henry I., Jr., and Ralph W. Donnelly. *Blacks in the Marine Corps*. Washington, DC: USMC, 1975.

Shore, Capt. Moyers S. II, USMC. *The Battle for Khe Sanh*. Washington, DC: USMC, 1969.

Shulimson, Jack. *U.S. Marines in Vietnam: An Expanding War, 1966*. Washington, DC: USMC, 1982

Shulimson, Jack, et al. *U.S. Marines in Vietnam: The Defining Year, 1968*. Washington, DC: USMC, 1997.

Simmons, Brig. Gen. Edwin H. Simmons, USMC. *The United States Marines, 1775–1975*. New York: Viking, 1976.

Sledge, Eugene B. *With the Old Breed at Peleliu and Okinawa*. New York: Oxford University Press, 1990.

Smith, Charles R. *U.S. Marines in Vietnam: High Mobility and Standown, 1969.* Washington, DC: USMC, 1988.

Smith, Gen. Holland M. *Coral and Brass.* New York: Scribners, 1949.

Stremlow, Col. Mary V., USMC. *A History of Women Marines, 1946–1977.* Washington, DC: USMC, 1986.

Tefler, Maj. Gary L., et al. *U.S. Marines in Vietnam: Fighting the North Vietnamese, 1967.* Washington, DC: USMC, 1984.

United States Marine Corps. *Small Wars Manual.* Washington, DC: USMC, 1940.

Vandegrift, Gen. Alexander A. *Once A Marine.* New York; W.W. Norton, 1954.

Walt, Gen. Lewis W., USMC. *Strange War, Strange Strategy: A General's Report on Vietnam.* New York: Funk & Wagnalls, 1970.

West, Bing and Maj. Gen. Ray L. Smith. *The March Up: Taking Baghdad with the 1st Marine Division.* New York: Bantam Books, 2003.

West, Capt. Francis J. West, Jr. *Small Unit Action in Vietnam, Summer 1966.* Washington, DC: USMC, 1967.

Wheeler, Richard. *The Bloody Battle for Suribachi.* New York: Crowell, 1965.

Wood, David Browne. *A Sense of Values: American Warriors in an Uncertain World.* Kansas City: Andrews and McMeel, 1994.

Acknowledgments

American Spartans is largely a work of synthesis. As such, it owes a great debt to the many fine historians who have written books and articles on specific aspects, battles, and wars in Marine Corps history, especially historians associated with the History and Museums Division of the Corps in Washington, D.C. The works of these historians—Edwin Simmons, Henry I. Shaw Jr., Benis Frank, and Lynn Montross, to name a few—appear with frequency in the source notes to the text.

Every serious student of Marine history, myself included, holds Allan R. Millett's definitive scholarly history, *Semper Fidelis: The History of the United States Marines*, in high regard. It is an indispensable study, based on prodigious research. I relied on both its text and bibliography heavily.

Active-duty Marine public affairs officers and their staffs provided excellent support and cheerful companionship during stays at Camp Lejeune and Camp Pendleton, at Marine Corps Base, Quantico, and aboard the USS *Peleliu*. I'm grateful especially to Captains Bill Pelletier, Justin Wilson, Mikail Rahseed, and Carrie Batson for their help in arranging my participation in various exercises and for securing interviews with scores of Marines during my visits to these bases.

A number of retired and former Marines graciously agreed to in-depth interviews. Major General Fred Haynes was generous beyond measure in sharing his time and considerable wisdom over the more than four years it took to write the first draft of this book, and he offered many useful comments. His impact on my thinking about Marine history and culture over those years has been large indeed. When you read the quotations from the Haynes interviews in the book, you will see why.

The novelist James Webb and Lieutenant General Bernard Trainor, a prominent military analyst and writer, were also generous with their time and thoughts. Both men saw extensive action in Vietnam, and both have a profound knowledge of the Corps and its place in American history. Andy Wehrle, Tim Jorstad, and Seth Haines, Marine veterans all, shared their views on the Corps on many occasions. So did retired Marine Cliff Chappel, a fellow Rhode Islander who has an extraordinary loyalty to the Corps and its values. Cliff put me in touch with two active-duty Marines at the Naval War College who played key roles in Operation Iraqi Freedom in spring 2003: Lieutenant Colonel Stacey Clardy and Lieutenant Colonel Fred Padilla. Both kindly agreed to in-depth interviews. Their stories form a critical part of the narrative covering the three-week drive on Baghdad — the last operation discussed in the book. I am grateful to them all.

Writing is a solitary and at times discouraging activity. It requires the moral support of friends. Over the course of writing this book, I relied more than I can say on the support of the following people: Mark Sutton and Karen Irving; Peter and Helen Flynn; Tom Verde and Kate Robins, Craig Crawford and Tom Ginnerty, Patrick Tracey, Lance King, Chester Gillis, George Sullivan, Blanche Gelfant, and Amy Lipman.

Bruce Nichols, my editor at Free Press, provided superb editorial guidance throughout, along with a great deal of patience and understanding during difficult times. He improved the draft manuscript in all sorts of ways.

The book never would have been written if it hadn't been for the constant encouragement and support of my friend and agent, John F. Thornton, who believed in the book from the outset, and, more important, believed in me. John truly lives and works by the motto of the Marines: *Semper Fidelis.*

Index

About the Author

James Warren is a freelance writer specializing in modern American military history. He has written books on the Vietnam War and the cold war, and he contributed the chapter on the Vietnam War to the *Atlas of American Military History* (Oxford, 2003). His reviews and articles have appeared in MHQ: *The Quarterly Journal of Military History, The Columbia Companion to the Twentieth-century American Short Story,* and *The Providence (RI) Journal.* James Warren was educated at Brown University and lives in Narragansett, Rhode Island.